The Guadalupan Controversies in Mexico

The Guadalupan Controversies in Mexico

Stafford Poole, C.M.

STANFORD UNIVERSITY PRESS

Stanford, California 2006

Stanford University Press
Stanford, California

Printed in the United States of America on acid-free,
archival-quality paper

Library of Congress Cataloging-in-Publication Data
Poole, Stafford.
   The Guadalupan controversies in Mexico /
Stafford Poole.
      p.   cm.
   Includes bibliographical references and index.
   ISBN-13: 978-0-8047-5252-7 (cloth : alk. paper)
   ISBN-10: 0-8047-5252-4 (cloth : alk. paper)
   1. Guadalupe, Our Lady of.   I. Title.

BT660.G8P65   2006
232.91'7097253—dc22

Typeset by BookMatters in 10/12 Sabon

To
Stephen, Emily, Brent, and Taryn
with love from
their great-uncle

Contents

Preface

There can be no doubt that devotion to Our Lady of Guadalupe is one of the preeminent religious phenomena of recent history. Originating in Mexico in the seventeenth century, it has spread throughout the world. The Mexican people have forged an almost mystical relationship with the Virgen Morena, or Dark Virgin. "Mexico was born at Tepeyac" is how this is often phrased. This devotion is based on the story of the appearances of the Virgin Mary to an indigenous neophyte named Juan Diego in which the Virgin directed him to have a church built on the site of the apparitions, the hill of Tepeyac. Yet this simple and poignant story has been at the center of a firestorm of controversy that began in the seventeenth century, reached a fever pitch in the last quarter of the nineteenth, and continues unabated to our own day. In all of this, there has been a high cost in personal tragedy, ruined careers, and an often unedifying spectacle of churchmen in strident disagreement.

This present study grew out of a previous one by this author on the history and sources of the tradition of Our Lady of Guadalupe, published in 1995.[1] Part of the preparation for that book involved research into the famed letter that the Mexican historian Joaquín García Icazbalceta wrote to the archbishop of Mexico, Antonio Pelagio de Labastida y Dávalos, in October 1883. As so frequently happens in historical studies, one point of research led to another until, by a strange concatenation of circumstances, the author found himself personally involved in the contemporary phase of the controversy. It will also be obvious that in the first chapter of this work there is a great deal of dependence on his earlier book on the origins and sources of the Guadalupe devotion. This was unavoidable, and it is hoped that the reader will not find it tiresome. It was the author's original intention to write the history only of the nineteenth-century controversy. It quickly became apparent that that was only one part of a continuum.

Though the term "controversies" in the title is given in the plural, it is the author's belief that there has been only one controversy, one that began in the seventeenth century and has continued substantially unchanged to the present day. Its history can be divided into five more or less distinct stages. The first began in 1648 with the publication of Miguel Sánchez's account of the apparitions. In this stage, the objections to the account were implicit, that is, they had to be reconstructed from the defenses that apologists wrote. The second stage began in 1794 with the first public attack on the apparition story, the dissertation that the priest Juan Bautista Muñoz presented before the Royal Academy of History in Madrid. Muñoz's critique had great impact, and its basic line of argumentation has been followed by anti-apparitionists to this day. In this stage most apologias for the apparitions were directed against Muñoz. The third and increasingly bitter stage can be dated from the composition of García Icazbalceta's letter in October 1883 until 1896. This came to include not only the historicity of the account but also the question of Roman approval of it and the coronation of the image. The fourth stage, called "An Uneasy Calm" in this study, lasted from 1896 until 1982. It was less polemical and involved the publication of histories and popular works both for and against the traditional account. The fifth stage can be said to have begun with the campaign for the beatification of Juan Diego in the early 1980s. This stage became most virulent after 1995 with the publication of the views of Monseñor Guillermo Schulenburg Prado, the abbot of Guadalupe. It eventually centered on the campaign to prevent or at least postpone the canonization of Juan Diego.

A major difficulty in the composition of this work, specifically with regard to the period from 1883 to the present, has been the author's inability to consult all the sources he would have liked. The volatile nature of the dispute and the deep feelings it has aroused have prevented him from having access to many vital documents. When he applied to the archive of the Basilica of Guadalupe in April 2003, he was told that no one was being granted access because the archive was being restructured and also because there was no priest or canon supervising the archive. "Restructuring" was the same answer he had received in 1991 when he was working on his first Guadalupe book. Also, it is not immediately clear why the supervision of a priest or canon is necessary for the archive to function. When Leo XIII opened the Vatican Archive to researchers, he is reputed to have said that the Church had nothing to fear from the truth. Unfortunately, that enlightened approach has not yet been fully accepted.

This story is necessarily written from the viewpoint of the author's research and experience. It is clear that he brings his own perspectives to bear on this study, most particularly in the account of the canonization controversy. As much as possible he has striven to let the facts speak for themselves. The full story will never be told until all the documents in diocesan archives and in the Vatican have been consulted, an eventuality that will not come about for many years. For this reason also, a disproportionate number of references are to newspaper and journal articles. The Guadalupan controversy of the past century and a quarter has been largely fought out in the media, primarily the press. In recent years, this has also included radio, television, and wire services, but even now the press has been the principal forum, especially for defenders of the tradition. Thus, the story of the controversy is necessarily incomplete.

As the author did his research, he was unprepared for the intensity, even viciousness, of the dispute and the stridency of its tone. This has not been a sterile argument over historical or theological minutiae, confined to the esoteric world of scholars and churchmen. It reaches to the depths of national feeling and identity. "Without Guadalupe we would cease to be Mexicans."[2] There is much about this that is sad and disconcerting. Tragically, Our Lady of Guadalupe, in addition to all her other meanings for the people of Mexico, is also a sign of contradiction.

It should be noted that the word *cultus* is used throughout this study in relation to devotion to Our Lady of Guadalupe. The English word "cult" has taken on somewhat sinister connotations in recent years, whereas the Latin *cultus* refers to any act of worship or religious devotion in general. Most commonly, it refers to acts of public devotion or prayer.

All translations from Latin and Spanish are the author's. The translation and publication of the letters in Appendices 2 and 3 are made with the kind permission of Señor Luis Guillermo Robles of Random House Mondadori, in Mexico. The author also wishes to express his deep appreciation to friends and colleagues who have sent him materials from around the world and given him needed help and encouragement: Professor Susan Schroeder of Tulane University, New Orleans; Professor W. Michael Mathes; Señora Carmen Boone de Aguilar; Professor John Frederick Schwaller of the University of Minnesota, Morris; Licenciado Oscar Philibert; Professor Iván Escamilla González; Doctor Magnus Lundberg; Canon José Martín Rivera; Señor Angel González and the staff of the Biblioteca Miguel Lerdo de Tejada in Mexico City; Señor Liborio Villagómez and the staff of the Biblioteca Nacional at the National and Autonomous University of Mexico; the staff of the Biblioteca Lorenzo Boturini Benaduci at the Basilica of Guadalupe; and the staff of the Bancroft Library, University of California at Berkeley. A special word of thanks is due to Monseñor Guillermo Schulenburg Prado, twenty-first and last abbot of Guadalupe.

Without Guadalupe we would cease to be Mexicans.

— *Prisciliano Hernández Chávez*

The Guadalupan Controversies in Mexico

CHAPTER ONE

From the Beginning

❖

In 1648 a Mexican priest named Miguel Sánchez published a book titled
*Imagen de la Virgen Maria, Madre de Dios de Gvadalvpe, milagrosa-
mente aparecida en la civdad de Mexico . . .* (Image of the Virgin Mary,
the Mother of God of Guadalupe, Who Appeared Miraculously in the
City of Mexico . . .).[1] This was the first known account of the apparitions of Our Lady of Guadalupe. In it he described how at the beginning
of December 1531 the Virgin Mary appeared to a neophyte native named
Juan Diego at the hill of Tepeyac outside Mexico City and ordered him to
go to the bishop of Mexico, the Franciscan Juan de Zumárraga, with a
message that he should build a church to her at that site.[2] He did as he
was directed, but Sánchez did not describe their meeting. Juan Diego
returned to Tepeyac, where he encountered the Virgin again and spoke to
her with Baroque imagery. "Señora and my mother, I obeyed your command, not without effort did I enter to visit the bishop, at whose feet I
knelt. He received me kindly, he blessed me lovingly, he heard me atten-
tively, and answered me lukewarmly, saying, 'Son, on another day, when
it is convenient, you can come, I will hear you more at length for your
claim and I will learn at the root what your embassy is.'"[3] Juan Diego
asked her to send someone else who would have more credibility. She
refused, saying that her message was for the humble and directed him to
return to Zumárraga on the following day.

Sánchez did not describe Juan Diego's second interview with Zumárraga.
Rather, he had the native relate it to the Virgin during the third apparition. This time, Juan Diego described the bishop as being somewhat
severe and abrupt. The Virgin promised that she would give a sign that
would cause Juan Diego to be believed. The bishop, however, had ordered

some of his servants to follow the native to see where he went and to whom he spoke. Juan Diego disappeared from view at the bridge at Tepeyac, and they returned full of anger and ready to discredit him with Zumárraga.

On the following day, Juan Diego was supposed to return to Tepeyac to receive a sign for the bishop but was unable to do so. His uncle was dying of *cocolistli*, a generic term for illness, whose precise meaning in this context is unclear. A physician had applied medicines but to no avail. So on this, the third day after the first apparition, Juan Diego set out for Tlatelolco to find a friar to minister to his uncle.

On coming to Tepeyac he attempted to take a different route so that the Virgin would not meet or detain him. Nevertheless, she saw him from the top of the hill and came down to intercept him. He knelt before her and wished her good morning. She assured him that he need not fear for his uncle, since he was already cured. He asked her for a sign to carry to the bishop, and she directed him to go to the top of the hill and collect the flowers that he would find there. As he did so, "instantly there appeared before his eyes diverse flowers, blooming by a miracle, born by a prodigy, uncovered by a portent, the roses inviting with their beauty, the lilies offering tribute of milk, the carnations blood, the violets ardor, the jasmines amber, the rosemary hope, the iris love, the broom captivity, rivaling each other eagerly and, seemingly, speaking to his hands, not only in order that he would cut them but that he would prefer them and with secret impulses divining the glory for which they were being cut."[4] He collected the flowers in his mantle and brought them to the Virgin, who took them and then returned them to Juan Diego with instructions that he was to show them to no one but the bishop.

Juan Diego returned to the bishop's palace, where he was delayed by Zumárraga's servants, who were still angry with him. After a long wait, the attendants, aware that he carried something in his mantle, attempted to see what it was. Juan Diego was unable to prevent them, but when they attempted to take some of the flowers, which Sánchez now called roses, they found them to be painted or embroidered. When he was finally admitted into the bishop's presence, Juan Diego related all that had happened. He then opened his mantle, and the many kinds of flowers fell to the floor. Imprinted on the mantle was the picture of the Virgin, "which today is preserved, kept, and venerated in her sanctuary of *Guadalupe* of Mexico."[5] All looked on it "in ecstasy astonished, in astonishment bewildered, in bewilderment lifted up, in lifting up stirred, in stirring entranced, in entrancement contemplative, in contemplation sweetened, in sweetness joyful, in joy mute."[6]

The bishop removed the mantle from Juan Diego and took it to his private oratory. He arranged that the native would return to Tepeyac together with others in order to point out the site for the sanctuary. Then they went to Juan Diego's town (whose name Sánchez did not give), where they found his uncle, whose name Sánchez gave for the first time as Juan Bernardino, totally cured. The Virgin had appeared to him and restored his health. It was to him, not Juan Diego, that she revealed that the sanctuary was to be called Guadalupe. Zumárraga hastened to have an *ermita*, or chapel of ease, built on the spot. In the meantime, the image was put on display in the Cathedral. After consulting both the ecclesiastical and civil *cabildos*, Zumárraga designated the Tuesday after Christmas, a scant two weeks after the appearance of the image, for a solemn procession and installation of the mantle in the *ermita*.[7] Juan Diego asked permission to live at the *ermita* as its guardian, and this was granted. He died there in 1548. Sánchez included in his account a description of the image and of the *ermita*, together with a series of miracle stories.[8]

The book was written in a florid style typical of the Baroque, filled with exaggerated conceits and contorted figures of speech, as the quotations given above abundantly show. Juan Diego's speeches to the Virgin were long and elaborate. Like the story itself, they were European in form and structure. They showed no signs of a Nahuatl substratum, something that one would expect if Sánchez had been working from an oral tradition. The *Imagen* was also characterized by an extravagant *criollismo*, which saw the people of Mexico as a new chosen people and Mexico City as a new Jerusalem. Though it would seem natural that the indigenous peoples were the special objects of the Virgin's love, they played little or no role in Sánchez's book. The story of the apparitions originated with him, and from it came the controversy that has swirled around the devotion to the present day.

Laso de la Vega and the Nican mopohua

In 1649, a mere six months after the publication of Sánchez's work, the vicar of Guadalupe, Luis Laso de la Vega, published a somewhat different account in Nahuatl (Aztec), with the Indians as the intended audience. It bore the title *Huei tlamahuiçoltica* . . . (By a Great Miracle . . .), and in addition to the apparition account contained prayers, exhortations, a life of Juan Diego, a description of the image, and a series of miracle stories.[9] The actual narration of the apparitions is now known by its opening words, "Nican mopohua" (Here is recounted). Though Laso de la Vega retained the basic European form of the apparition genre, his account was more native in style and expression. Juan Diego's dialogues with the Virgin now reflected formal Nahuatl speech, including polite inversions and expressions of self-deprecation. Other native elements included the description of the hill on which the Virgin was standing and Juan Diego's wonderment at what he heard and saw: "Where am I? Where do I find myself? Am I just dreaming it? Am I imagining it in sleepwalking? Is it in the land of the flowers, the land of plentiful crops, the place of which our ancient forefathers used to speak? Is this the land of heaven?"[10] Laso de la Vega departed in other ways from Sánchez: his account omitted one apparition, when Juan Diego returned to the Virgin after the initial interview with Zumárraga; and Sánchez had seven miracle stories, whereas Laso de la Vega had fourteen.

There are two key questions about the *Nican mopohua*. First, was Laso de la Vega truly the author or was he merely publishing a much earlier native account? He clearly stated four times in his introduction that he was the author of the apparition account, and he made no reference to either written documents or published works, including Sánchez's. A recent study by three scholars has come down strongly on the side of unitary authorship.[11] He was, however, most probably helped by native assistants. The *Nican mopohua* shows no signs of being a translation from Spanish, whereas the miracle stories (the *Nican motecpana*, "Here is an orderly account") show every sign of a Spanish original. The second question is: Was Sánchez's account based on Laso de la Vega's, or vice versa? Those who wish to give the *Nican mopohua* pride of place see it as the basis of Sánchez's account. This cannot be proven, and certainly the *Imagen* shows no sign of being a translation of a Nahuatl original. Though the probability favors Sánchez's account as being the original one, the question cannot be definitively resolved at this time.

One thing that is clear about both accounts is that they were not based on any documentary evidence. Sánchez gave only the vaguest description of his sources. In the prologue to his book he admitted that he had been unable to find documentary proof for the apparition story, though he had searched through various archives and repositories. Finally, he had recourse to the memories of older people, especially natives, which he cited in a rather vague way as the source or proof of the truth of what he was writing.[12] Sánchez laid the groundwork for two consistent themes that have run through the Guadalupe tradition down to the present day: the lack of any clear documentary evidence for the apparitions, and the appeal to an unwritten tradition dating back to the year 1531. In a real sense, the controversy over the authenticity of the Guadalupe apparitions began with the work that first made them known.

Sánchez's contemporaries, including Laso de la Vega, Juan de Poblete,

Francisco de Siles, Antonio de Lara Mogrovejo, Pedro de Rozas, and Antonio de Robles, all testified to the fact that the story of the apparitions had been unknown or forgotten in Mexico prior to 1648.[13] Writing in the following century, Gutiérrez Dávila expressed surprise that such a great event could have been forgotten. "The forgetting of such a great benefit that the Empress of Heaven did for our America, and especially for Mexico, was certainly something worthy to be pondered."[14] In 1666 Sánchez claimed that a paper shortage in New Spain had caused the theft of many documents from the archdiocesan archive, including those that dealt with Guadalupe. There was, indeed, a paper shortage in New Spain about the year 1621, but there is no record of the extremities that Sánchez mentioned.[15] Similarly, Laso de la Vega was clear that he did not have any written sources from which he drew his account. He declared, "But a great deal has been left out, which time has erased and no one at all remembers any more, because the ancients did not take care to write it down when it happened."[16]

Though the lack of written evidence caused difficulties from the very beginning, there is no evidence at this time of overt doubts about the historical reality of the apparitions. These can be inferred, however, from the repeated attempts of apologists to find a solid basis that would render the account impervious to historical criticism, specifically, a long-standing oral tradition. The first serious attempt at confirming such a tradition was made by the Cathedral chapter of Mexico in 1665–66. During a period when it was ruling the archdiocese in the absence of an archbishop, it decided to ask the Holy See to have December 12 declared a feast day for all New Spain and that the feast have its own proper mass and office. To lay the basis for this request, the chapter ordered an inquiry.[17] The officials of the inquiry were appointed in December 1665 and a detailed questionnaire was drawn up. The investigators questioned twenty witnesses: one mestizo and seven Indians from the town of Cuauhtitlán (named by Laso de la Vega as Juan Diego's hometown), ten Spanish clerics and religious, and two Spanish laypersons. All the witness statements agreed on the existence of a tradition that went back through many generations, testifying to the reality of the apparition story. The testimonies were forwarded to Rome together with other supporting documents, but the entire case went into the limbo of Vatican bureaucracy.

At first reading, the testimonies given in the inquiry seem quite persuasive, a fact that has made this investigation of major importance to apologists for the apparitions. They were marred, however, by a number of inconsistencies and anachronisms that seriously weakened their credibility.[18] More important was the fact that the inquiry was not an examination into the truth or falsity of the apparitions, nor an investigation of the existence or non-existence of an historical fact. On the contrary, the truth of the apparitions was presupposed. All of those involved in the inquiry were enthusiastic *guadalupanos*. The purpose was to seek evidence that would persuade the Holy See to grant the request for a proper feast day and mass and office. It was not, therefore, an objective investigation. It appears not to have persuaded officials in Rome, because for the next century they showed a decided reluctance to grant any privileged status to the Guadalupe devotion.

One important result of the inquiry was the testimony of a key witness, Luis Becerra Tanco, a diocesan cleric and a learned man who was also an expert in Nahuatl.[19] He submitted his testimony in writing and later in that same year of 1666 published it under the title of *Origen milagroso del santuario de Nuestra Señora de Guadalupe* (Miraculous Origin of the Sanctuary of Our Lady of Guadalupe).[20] Shortly thereafter he revised the work but was unable to have it published for lack of money. In 1675, through the agency of a friend, it was published posthumously in Spain under the title *Felicidad de México* (Mexico's Happiness)[21] and republished in 1685 and 1745. The two versions contained substantial variations.[22] His two works were the first true apologias for the Guadalupan apparitions.

Becerra Tanco admitted the lack of any contemporary documents that corroborated the apparition story. He attributed this to the fact that in 1531 there was no diocesan archive and because of the general disdain that peninsular Spaniards had for anything that came from the Indies. For him, the strongest proof of the authenticity of the account was in the constant tradition handed down from father to son. It is significant, however, that he admitted that there was no explanation of how the tradition had been transmitted, since "neither one [Sánchez or Laso de la Vega] explained the way in which it was ascertained or how this information came down to us."[23] Despite his assertion about the lack of documentary evidence, Becerra Tanco claimed to have seen indigenous maps and pictures that depicted the miracle. Even more, he went beyond the reliance on an unwritten tradition and was the first to claim the existence of a written account of the apparitions in Nahuatl. The descriptions he gave in the two versions of his work were somewhat different. In his testimony of 1666, Becerro Tanco spoke of

. . . a notebook written in the letters of our alphabet in the hand of an Indian, in which were described the four apparitions of the Most Holy Virgin to the Indian Juan Diego and the fifth to his uncle Juan Bernardino. It was the one that was published in the Mexican language in 1649 by order of Licenciado Luis Laso de la Vega, vicar of the sanctuary of Our Lady of Guadalupe.[24]

But in *Felicidad de México*, published in 1675, he wrote:

[Fernando de Alva Ixtlilxochitl] had in his possession a notebook written in the letters of our alphabet in the Mexican language, in the hand of an Indian who was one of the earliest graduates of the Colegio de Santa Cruz, which was mentioned above, in which reference is made to the four apparitions of the Holy Virgin to the Indian Juan Diego and the fifth to his uncle Juan Bernardino.[25]

The two variations are that, in the revised work, (1) the author was identified as a graduate of the Franciscan school at Tlatelolco, and (2) Becerra Tanco suppressed the identification of this Nahuatl document with the *Nican mopohua*. It is not clear why, though it can be surmised that as a student of Nahuatl he knew that the two documents were not the same. Four points should be noted about this now unknown Nahuatl account: (1) Becerra Tanco did not give the name of the author of this account in either version of his book; (2) he moved away from identifying it with the *Nican mopohua*; (3) he gave the document a Franciscan provenance at a time when the Franciscans were known to be hostile to Guadalupe; (4) he did not identify it as the one that he used in his own narration of the apparitions earlier in both works. At the same time, his assertion concerning this account laid the groundwork for the present-day claim that a native composed the *Nican mopohua* and that it was nearly contemporaneous with the events it narrated.

Francisco de Florencia

The problem of written sources was approached again by the next apologist for the apparitions, the Jesuit Francisco de Florencia (1619/1620–1695), in his book *La estrella del norte de Mexico . . .* (The North Star of Mexico), published in 1688.[26] It was the most complete apologia for Guadalupe up to that time and has continued to be influential down to the present day. Florencia garnered all the information that he could concerning the apparition account and the miracles worked by the image, with the result that his work is often repetitious and ill organized. His historical approach was that of the Baroque in New Spain — traditionalist, moralistic, and uncritical. Thus, he was going against a growing tendency in Catholic historiography, represented by the Benedictines of Saint-Maur (especially Jean Mabillon) and the Jesuits of the Bollandists, who were more critical and skeptical of traditional devotions and demanded evidence for their authenticity.

Like others, Florencia attempted to compensate for the lack of documentation, both by insistence on a constant tradition and by appealing to now unknown native accounts. In an introductory letter to the book, the bachelor Jerónimo de Valladolid admitted the lack of official documentation. "No authentic document on this holy image is to be found among the official papers of this holy church [the Cathedral] of Mexico."[27] Because of the lack of written sources, he emphasized that the existence and preservation of the image were testimony enough. Documents, therefore, were unnecessary. Thus, he introduced a third argument into the armory of the apologists. The first censor of the book, Antonio de Gama, emphasized tradition as compensating for the weakness of the human memory.[28] "For our ancestors evidence was the clearest testimony of these signs, just as tradition is for us. And so it seems that it was not just human carelessness, but also the foresight of divine providence that for us the only proof of those signs should be tradition, which, supported by the fragility of our memory, should serve continually to awaken our distrust of its forgetfulness."[29] The second censor, Carlos de Sigüenza y Góngora, echoed this theme: "The fact that we do not know how we possess such a sovereign wonder is the result of our innate carelessness . . . and after so many years what by the lack of individual notices is made known to the world with such clarity that only among the pusillanimous may it be considered doubtful."[30]

Despite these clear assertions, Florencia attempted to show that there were authentic documents that proved the historicity of the apparitions. He described two different Nahuatl accounts of Guadalupe, but his descriptions have created as many problems as they attempted to solve. In addition, his writing on this subject was rather confused. The first of these native accounts was entitled *Relación de Nuestra Señora de Guadalupe*, of which a Spanish paraphrase had been lent to him by Sigüenza y Góngora. Florencia believed that it had come from some very ancient papers of an Indian and that it had been translated from Nahuatl by the native scholar Alva Ixtlilxochitl. He estimated the translation to be at least seventy or eighty years old and the original Nahuatl to be about one hundred.

Florencia gave numerous quotations from the *Relación* and cited some of the data given in it. Regarding the celibate marriage of Juan Diego and María Lucía (the name traditionally given to his wife) and his subsequent widowhood, Florencia quoted the author of the document as saying, "He was a widower two years before God and his Most Holy Mother chose him for such a singular task. His wife, whose name was María Luisa [*sic*], had died. He had no children because according to what I learned through many inquiries and investigations, he and his wife always observed chastity."[31] As for the identity of the author, Florencia stated in a marginal note that "it seems from the *Relación* itself that the author was a contemporary of the time of the apparitions."[32] He then deduced that the author was a Franciscan, quoting lines from the document such as "the very exemplary and seraphic fathers of our glorious seraphic Francis," "[Motolinía,] a holy religious of our order of Saint Francis," and "[Zumárraga] belonged to the order of Our Holy Father Saint Francis." By a process of elimination, he concluded that the author was Gerónimo de Mendieta.

Florencia's description of this *Relación* contained elements not found in other accounts or as part of the standard tradition. When Juan Diego left Zumárraga's house, he was late for mass at Tlatelolco and humbly accepted the blows with a stick that in Florencia's day were still given to tardy natives. When Zumárraga asked him for a sign, Juan Diego replied with perfect confidence that "he should ask for any sign whatever, that he would go and ask for it in order that he might see that what he was asking was the truth." The *Relación* stated that some people went to Tepeyac at a later date, after the apparitions, in order to find the exact place where the Virgin had appeared so as to pray there. When they approached the spring, which in Florencia's day was called the Pozo de la Virgen, it gushed forth. This was taken as a sign that it was the site of the apparitions. Finally, Florencia believed that this *Relación* was the same one from which Miguel Sánchez and Becerra Tanco got their accounts. Yet from all of Florencia's quotations and references it is abundantly clear that the *Relación* was different, not only from the *Nican mopohua* but also from both Sánchez's and Becerra Tanco's accounts. This *Relación* does not exist today and, most importantly, it is clearly different from any known account of the apparitions. Florencia promised to publish this *Relación* in the *Estrella del norte de México* but did not do so because, he claimed, his book was already too long. Therein lies the problem: it is impossible to identify it with anything known today. Florencia never saw the original nor, as far as is known, did he know Nahuatl. It clearly was not the source used by Sánchez, Laso de la Vega, or Becerra Tanco. Yet, as will be seen, this account has come to be identified by some with the *Nican mopohua*.

There was, however, a second account, which Florencia did identify with the *Nican mopohua*. In words similar to those of Becerra Tanco, he described a Nahuatl account written in the Latin alphabet by an Indian, a graduate of Santa Cruz de Tlatelolco, that was in a notebook that was in the possession of Alva Ixtlilxochitl. Unlike Becerra Tanco in the *Felicidad de México*, however, Florencia identified it with the one published by Laso de la Vega. It seems probable that Florencia had no first-hand knowledge of this document, that he was simply repeating what Becerra Tanco said, and that he arbitrarily made the identification with the *Nican mopohua* or took it from Becerra Tanco's testimony of 1666.

Sigüenza y Góngora and the Nican mopohua

Florencia's identification of Mendieta as the author of the *Relación*
brought a sharp rebuttal from Carlos de Sigüenza y Góngora (1645–
1700), one of the staunchest defenders of the Guadalupe tradition.[33] In
1689 he wrote *Piedad heroyca de D. Fernando Cortés* (The Heroic Piety
of Don Fernando Cortés), though it was not published until much later.[34]
Although it was intended primarily to be a panegyric of the conquistador,
it also contained references to the apparition account. In a lengthy digres-
sion, Sigüenza y Góngora attempted to establish the definitive location of
Zumárraga's residence, where the miracle of the image took place, and to
disprove a differing assertion by Florencia. After describing how Juan
Diego had been sent to the bishop's house with the flowers and had there
revealed the image, he stated that "as uniformly declare all those historical accounts that have been printed up to the present time, and especially
a very ancient one of which I still have the manuscript and that I value
very much, and it is the same one that I lent to the Reverend Father
Florencia to embellish his history."[35]

He claimed that the identification of Mendieta as the author of the
Relación was not in the manuscript of Florencia's book that he had read
and approved. He then went on to make the following statement:

Not only is the said [*Relación*] not by Father Mendieta, but it cannot be so
because it recounts miracles and events in the years after the death of that religious. I declare and I swear that I found this account among the papers of Don
Fernando de Alva [Ixtlilxochitl], all of which I have,[36] and that it is the same one
that the Licenciado Luis de Becerra in his book (page 30 of the Seville edition)[37]
had seen in his possession. The original in Mexican [Nahuatl] is in the handwriting of Don Antonio Valeriano, an Indian, who is its true author, and at the end are
added some miracles in the handwriting of Don Fernando, also in Mexican. What
I lent to Father Francisco de Florencia was a paraphrased translation that Don
Fernando made of each, and it is also in his handwriting.[38]

The elements of his declaration are: (1) the *Relación* referred to was written in Nahuatl in the hand of its author, Antonio Valeriano; (2) it was in
the papers of Alva Ixtlilxochitl; (3) it was the same as the *Relación* mentioned by Becerra Tanco in his *Felicidad de México* and described by
Florencia; (4) this *Relación* narrated miracles and events that took place
after the death of Gerónimo de Mendieta (1604); (5) Alva Ixtlilxochitl
had made a paraphrased translation of it; (6) there was added to it a separate account of miracles in the hand of Alva Ixtlilxochitl (and perhaps
composed by him); and (7) he made no mention of Laso de la Vega or the
Nican mopohua.

Although on first reading Sigüenza y Góngora's declaration seems clear and straightforward, it is actually quite confused. His two statements contradicted his earlier assertion that the origins of the tradition story were unknown. In the first quotation, he implied that he lent Florencia the original document, whereas in the second he specified that it was a Spanish paraphrase.[39] This statement identified the paraphrased *Relación* that he lent to Florencia with the account mentioned by Becerra Tanco in the *Felicidad de México*. The reason given by Sigüenza y Góngora for denying Mendieta's authorship, that is, that the account narrated miracles that occurred after Mendieta's death in May 1604, would also exclude Valeriano, who died in August 1605. The confusion is almost total, and it is impossible today to make sense of it. It is clear that the original Nahuatl version of the account was seen only by Becerra Tanco and Sigüenza y Góngora. Florencia saw only a Spanish paraphrase of this *Relación*, an account that is clearly not the *Nican mopohua*, and he also made a complete hash of his identifications. Worse, he did not take the trouble to publish a document of supreme importance for the Guadalupan devotion. As Xavier Noguez observed, "We could not conclude now whether Florencia had a clear idea of the origin and content of the Guadalupan documents that had been given to him to write his *Estrella del norte*."[40] If such accounts ever existed, they no longer do so today. Incredibly, however, even at the present time, Sigüenza y Góngora's statement continues to be quoted in support of the claim that Antonio Valeriano was the author of the *Nican mopohua*, a claim that has been accepted even by some anti-apparitionists. Sigüenza y Góngora, however, did not identify this account with the *Nican mopohua*. As has been mentioned, the quotations given by Florencia show that the *Relación* and the *Nican mopohua* were two different accounts, and that the *Relación* also differed from Becerra Tanco's account.

Florencia and Sigüenza y Góngora were two of the most influential defenders of the Guadalupe tradition in the seventeenth century. Their influence has endured, and they are still cited today. Unfortunately, their works are flawed, especially in their failure to publish or give more information about the mysterious *Relación*. Many subsequent defenders of the apparitions have put their faith in a document that only two people saw, and that, if it ever existed, has not survived to the present day.

The Century of Lights

In the eighteenth century, the two trends of historiography, the Baroque and the Catholic Enlightenment, were becoming clearly differentiated. As was to happen again at the end of the nineteenth century, *guadalupanos* viewed the newer approaches to historical research as threatening, and their reaction was defensive. The new historiography was feared as an opening wedge for the intrusion of Enlightenment thought and the destruction of religion and its pious traditions. The counterarguments of the apologists also assumed the form that they have retained to the present day. These were (1) that though there was no documentary evidence, there was an immemorial tradition; (2) that the image itself, in its beauty and preservation, was the best argument for its supernatural nature; (3) that the Holy See's approval of a feast day and proper mass and office confirmed the historicity of the Guadalupan events; (4) that despite the nearly universal agreement on the lack of documentary sources, there was in fact written evidence that supported the apparition tradition.

A major step in the history of the Guadalupan devotion in New Spain came with a calamitous but historically significant event, the epidemic of 1736. Like an earlier one in 1576, it was called the *matlazahuatl*, though its precise nature was unclear. The reaction of rulers and people alike was to take refuge in prayers and processions. Following a standard practice of that time and place, there was a "serial" invocation of saints, that is, first one saint was invoked against the disease and if that failed, then another. The city authorities of Mexico City decided to invoke the Virgin of Guadalupe, specifically by taking an oath proclaiming her the principal patroness of the city. After this was done on May 27, 1737, the epidemic began to abate. As a result, other cities in New Spain followed the lead of the capital.

One result of this was a special volume, a detailed history and defense of Guadalupe written by Cayetano Cabrera y Quintero and published in 1746 with the title *Escudo de armas de México* (Coat of Arms of Mexico). Cabrera's approach was quite learned and precise and in some ways resembled that of the new historiography. However, when he had to choose between Baroque history, with its emphasis on moral teaching and the formal, literary aspect of history, and the newer scientific history, he chose the former. Though he was critical of some assertions in Becerra Tanco and Florencia, he still admired and imitated them. With regard to Guadalupe, he asserted that the first argument in its favor was the image itself, miraculously preserved over the course of time. At the same time, he thought that there should be a better and more scientific examination of it than had been done in 1666. The second argument in favor of the apparitions was the one that began with Miguel Sánchez and has continued to the present day, the tradition, transmitted orally from generation to generation, that had greater authority than written sources. As for the latter, since Cabrera was unable to find any accounts in the archdiocesan archive, he fell back on the Nahuatl account that was seen by Becerra

Tanco, Sigüenza y Góngora, and in a Spanish paraphrase by Florencia, but by no one else.

Cabrera included a bitter attack on the Italian scholar Lorenzo Boturini Benaduci, whom he called "an extractor of maps" and a thief of native documents. At first sight, Cabrera's hostility toward Boturini is difficult to understand because the latter was a zealot for the cause of Guadalupe. He was, however, also more of a scientific historian in the mold of the Enlightenment, and hence his approach was viewed as dangerous. For Cabrera a man like Boturini was a "Trojan horse," introducing dangerous novelties into the history of the apparitions and criticizing the historians whom Cabrera honored.[41]

Boturini Benaduci

Lorenzo Boturini Benaduci, a Milanese nobleman, was strongly influenced by Giambattista Vico, a pioneer in the area of scientific history. This in itself was probably sufficient to arouse Cabrera's ire. Boturini Benaduci came to New Spain in 1736 on a pension from a descendant of Moteucçoma II. A man of insatiable curiosity and unbounded enthusiasm, he quickly became interested in the history of New Spain, and especially that of Guadalupe. In an effort to find evidence for the apparitions, he traversed the colony from end to end, gathering documents, pictures, and maps of every description, laying the basis for Cabrera's accusation of theft. The result was a collection of some five hundred manuscripts, both pre- and post-conquest, that dealt not only with the apparition but also with different aspects of indigenous history and culture.

In his enthusiasm for Guadalupe he devised a scheme to have a solemn coronation of the image. This was an innovation, since there had never been any such ceremony in the New World. To bring this about, he undertook an unauthorized fundraising campaign that quickly alarmed the Spanish authorities. He was arrested in 1743, and his collection of documents was confiscated. He was sent back to Spain, where he was exonerated and then appointed official historian of the Indies. He was unable, however, to regain his collection of documents.

Like others, Boturini Benaduci embraced the contradictory positions that there was no documentary evidence for the apparitions and that there was. In the introduction to his book, *Idea de una nueva historia general de la América septentrional* (Plan for a New General History of North America), he clearly stated, "I found their [the apparitions'] history founded on tradition alone, without there being any knowledge of where or in what hands the sources of such a rare portent had stopped."[42] Yet at the same time he claimed that there was an authentic account in Nahuatl, composed by Antonio Valeriano, which he identified with the *Nican mopohua*. A necessary corollary of this was that Laso de la Vega was not the author of the entire *Huei tlamahuiçoltica*.

Spread of the Devotion

In 1746 the Virgin of Guadalupe was declared by a general oath to be the patron of all New Spain. The last part of the text of the oath committed those taking it to continue their efforts to seek the Holy See's approval of the *patronato* and the grant of a proper office and mass for her feast. It was believed that such a grant would be the equivalent of a definitive confirmation of the authenticity of the apparitions.[43] This line of thought, deriving from the capitular inquiry of 1666, has remained a constant in apparitionist belief down to the present time. To obtain these grants, the civil and religious corporations of Mexico City commissioned the Jesuit Juan Francisco López, the representative, or proctor (*procurador*), of the Mexican province of the Jesuits, to go to Rome in 1752. López took with him a copy of the image of Guadalupe, which, according to a popular story, prompted the pope, Benedict XIV, to quote Psalm 147, "Non fecit taliter omni nationi" (He has not done the like for any other nation). López, in his last petition to the Holy See, had to admit that there were no contemporary testimonies for the apparitions. Hence, in the absence of written evidence, the existence of a pious tradition continued to be the principal support for the miracle. Whatever the reason, the pope granted the proper office and mass and designated December 12 a feast of high rank. The grants were celebrated throughout New Spain.[44] Unfortunately for the hopes of the apparitionists, the reality fell short of their desires. Rather than making a definitive pronouncement on the authenticity of the apparitions, the pope had merely certified that there was an ancient tradition. Similarly, there was no declaration of the miraculous character of the image itself, which in the absence of probative documents, was a major testimony to the truth of the accounts.

At mid-century the newer, more critical approach to history began to gain ground as the Baroque world "began its slow death throes."[45] Among the Jesuits, Francisco Javier Clavigero and Francisco Javier Alegre were representative of the new spirit, as were Archbishop Francisco Antonio Lorenzana of Mexico and Bishop Fabián y Fuero of Puebla. All of this caused the apparitionists to search even more zealously for written evidence for the miracle. It also revived the reputation of Boturini Benaduci and brought about a species of rehabilitation. The newer school of Guadalupan historians was intent on preserving whatever sources or documents could be found, and this led not only to a renewed appreciation for Boturini's work but also to the publication of other works that, it was feared, might be lost.

Testimony to the lack of written sources was given by the noted scholar José Ignacio Bartolache y Díaz de Posadas (1739–90). His book, *Manifiesto satisfactorio u opúsculo guadalupano* (Manifesto in Satisfaction, or a Guadalupe Tract), the first on Guadalupe not written by a cleric, was published posthumously. In it, he examined and gave a critique of every Guadalupan publication up to his time and in so doing gave further witness to the lack of documentary evidence. He criticized Miguel Sánchez for failing to identify his sources. "I wish that its pious author, in place of the many texts that he copies from Holy Scripture and the holy fathers . . . had given us a simple historic narration of the miracle, backed up with some good document."[46] Similarly, when citing Sánchez's claim that he found "some" among the Indians, he writes, "The bachelor Miguel Sánchez would have done very well in having said what papers those were that he found and where."[47] In discussing Laso de la Vega, Bartolache disagreed with Boturini Benaduci's claim that Laso was not the author of the *Nican mopohua*.

The Attack of Juan Bautista Muñoz

At the end of the eighteenth century came the first major and public attack on the apparitions. It was made by a peninsular priest and would have great staying power. Juan Bautista Muñoz (1745–99) was a student of philosophy, theology, and history. In 1779 he was given the task of revising the history of the New World that had been entrusted to the Real Academia. Influenced by the Enlightenment, he had a modern sense of history and was a precise and critical thinker.[48]

In 1794 he read a paper before the Real Academia titled "Memoria sobre las apariciones y el culto de Nuestra Señora de Guadalupe de México" (Memorial on the Apparitions and Cultus of Our Lady of Guadalupe of Mexico).[49] He began by emphasizing the freedom of individuals to believe or not to believe in visions and prodigies that were not of divine faith. "We are obliged to believe them in general, but in particular cases we are free to doubt any teaching and facts not contained in the canonical books nor in the primitive, universal and constant tradition."[50] Muñoz surveyed the various chroniclers and writers of the sixteenth and seventeenth centuries whose silence on Guadalupe was considered significant. Among these were Zumárraga, Torquemada, Motolinía, and

Mendieta. "Thus, either the tradition that we are dealing with did not exist in their time, or, if there was some rumor among the populace, [they] paid no attention, as sound reason says should be done with the populace's stories that do not have an ancient origin."[51] He rejected all proofs based on songs, maps, and manuscripts. The *Relación* mentioned by Sigüenza y Góngora and Florencia he dismissed as being of a later date than the apparitions, and he posed the key question that is still valid today, "And why has it never been published?"[52] He cited Martín Enríquez's letter of 1575, the first to do so, in which the viceroy credited Alonso de Montúfar, the second archbishop of Mexico, with being the founder of the shrine.[53]

Muñoz believed that the story resulted from the great flood of 1629–34, when the image of Guadalupe was credited with ending the catastrophe. "That it was invented long after the fact is proved by the irrefutable testimonies of Father Sahagún and the Viceroy Enríquez. It is the obligation of its defenders to exhibit more ancient and less suspicious documents than those that they have produced up to now."[54] In his conclusion, he made a clear distinction between the devotion, "which is reasonable and all right," and the apparitions.[55]

Muñoz's "Memoria" was not a detailed scientific treatise. It dealt with a variety of topics without going deeply into particulars. It is significant, first, as being the first known public attack on the historicity of the apparitions, and, second, as using a line of argumentation that would endure to the present day. Central to this was the silence of so many individuals who would have been expected to comment on Guadalupe. His treatise, however, did not become known in Mexico until 1817. From then until the letter of García Icazbalceta in 1883, it was the principal target of rebuttals by apologists for the apparitions. Even today, those who reject the historicity of the apparitions are accused of merely repeating Muñoz's arguments.

The Fevered Speculations of Fray Servando

One of the more eccentric figures in the history of the Guadalupan controversies was the Dominican friar Servando Teresa de Mier Noriega y Guerra (1763–1827). A man of febrile imagination, he derived many of his ideas on Guadalupe from a lawyer of the royal *audiencia*, Ignacio Borunda. The latter had spent many years studying native languages and antiquities, but in the process had devised some rather bizarre theories. Beristáin de Sousa said of him that he was "very learned in the language and antiquities of the Mexicans, although often exotic and capricious in his ideas and arbitrary and superficial in his interpretations."[56] In an interview, Borunda expounded these to Mier.[57] His thesis was that Saint Thomas the Apostle had come to Mexico to preach Christianity and that he was the Quetzalcoatl of native lore. The *tilma* was not the mantle of an Indian but the cape of Saint Thomas himself. It was decorated in the native style and contained all the articles of Christian faith in a system of hieroglyphics. Therefore, it was not miraculous. During times of persecution, it had been hidden, and the story of Juan Diego was the story of its recovery.[58] Mier enthusiastically embraced these ideas and promised to include them in a sermon which, it was hoped, would bring in funds that would enable Borunda to publish his ideas.

At the invitation of the city council of Mexico, Mier gave the annual sermon in the church at Guadalupe on December 12, 1794, in the presence of the viceroy, the archbishop, and the notables of the city. At that time, tensions were high because of reports from Europe on the progress of the French Revolution and the fear of revolution in the New World. Spain appeared headed for defeat in its war against the French republic. Probably to the surprise of his sponsors, Mier expounded Borunda's claim about the apostle Saint Thomas and the image. Much more important for the history of the controversy were the six letters that Mier wrote to Juan Bautista Muñoz in 1797.[59] Included with a multitude of topics and amid much verbiage were clear and cogent attacks on the Guadalupe tradition. Each letter was less correspondence than a minor treatise. In his haste, Mier was often inaccurate, but his arguments, like those of Muñoz, were to be very influential. He strongly denied that he did not believe in the apparitions, only that he believed that the cultus of Tepeyac antedated the conquest.

Mier accepted Valeriano's authorship of the original Guadalupe account, though his writing is unclear. He claimed to have in his possession a manuscript of Sigüenza y Góngora, written when the latter was administrator of the Hospital de Jesús in Mexico City, which contained the accounts of all the churches in the diocese but without any reference to Guadalupe. He pointed to the silence of writers, with special emphasis on Bartolomé de Las Casas, Antonio de Remesal, Gil González Dávila, and other mendicants. He cited Torquemada as saying that all the images venerated in New Spain came from the school of painting established by Pedro de Gante for the Indians of New Spain, and he denied any role to Guadalupe in relieving the flood of 1629.

Despite his exaggerated writing style, Mier expanded on the original points made by Muñoz and added some of his own. These have remained part of the anti-apparitionist stance down to the present day. With these two, it can be said that both the apparition tradition and the arguments against it had been fixed. Many authors would write about this in subsequent years and engage in often heated controversy, but they would not substantially change the question.

Fernández de Uribe

Reacting strongly to Mier's sermon, church authorities in Mexico sought a defender and found him in José Patricio Fernández de Uribe (1742–96). A man of prodigious learning who held many important posts in the archdiocese of Mexico, he shared some of the Enlightenment prejudices against popular religion and Baroque religious practices, but he drew the line at the religious skepticism of the century. He was a man of the Enlightenment but only up to a point.

Uribe first defended Guadalupe in a sermon he preached in the church at Guadalupe on December 14, 1777.[60] Instead of presenting the usual tired phrases and eulogy, Fernández de Uribe defended the historical veracity of the apparition tradition. He also attacked Enlightenment thought and attitudes, characterizing the era as "an age whose favorite profession is a rashly free philosophy for which devotion is superstition, miracles illusions or fables, the most pious traditions ignorant concerns of childhood, with which we blindly follow the errors of our ancestors."[61] With regard to the documentary basis of the apparitions, Uribe (as he often called himself) mentioned the various writings he had seen and which dated from 1640, especially two of them:

... the history of this same in the Mexican language kept at that time in the archive of the Royal University. Its antiquity, although not known precisely, is known to date from times not very distant from the apparition, both by the quality of the handwriting, and also by its material, which is maguey pulp, which the Indians used before the conquest; the testament of Gregoria Morales dated 1559, twenty-eight years after the apparition, in which there is precise reference to this prodigy, an instrument written on the same paper, so old and worn out that not even with the finest lenses have translators been able to decipher it in many places, all are respectable documents that testify to the antiquity of this cultus.[62]

Uribe offered no clarification about the first document. With regard to the second, it is clear that he was referring to the so-called will of Gregoria María but confused the supposed name of the testator with that of the notary.[63]

Uribe received two requests to respond to Mier's sermon. One was from the archbishop of Mexico, Alonso Núñez de Haro y Peralta, who commissioned Uribe and Manuel de Omana y Sotomayor to draw up a critique or censure of it.[64] Their report, which was submitted to the archbishop on February 21, 1795, was long and exhaustive. The two examiners claimed that Mier had obtained most of his ideas from Borunda, who had written an unpublished manuscript called "Clave historial" (Key to History). According to Uribe and Sotomayor, Borunda's ideas about Guadalupe were delirious and frenzied and smacked of Don Quixote's delusions. They devoted a large part of their report to rebutting Borunda's claim that the Apostle Thomas had come to the New World, while at the same time they offered a lengthy defense of the apparitions. The final recommendation was that the archbishop forbid the preaching of any version of the Guadalupe story that was not sanctioned by tradition. This he did in 1795. This decree was published in all the churches of the archdiocese on March 25, 1795. It was reproduced in the *Gaceta de México*, copies were sent to all the dioceses in New Spain, and it was finally published in pamphlet form.[65]

The second request came from the Chapter of the Collegiate Church of Guadalupe, which on December 16, 1794, asked Uribe to respond to Mier.[66] He agreed, but as happened with so many writings at this time, his *Disertacion historico-critica*, which was an expansion of his sermon, was not published in his lifetime. After his death, the executor of his will, Juan Francisco de Castañiza, found both it and the sermon among Uribe's papers. They were published posthumously in 1801. Uribe acknowledged the lack of any documentary evidence for the events of Tepeyac, saying that the knowledge of the apparitions had been maintained by tradition for a hundred years after the event and had then begun to be published from 1640 [*sic*] onward. He admitted that Zumárraga had left nothing in writing about the occurrence and attributed this to the fact that the bishop was too busy to have composed a juridical instrument. "Recourse was had to ancient or contemporary historians or those immediately at that time and neither was there found in them clear and individual notices of the prodigy. These two points — the lack of the former and this silence — have always served, if not as stumbling blocks to piety, as reasons for bitter feelings."[67] Admitting the lack of early or contemporary documentation, Uribe also testified to the existence of arguments against the apparition. "It seemed to us opportune not to omit what has been commonly discussed about this lack, although on the opposite side, in order on all sides to cover the apparition with an unjust suspicion."[68] He countered by claiming that the fact that none had survived did not prove they had not been written. They could, he said, have been lost with the passage of time or in the many floods that Mexico City suffered.

Beginning with chapter 8, Uribe attempted to prove the apparition tradition from authentic and indisputable documents. In chapter 9 he discussed the various historians whose works proved the apparitions, but

none of these antedated Sánchez. Like Becerra Tanco, he criticized
Sánchez for failing to give accurate notice of his sources.

This respectable author would have done a great service for posterity if he had left
us a precise notice of those documents that he used for his work. But either
because he did not judge this useful work necessary for proving a tradition that
he found universally accredited in the common and general concept of the miracle or because his design (as it is explained) was more to proclaim it as an orator
of the apparition than to detail it as an historian, he contented himself with just
the common notice and with assurances that he had before him ancient and curi-
ous documents, examined well and at length, in agreement with the information
in the most ancient and trustworthy and sufficient ones in order to go forward in
security with the historic eulogy that he contemplated.[69]

Uribe, however, did consider Laso de la Vega's account to be a translation, literal or paraphrased, of a very ancient Nahuatl account. He then
went on to make one of his most important, and enduring, assertions.
"The bachelor Luis Laso copied and made known this [Nahuatl account]
(as everyone has generally believed after Father Florencia) . . . and [other
authors] have worn themselves out in useless conjectures about the original author of this history, when it is evident who it was, enough to give
it the greatest authority."[70] Uribe's conclusion was that Antonio
Valeriano, a contemporary of the apparitions, had written a creditable
account of the event. Laso de la Vega "saw it, copied it, and published it,
as Luis Becerra affirms."[71] The identification of Valeriano as the author
of the *Nican mopohua* was complete.

Uribe's sermon and *Disertacion* are extremely important for two
reasons. The first is that in his sermon he made the first clear references
to the doubts and questions raised by opponents of the apparitions
(Muñoz's "Memoria" was not yet known in New Spain). He made
explicit what had been implicit in the works of other authors. The second
reason is that in his *Disertacion historico-critica* he was the first person
positively to identify the so-called *Relación* of Antonio Valeriano with the
Nican mopohua. Uribe was highly critical of those who denied the
apparitions, equating them with the skeptical and rationalistic spirits of
the Enlightenment, and in general he followed the standard argumentation of the defenders of the traditional account.

Guadalupe and Nationhood

When Father Miguel de Hidalgo y Costilla raised the banner of revolution on September 16, 1810, he chose the Virgin of Guadalupe as his symbol. In so doing, he consolidated a process that had begun with Miguel

Sánchez, though now she was identified not with *criollismo* but with Mexican nationhood. The symbolism of Guadalupe played an important role throughout the campaign for independence. After Hidalgo's defeat and execution in 1811, the leadership of the movement fell to another priest, José María Morelos y Pavón, also a devoted *guadalupano*. In 1815, he too was defeated and executed, after which the movement fell into sporadic guerrilla warfare. The situation changed dramatically in 1820 when a military revolt in Spain brought a liberal and mildly anticlerical government to power. This turned the conservative elements of New Spain toward independence. "Ironically, a conservative colony would thus gain independence from a temporarily liberal mother country."[72] The defection of the Royalist general Agustín de Iturbide sealed the fate of Spanish rule, and independence was formally recognized by the Treaty of Córdoba in 1821. A junta was formed to rule the country and a regency to seek a European prince to become king or emperor. In less than a year, however, Iturbide overthrew both and proclaimed himself emperor as Agustín I. As Simón Bolívar bitingly commented, he ruled "by the grace of God and bayonets."

Iturbide, in turn, was deposed in February 1823 by Republican forces under the leadership of General Antonio López de Santa Anna. In the following year, a new constitution was enacted, and one of the revolutionary leaders, Félix Fernández, who had changed his name to Guadalupe Victoria, became Mexico's first elected president. This did not bring stability, as Mexico was bitterly divided between federalist (here meaning decentralizing) and centralizing forces. The new constitution was federalist, in imitation of that of the United States. The leaders of Mexico were, for the most part, members of two opposed Masonic lodges, the York Rite (Yorkinos) and the Scottish Rite (Escoceses). Victoria was able to serve out his term, one of the few presidents to do so in that century, but Mexico entered a long period of turbulence and civil disturbance. Much of this centered around the enigmatic figure of Santa Anna (1794–1876), who actually served in the presidency on eleven different occasions. The low point was reached in the revolt of Texas (1835–36) and the disastrous war with the United States (1846–48). As a result, Mexico lost almost half its territory. It was a supreme irony, and humiliation, that the treaty ending that war, the Treaty of Guadalupe-Hidalgo, was signed at Tepeyac. The instability continued through a musical-chairs series of governments. It is instructive to note that the early years of almost all the protagonists in the Guadalupan controversy were spent against the background of war, revolution, and political instability.

Throughout this period, Guadalupe continued to be the preeminent symbol of Mexican nationality. After independence, an image of Guadalupe was placed in the meeting hall of the Chamber of Deputies.[73] Iturbide professed devotion to *la guadalupana*. Throughout the nineteenth century, this identification grew closer and, with it, the need to defend the authenticity of the image and the apparitions against all critics. After Muñoz's "Memoria" became known in Mexico City in 1819, apologists for the apparitions would spend the next thirty years directing their rebuttals against it.

One of the first responses was by Manuel Gómez Marín, published in that same year of 1819, under the title *Defensa guadalupana . . .* (Defense of Guadalupe). He used what were by this time the standard arguments in favor of the apparitions, but also included some strong attacks on Muñoz. Another early apologist was the priest José Miguel Guridi y Alcocer (1763–1828), who published two major works in defense of Guadalupe. The first was a sermon preached before an assembly of lawyers in 1804.[74] His purpose was to "dispel the latest objections that biting criticism has produced in our days against the miracle, as against all and many others because the eighteenth century from which we have emerged, although called [the century] of Lights because of its scientific advances, could rather be called 'of darkness' because of the shadows with which it has sought to obscure the truths of religion and piety."[75] For him, the beauty and perfection of the image together with a constant tradition were the two principal arguments in favor of the authenticity of the apparition story.

In a note to this sermon, Guridi y Alcocer added his bit to the identification of Valeriano as the author of the *Nican mopohua*. Surveying the different works on the tradition, he wrote, "Don Luis Laso de la Vega, chaplain of the sanctuary and later prebendary of Mexico, made known a history of the miracle, written in Mexican [Nahuatl], which was published in 1649 in Mexico, and it is a paraphrase of that of Don Antonio Valeriano."[76]

Guridi y Alcocer's second work was *Apología de la aparición de Nuestra Señora de Guadalupe de Méjico: En respuesta a la disertación que la impugna* (Defense of the Apparition of Our Lady of Guadalupe of Mexico: In Response to the Dissertation that Impugns It), published in 1820. The "Disertación," of course, was that of Juan Bautista Muñoz. On the supposition that not all his readers would have access to Muñoz's original text, he included it verbatim in his refutation. He followed Muñoz point by point, disputing the latter's claim of the silence of authorities, citing Becerra Tanco and Florencia. In addition, he included the usual appeal to tradition which was kept in the memories of hearts of both Spaniards and Indians.[77] He likewise emphasized that the papal approval of the proper mass and office constituted a proof of the authenticity of the apparitions. As with his sermon, Guridi y Alcocer appended a list of authors and documents that corroborated the apparitions.

In this work, he returned to the authorship of the *Nican mopohua*.[78] "And although the writers disagree about the original — Florencia attributes it to Fray Jerónimo Mendieta and Cabrera to Fray Francisco Gómez — the most common and probable opinion considers it to be that of Antonio Valeriano, governor of Tlatelolco, followed by Becerra, Sigüenza, Boturini, and Uribe, who establishes it firmly."[79] In fact, as has been shown, the first two did not identify Valeriano as the author of the *Nican mopohua*. Guridi y Alcocer also demonstrated the importance of the identification as a compensation for the lack of documentary evidence when he spoke of how Uribe "shows at length the moral certainty that a very ancient history was written by Don Antonio Valeriano, who was a contemporary of the apparition and who was endowed with the talents that guarantee his credit as an historian."[80] This, of course, became the predominant motive for the identification, since it rebutted the accusation that there was no document that verified the miracle.

Probably the most magisterial defense of the apparitions in the early part of the century was that of Carlos María de Bustamante (1774–1848). A lawyer by training, he was also a journalist and prominent in public and political life. There is a certain amount of confusion about his works in defense of Guadalupe. In 1840 he published *La aparicion de N.tra Señora de Guadalupe de México . . .* (The Apparition of Our Lady of Guadalupe of Mexico). This, too, was a refutation of Muñoz's "Memoria," especially the parts that cited Sahagún's *Historia general*. The first part of the work, called "Disertación guadalupana" (Guadalupan Dissertation), is twenty-two pages long and is the part that is specifically devoted to Guadalupe. The rest of the work, however, is a translation of Sahagún's account of the conquest of Mexico, taken from chapters 1 through 42 of the *Historia general*. This section has no connection whatever with Guadalupe.[81]

Further confusion arises with Bustamante's works as reproduced in the *Testimonios históricos guadalupanos*. The editors have placed two works together under Bustamante's name with the overall title "Elogios y defensa guadalupanos" (Praise and Defense of Guadalupe). The first of these works is titled "La aparición guadalupana de México," which was originally published in 1843.[82] It is an entirely different work from the one published in 1840 with a similar title. Grajales and Burrus in their Guadalupan bibliography attribute it to Juan Francisco Valdés.[83] The first part of this work covered pretty much the same material as the previous work. Bustamante began with a detailed description of the chaotic state of New Spain in 1531 in order to answer the question, "*Is there a basis*

*for doubting the apparition of Guadalupe because there is no reference in
the writings of Señor Zumárraga or did he produce any account of it, and
because this prelate did not make the event known, the most portentous
that has occurred in this New World?*"[84] He then immediately added
another question, which he called the central point of his dissertation:
"*Will the arguments that Sr. D. Juan Bautista Muñoz . . . presents to us
against this apparition be enough to destroy the general belief that we
have regarding this miracle?*"[85] He believed that one reason for Zumárraga's silence was the unsettled condition of New Spain and his fear of
what his enemies would do with any judicial act. The author also fell
back on the familiar documents, such as the Valeriano account and the
will of Gregoria Morales. Most of his arguments were taken from Uribe.
He also cited the capitular inquiry of 1666 and devoted considerable
space to Indian songs and dances.

The second work under Bustamante's name in the *Testimonios histori-
cos guadalupanos* is titled "Manifiesto de la Junta Guadalupana a los
mexicanos, y disertacion histórico-crítica sobre la aparición de Nuestra
Señora en Tepeyac" (Manifesto of the Guadalupan Committee to the
People of Mexico and Historical-Critical Dissertation on the Appearance
of Our Lady at Tepeyac).[86] It was written in 1831 on the occasion of the
three-hundredth anniversary of the apparitions. This was the work of a
committee of prominent citizens of Mexico City appointed by the city
government for the purpose of arranging a proper celebration of the
anniversary. The minutes of the committee's meetings are given in full.
After these, there is a brief refutation of Muñoz by Bustamante, dated
December 7, 1831, followed by a description of the festivities celebrating
the anniversary.

Bustamante repeated and strengthened the identification of Valeriano
as the author of the *Nican mopohua*. At first he wrote somewhat tenta-
tively, "but this lack [of documentation] can be supplied by the account
of the miracle which Don Antonio Valeriano did, if not as the author, at
least as the translator. . . . He wrote many Latin letters, and Don Carlos
de Sigüenza y Góngora makes him the author of an account in the
Mexican [Nahuatl] language of the image of Our Lady of Guadalupe
painted miraculously with *flowers* in the presence of the archbishop of
Mexico. It begins thus, 'Nican mopohua.'"[87] In 1835, as one of three persons commissioned by the Cathedral chapter of Mexico to make a report
on a tradition that the *tilma* had been laid on a table owned by
Zumárraga at the time that the image was formed, Bustamante was less
hesitant. "Besides, let us reflect that we have an ancient account in
Mexican, written in the hand of *Don Antonio Valeriano*, which begins,

'*Nican mopohua.* . . . Here is an original document of that period of the apparition."[88]

Even in the first half of the century there were those prominent men who had doubts about or looked askance at the apparition tradition. Lucas Alamán, a leading Conservative in the early days of independence, wrote, "I have also believed that I ought to abstain from talking about all those pious traditions, which have been the object of persistent dispute among writers and which ought to be more a matter for respect than of discussion."[89] In 1849 there appeared an important work in defense of the apparitions that is often overlooked by historians of the Guadalupe phenomenon. This was *La aparición de Nuestra Señora de Guadalupe de México, comprobada con documentos históricos y defendida de las impugnaciones que se la han hecho* (The Apparition of Our Lady of Guadalupe of Mexico, Proven with Historic Documents and Defended against the Impugnations That Have Been Made Against It), by José Julián Tornel y Mendívil (1801–60).[90] In part, this was intended as a collection of all documents that proved the historicity of Guadalupe and, in fact, is quite complete. Tornel y Mendívil drew his account of the apparitions from Becerra Tanco.[91] He also accepted Valeriano as the author of the *Nican mopohua* and included the entire capitular inquiry of 1665–66. He gave special attention to all the archbishops and bishops of Mexico who had a particular devotion to Guadalupe. In the second volume, he concentrated more on the arguments from silence and gave a point by point refutation of Muñoz. Referring to Archbishop Haro's reaction to Mier's sermon, he wrote, "Until that time there had not been any author, native or foreign, who would have dared to challenge publicly the Apparition of Our Lady of Guadalupe."[92] In 1859, José Fernando Ramírez (1804–71), a Liberal politician who would serve under Maximilian, said of the apparitions that they were "an event which is not based on any historical foundation but which originates in the middle seventeenth century."[93]

The first half of the nineteenth century was the formative period for the identification of *guadalupanismo* and *mexicanidad*. This identity became so fixed that from that time to the present any criticism of the former was viewed as an attack on the latter. Even the scholarly critic of the apparitions ran the risk of being considered a traitor to his nation and people.

CHAPTER TWO

The Controversy Is Ignited

❖

In the late nineteenth century the dispute over Guadalupe was involved with major developments in both church and state in Mexico. For the state, this meant the restoration of a measure of peace with the long rule of Porfirio Díaz (1876–80, 1884–1911). For the church, it meant the growth of the papal monarchy and the Romanization of Catholicism in Mexico.

The final downfall and exile of General Antonio López de Santa Ana in 1855 saw a flurry of anticlerical legislation that came to be known globally as the Reform (La Reforma). Laws were enacted that abolished clerical immunity from civil courts (Ley Juárez), forced the sale of church lands not actually used for religious purposes (Ley Lerdo), put all vital records and cemeteries under the jurisdiction of the state, and abolished certain fees for the administration of the sacraments (Ley Iglesias).[1] These laws were codified in the Constitution of 1857. The clerical and Conservative reaction led to three years of civil war (1858–61), known as the War of the Reform, in which the Liberal forces under Benito Juárez were victorious. The laws of the Reform remained intact, and Juárez exiled a number of bishops. The victory, however, was soon interrupted when the French intervention and the puppet empire of Maximilian (1863–67) ushered in a brief period of Conservative reaction. The overthrow of the empire and the execution of Maximilian in 1867 brought Juárez back to power, and the Liberal, anticlerical republic was triumphant. After Juárez's death in 1872, the anticlerical policies became more radical under his successor, Sebastián Lerdo de Tejada. In 1876 the government was overthrown by Porfirio Díaz, hero of the battle of Puebla on May 5, 1862 (Cinco de Mayo). He ruled Mexico as president from 1876 to 1880. After a four-year interim, he was again president from 1884 until overthrown by the Revolution led by Francisco Madero in 1911. To the outside world, Mexico was a model of an economically and socially progressive state, but beneath the republican facade Díaz was a dictator who ruled through a system of local governors and political bosses (*jefes políticos*). The Porfiriato, as his rule was called, was marked by human rights abuses and the expropriation of native lands. For the upper classes, the emerging bourgeoisie, conservative Catholics, and foreign investors it was a time of peace, stability, and growth. Those who were excluded from this progress characterized the Porfiriato with the ironic comment that Mexico was a mother to foreigners, a stepmother to Mexicans.

Díaz kept a fine balance between the church and the anticlericals, and while there was relative peace for the former, the memory of the recent struggles was still fresh. Liberal educational reforms, the increasing influence of positivism, and Protestant missionary activity put the Catholic Church in Mexico on the defensive. Toward the end of his rule, Díaz became more conservative and began to seek an accommodation with the church, a move that came to be known as the policy of conciliation. Díaz also cultivated good relations and even friendships with several of the Mexican bishops. As a result, there was a bloc of Catholics who were willing to accept the basic tenets of nineteenth-century liberalism and accommodate themselves to the Porfiriato. Others, known as social Catholics, rejected compromise with the regime and focused on the plight of the working man and the poor.[2]

At the same time, there were deep changes within the worldwide Catholic Church. Partly as a result of the chaos unleashed by the French Revolution, there was an accelerated move toward centralization and enhanced papal monarchy, a movement known as Ultramontanism (from the Latin, meaning "beyond the mountains" and referring to the view of Rome from France). During the long pontificate of Pius IX (1846–78), the conservative, ultramontane forces came into the ascendancy and achieved a major, if not entirely creditable, victory in the definition of papal infallibility at the First Vatican Council (1870–71). The subsequent pontificate of Leo XIII (1878–1903) brought little change, and Roman centralizing tendencies continued unabated. A corollary to this was that popes could not admit to mistakes or errors, nor could they change or contradict the teachings of their predecessors.

Philosophical and theological differences within the church ran deep. The general tendency in this period was to substitute authority, specifically papal authority, for tradition and history. Teaching authority in the church became primarily a papal prerogative. The popes of this period sought to bring about a Catholic restoration, but one that would be totally under the guidance of the papacy. It was also highly clerical and hierarchical, with the laity having no active role except under the guidance of the pope and the bishops. Theology came to be dominated by the neo-scholastic and neo-Thomistic revival, with the Jesuits as the chief proponents, which emphasized speculative thought at the expense of historical context and development. This school of theology was divorced from historical studies and existed in a kind of time warp, oblivious to the evolution of dogma and institutions. One leader in this development, the Jesuit Camillo Mazzella, would play an important role in the approval of a new office for the Feast of Guadalupe. He and others sought to develop a philosophical system that would be self-contained and independent of contemporary thought.[3] Mazzella himself cheerfully confessed to an almost total ignorance of science.

The extreme conservative, ultramontane forces, resistant to all change or accommodation with contemporary thought, were known as integralists. The church was seen as the depository of absolute truth that needed to make no accommodation to the contemporary world. Integralists believed that the church should have a special role in any society, harking back to the union of throne and altar that existed in many countries prior to the French Revolution. There was an ongoing dispute over the "independent rights" of history, that is, the extent to which historians were free to pursue their research. This went beyond matters of dogmatic and moral teaching and embraced the issue of whether historians could question long-standing practices, devotions, and legends. In September 1863 a conference of eighty-four Catholic scholars, organized by the noted German priest-historian Ignaz von Döllinger, met at Munich. One purpose was an attempt to find a modus vivendi between ecclesiastical authority and free inquiry. Pius IX responded on December 21 in the letter "Tuas Libenter," in which he used for the first time in a papal document the phrase "ordinary magisterium" and commanded conformity with it. This was often given a narrowly authoritarian definition. Anything that tended to limit or threaten the authority of the church, increasingly identified with the authority of the pope, was to be rejected. Thus, Catholic historians were obliged not just by the dogmas of faith but also by the decisions of the Roman congregations and the opinions commonly accepted in the schools. This presented difficulties since these decisions and opinions were at times notoriously non-historical. One modern author has claimed, with some exaggeration, "Catholics everywhere were particularly suspicious of historical study, because, as the study of facts, it was less amenable to authority and less controllable by interest than philosophical speculation."[4] The negative attitude of the papacy

resulted in the Syllabus of Errors (1864), the condemnation of American-
ism (1899), which is sometimes called the "phantom heresy," and even
more strongly, the condemnation of Modernism (1907), which had long-
lasting and detrimental effects on Catholic scholarship and intellectual-
ism. The anti-Modernist movement intensified the suspicion of historical
studies and the attempts to control them. The Jesuits of the nineteenth
century represented a strongly neo-scholastic, theologically conservative
force, especially through their Roman journal *La Civiltà Cattolica* and
their teaching at the Gregorian University in Rome. Like other ultramon-
tanes, their ecclesiology was monolithic, hierarchical, centralized, tri-
umphalistic, and ahistorical.

The hierarchy and clergy of Mexico were generally conservative in outlook, and as the nineteenth century progressed, increasingly ultramontane.
Bishops tended to follow similar career patterns and were sometimes
interrelated, as in the cases of the Labastida/Plancarte family and the
Camacho García brothers, who were successively bishops of Querétaro —
Ramón Camacho García from 1868 to 1884, and Rafael Sabás Camacho
García from 1885 to 1908. Clerical formation had suffered during the
years of war and turbulence. The papacy and Roman curia tended to look
askance at many aspects of the Latin American clergy, whom they considered to be too independent and undisciplined. A particular concern
was the various Cathedral chapters, powerful corporate bodies since
colonial times, often at odds with their bishops, frequently in financial
matters. Rome's centralizing tendencies, especially during the pontificate
of Pius IX (1846–78), sought closer control of the churches in Latin
America. One tool in this control was the formation of clergy and the
appointment of bishops. Throughout the colonial period, both had been
under the control of the *patronato real*, which had left them almost
totally independent of the Holy See. "In many cases the clergy was portrayed as reduced in number and with insufficient formation, undisciplined, with a questionable morality and not very submissive to the
church authority. The hierarchy was described as not very attached to the
Holy See and accustomed to managing the business of ecclesial administration and discipline with excessive independence. The faithful were seen
as alienated from religious and ecclesial life, with little pastoral attention,
an incomplete evangelization, and relaxed moral conduct."[5] In addition,
there was a movement toward starting a Mexican national church that
would be independent of Rome. Eventually it came to naught, but was
threatening enough to cause concern.[6] For integralists and conservative
Catholics in general, the term "liberal" denoted all that was irreligious,
anti-Catholic and incompatible with the history and traditions of Mexico.

One of the most important ways of inculcating *romanità*, or the

Roman spirit, was education at the various national colleges in the Eternal City. Prior to the last quarter of the century the majority of bishops and clergy had received their formation and training in Mexico, under a system unchanged for centuries. Gradually, however, the ranks of the ultramontanists and "reformers" began to swell. One of the key instruments in this change was the Colegio Pío Latinoamericano in Rome, founded by the Chilean priest José Ignacio Víctor Eyzaguirre in 1858.[7] Both he and its patron, Pius IX, for whom it was named and who was the first pope to have visited the New World, saw it as a means of binding the clergy of Latin America more closely to Rome. In his petition to Pius IX in January 1856, Eyzaguirre said that one of the purposes of the college would be to prepare seminary professors for the various Latin American dioceses "who would model the doctrine, opinions, and customs of the clergy according to what they had learned in the school of Rome."[8] He saw a special need for this in Latin America. "If ever a country had need of strengthening more and more its bonds of union with the center of Catholic unity it is, without doubt, America, since it is the most distant by reason of its geographical location and the most exposed to the influences of evil passions, with few means of confronting them."[9] From the beginning, the Colegio's stated purpose was to promote the Romanization of the Latin American churches.

The Colegio was primarily a residence, with the students taking their courses at the Gregorian University under the direction of the Jesuits. As a result, their education was strongly ultramontane and theologically conservative. This outlook was all the easier to impart because of the youth of the candidates. Until about 1900, entering students could be no older than fifteen, and one student, Juan Herrera y Piña, the future bishop of Monterrey, entered the Colegio at the age of eleven. Facility in both Spanish and Latin was stressed, with most of the students also becoming fluent in Italian. This attempted restoration created a division within the Mexican clergy. The *piolatinos* or *romanos* formed an elite, or "old boy," network that was resented by other sectors of the Mexican clergy.

The division in the Mexican Church between the older and newer ways was well described by Francisco Plancarte y Navarrete, who belonged to the *romano* faction. He pictured the clergy and laity of Mexico as forming

a school that we can call conservative, whose principal tendency was to preserve the usages, customs, and let us also say it, the abuses, of the old regalistic Spanish church, in the ceremonies of worship, in religious practices, and in the education of children, in schools, colleges, and seminaries. Many persons adhered to it, especially the higher and lower clergy of the nation who, although they were of the purest lives, sound doctrine, and refined virtue, had not seen any horizons beyond those of the mountains of the cordillera of the Sierra Madre. With them were the older clergy, a part of the younger clergy who owed their formation to them or constantly listened to their voice, and the laity who in the same situation of lacking a broad horizon, gathered around them.[10]

The *romanos* were fewer in number and consisted of younger clergy who had been educated in Europe. Once the political ties with Spain had been broken, they also wanted to break "the chain of liturgical usages and customs in order to be more closely united to Rome, the center of Catholicism and the light from which emanates all truth."[11]

The first Mexican students were sent to the Colegio in 1869 by Father Antonio Plancarte of the diocese of Zamora, who together with Eulogio Gillow, bishop of Oaxaca, was a major supporter of the college. In that year, five students, including Plancarte's own nephew, set sail for Rome. On the ship, someone asked Plancarte, "What are you going to do with these boys?" He answered, "I am taking them to Rome so that they can study to be bishops."[12] This statement contained more truth than jest, since at least four of the students did eventually become bishops. Attendance at the Colegio soon became a stepping-stone to bishoprics. Among the alumni who became prominent in the Mexican hierarchy were José Mora y del Río (Tehuantepec, Tulancingo, Mexico City), Francisco Plancarte y Navarrete (Campeche, Cuernavaca, Linares), Martín Tritschler (Yucatán), Francisco Orozco y Jiménez (Chiapas, Guadalajara), Ramón Ibarra y González (Chilapa, Puebla), Filemón Fierro (Tamaulipas), Leopoldo Ruiz y Flores (León, Michoacán), Juan Herrera y Piña (Monterrey), Gerardo Anaya y Díez de Bonilla (Chiapas, San Luis Potosí), Manuel Fulcheri Pietrasanta (Cuernavaca, Zamora), and Othón Núñez y Zárate (Michoacán).

It is understandable, then, that the bishops, priests, and laity of Mexico felt intense sensitivity toward any historical critique of the Guadalupe tradition. It not only struck at a keystone of Mexican nationalism but opened the Church to the accusation of obscurantism and the manipulation of the devotion as a means of keeping control of a docile native population. In the late nineteenth century the controversy became especially bitter.

Early on, however, there were indications of sensitivity on the part of church officials to criticism of Guadalupe. In a circular letter of November 21, 1871, the archbishop of Mexico spoke of something new that was compromising the faith.[13] "I refer to the tenacious and open warfare that the enemies of God and his Most Holy Mother have begun to wage against the cultus of the Immaculate one and especially in her admirable invocation of Guadalupe." The Italian Jesuit Esteban Antícoli said that this referred not only to Protestants but to some within the church, including those who denied the miracle simply by not mentioning it.[14]

Vicente de Paúl Andrade

One of the major participants in the burgeoning controversy was Vicente de Paúl Andrade, who was responsible for the publication of Mier's correspondence with Muñoz in 1875. He was born on February 23, 1844, in Mexico City of a socially prominent family.[15] His father, Manuel Andrade, was a celebrated physician and surgeon, and an uncle, José María Andrade, was a well-known bibliographer and scholar. Vicente's father had been instrumental in introducing both the Vincentian Fathers (Padres Paúles, the Congregation of the Mission of Saint Vincent de Paul) and the Daughters of Charity of Saint Vincent de Paul into Mexico. His fondness for these communities and their founder led him to name his youngest son after the saint, and he entrusted the early education of three of his sons to the *colegio-seminario* directed by the Vincentians in León. Young Vicente entered the seminary in 1856, but in the following year it was closed because of a dispute between the governor of the state (Guanajuato) and the bishop of Michoacán. He then continued his studies in Pátzcuaro. He returned briefly to León when there were prospects that the seminary would be reopened, but that did not happen. The young Vicente shared his father's appreciation of the Vincentians, who had a strong influence on his life and development, and he entered that community on November 12, 1863, becoming a member of what a biographer called "one of the most amazing religious communities that has ever been able to exist."[16] In November 1856 he went to Jalapa, both to make his internal seminary and to teach Latin.[17] Sent to Paris to complete his theological studies, he was ordained to the priesthood there on December 19, 1868.[18] After spending time on the parish missions in Mexico and Veracruz, he was assigned to the seminary of Jalapa in 1869,[19] then the seminary of Zacatecas in 1871.[20] He returned to Jalapa in 1874, was at Mexico City in 1875, then went to Puebla (July 3, 1876–April 23, 1877), and the central house of San Lorenzo in Mexico City as provincial treasurer and secretary to the provincial, Agustín Torres, in 1877.[21]

There was an abortive attempt to have Andrade named a bishop. In a private interview and under secrecy, Archbishop Labastida y Dávalos told Torres that the new diocese of Tabasco was going to be created out of Yucatán. Andrade had been commissioned by the bishop of Yucatán, Leandro Rodríguez de la Gala, to handle the details of the division. This required his going to Rome, entrusted with not only diplomatic details but also a large sum of money. The division was made on May 26, 1880, for which the bishop publicly thanked Andrade in a pastoral letter (December 30, 1881). Andrade was proposed to be the bishop of Yucatán or the first bishop of Tabasco, and a canonical inquiry was undertaken. Torres asked the archbishop of Mexico to prevent the appointment if at all possible. It seemed, however, to be an accomplished fact. Andrade's elevation to the bishopric of Tabasco was initially approved by the Consistorial Congregation, which in 1880 reversed itself for reasons unknown, and Torres was named instead.[22]

Andrade had a reputation for being an intriguer and a rather crude practical joker. Though scholarly, he was also undisciplined. He was probably responsible for one of the opening salvos in this stage of the controversy, which can be said to have begun with the publication in 1875 of Mier's correspondence with Muñoz. The publication of these letters was probably Andrade's work. He would also be deeply involved in the disputes of the ensuing years.

The Letter of García Icazbalceta

It was Joaquín García Icazbalceta (1825–94), one of the foremost historians in the history of Mexico, who reluctantly launched the most authoritative attack on the authenticity of the Guadalupe apparitions.[23] Though he was a native of Mexico City, his father, Eusebio García Monasterio, was Spanish, his mother, Ana Icazbalceta y Musitu, Mexican. Classified as Spaniards because of the father's nationality, they were compelled to leave the country in 1829 when all Spaniards were expelled by the newly independent Mexican government. They reached Spain via the United States and settled in Cádiz, where the young Joaquín became a Spanish citizen. In 1836 the family returned to Mexico, and he fought in the war against the United States (1846). His family was well-to-do, and he inherited extensive landholdings, especially sugar plantations in Morelos. As a boy he had been educated by tutors from whom he claimed to have learned nothing, but he eventually learned Latin, English, French, Italian, and some German.

At about the age of twenty-one he developed an interest in historical studies and collected a large library, often from books dispersed or confiscated from ecclesiastical libraries during the Reforma. In this he was encouraged by the Mexican scholar and conservative statesman Lucas Alamán. García Icazbalceta was part of a renaissance of historical studies in Mexico that included such scholars as José María Andrade, José María Agreda y Sánchez, José Fernando Ramírez, Federico Gómez de

Orozco, and Manuel Orozco y Berra. He was primarily an autodidact, and his historical studies based on original sources were fewer than his publications of hitherto inaccessible but important works, such as Gerónimo de Mendieta's *Historia eclesiástica indiana*. In part, this was deliberate, because he believed that he had to help preserve and make known Mexico's historical patrimony and pave the way for other historians. At that time many valuable collections, such as those of Ramírez, Andrade, and Agustín Fischer, were taken out of the country, dispersed, and sold to depositories in France, Britain, and the United States. By a cruel irony García Icazbalceta's own library of books and manuscripts was sold to the University of Texas in 1937.

In 1849 he published a Spanish translation of William Prescott's *History of Peru* and eventually carried on an extensive correspondence with the noted North American historian. He was deeply interested in printing and kept a press in his home. In 1852 he printed with his own hands a devotional work he had composed, *El alma en el templo* (The Soul in the Church), the proceeds of which went to the poor.[24] In 1854 he married Filomena Pimentel y Heras, by whom he had two children, Luis and María. His wife and third child died in childbirth on June 16, 1862. The loss affected him strongly for the rest of his life, and he never remarried.[25] He also served as director of the Academia Mexicana Correspondiente de la Española. Wagner, however, has pointed out that "the institution in which he was principally interested was the Sociedad de San Vicente de Paul."[26] This was an association of Catholic laymen, founded in France by Blessed Frederic Ozanam, dedicated to helping the poor. His involvement in this organization began after his wife's death and lasted to the end of his life. He was elected national president of the organization in 1886. He never held any public or political post or even an academic one.

García Icazbalceta has been accused of racism. Benjamin Keen was critical of him, saying "[his] holdings had increased at the expense of neighboring Indian communities." He also considered him to have been a racist and Darwinian (without using that term) in his attitude toward the Indians.[27] It is doubtful that a man of García Icazbalceta's conservative religious beliefs would have found much to favor in the theories of Darwin. Some modern authors have also considered him to have been a racist, but as will be seen in Chapter 7, their judgment is hardly unbiased.[28] The *Diccionario Porrúa*, in contrast, states that his actions on his estates anticipated the social legislation of the later Mexican Revolution.[29] Similarly, Bishop José Ignacio Montes de Oca of San Luis Potosí, in a eulogy for García Icazbalceta delivered to the Saint Vincent de Paul Society in 1894, strongly defended his sense of social justice.[30]

His life was long and he employed it in spreading good works. Wealthy from the cradle, he conserved and increased his property without ever exploiting the poor, without taking undue advantage of their labor, without ever practicing usury, that plague of our society which seems to tempt most those who have most and that is clearly cursed by the gospel. In his vast possessions there was never known that covert slavery, so common in some regions of the country, which chains the peon all his life to a specific master and a specific land without hope of bettering his most sorrowful fate. . . . The works of mercy that he exercised with his own people he practiced equally with strangers. For long years the conferences [of the Saint Vincent de Paul Society] of Mexico saw him visiting the homes of the poor and helping them generously, and when he was its president he exercised his influence inside and outside the capital, keeping the fervor of the older members and attracting new ones with his fine treatment, his opportune requests, his prudent insistence.[31]

Victoriano Agüeros asserted the same thing, saying that García Icazbalceta practiced social justice even before Leo XIII's encyclical on social justice, *Rerum novarum*.

Señor García Icazbalceta was before all else and above all else a man of charity. Great amounts of money passed from his hands to those of the poor. These were the true masters of his bounteous riches. . . . Even before Pope Leo XIII wrote his famous encyclical on socialism, he practiced the very wise counsels that the immortal Pontiff gave to the rich for the behavior that they ought to observe toward the poor, the workers, the servants on their farms. In his haciendas in the hot lands, Señor García Icazbalceta had implanted for many years a system of work and payment that left his workers content; they saw in him a father, always attentive to their needs: just, fair, open handed, and generous.[32]

He was probably paternalistic in dealing with his workers, but hardly racist or exploitive. On the contrary, he seems to have been a man of strong social conscience.

In 1881 García Icazbalceta published his classic biography of Juan de Zumárraga, first bishop and archbishop of Mexico, to whom Juan Diego was said to have brought the message of the Virgin of Tepeyac. This caused a stir because of its failure to mention the Guadalupe apparitions. The reason for this was that there was no mention of the apparitions in any of the records or documents of Zumárraga's life, including, most significantly, his will. There is evidence that García Icazbalceta had originally intended to include a chapter dealing with the bishop's silence on the apparitions. In the panegyric mentioned above, Bishop Montes de Oca said that, at the request of a bishop, "he removed a chapter, an entire chapter, from the work he loved best of all his works, a chapter that had cost him long years of study and sleepless nights."[33] Confirmation of this can be found in two letters quoted by Esteban Antícoli, an Italian Jesuit living in Mexico and one of the most fervent defenders of the apparitions, in his book, *Defensa de la aparicion de la Virgen Maria en el Tepeyac.* These were written by Francisco de Paula Verea y González, bishop of Puebla.[34] The letters are significant for highlighting the ahistorical attitudes and subjugation of historical research to the demands of popular religion. The first was written on February 6, 1880, "a un sugeto," prior to the publication of the Zumárraga biography:

I do not agree with the idea that the biographer-historian should content himself with not impugning the apparition of Our Lady of Guadalupe. . . . To write the life of the Venerable Zumárraga and to omit one of the principal and most serious acts attributed to him, what does that suppose? Bad faith? Ignorance, fear of the truth, wretched self-interest? Think about it. I judge that to say as the Church, the most prudent teacher, and to weave together very briefly what has been said and written and to conclude that episode by praising the popular piety and devotion to the Most Holy Virgin, would that not be better?[35]

In a second letter of September 30, 1881, the year in which the biography was published, the bishop of Puebla wrote, apparently to García Icazbalceta,

I take this opportunity to beg you earnestly and with every confidence that you not write or say a single word relative to the apparition of Our Lady of Guadalupe, in reference to the publication of the biography of Señor Zumárraga. The prejudice that the people's piety will suffer, *what saddens the bishops, as they have made clear to me,* you can consider better than what I can earnestly recommend. . . . *My pastoral duty,* my love of the Most Holy Virgin, and the confidence that I have in your good judgment impels me to make this request.[36]

Whatever the reason, the biography contained no reference to Guadalupe. This, however, did not spare García Icazbalceta from attacks by the apparitionists. His silence, of course, was regarded as significant. An article in *La Patria* on February 16, 1884, summarized its importance. "Señor Icazbalceta is a very illustrious person, and his silence on the apparition of the Virgin of Guadalupe is more significant than anything we could say against it. On the other hand the said gentleman cannot be suspect as far as his religious ideas are concerned . . . a guarantee of them being the esteem with which Archbishop Labastida favors him."[37] A similar opinion was voiced by the noted Liberal politician and writer Ignacio Manuel Altamirano. "In his authoritative book he does not say a single word about the apparition of the Virgin of Guadalupe of Mexico, and although such a silence constitutes only a negative argument, it is worthy of the greatest attention in the case of a writer as scrupulous as Señor García Icazbalceta, of a book as meticulous and researched as his, and of a tradition as interesting as that of the Virgin of Guadalupe in which Bishop Zumárraga appears involved in a special way."[38]

Antícoli responded with a short treatise published anonymously in Puebla in 1882.[39] He did not mention García Icazbalceta by name, but gave five arguments in favor of the apparitions and three dialogues refuting objections to them. The arguments were ones that by then had become standard among defenders of the apparitions: the constant tradition of the Mexican Church, the miracles worked by the image (miracles cannot be worked in favor of falsehood), the approval of the Holy See, the image itself, and the various maps and chronicles. In the dialogues, "Bonifacio" and "Guadalupano" discussed the principal arguments against the apparition tradition and, of course, Guadalupano successfully rebutted them. García Icazbalceta realized that he was the Jesuit's target and described the book as anonymous and virulent.[40] Antícoli would be one of the most energetic and important participants in the ensuing controversy.

In 1883 José María Antonino González, a canon of the collegiate chapter of Guadalupe, sought the approval of Archbishop Antonio Pelagio Labastida y Dávalos to publish a book he had written, titled *Santa María de Guadalupe: Patrona de los mexicanos* (Saint Mary of Guadalupe: Patroness of Mexicans). Though the title made it sound like a devotional work, it was actually a defense of the apparitions against critics. The archbishop sent the manuscript to García Icazbalceta for evaluation. The latter promptly returned it, saying that he was neither a theologian nor a canon lawyer. The archbishop responded that he was not seeking his opinion in either of those capacities but as an expert in Mexican history, and that "he was asking him as friend and commanding him as prelate."[41] Reluctantly García Icazbalceta yielded, and the result was the famous letter of October 1883, a landmark in the history of the Guadalupe devotion.[42] At the same time, José María Andrade sent the archbishop a number of books and manuscripts that served to bolster García Icazbalceta's arguments.

In the letter, the eminent historian did not evaluate González's manuscript, but rather examined in detail the historical questions attached to the Guadalupe tradition. "In my youth I believed, like all Mexicans, in the truth of the miracle; I do not remember where my doubts came from and in order to remove them I went to the apologias; these turned my doubts into the certainty that the event was false."[43] He also emphasized that he was writing the letter only in obedience to the archbishop, in violation of his resolution never again to write a word on the subject.[44] Somewhat surprising, in view of the subsequent scandal caused by the letter, is the fact that much of it was not original. Many of his arguments were expansions of those of Muñoz and Mier, and even his final conclusion, that the *Nican mopohua* was an *auto sacramental* (a form of Spanish religious drama), had originally been offered by Mier. The letter was not, nor was it intended to be, a scientific historical treatise, but rather a survey of the principal difficulties in the apparition tradition, especially the silence of so many chroniclers and churchmen. It contained quotations without citations and some minor errors. Although much has been made of these by apparitionist critics, the bulk of García Icazbalceta's arguments have remained valid to the present time.

Nothing is known about the archbishop's reaction to the letter, and there is no evidence that it caused him shock. Neither did he rebuke or criticize García Icazbalceta. In fact, there are indications that he already knew the historian's views on the matter. He once asked the historian Francisco Sosa, who had written a history of the Mexican episcopate, why he had not mentioned Guadalupe in reference to Zumárraga.[45] He explained why, and the archbishop seemed satisfied with the answer. Labastida said later that the omission by Sosa, a Liberal, was understandable, but that by García Icazbalceta, a Catholic, was not. So García Icazbalceta explained his disbelief to the archbishop who, apparently, accepted it.[46] Agreda y Sánchez related a somewhat similar story.

An elderly canon of La Villa[47] told me once "Señor Labastida was in La Villa de Guadalupe, he told me that the Congregation of Rites did not grant the new office and mass that had been requested in view of some writings that Señor García Icazbalceta and you sent." After the death of Señor Labastida some bishops insisted again that Rome should grant the new office and mass. The promoter of the faith gave a report [*dictamen*] against it. Señor García Icazbalceta showed me that report; he approved the reasons on which it was based; and later, when it was learned in Mexico that the concession had finally been given, Señor García Icazbalceta regretted it, foreseeing the abuse that the clergy was going to make of Rome's graciousness. Today we see how right Señor Icazbalceta was.[48]

González submitted his book to Archbishop Pedro Loza y Pardavé of Guadalajara for approval and publication.[49] The task of examining it was given to Rafael Sabás Camacho García, at that time a canon of the Cathedral and a fervent apparitionist. It was published anonymously in 1884 and dedicated to Ramón Camacho García, bishop of Querétaro, and his brother, Rafael Sabás Camacho, who succeeded him as bishop (1885).[50] There is no known reason why the book was published anonymously in another archdiocese. Iguíniz speculated that Archbishop Labastida y Dávalos suggested it as a way of not injuring García Icazbalceta's feelings, and that the anonymity was to prevent any publicity about the letter.[51]

The introduction to the book was written by the archbishop of Guadalajara. He observed that it was a time "when not just simple criticism, however baseless and reckless, such as appeared in times past, but unmasked unbelief has raised its impious voice against that prodigy, wounding to the quick the piety and religious feeling of Mexicans."[52] There was a second letter of approval from Bishop Camacho García of Querétaro. The book was rather lengthy. On the whole, the author repeated the standard arguments, including those of Muñoz. A major part of the book was in semi-dialogue form with a Mr. N, a non-Catholic, who acted as the devil's advocate, though eventually he was converted. González also had the standard arguments about miracles, tradition, the Holy See's approval, and the capitular inquiry. One original contribution was his reference to the Montúfar and Bustamante *Información*, which he had not seen personally but which he had been told about.[53] It was the first time that anything about this incident had appeared in print. His informant was "worthy of our greatest confidence because of his sincerity and good faith, notable for his faculties, especially for that of a great memory and facility."[54] González went on to quote from his informant, and the quote was quite accurate. "Around here rumors are running relative to a manuscript of the year 1556."[55] "One thing above all called attention and caused surprise: a witness, a priest, asked the archbishop not to order him to give testimony in this business because he was a chaplain of the viceroy and the *audiencia*, and the bishop had to repeat the command under penalty of excommunication."[56] In his refutation, González attributed all of Bustamante's criticisms to passion and hatred, and hence deemed them not credible. More details will be given about this incident below.

Apparently, Archbishop Labastida y Dávalos kept his promise not to divulge the letter, but García Icazbalceta himself showed it to friends, including some of Mexico's foremost scholars. Francisco Sosa declared, "I knew about it many years before it was published and if its author did not publish it before that time it was because he did not want to attract hostility."[57] Another historian, Jesús Galindo y Villa, said, "I read Señor García Icazbalceta's letter for the first time in 1889, together with my learned friend Don José María de Agreda, who then had the kindness to ask for it from Señor Icazbalceta in order to show it to me. The original was written entirely in the hand of the author himself, whose handwriting was then perfectly familiar to me."[58] Agreda y Sánchez claimed that he had been the first of García Icazbalceta's friends to read it and that he was given permission to copy it. "Certainly during the time that the letter was in my keeping, Señor García Icazbalceta came on three different occasions to show me some data that, in his own words, 'had remained in the inkwell,' and to point out to me where in the manuscript they were to be included." Agreda y Sánchez persuaded García Icazbalceta to let Paso y Troncoso read it also. The latter, apparently without the author's permission, made a copy, "which disappeared one day from his waste basket." More will be said about the theft of the copy below.

With García Icazbalceta's permission, Agreda y Sánchez also showed the original to a Carmelite, Fray José María de Jesús. Others who saw it were José María Vigil, Luis González de Obregón, Fernando Espinosa y Agreda, Nicolás León, and Bishop Ignacio Montes de Oca of San Luis Potosí.[59] Within a few years, the existence of the letter seems to have been known to others in the Mexican scholarly community.

The Montúfar–Bustamante Interrogatory

Though a small and elite group of scholars were aware of the letter, its existence was still not generally known and so it generated no controversy. That situation changed in 1888 with the publication of the Montúfar–Bustamante interrogatory of 1556. Until that time, almost nothing was known about this significant incident in colonial Mexican history. On September 6, 1556, the second archbishop of Mexico, Alonso de Montúfar, gave a sermon in which he praised the devotion to the Virgin of Guadalupe at Tepeyac and spoke of the miracles performed at the sanctuary. Two days later, the Franciscan provincial of Mexico, Francisco de Bustamante, delivered an angry rebuttal to the archbishop, condemning the devotion as neo-idolatry and claiming that the image had been painted by an Indian. On September 9, the archbishop initiated a secret investigation of Bustamante's sermon, in the course of which many witnesses gave testimony, but without once mentioning the story of the apparitions or Juan Diego.[60]

The subsequent history of the investigation involves some tantalizing mysteries. The mendicant historians who wrote the life of Bustamante did not mention it. The documentation of the inquiry disappeared and was not known again until the nineteenth century. The following account of the papers' fate was given by Agreda y Sánchez. According to him, the incident remained unknown until 1846. On April 30 of that year José Fernando Ramírez went to visit the archbishop of Mexico, Manuel Posada y Garduño, a few months before the latter's death.[61] During a conversation about the origins of Guadalupe, the archbishop showed him a packet of papers, saying, "What is certain about this matter is contained in this small folder, but neither you nor any other person will see it."[62] He gave no indication as to where the papers had come from or how they had been discovered. The archbishop then had them locked away in a reserved archive in the secretariat of the archdiocese. After his death on April 30, 1846, the see of Mexico remained vacant for more than four years, until Lázaro de la Garza y Ballesteros was appointed archbishop

(September 20, 1850). He took possession on February 11, 1851, and died in exile in Spain during the War of the Reform, on March 11, 1862. On July 6, 1863, Labastida y Dávalos took possession of the see, which he ruled until 1891.

In the vacancy following Archbishop Posada's death, José Braulio Sagaceta acted as secretary for the interim administration. He discovered that unauthorized persons were entering the reserved archive, and so he took the key to himself.[63] On checking through the archive, he found the papers of the Montúfar–Bustamante *Información*, but was unable to read the ancient script. He guessed, however, that the contents went against the Guadalupe apparitions. He took the papers to his home, where he kept them for more than twenty years. Fearing what would become of them after his death, he made plans to take them to the officials who were administering the archdiocese while Archbishop Labastida y Dávalos was in Europe attending the First Vatican Council. These were the dean, Manuel Moreno, and a canon, Eulogio María Cárdenas. In 1869, in order to be able to give them a verbal summary of the contents, he asked Agreda y Sánchez to read and summarize them. The latter took them home and after a month gave Braulio Sagaceta a verbal summary. Two months later, Braulio Sagaceta returned the documents to Agreda y Sánchez, asking that he make a written summary since the two administrators were not satisfied with the verbal one. After another month, Agreda y Sánchez gave him a written summary for the two administrators.[64] Shortly thereafter, the Jesuit historian Andrés Artola, a Spaniard by birth, told Agreda y Sánchez that the administrators had given him the original folder to take home and read. His reaction was that it was the final proof against Guadalupe. Later, Braulio Sagaceta, through Agreda y Sánchez and Artola, dissuaded the two administrators, who believed that the documentation favored the Guadalupe tradition, from having it published. When Archbishop Labastida y Dávalos returned to Mexico in 1871, the two administrators gave him the *Información*.

Word of its existence reached García Icazbalceta and his friend, José María Andrade, Vicente de Paúl Andrade's uncle. García Icazbalceta borrowed it from the archbishop. It eventually came into the hands of Vicente Andrade, although it is not at all clear how. He arranged for its publication in 1888.[65] In an introduction, he wrote that he had first heard about the documents from González's book in 1880. The title page said that it was printed in Madrid, but it was actually printed in Mexico City by the press of Albino Feria. The cost of the printing was subsidized by Andrade. The text was preceded by a letter of Agreda y Sánchez relating the history of the *Información* given above and followed by notes and "*aditamentos*," strongly anti-apparitionist in tone, that were probably the work of Francisco del Paso y Troncoso and that showed a dependence on García Icazbalceta.[66] The book had such an impact that it was soon known as the *libro de sensación*.[67] Andrade arranged for it to be reprinted in 1891 as part of his effort to prevent the granting of a new mass and office for the feast of Guadalupe.

In recent times, the truth of Agreda y Sánchez's account and the authenticity of the *Información* have been challenged.[68] There was no contemporary reference to the controversy, and none of the mendicant chroniclers who gave data on Bustamante made mention of it.[69] On the other hand, the inquiry was conducted in total secrecy. One reason for caution about the *Información* was that there was no indication of where or from what archive the original document came; it simply appeared out of nowhere. There was no mention of or reference to it prior to 1846. The idea that Braulio Sagaceta could have kept the document in his private possession for twenty years seems implausible. On the other hand, Agreda y Sánchez did name a number of persons who could have supported or rebutted his testimony. One should also keep in mind García Icazbalceta's evaluation of Agreda y Sánchez. "No one can doubt the rectitude and probity of Señor Agreda, who is at the same time in matters of our ecclesiastical history the most competent person I know."[70] At this time, it is difficult to make a final decision on the question.

To add to the mystery, the papers have again disappeared and their present location is unclear. Histories and works that quoted from them, including the *Testimonios históricos guadalupanos*, never cited their original location. Miranda Godínez did not have access to the originals in making his transcription, but had to make use of photocopies.[71] He quoted the former archivist, José de Martín Rivera, as saying that they were in the archdiocesan archive. He also said that he was told by the Swedish scholar Magnus Lundberg that they were no longer available to researchers.[72] According to an informant in Mexico City, they had been in the archdiocesan archive and Archbishop Corripio Ahumada had asked the archivist to give them to him. The archivist asked for a request in writing with the archbishop's signature, since the papers belonged to the archdiocese, not the archbishop personally, whereupon Corripio Ahumada bluntly ordered him to hand them over. He then gave them to Joel Romero Salinas for his book *Eclipse guadalupano*. Another informant said that they had been given to Roberto Salazar Salazar, the first postulator for the cause of Juan Diego. According to Grajales and Burrus, the original papers are in the Museo Nacional in Mexico City, but that does not appear to be accurate.[73] If anyone knows the location of these valuable documents, he or she is not speaking.

A New Mass and Office

At about the same time, there were two other developments that were to play important roles in the burgeoning controversy: a revival of a plan first proposed in the eighteenth century by the Italian scholar Lorenzo Boturini Benaduci to have a solemn coronation of the image, and a campaign to have Rome approve a new proper mass and office for the feast.

In 1884 Rafael Sabás Camacho García, at that time a canon of the Cathedral chapter of Guadalajara, conceived the idea of petitioning Rome for a new office and mass for the Feast of the Virgin of Guadalupe, December 12.[74] When he discussed the matter with Esteban Antícoli, he was surprised to find that the Jesuit had already composed a new office. When Sabás Camacho mentioned this to Archbishop Loza y Pardavé of Guadalajara, he was even more surprised to learn that the archbishop had commissioned Canon Agustín de la Rosa to do the same.[75] The idea was definitely in the air. The reason for this was the desire to have a strong statement of the validity of the apparitions in the historical lessons of Matins.[76] Those that had been granted by Benedict XIV in 1754 had been circumspect, using qualifiers such as *fertur* (it is reported) and *dicitur* (it is said) to describe the apparitions and making no reference to the miraculous nature of the *tilma*. Roman approval of a more unconditional wording would be seen as verification of the tradition itself.

It was the request for a new mass and office that occasioned the first publication, in garbled form, of García Icazbalceta's letter. In 1887 Vicente de P. Andrade, who in that year was named a canon of the collegiate church of Guadalupe by Archbishop Labastida y Dávalos, was living in the same apartment building as Paso y Troncoso, who at that time had a copy of García Icazbalceta's letter in his possession. Despite Andrade's requests, Paso y Troncoso refused to let him see it because of a promise he had made to García Icazbalceta. Taking advantage of one of Paso y Troncoso's absences, Andrade slipped into his study and went through his papers.[77] He finally found the letter by turning over a work table and extracting it from a hidden drawer. He then copied the letter rapidly and returned it to its hiding place. Not unnaturally, the copy contained errors and omissions, although on the whole it was faithful to the original. Together with his friend, Antonio Icaza, pastor of the parish of Santa Catarina de México, Andrade made a Latin translation, changing the format from that of a letter to that of a treatise — expunging some paragraphs, changing others. Both Antícoli and Francisco Plancarte y Navarrete (great-nephew of Archbishop Labastida y Dávalos) considered the Latin to be barbarous and ungrammatical, but theirs were hardly unbiased judgments.[78] This translation was published in Mexico City in

1888 under the title *De B. M. V. apparitione in Mexico sub titulo de Guadalupe exquisitio historica* (Historical Inquiry Concerning the Appearance of the Blessed Virgin Mary in Mexico under the Title of Guadalupe). This work did not mention García Icazbalceta by name or credit him with being the author.

The reason for publishing the work in Latin was obviously to influence Rome. In fact, Andrade sent copies of the work to all the members of the Congregation of Rites. He also sent copies to others, including Cardinal Mariano Rampolla (papal secretary of state); Rémi Siméon (a well-known Nahuatlato and author of a Nahuatl-French dictionary); Archbishop Labastida y Dávalos; the archbishop's nephew, Antonio Plancarte y Labastida (who was also destined to play a major role in the controversy); and the historian Genaro García. It should be noted that the letter was not published with a view to distribution to the general public. Rather, it was part of a major push by the anti-apparitionists to thwart Roman approval of a new mass and office. It came to the attention of Fortino Hipólito Vera, a priest of the diocese of Amecameca who had already published three books on Guadalupe and who was the first to attempt to refute the *Exquisitio*. In 1887–89 he published a compilation of Guadalupan documents titled *Tesoro guadalupano*.[79] He did not include the full text of the *Información*, but only the summaries as found in González and Antícoli. Apparently, it was his hope that García Icazbalceta would write the introduction, but he refused.[80]

In 1890 a group of bishops who had gathered in Mexico City for the golden sacerdotal jubilee of Archbishop Labastida y Dávalos examined the texts written by Antícoli and Rosa for the proposed mass and office and decided to send them to the master of ceremonies of the Congregation of Rites for an opinion as to which would more easily gain approval in Rome or if the two should be combined and presented for approval.[81] According to Antícoli and Velázquez, he chose Rosa's office and returned it to the bishops.[82] According to Tapia Méndez, however, the consistorial advocate, Angelo Mariani, combined the two texts of Rosa and Antícoli, but before submitting them to the Congregation of Rites wanted the metropolitans of Mexico to approve them.[83]

The death of Archbishop Labastida y Dávalos on February 9, 1891, delayed the request. According to Tapia Méndez, the two metropolitans and the vicar capitular of Mexico (Próspero María Alarcón y Sánchez de la Barquera, who ruled the archdiocese *sede vacante*) entrusted the matter to Plancarte, who in turned entrusted it to Enrique Angelini, the Mexican consul in Rome.[84] On December 17 of that year, Alarcón was named archbishop of Mexico, and he was consecrated on February 7, 1892 in the Cathedral of Mexico. Almost immediately (February 12, 1892), the campaign was renewed by the three archbishops of Mexico in the name of all the nation's bishops.[85] The anti-apparitionists, in turn, sent a special representative to Rome to work against it.[86] Together with other objections sent to Rome by anti-apparitionists, the *Exquisitio* succeeded in delaying approval of the new office and mass. As mentioned above, there is an indication that García Icazbalceta sent a letter opposing the grant, and that Labastida y Dávalos himself was not enthusiastic about the request.[87] The request definitely encountered opposition in Rome.

According to Velázquez, the petition of the three archbishops went to the Congregation of Rites, where Cardinal Vincenzo Vannutelli accepted the position of *ponente,* or relator of the cause.[88] He arranged for the publication of the papers so that they could be distributed to the cardinals who composed the Congregation of Rites. Included were a *disertación,* or position paper, by Mariani, the request of the three archbishops, Leo XIII's decree about the coronation, the office and mass approved by Benedict XIV, and a copy of the proposed new office. After an examination of the papers, the Congregation decided that it would approve the new office, except that it would retain the old lessons, precisely the part that the apparitionists wanted to change.[89] The three archbishops persisted and sent another request to Rome together with a copy of the capitular inquiry of 1666, from which they had taken the new lessons.[90] Cardinal Gaetano Aloisi-Masella, the prefect of the Congregation and a staunch opponent of the new office, argued that consideration would have to be given to certain anonymous letters that had come to the Congregation some time before. His tactic was delay. In their meeting of April 15, 1893, the cardinals decided: "Dilata reproponatur cum Adnotationibus S. Fidei Promotoris" (Delayed, to be returned with observations to the Promotor of the Holy Faith). This person was Monsignor Agostino Caprara, who drew up a list of thirty-four objections, all but two of them drawn from the *Exquisitio historica.*[91] According to Agreda y Sánchez, García Icazbalceta had a copy of this *dictamen.*[92] Most of the objections centered on the silence of contemporaries and the lack of documentation. These observations and difficulties were sent to the archbishops and bishops of Mexico early in 1893.

These, in turn, consulted Bishop Camacho García of Querétaro about the best form of response. Eventually, some of the bishops entrusted their responses to Antícoli, while others responded on their own. In November 1893 Francisco Plancarte y Navarrete set sail for Rome to act as the bishops' representative for gaining the approval, with his expenses subsidized in part by the bishop of Querétaro.[93] Archbishop Alarcón sent Antícoli's response with Plancarte, together with a request for the approval of the entire office. It was said at that time that numerous letters from Mexico denying the supernatural origin of the devotion arrived in Rome. Some were anonymous, but one, which was not, said that "Mexicans could abuse the new approbation in order to say that it would have been a definition and that the *guadalupanos* with the new approbation by the Congregation of Rites would want to raise the apparition to a dogma."[94] It was also known that a very important and highly placed official in Rome was opposed to both the devotion and the request. This was probably Cardinal Aloisi-Masella. Sabás Camacho, bishop of Querétaro, also testified to the impact of the *Exquisitio* in a letter to Vera dated January 22, 1894. "I had already seen what Father Plancarte wrote to the Illustrious Señor Alarcón, and through it was impressed by the great evil that the 'Exquisitio Historica' caused in Rome. But I hope in God, Our Lord, that the good cause will triumph."[95]

In Rome, Plancarte y Navarrete found himself plunged into the morass of Vatican politics.[96] On the day of his arrival (December 4, 1893), he had interviews with both the substitute secretary of the Congregation of Rites and the Promotor of the Faith, Caprara, and both said that the business was going well. Cardinal Vannutelli later told him the same thing. This turned out to be far too optimistic. By mid-December Plancarte y Navarrete had concluded that a prompt resolution of the business would depend on the *abogado defensor* and as well as on the intrinsic difficulties of the cause. The *abogado defensor*, or defending advocate, was responsible for responding to and refuting objections brought against a petition. Plancarte y Navarrete went to see the advocate, Angelo Mariani, and they arrived at an agreement as to what needed to be done. One difficulty was that the advocate did not know Spanish and was concerned that he could not base his defense on the papers that had come from Mexico. The books that the bishop had brought lacked ecclesiastical approval, and the documents in general were not in proper legal form. Ordinarily the advocate would have responded to the objections of the Promotor of the Faith, but because of the irregularities in the documents, the objections were sent back to the Mexican bishops. What was needed was authentic documents from the bishops on which to base the defense. It had been expected that the responses would be in Latin, something that would have overcome the language difficulty.[97]

Shortly after his arrival in Rome, Plancarte y Navarrete learned of the impact of the *Exquisitio*. He wrote to Archbishop Alarcón:

Your Excellency cannot guess the evil that has been done by the anonymous Latin writing that the opponents of the apparition sent here. Since it is written with a certain critical and learned apparatus, and since on the other hand they are completely ignorant here of the fundamentals of the apparition, the bad seed fell on virgin soil, germinated, and is growing, and if God does not provide a remedy, it will suffocate the good. In the meantime the theological arguments of the defenders do not please them very much. I heard it said that it is an historical question that should be resolved in an historical way. . . . Here theology will have to be the support of history, but the latter is in the forefront.[98]

Despite the fact that not all of the bishops' answers had yet arrived, Plancarte y Navarrete determined to proceed with the case. "However, the road is not as smooth as it seemed at first sight."[99] He also intended to have a meeting with Vannutelli and Caprara, but first had to prepare a long presentation in Latin or Italian in which he would give the arguments brought forward by the apparitionists and resolve the difficulties raised by the Promotor of the Faith.

By January of 1894 the business had made little progress. Rome tended to move slowly, and this case was no exception. Plancarte y Navarrete had learned that the cardinals would not meet before the second week of Lent and that it was possible that the Congregation would not meet until even later.[100] He was encouraging the advocate to finish the defenses and have them printed. By February, the responses of the bishops had arrived. This encouraged Plancarte y Navarrete. Since his arrival in Rome he had become discouraged about a successful outcome and believed that the Vatican's answer would be negative. Now, he was becoming more hopeful. Both the advocate and the Promotor of the Faith were impressed by his work. His hope was that the cardinals would be equally so. He was in the process of correcting the page proofs of the responses he had drawn up and which had been condensed and put in order by Mariani. They were to be distributed to the cardinals on February 10, and the question would receive definitive treatment on March 6.

To save time and money, Caprara wanted Mariani to condense Plancarte's dissertation, which he had originally written in Italian, and translate it into Latin.[101] This was done, but since some parts were not clear, it was decided that Plancarte y Navarrete should see each one of the cardinals individually in order to explain the more obscure sections. "This is what I have begun to do now, arming myself with the patience of Holy Job to accept the snubs of doorkeepers and servants and to spend two or three hours in waiting rooms in order that they might tell me to return tomorrow or things like that."[102] He had several interviews with Cardinal Vannutelli, who showed himself devoted to the cause. Both the Jesuit Cardinal Camillo Mazzella (who had taught him theology at the Gregorian) and Cardinal Raffaele Monaco (who ordained him to the priesthood) promised all their help. He had yet to see the other thirteen, but "I will go tempt fate, as they say here, to see if one or another will receive me or at least give me an appointment."[103]

Mariani's position paper, or "Disertación," that Plancarte y Navarrete presented to the cardinals consisted of four parts. The first was a reprint of the request and the summary of the inquiry of 1666 that had been discussed by the cardinals on April 15, 1893. The second consisted of the thirty-four observations by Caprara. The third was seventy-four pages of responses to these observations, probably by Plancarte y Navarrete and Mariani. The fourth part was a summary of other key documents: Benedict XIV's letter of 1754, the *Nican mopohua* translated by Agustín de la Rosa, and five testimonies taken from the capitular inquiry of 1666. As March 6, the meeting day, approached, Plancarte y Navarrete felt great anxiety because he knew that Cardinal Aloisi-Masella, the Cardinal Prefect of the Congregation, was opposed to the grant. The bishop had sought to see the cardinal in order to find out the reasons for his opposition, but after an appointment had been made the cardinal refused to see him. Plancarte y Navarrete went to Caprara, who said that he personally had no quarrel with the bishop's responses but that Aloisi-Masella had told him that he intended to prevent the grant. Plancarte y Navarrete was still unable to learn the reason for the cardinal's stance, either because Caprara did not know or because he did not want to tell him. He went to see Cardinal Mazzella, who said that Aloisi-Masella had attempted to win him over to his side. Plancarte y Navarrete could be sure only of the votes of Mazzella and Monaco, but that counted little against the influence of the Cardinal Prefect. He then went to see Cardinal Lucido Parocchi, who was busy but promised, contrary to his custom, to receive him on Sunday. Plancarte y Navarrete felt encouraged by this. He was even more encouraged when in a subsequent interview Parrochi not only promised his vote but said that he would speak in favor of the petition at the meeting. Parrochi was very influential among the other cardinals. After visiting Cardinal Luigi Ruffo Scilla, Plancarte y Navarrete could count on five votes. He feared, however, that not all would show up for the meeting. "Having exhausted all human means I turned to divine ones, making prayers and promises to the Virgin, to Saint Anthony, and all the saints to whom I am devoted, in order to interest them in the cause that I was defending."[104]

At noon on March 6, Plancarte y Navarrete awaited the outcome of the meeting at Vannutelli's residence. The cardinal returned to tell him that the vote was affirmative. The word *fertur* had been removed from the lessons and the phrase *antiqua et constans traditio docet* (an ancient and constant tradition teaches) had been adopted. Cardinal Mazzella had spoken so eloquently in favor of the grant that even Aloisi-Masella had voted affirmatively. "After a hard-fought battle the sixth of March arrived, a day on which hopes had changed to fears, but which was suddenly to bring the most complete victory."[105] However, all was not over. Aloisi-Masella found other reasons for delaying the decree of approval. He said that since the sixth lesson made reference to the coronation of the image, a complete description of the ceremony should be included. Until this was done he would not give permission for printing the office. Finally, however, on March 19, Plancarte y Navarrete had the printed office in his hands. He had won out, he said, over Italian diplomacy.[106]

José Antonio Plancarte y Labastida

Paralleling the campaign for a new office and mass was the move to have a solemn coronation of the image.[107] The chief proponent of this was Father José Antonio Plancarte y Labastida, a man destined to play a leading role in the Guadalupan controversy. Though his parents were from Zamora, he was born in Mexico City on December 22, 1840.[108] He was the tenth and next-to-last child of Francisco Plancarte and Gertrudis Labastida. The family was devoutly Catholic, with roots extending back to colonial times. It was also wealthy and prominent in the Mexican Church; the name Plancarte can be found among numerous priests, scholars, and canons. José Antonio Plancarte's maternal uncle was Archbishop Labastida y Dávalos, and Antonio's own nephew, Francisco Plancarte y Navarrete (1856–1920), was later bishop of Campeche and Cuernavaca and archbishop of Monterrey (Linares).[109] Two prominent priests and scholars in Mexico, Gabriel (1905–49) and Alfonso (1909–55) Méndez Plancarte were sons of Perfecto Méndez Padilla and María Plancarte, daughter of Luis Gonzaga Plancarte y Labastida, Antonio's younger brother.[110] Antonio received his earliest schooling in Morelia and Guadalajara, where his parents had moved. In 1852, he entered the Seminario/Colegio of Morelia, where his uncle, the future archbishop of Mexico, was rector and his brothers were already studying. Such institutions received both clerical and non-clerical students, and were a principal means of education for sons of the upper class.[111] The seminary of Morelia had produced some notable alumni, including José María Morelos, Agustín de Iturbide, and Plancarte's own uncle. A future alumnus would be José María Cázares, who would become bishop of Zamora and an implacable enemy of Antonio Plancarte. In 1854, Antonio's father died, and the following year his uncle became bishop of Puebla and was succeeded in the seminary by Ramón Camacho. Antonio and his brother, Luis Gonzaga, entered the seminary in that city in 1856, but remained for only a short time.[112]

Despite his attendance at these seminaries, Plancarte had no intention of becoming a priest. Rather, he was inclined to undertake a career in business. In 1856, he accompanied his uncle when the latter was exiled by the government of Ignacio Comonfort. By that time, he had decided to go to England to the college of Saint Mary of Oscott, near Birmingham. Though the college acted as a seminary, its primary purpose was to educate upper-class Catholic men at a time when Catholics who sought a higher education had to go to the Continent.[113] Together with his brother Luis he arrived at Oscott in August 1856. Antonio took an easier, accelerated course of studies, with the object of following a business career and of taking care of the family properties. Despite this, his first years there were not easy. At Oscott he became a close friend of a fellow Mexican, Ignacio Montes de Oca y Obregón, who was destined to play a prominent role in the Mexican Church.[114] Though they spent only one year together at Oscott, they remained friends for the next forty years. Eventually, Plancarte learned to love Oscott, and it left him with a lifelong appreciation of English education.

His friend Montes de Oca, after returning from England, spent two years in the Seminario Conciliar of Mexico City. Then, on an ocean voyage, he met Father Eyzaguirre, who persuaded him to study at the Colegio Pío Latinoamericano.[115] By about the age of twenty, Plancarte also decided to embrace the ecclesiastical state. This decision caused him some conflict with his family, especially his older brother, José María, who had become head of the family after their father's death. The stress gave Antonio stomach trouble that was to plague him for the rest of his life.[116] In 1862 he was admitted to the Pontifical Academy of Noble Ecclesiastics. Montes de Oca and Eulogio Gillow, another person destined to be a friend and confidant throughout his life, were also there. The purpose of the academy was to train diplomats for the Vatican's diplomatic corps, though Plancarte apparently had no intention of following such a career. The academy was well named, for genuine noble descent was a requirement for acceptance; Antonio was admitted because of his uncle. The students took their theology courses, however, at the Gregorian University (or Colegio Romano) under the Jesuits.[117] Throughout his stay in Rome, Plancarte was bothered by poor health, but he was ordained to the priesthood on June 11, 1865.[118]

Antonio's older brother was not the only one who had reservations about his priestly vocation. His uncle wrote to José María:

Antonio insists on following an ecclesiastical career, and only a transformation that would be clear to us would make him change. Having been educated in England he has deeply absorbed the spirit of individual independence, and neither you nor I nor the entire Society of Jesus nor all the fathers, calced and discalced, are capable of making him change nor would we have been able to have any influence. He caused me irritation in Paris and causes it to me here sometimes, seeing his indifference and even his repugnance for all worldly matters. He has no liking or interest for other things except those that have some aspect of the ecclesiastical and divine.[119]

Antonio himself admitted that he had a passion for glory, acceptance, and fame, which he always fought against. He liked to be in charge of things, and the spirit of independence that he had absorbed in England often caused him to act as an individual agent.[120] During his stay in Rome he had also absorbed the spirit of *romanità*, of everything Roman. This meant not just theology and ultramontanism, but a way of thinking, living, and even dressing. Pictures of him as pastor of Jacona show him dressed like a typical Roman cleric: cassock with shoulder cape and buttoned upper sleeves, a wide cincture tied on the left with a pom-pom on the bottom, shoes with silver buckles, a long cape, sometimes the zuchetto (skull cap). He later gave up the shoulder cape and sash except for solemn occasions.[121] His fondness for things foreign, for *extranjerismos*, alienated him from many conservative clergy and laity. The dislike for *malinchismo* was strong in Mexican society.[122]

In 1865 he returned to Mexico after an absence of almost ten years. Though his uncle was archbishop of Mexico, Plancarte went to Zamora, where the family properties were located. The bishop of Zamora, José Antonio de la Peña y Navarro, was a former teacher of Archbishop Labastida y Dávalos, who was responsible for his appointment as bishop.[123] In 1866 he named Plancarte pastor of Jacona, Michoacán (now known as Jacona de Plancarte), not far from Zamora near the family properties. Plancarte tried to refuse but eventually accepted the post, which he held for fourteen years.[124] His numerous undertakings during that time showed the spirit of independence and entrepreneurship he had imbibed in Europe. He rebuilt the sanctuary of Our Lady of Hope (also called Raíz), reconstructed the cemetery, paved the streets of Jacona, and founded three schools: the Colegio de San Luis Gonzaga for boys, La Purísima for girls, and the Asilo de San Antonio for orphans.

Plancarte became deeply involved in educational issues and stirred up controversy because of his criticisms of Catholic education in Mexico. His educational efforts encountered resistance because he was thought to be, or actually was, introducing European methods and removing native ones. He was also criticized for using theater as an educational tool, something else that he had learned at Oscott.[125] It was also believed that he allowed the girls of La Purísima too much freedom. In 1875 he was nominated to the Cathedral chapter of Zamora but refused the position.

Plancarte was known as a seminary reformer and as very ultramontane. He was part of the "new breed" of church reformers who looked to the papacy for leadership and direction.

Plancarte had many difficulties with his school for boys, San Luis Gonzaga, partly because he wanted to introduce the teaching methods of Oscott.[126] Many complaints were sent to the bishop, and on August 31, 1876, the school was closed after an existence of eight years.[127] Plancarte then took the student body to Mexico City, where they were joined by Francisco and Mauro Navarro and José Juan and Jesús Herrera y Piña.[128] Plancarte had conceived the idea of sending the best students to study at the Colegio Pío Latinoamericano. Later that year he set sail for Rome, accompanied by José Mora y del Río, Nicanor Mora, Luis Gonzaga, and Francisco Orozco y Jiménez. Also going with him were his nephews Pelagio, Agustín, and Adrián, sons of his brother Gabriel and María Josefa Alvarez, and another nephew, Miguel Plancarte, son of Miguel Plancarte and Modesta Garibay.[129]

Because of his many talents and accomplishments, it seemed that Plancarte was destined for higher positions in the church. In this regard, Montes de Oca related an interesting comment by Archbishop Labastida y Dávalos: "It would be easy for me to heap honors on him, and at the slightest request on my part the Holy See would give him to me as a coadjutor. But dignities were not made for Antonio, and he neither seeks them or wants them. A bishopric would clip his wings, and taking him to an unknown land would keep him from doing good on the vast scale that staggers our imagination. Let us leave him, let us leave him peaceful in our beloved town, and not seek to force the hand of providence."[130] Unfortunately for Plancarte, he was not to be left in peace.

Plancarte returned to Mexico in 1877 and in the following year helped organize the building of the Zamora-Jacona railroad, a project which received much criticism.[131] Though he is sometimes described as the builder of the railway, he was actually the leading figure in a consortium. The project encountered opposition on the grounds that it was unnecessary. Since the two towns were rather close (today they are linked by urban sprawl), the railway was probably rather short. Almost nothing is known about its subsequent history.

More ominously for him was that on July 15, 1878, a new bishop was named for Zamora, José María Cázares. Cázares had been a lawyer and a judge before becoming a priest.[132] His was an enigmatic personality, to such an extent that there were doubts in his later years as to his mental competence. He had reputation for holiness and for being apostolic, but he was a mystic, somewhat timid, an enemy of what he considered materialistic civilization. He even believed that railroads and newspapers were instruments of the devil. He was a traditionalist and authoritarian who lived in the past and possessed neither coach nor horse.

It was inevitable that he would have conflicts with Plancarte, and they were not long in coming. The situation was not helped by the fact that Cázares's appointment to Zamora had been opposed by Archbishop Labastida y Dávalos. On one of his first visits to the girls' school, Cázares wanted Plancarte to close the door between the school and the rectory because of rumors that Plancarte was overly familiar with the girls. Plancarte refused, saying it would lend credence to the rumors, and demanded to know the names of his accusers. Cázares refused.[133] The bishop was also unhappy over the construction of the railroad, although, paradoxically, he had blessed it on December 6, 1878.[134]

On another occasion, Cázares denounced Plancarte to his uncle, the archbishop of Mexico, for not having given him a legacy that had been left for the poor by Clemente de Jesús Munguía, archbishop of Michoacán.[135] On May 18, 1880, Labastida y Dávalos wrote him that Cázares had complained to him that when he asked Plancarte for money from the estate of the late bishop, Plancarte answered that he had already spent it on the Asilo de San Antonio in Jacona. He also claimed that Archbishop Labastida had received permission from the Holy See for him to do this, and that the local curia had never asked for the money. Despite this, the archbishop wrote a harsh rebuke to his nephew.[136] Ultimately, it seems, Plancarte was vindicated, but these incidents left a lasting hostility between him and the diocesan authorities of Zamora. Plancarte himself was so discouraged that he seriously thought about migrating to the United States or joining the Jesuits.[137]

The real conflict, however, would come over Plancarte's newly established congregation of nuns. When he founded the Asilo de San Antonio for orphans in 1875, he had offered the direction of it to the Daughters of Charity, who placed unacceptable conditions. In that same year, however, the Daughters of Charity were suppressed in Mexico. These events encouraged Plancarte to found his own order. In September 1873 he spoke with seven girls who aspired to the religious life and invited them to take their vows with the intention of forming a women's congregation for the education of Mexican youth.[138] It would be several years, however, before the foundation came about. Finally, in 1878, he established a religious congregation of nuns at Jacona, the first founded in Mexico.[139] It was initially called the Religious of Guadalupe, but in 1885 the name was changed to the Daughters of Mary Immaculate of Guadalupe.[140] Its principal function was the education of young girls. About the year 1881, Archbishop Labastida y Dávalos suggested to his nephew that the best way to preserve the existence of his community was to unite it with the

Hermanas Josefinas, founded by the former Vincentian José María Vilaseca as a replacement for the Daughters of Charity. Apparently, the two founders could not agree on the terms of the union. In 1882, Plancarte and Vilaseca went to Rome to seek approbation for their communities and to discuss merger. They were, however, at total cross purposes and could not agree on the rules and nature of the two institutes.[141]

Plancarte's fledgling community involved him in difficulties that eventually led to his departure from Jacona and the diocese of Zamora. The accounts of what happened vary in detail but are in substantial agreement about the following points. In 1880, Plancarte's nuns directed a college for girls in Jacona, La Purísima. One girl, Concepción Calderón, wanted to join the community but was removed from the Colegio by her father and dying mother. She refused to return home and took refuge with Plancarte's brother. She also appealed to the Holy See and the local civil government. Her father appealed to Bishop Cázares, who ordered an ecclesiastical trial. In February 1882, the diocesan curia found in favor of the father and ordered the return of the girl. To avoid this, she fled to Mexico City. Shortly thereafter, Plancarte moved the school there.[142] Additional details were given by a priest named Wilde, who had been a teacher at San Luis Gonzaga and was favorable to Plancarte.[143] According to him, the girl wanted to join Plancarte's nuns but her father wanted her to marry a young man who was not religious and who was said to be a mason. Wilde said that he had read Plancarte's testimony and believed that the weight of justice was on his side, though in some ways he may have gone too far. One result of this case was a lasting enmity of the bishop and diocesan authorities toward Plancarte.[144] A slightly different version was given by Cesáreo Munguía, who claimed to be quoting from Plancarte's diary. According to this version, Plancarte had an interview in mid-1882 with Bishop Ramón Camacho García of Querétaro, who told him that he had hoped for just such an eventuality. "In Michoacán they will never forgive you for having done better than they."[145] The bishop recommended selling the college buildings and moving to Mexico City, where Plancarte would be better received and would do more good.

Tapia Méndez's account of the incident differs from the others.[146] According to him, in February 1880 Ramón Calderón, and then Ignacio del Río, presented to the diocesan curia a *demanda* accusing Plancarte of keeping their daughters, Concepción Calderón and Guadalupe del Río, in his congregation contrary to the wishes of their parents.[147] The diocesan court decided that though the girls had genuine religious vocations, they were not yet religious in the canonical sense and so were still subject to parental authority.[148] Because they were still resolute, Cázares had them confined to an *asilo* in Zamora. Plancarte devised another way of freeing

Concepción from parental authority. When José María Orozco asked Plancarte to free one of his farms from a mortgage he held, Plancarte agreed, on the condition that Orozco marry Concepción. Orozco accepted and public notices were posted. However, the legal marriage never came about. A canon told Orozco that he would be excommunicated. But Plancarte told him not to pay any attention and that he thought it was a good way out of all the difficulties, especially of keeping the case out of the civil courts. Plancarte's enemies accused him of favoring civil marriage.[149] Concepción escaped from the *asilo* and sought asylum with Plancarte's younger brother, Luis Gonzaga. Guadalupe del Río was removed deceitfully from the *asilo* by her father, who then kept her sequestered at home. A canon sought an opinion from all the confessors in Zamora, who said that Concepción should not be absolved in the confessional. Plancarte and Mora y del Río replied that she had incurred no canonical penalty. Concepción sought the protection of the civil law. She also appealed to Rome, though Cázares refused to forward her appeal. On April 24, 1882, Cázares removed Plancarte as pastor of Jacona. The position was then offered to Mora y del Río, who declined it. In an interview, Plancarte asked Cázares that his accusers be summoned under oath, but Cázares refused and said that he had no need for the schools. Plancarte had also been denounced because, after a celebration in Jacona, he had been *solus cum sola* with Concepción.

This series of events was not the only thing that cast a shadow on Plancarte's reputation. While he was still pastor at Jacona, his brother, Gabriel Plancarte y Labastida, gave him a substantial sum of money in cash and orders of payment as a confidential deposit, on condition that the money eventually be repaid to Gabriel's three sons when they returned from their stay in Europe (see above). During that time, the money was supposed to return a moderate interest, though the method of earning the interest was not specified. A few days after receiving the money, Antonio Plancarte departed for Rome.[150] On his return, he was asked for the money but denied the debt. An appeal was lodged with Bishop Cázares, but, in the words of Gabriel's son, the bishop did not want to take action because "in those days there began the scandalous schism provoked by the pastor Plancarte against both the civil and ecclesiastical authorities of Zamora over the matter of señorita Calderón."[151] Shortly after, Plancarte was "expelled" from the diocese of Zamora, "escaping from the claws of the federal justice together with señorita Calderón."[152]

Because Antonio had taken refuge with his uncle, the archbishop of Mexico, Gabriel lodged a formal accusation of theft and abuse of confidence before the archbishop against Antonio. Wanting to avoid another family scandal, the archbishop offered to pay the sum asked for but asked for an extension of the deadline. Apparently, the money was not forth-coming, because after Antonio's death in 1898 his nephew sought repay-ment from Antonio's executors.[153] The heirs eventually had to appeal to Cardinal Mariano Rampolla, the papal secretary of state, while threaten-ing to make the matter public if justice was not done. One of them pointed out to Rampolla that the amount of money in contention was insignificant compared with the immense riches in cash and lands that Antonio Plancarte had left, "which without fear of mistake and being considered a liar I can affirm are the profits from robberies and illegal combinations" by the man whom the rest of the family considered an "upstart."[154] The accusation that Antonio Plancarte was not scrupulous in the handling of money is strengthened by creditors' attempts to secure payment from him at the time of the coronation.[155] Some of these attempts may also have stemmed from Placarte's tendency to act as an independent agent, the "independencia individua" that he had learned in England.

For whatever motives, Antonio Plancarte went to Mexico City in 1882, where he put his works under the protection of his uncle, the arch-bishop.[156] His uncle gave him and his community charge of a school for boys, San Luis Gonzaga, in Tacuba. Concepción Calderón, who had been living with another group of nuns since 1877, also came to Mexico City. In 1884, she became mistress of novices of her congregation.[157] It was in Mexico City that uncle and nephew became involved in a plan to amal-gamate clerical education in the archdiocese. There were three seminaries in the city. One was the Colegio Clerical of San José, which had been founded by José María Vilaseca in 1873 for the formation of the Padres Josefinos and diocesan clergy. The second was San Camilo, directed by the diocesan clergy. The third was San Cosme, or Mascarones, directed by the Vincentians.[158] These reflected a diffusion and overlapping of resources, and they seemed to be at odds in their approach to clerical edu-cation. Plancarte had an idea, which never came about, of having just one grand seminary in Tepozotlán under the direction of the Jesuits. Uncle and nephew devised a plan to merge all the clerical colleges into one. In 1883, Plancarte was named rector of the Colegio Clerical de San José. The archbishop then sought to separate the formation of diocesan clergy from that of the Josefinos. In 1884, he founded a new clerical college, San Joaquín, to replace all the others, with his nephew as rector, a move that aroused intense opposition. The administration and faculty of San Camilo flatly rejected the idea, but San Cosme was terminated in 1885, as was San José at approximately the same time, much to Vilaseca's anger. The archbishop ordered that all candidates wishing to enter the seminary had to attend San Joaquín rather than San Camilo.[159] Again, this seemed to reflect a conflict between the conservatives and the *romanos*. Plancarte y Navarrete described San Joaquín as "a little Gregorian university."[160] After the archbishop's death in 1891, his successor, Archbishop Alarcón, suppressed San Joaquín (February 1892).[161] The students were transferred to the Seminario Conciliar of Mexico.[162]

CHAPTER THREE

Coronation and Controversy

❖

The triumph and cross of Plancarte's life was to be the coronation of the image of Our Lady of Guadalupe. The placing of a crown on an image was a rare and splendid ceremony that required permission from the Holy See. Before this happened, however, Plancarte would be involved in another major project, the construction of the "*templo expiatorio*" of San Felipe de Jesús. In 1884 the Englishman Kenelm Vaughn had collected alms in Mexico for a church of expiation to be built in London, where prayers would be offered day and night for the sins of the world. Plancarte conceived the idea of a similar one in Mexico City, dedicated to San Felipe de Jesús, to make expiation for the anti-religious sins of Mexico. The uncle/archbishop approved.[1] Plancarte planned to use family funds and also began looking for money among friends and the faithful. The cornerstone was laid on August 2, 1886.[2] The project aroused great opposition in the liberal and anti-Catholic press. Plancarte was even accused of being a foreign Jesuit.[3] The church was dedicated on February 3, 1897.

While the campaign and construction were going on, Plancarte became involved in the even more grandiose project of the coronation of the image of Guadalupe. It was preceded by the coronation of Our Lady of Hope in Jacona, the first such ceremony in the New World.

One of Antonio's Plancarte's nephews, Miguel Plancarte Garibay, claimed to have had the original inspiration for this coronation. As a student in Rome, he had been impressed by a coronation in a Jesuit Church, and his first thought was to do the same for Guadalupe. But since Guadalupe had a collegiate chapter that was jealous of its prerogatives, it would have been difficult, and so he thought it would be best to start with Jacona. Antonio Plancarte was enthusiastic over the suggestion.[4] A brief was secured from the pope and the permission of the bishop of Zamora.

In 1886 Plancarte was back in Jacona, at least briefly. He and his nephew, Francisco Plancarte y Navarrete, made the arrangements for the coronation, an event that took place on February 14 of that year. It was an elaborate ceremony accompanied by various celebrations. At the banquet after the coronation, Archbishop Labastida y Dávalos declared, "This has been a rehearsal for the coronation of the Most Holy Virgin of Guadalupe."[5] After some consultation, the three archbishops of Mexico [City], Michoacán, and Guadalajara sent the request to Rome (September 24, 1886).[6] The only bishop who did not want to endorse the request was Eduardo Sánchez Camacho of Tamaulipas, whose role in the controversy will be detailed later.[7] The original intention was that it should correspond with the golden anniversary of Pope Leo XIII's ordination to the priesthood, December 1887. The pope gave his approval in a brief dated February 8, 1887.[8]

In the enthusiasm over the coronation, a decision was made to refurbish the collegiate church. The archbishop put his nephew in charge of collecting money for the project and overseeing it, while at the same time he was doing the same for the church of San Felipe de Jesús. Plancarte led a committee of engineers to inspect the building for the purpose of giving a report to the archbishop.[9] The original intention was to have the work done by the time of the coronation, but it proved to be more extensive than originally planned, and, in fact, turned into a major reconstruction project. This necessitated a delay in the coronation, to which the pope gave his assent. The date for completion was set for October 12, 1892, the fourth centenary of Columbus's arrival in America. Even this date, however, proved impossible to meet because of the extent of the reconstruction. The death of Archbishop Labastida y Dávalos in 1891 caused further delays.

Plancarte published a pamphlet (November 12, 1886) explaining the coronation and the plan for collecting money.[10] In it he stressed the obligation of the faithful to give money, because of the "substantial costs." These included the throne and the crown, "which should be the richest possible." Other expenses were the repair and refurbishing of La Colegiata, as the collegiate church was commonly called, and the solemnities of the coronation, "which ought to be splendid." In addition, there was a gift to be sent to the pope in gratitude for his concession of the coronation. How would this money be raised? Plancarte said that the archbishop would send to all the clergy in his ecclesiastical province copies of the image with his seal and that of the local parish, with space for twelve names at one peso per name. Indians could contribute a centavo. Another way would be to contribute jewelry containing gold, silver, or precious stones, which would be used in the crown. For this purpose, he made a special appeal to women. Plancarte's use of such gifts would later be the source of controversy.

An invitation was sent to all architects and engineers of the republic to present plans and suggestions for the altar and the *baldachino*, or permanent canopy, over the altar (March 13, 1887). Apparently, the old church did not have one and Plancarte was introducing a Roman custom. The three archbishops sent out a circular letter urging Catholics to contribute and to support the project (March 19, 1887). Plans for the altar and *baldachino* were received on April 12, and the junta unanimously approved those of the sculptor Calvo. The proposal was made to lengthen the church to give it more room, but this idea was strongly opposed.

On February 23, 1888, the image was removed to the nearby church of the Capuchin nuns, where it remained until September 30, 1895.[11] When it was removed from its protective frame, onlookers were surprised by the fact that there was no crown on the Virgin's head.[12] This led to another of those mysteries that have bedeviled Guadalupe throughout its history. Until the nineteenth century, all representations of the image, with the exception of the frontispiece to Becerra Tanco's *Felicidad de México*, published in Spain in 1675, depicted the Virgin with a ten-pointed crown. Antícoli claimed that the crown was still visible in 1838 and that no one knew how it had disappeared.[13] According to another story, the absence of the crown was noticed in mid-1887 when the *tilma* was photographed with the intention of printing stamps of the image for sale as a means of raising money for refurbishing the church. In June 1887, Plancarte described this to Crescencio Carrillo y Ancona, bishop of Yucatán: "He [Plancarte] immediately noticed that the photograph did not have a crown" and he went to tell his uncle,[14] who maintained that the original did have it. Vicente de Paúl Andrade and his associates circulated the story that Plancarte and José Salomé Pina of the Academia San Carlos had erased it.

On his deathbed, the painter Rafael Aguirre, a student of Pina, told the *guadalupano* historian Antonio Pompa y Pompa that Plancarte had come to the academy and taken Pina to Guadalupe, where he erased the crown.[15] Plancarte denied the story and threatened to sue anyone who circulated it. He also offered to pay six thousand pesos to anyone who could substantiate the story. Plancarte and others are supposed to have secured an *acta notarial* on September 30, 1895, the eve of the coronation, stating that the crown had never existed but that "just as God painted it, so he took it away."[16] The question arose again when the image was returned to La Colegiata. Gabino Chávez wrote a pamphlet on the disappearance of the crown in which he said that neither time nor climate could have erased it. Human hands could not have done it because no one could have gotten close enough to the image. This would also have required time and instruments. Erasure would have left traces, hence only God could have done it.[17] Velázquez wrote, "That it had a crown is indisputable; that now it does not have it is beyond doubt; but it is not known when it disappeared."[18]

A key point in the refurbishing of La Colegiata was the removal of the *coro*, the semi-enclosed area where the canons sang the canonical hours each day. As in Spanish cathedrals and collegiate churches, this was situated in the middle of the center nave, thus blocking the view of the altar for most of the laity. At La Colegiata, the *coro* in the middle of the central nave was removed and placed behind the main altar to provide more room for viewing the image. This, in turn, exposed defects in architecture and construction in the central area of the church. As a result, it was necessary to enlarge the naves, straighten the lines of the interior, construct a spacious apse, and especially to strengthen some of the vaults and walls.[19]

As it turned out, the restoration was extremely ambitious and cost enormous sums of money. In 1889–90 Plancarte undertook a fundraising tour that carried him through almost all of Mexico and aroused a great deal of controversy. His enemies circulated stories about the real motivation for the tour and invented a term, *plancartear*, meaning to defraud or swindle. In 1891, Plancarte went to Europe to arrange for some of the artwork for the restoration. Since the arches and vault of the *baldachino* could not be cast in Mexico, it was necessary to obtain them from Belgium. The altar and *retablo*, where the image was displayed, were made of Carrara marble and were carved by the Roman sculptor Carlo Nicoli. He also carved the statues of Zumárraga and Juan Diego kneeling in prayer.[20]

Similarly, it was necessary to turn to Europe to have the crown made. In July 1891 Plancarte went to Rome to take care of some of the business of his uncle's estate.[21] While in Europe, he went to France to see Edgar Morgan, a British jeweler headquartered in Paris. It was Morgan who made the crown according to a design by Rómulo Escudero and Salomé Pina. The work on the crown took two years and eventually cost 80,000 francs (about 30,000 Mexican pesos at that time), not counting the jewels. Because the original crown would probably tarnish when exposed to the open air, a silver crown of the same design, intended for permanent display, was made in Mexico City by the jeweler Dienner. The gold crown was brought from Europe to Mexico in May 1891.[22]

Presently, it is not certain if the original gold crown contains real jewels or paste. As of this writing (February 2004), it is not on display in the museum at Guadalupe. This has led some to claim that Plancarte substituted paste for real jewels.[23] A more serious accusation was that Plancarte did use the jewels donated by the ladies of Mexico for the crown but sold them in order to purchase stones that were more appropriate.[24] Tapia Méndez also says that some of the original jewels were sold in order to buy better ones that were also consistent with those already in the crown.[25] López Beltrán simply states that jewels for both the gold and silver crowns were donated by distinguished Mexican ladies.[26]

The undertaking encountered opposition, both on theological grounds (why crown an image that had been crowned by God himself?) and practical ones (the great expense involved). Plancarte's reliance on foreign materials and craftsmen aroused criticism, and he was accused of being a *malinchista*, a derogatory Mexican term for anyone who consorts with foreigners or is too fond of things non-Mexican. The response, of course, was that neither the materials nor the craftsmen could be found in Mexico.

The canons of La Colegiata strongly opposed the proposal to move the *coro* to the back of the church. Some of them began a campaign against Plancarte's plan. Three of the canons, who were opponents of the proposed coronation and claimed to be acting on behalf of the entire chapter, enlisted the help of *El Nacional*, a newspaper of Catholic sympathies. An article that appeared on January 23, 1887, accused Plancarte of manipulating his aged uncle into the coronation and of planning a restructuring of the church that would destroy its original character. An open letter to the archbishop, signed by a large number of Catholics, called for no change to be made in the church (January 29 and 30, 1887). The archbishop's response, written on January 27 but published on February 1, was curt and authoritative. "You can suspend your call to Catholics and especially the representation that you intend to send me because it is useless, with the single warning that there is not nor has been any other person who has undertaken the improvements that are intended to be done to La Colegiata than your humble prelate."[27] He followed this up on February 4 with a long letter defending the changes and his authority. The editors responded by reiterating their objections. In contrast, on April 24, 1889, *El Tiempo* ran a long article on the repairs to be made to La Colegiata and the need for them.

Further accusations appeared in the newspapers *El Nacional* and *El Partido Liberal*, as well as in leaflets and pamphlets. Some of the accusations were outlandish — for example, that Plancarte and his associates were planning the overthrow of Porfirio Díaz and were using money collected for the coronation to pay for it. López Beltrán related a truly bizarre story.

The enemies of [Plancarte], cleric and lay, met in secret — as in a diabolic witches' Sabbath — in order to weave their embarrassing villainy. They sought out a hidden place, and made up in the manner of the theater false impersonators meeting in a so-called session presided over by a pseudo Father Antonio Plancarte. The inspector general of police, General Carballeda, sent a secret agent, who from a hiding place which they had previously prepared for him, watched the session, headed by a fake Father Plancarte. This ridiculous and absurd meeting was attended by other figures disguised as clerics, a fake doctor, a fictitious lawyer, and the aforesaid old general or, better, an individual made up and changed into the general, as is usually done in theaters, comedies, and farces. They all gave an account of their apparent commissions, leading to the overthrow of Don Porfirio Díaz."[28]

The policeman, who apparently knew the real Plancarte, saw through the charade and reported it to General Carbelleda, who informed the real Father Plancarte.

Plancarte had a talent for making enemies. According to some sources, his strongest opposition came not from his open enemies but from those who claimed to be his friends. Jesús García Gutiérrez was quoted as saying, "Those from whom he had the most to suffer appeared to be his friends, those who walked together with him in the house of the Lord."[29] This may have been a veiled reference to the canons, especially Andrade, who was regarded as one of Plancarte's fiercest enemies.[30] In Plancarte's correspondence Andrade was referred to as "inimicus homo," and Bishop Cázares as "Señor X."[31] Despite the opposition, the work of restoration began on April 25, 1887.

The Rebuke of Bishop Sánchez Camacho

Another focus of opposition to the coronation was the city of Victoria, where the bishop of Tamaulipas, Eduardo Sánchez Camacho, and others wrote against it in the newspaper *La Verdad*. Camacho was born in Hermosillo, Sonora, in 1838, and later claimed that he had made his first studies among the "Apaches" of Northern Mexico.[32] By his own account, he finished his studies at the seminary of Culiacán and then went abroad with an exiled bishop, where they hardly knew a word of the language spoken. Then they went to Rome, "and there we were scarcely able to make ourselves understood by the Italians . . . and whom we had the misfortune of knowing and dealing with."[33] Another source said that Sánchez Camacho made his first studies in "California" and then went to Sonora, attracted by Bishop Loza y Pardavé.[34] There, he was ordained to the priesthood in 1862.[35] Sánchez Camacho then followed Loza y Pardavé to Guadalajara, where he earned a doctorate in canon law at the

Pontifical University. After serving in different functions in the archdiocese of Guadalajara, he was named second bishop of Tamaulipas in 1880, succeeding Montes de Oca, and took possession of his diocese the following year.[36]

It was Montes de Oca who promoted Sánchez Camacho's appointment to the see over the opposition of Archbishop Labastida y Dávalos, a fact that led to a cooling of relations between the two. Montes de Oca, who had been close to Sánchez Camacho, soon had occasion to regret what he did. He wrote in his diary, "The ingratitude of my successor in Tamaulipas, Eduardo Sánchez, a protégé of mine; it is not good that he became a bishop; he turned against me; and just recently I received an infamous letter that caused me very much pain."[37] Loza y Pardavé also had occasion to regret it. Sánchez Camacho celebrated three diocesan synods, in 1882, 1883, and 1885, that not only dealt with diocesan questions but also attempted to make some accommodation to the laws of the Reform. He was an ardent Mexican patriot but had an exaggerated respect both for civil government and civil laws. For this and other reasons he came to be regarded as tainted with liberal ideas. He opposed the pilgrimages that the poor of his diocese made to Tepeyac because of his belief that this was beyond their financial means. From that, he passed to the anti-apparitionist school.

In April 1887, Rafael Sabás Camacho García, recently named bishop of Querétaro and a fervent apparitionist, wrote to Sánchez Camacho to ask him to stay in line with the other bishops regarding the coronation. It was too late, for the bishop of Tamaulipas had just issued a pastoral letter against it (April 8).[38] In it he quoted the letter of the three archbishops to Pope Leo XIII and the pope's response.[39] "We do not want to appear, either now or at any time, as cooperating directly in the coronation of the Image of Tepeyac, nor in the consequences that such an act can have for the Catholic Church and its cause in the world or for the Mexican nation. . . . Therefore we have thought it appropriate and necessary to make known to our pastors and the faithful of our diocese that they are at complete liberty to contribute with their alms to the coronation of the Virgin of Tepeyac."[40] Sánchez Camacho claimed that he had forewarned Archbishop Labastida y Dávalos about the letter the previous year but had received no reply. On December 31 he wrote another, longer letter that was published the following year. This time he was more blunt. He declared that he had been opposed to the coronation from the beginning and that he did not believe that any educated Catholic could favor it. He was content to praise the piety of it, but said, "We condemn it and we qualify it as impious."[41] He believed that Mexicans were opposed to crowned heads and that the coronation was divisive and would cause problems with civil authorities. He then approached the most delicate problem, that of belief in the apparitions. "Belief in the Apparition of Our Lady of Guadalupe in Mexico is a purely pious belief in the widest sense of this word."[42] He then tried to demonstrate that the various papal approvals did not raise Guadalupe to the level of a dogma. He began to ramble as he pressed home his belief that denial of the apparitions did not constitute one "either as impious or much less as a heretic . . . and even less as anti-Christian," as a contemporary author, "worried and exaggerated," had claimed.[43] In a later part of the letter he dealt with the historical difficulties of Guadalupe.[44] "In a word, belief in the Guadalupan apparition is purely human, and no one has the obligation of accepting it under the pain of any sin."[45]

The archbishop sent the matter to Rome. Sabás Camacho drew up a short protest that he sent to all the bishops of Mexico. All signed it except Sánchez Camacho and Montes de Oca.[46] The matter was studied by the Roman Inquisition (now called the Congregation for the Doctrine of the Faith), which on July 9, 1888 sent a rebuke to Sánchez Camacho signed by Cardinal Monaco.[47] "The Most Eminent Cardinals who together with me are Inquisitors General . . . have deplored in the highest degree your manner of acting and speaking against the miracle or apparitions of the Blessed Virgin Mary of Guadalupe."[48] On August 10, 1888, immediately after receiving the reprimand, Sánchez Camacho publicly retracted all that he had said or written against Guadalupe.[49]

Sánchez Camacho later signed the letter that the Mexican bishops sent to Leo XIII to thank him for the grant of the proper office.

After the rebuke of Sánchez Camacho, the bishop of Yucatán, Crescencio Carrillo y Ancona, wrote to his priests, calling the Inquisition's action a new confirmation by Rome of the historical truth of the apparitions, a stance that almost all the apparitionists would take.[50] For him, the question of the historical veracity of the apparitions was now closed. This letter was published in 1888 with the title "Carta de la actualidad sobre el milagro de la aparición guadalupana en 1531" (Letter on the Current Situation of the Miracle of the Guadalupan Appearance in 1531).[51]

The letter was addressed to "N.N." in response to a letter of October 16 and was apparently part of an ongoing correspondence, possibly with Antonio Icaza. Carrillo y Ancona began by referring to Sánchez Camacho's pastoral letter in which he denied the apparitions of Guadalupe and said that he would abstain from supporting the coronation. This led to "the declaration, or better, the confirmation of that miracle on the part of an authorized tribunal of the Holy Roman Church."[52] As he had done in a previous correspondence, the bishop applied to Guadalupe the formula of the medieval Franciscan theologian John Duns Scotus in defense of the Immaculate Conception: "Potuit, decuit, ergo fecit" (He could do it, it was fitting that he do it, therefore he did it). He said that the same formula could be applied to Guadalupe and used to justify it. His correspondent had replied, "I am sorry to tell you that there is no parity," and went on to say, "I do not see Rome's resolution as a proof but only as a reprimand of the imprudence of the bishop of Tamaulipas."[53] Carrillo y Ancona replied that although the two miracles were not of the same nature, Guadalupe, like the Immaculate Conception in the Middle Ages, "had come equally in its turn to being declared and realized as a great and true miracle, and consequently as a sure historical fact."[54] Though it had once been lawful to deny the Immaculate Conception, it no longer was. In the same way, it had once been lawful to deny Guadalupe, but no longer. He claimed that in the rebuke to Sánchez Camacho the church declared the apparition to be real and effective. Otherwise, there would be no point in saying that it was a grave fault to speak against it. "The matter is finished. *Roma locuta, causa finita*" ["Rome has spoken, the case is closed," a statement attributed to Saint Augustine of Hippo].[55] He did not, as was later claimed, come out with a strong, unambiguous statement that the Inquisition's rebuke represented an infallible statement, but he did see it as raising Guadalupe to the status of an historical fact that could no longer be challenged. "If here the Church does not declare and confirm *the truth and cultus* of the miracle, what reason would it have for rebuking the imprudence?"[56]

Carrillo y Ancona sent a copy of his letter to García Icazbalceta, who tried to avoid any involvement in the issue. He argued that the issue raised by the bishop was outside his competence as an historian.

In the same way as the correspondent I believed that the rebuke referred to the manner of speaking and not to the very essence of the matter. But Your Excellency affirms, and this is sufficient for me to believe it, that the matter is finished, because *Roma loquuta causa finita*; and that being the case it would not now be lawful to enlarge upon purely historical considerations. This matter can be viewed on two levels: the theological and the historical. The first is forbidden to me by my well known incompetence; and if a declaration is made by whoever is able to do so that the fact is certain, we simple faithful cannot enter into the other.[57]

Some considered this to be a retraction, but others saw it only as a courtesy, especially since García Icazbalceta never changed his mind about the historical truth of the apparition tradition. In March 1889, he wrote to Nicolás León, "As for the question that is referred to in the *Carta de actualidad*, I avoid it like the plague."[58]

On January 4, 1889, *El Tiempo*, a Catholic newspaper of ultramontane sympathies, published a favorable article that claimed that Carrillo y Ancona's letter had destroyed all the anti-apparitionist arguments. The same newspaper carried a response to the letter, signed only with the initials E. B. y D., on January 29, 1889. Titled "Estudio Teológico sobre la Carta de Actualidad del Ilmo. Sr. Obispo de Yucatán, al Sr. Doctor Don N. N., México," it was actually the work of Father Antonio Icaza.[59] Everyone, he wrote, was assuring him that the Yucatecan bishop established the Guadalupan apparition as a matter of faith. "It was a fact: the Illustrious Señor Carrillo establishes in his letter that doubt about the Apparition is no longer lawful, and since this cannot take effect if it is not declared as a matter of faith by the infallible authority of the Roman Pontiff, we have the Illustrious Señor Bishop teaching that the Guadalupan apparition has been defined by the supreme authority of the Supreme Pontiff. That such has been his intention, his words prove at every step." Carrillo y Ancona derived this position from the rebuke of Sánchez Camacho. He believed that the wording of the rebuke contained a declaration by the church that it would no longer be lawful to doubt or deny the apparition. Icaza denied that the wording of the rebuke contained a definition. The essential conditions for a definition were missing. It was not something that involved faith or morals, and the pope was not speaking infallibly (*ex cathedra*). He also denied that the pope could make a definition about an historical fact. "Since the fact of the Guadalupan apparition is entirely foreign to faith and morals, and only an historical event, the Roman Pontiff can *never* declare and define it as true."[60] He concluded, "Please God, we may soon see *solidly* explained the complete silence of all contemporary historians about the event with irrefutable documents, rather than with fallacies, proving to us not the ancient cultus but the real and positive apparition on the slopes and summit of Tepeyac to the Indian Juan Diego, of that blessed and holy image, symbol of our independence and pledge of a happy future."

On February 9, 1889, *El Tiempo* ran a lengthy, unsigned attack on the "Estudio Teológico" that had originally appeared in *La Voz de México*. The article was verbose and extreme enough as to raise suspicions that it was written by the Jesuit Esteban Antícoli. The author went to great lengths to show that although Guadalupe was not defined as a dogma, it was authoritative and so could not be denied. "Did that author think about the implications of his manner of expressing himself — almost sacrilegious, at the least rash — against three and a half centuries of spotless piety, of most firm belief, against the supreme authority of the Church and that of all the prelates, religious orders, scholars of every kind, who have supported it, and against all the juridical and scientific inquiries that have been made to justify it?"[61]

A Paladin of La Guadalupana

From an early stage in the controversy, the Jesuit Esteban Antícoli played an increasing, and generally negative, role in the burgeoning dispute. He was born on December 26, 1833, in Monte San Giovanni, near Rome.[62] He entered the Society of Jesus in 1852 as a member of the Roman province. After studies at the Roman College, he taught philosophy at a seminary in Taranto. He returned to Rome in 1868 to teach at the German and Roman Colleges. Four years later he returned briefly to Taranto to teach logic, and in that same year went to Mexico, together with Father Andrés Artola (mentioned above), to teach in the seminary of San Camilo. In the following year, he was exiled together with the rest of the Jesuits to Texas, where he taught dogmatic theology for two years. In 1876 he went to New Orleans, Louisiana, where he taught philosophy for two years in the college of Spring Hill. Two years later, he returned to Mexico with the permission of Porfirio Díaz and changed his name to Victorio Suárez, though all documents of the Guadalupan controversy continued to call him Antícoli. It is clear that he came to identify very strongly with Mexican nationality and religion. In 1881 he was beset by a serious lung disease of which he was cured, he believed, through the intercession of the Virgin of Guadalupe. From that time on, he became one of the foremost, even exaggerated, defenders of the devotion. In 1885 he worked on the mission of New Mexico, and in 1889 returned to the college of Saltillo, Coahuila. In 1891 he taught theology in the seminary of San Luis Potosí, and then went to the Jesuit residence at Orizaba, Veracruz, in 1894.

Gutiérrez Casillas gave the following description of his confrere:

> The good Father was a good theologian and an observant religious; of a fiery and irascible disposition; somewhat irritating to his companions, since he could not endure contradiction. He attacked his opponent with excessive force and sometimes he gave vent to hurtful words. For all that, at heart, he had a good and humble temperament. Once the storm had passed, he sincerely asked pardon and humbled himself. His entire Guadalupan polemic was resented because of these defects. He ridiculed his opponents in a vulgar fashion, in part because of lack of knowledge of the language. His writings, simply because they were edited, came out less badly prepared. When he found himself involved in a matter, he turned into a fanatic. For him all those who denied the apparition were little less than protestants, impious, heretics, or rash in the theological sense, scornful of the authority of the Church, etc., etc.[63]

Unfortunately, this personal contrition did not extend to his written works, and there is no evidence of his having asked pardon of García Icazbalceta or others whose persons and reputations he had wounded —

even to the point of slander. *Res scripta manet*. Gutiérrez Casilla's assertion, repeated by Xavier Escalada, that "his zeal for the devotion to Our
Lady of Guadalupe was in every way edifying and worthy of being imitated" cannot be taken seriously.[64]

Antícoli conceived the idea of publishing a chronological history of the
apparitions but felt insufficiently prepared to do so. Instead, he recast his
previous works in book form and published the resulting work at
Guadalajara in 1884.[65] It not only covered the history and principal difficulties with the apparition tradition, but also ended with a new set of
dialogues between "Bonifacio" and "Guadalupano" which refuted the
"Memoria" of Muñoz and tried to prove that the *Información* of 1556
supported the apparitions. In 1892, he replied to Icaza's article in *El
Tiempo* in his book on Guadalupe and the magisterium of the Church,
which was published anonymously (as were all his books) and dedicated
to Bishop Camacho García of Querétaro.[66] Antícoli claimed that the three
approvals by the Holy See — the mass and office, the institution of
December 12 as a holy day of obligation, and the confirmation of the
oath of the *patronato* in 1754 — would not have been done without an
historical foundation.

He preached an extreme authoritarianism. His thesis was that a good
Catholic should obey even a hint of the church's will without questioning.
For him, it was the bishops who carried on the mission of Christ to evangelize the world. "To this right and authority that bishops have for teaching everything that belongs to the supernatural life or which is related to
it in some way there corresponds in the faithful the strict obligation to
obey and to hold as true what they teach."[67] The pope and the bishops
together constituted the teaching authority, or *magisterium*, of the
church, "from which it follows that to this teaching there corresponds no
longer *discussion*, as if it were a question of a private author but *submission*."[68] Since the Mexican hierarchy had always supported the devotion,
there could be no questioning of it. Referring to Icaza as "Don Estudio,"
Antícoli wrote, "Don Estudio of *lamentable* memory . . . by what he
added by way of conclusion to his condemned letter disobeyed completely
the authentic teaching of the bishops of Mexico: *he disobeyed his bishop*.
. . . Only a liberal Catholic could speak in this way, and we have painted
the portrait of the entire body of liberal Catholicism. *Poison* at the bottom, smoothness in *form*. . . . Heretics and liberal Catholics agree on *substance*, they disagree on *means*."[69] For Antícoli the magisterium extended
to everything in the supernatural order, including miracles such as
Guadalupe. Antícoli also claimed that Benedict XIV's approval of the cultus in 1754 was close to being a bull of canonization, though not quite the
same.[70] Anyone who denied Guadalupe was objectively a heretic. "If such

a one denies the competence of the Roman Pontiff in judging about the historical fact linked with the cultus, specifically, a limit is placed on the extent of the Church's magisterium, such a one is a *heretic*, at least objectively."[71]

In 1890 plans were afoot to republish the Montúfar–Bustamante *Información*. From what can be reconstructed of this process, it seems that in 1890 Paso y Troncoso was revising his *aditamentos*. One of the participants wrote, "It is a pity that he and Don Joaquín, who with their pens were able to do much good in this matter, are so intimidated. Don Joaquín fears that reproaches and excommunication will come upon him, and our friend [Paso y Troncoso] believes that if it becomes known that he is the author of our notes the defenders [of the apparition] will come after him and will wear him down in the press. He tells me that he does not have the vocation of a martyr."[72]

It seems that the apparitionists were aware of the intended republication. On October 15, 1890, Carillo y Ancona wrote to Vera,

I have seen the process against Father Bustamante or *Información* of 1556 by Señor Montúfar published in Madrid in 1888 with disgusting prologues, notes, and appendices in order to make the document work against the Guadalupan apparition.

Please tell me if the said process is authentic; if you know that it is true that the canon of Guadalupe, Señor Don V. de P. Andrade, is the one who published it, doing so in Mexico but making it appear that it was done in Madrid; and if you or anyone else has there the original of the process or an authentic copy. Señor Icazbalceta has one. Would it be the same?[73]

Carillo y Ancona went on to ask Vera to prepare a critical edition of the same work, with notes and appendices "that will make the reader see the true meaning that the document has, refuting and condemning the perverse and crazy intention of the anonymous author of the fraudulent edition." He assured him that Labastida y Dávalos would sponsor the publication. He expressed astonishment that the archbishop had not condemned the book. "And with regard to Señor Labastida, tell me, what does he think of that edition of 1888? Why does he not prohibit it as an evil book? If Rome rebuked a bishop, why does not the metropolitan, even consulting if he wishes with his suffragans and the other metropolitans of the nation, censure that booklet? Speak to him about this, even on my behalf if you think it appropriate."[74]

Vera's version of the Montúfar–Bustamante *Información* was published in 1890 as part of a work titled *La milagrosa aparición de Nuestra Señora de Guadalupe* . . . . In the following year the *Información* was republished by Vicente de P. Andrade with a provocative preface and the expanded *aditamentos*.[75] It also contained a critical commentary on some of the leading apparitionists, including Vera, Antícoli, and González.[76] There was also a lengthy notice on Marcos and other native painters of the sixteenth century, probably by Paso y Troncoso.[77] Teixidor said that the reprint, which was longer than the first edition, was subsidized by Licenciado Joaquín Baranda, at that time Secretary of Justice and Public Instruction, using funds from the Secretariat of Justice.[78] It is apparently this edition of 1891, and not that of 1888, that the editors of *Testimonios históricos guadalupanos* have reprinted.[79]

In response to this, Antícoli wrote a series of articles, intemperate in tone, for the Catholic newspaper *El Amigo de la Verdad* in Puebla de los Angeles (December 1891). These were published separately in 1892 under the title *Algunos apuntamientos en defensa de la Virgen del Tepeyac contra una obra recién impresa en México* (Some Notes in Defense of the Virgin of Tepeyac against a Work Recently Printed in Mexico). He also used them as the basis for his book *Defensa de la aparición de la Virgen María en el Tepeyac*, whose subtitle specifically stated that it was in response to the republication of the *Información*. In it he attacked García Icazbalceta by name. Of this work Nicolás León said that it was written "in a coarse and pedestrian style, a typical example of 'clerical' literature."[80] Antícoli followed this in 1893 with his *Defensa de la Virgen Maria en el Tepeyac*. The expenses of publication, like those of Vera's book, were paid for by Bishop Camacho García of Querétaro, who gloated to Vera, "Have you seen the other short treatise by the Reverend Father Antícoli, printed in Puebla, in which he puts ashes on Icazbalceta's forehead?"[81]

The book was an interesting example of the tendency of Catholic theologians and philosophers of the period to subjugate history to theology and church authority. Antícoli dedicated the first part of the book to refuting the arguments in the *aditamentos*. According to Antícoli, the event of Tepeyac was intrinsically and essentially supernatural and so could not be investigated as a strictly historical fact. There were three criteria for judging it: (1) the tradition that had been preserved and defended by the Church of Mexico, beginning with its bishops; (2) the miracles worked through the intercession of the Virgin of Guadalupe; and (3) approval by the Holy See. "There being, as there are, these arguments, it is now impossible that the apparition never existed and consequently the fact of the apparition is certain beyond doubt."[82] Thus, Antícoli removed Guadalupe from any empirical consideration, and by the simple assumption of its supernatural nature rendered it impervious to historical study. If someone should say to him that "this fact can be treated solely from the point of view of history," Antícoli would answer, "if the event is supernatural in itself and consequently theological, you cannot *in the concrete* prescind from the theological principles in the examination that you make of this fact."[83]

With regard to papal approbation, the fact that Benedict XIV approved the apparitions by his concession of the feast, the proper office and mass, and the title of principal patron of the Mexican nation, meant that "it is impossible that the apparition be false and that the Holy Image not be supernatural."[84] Stating his by-then familiar thesis, he launched into a vituperative attack on García Icazbalceta.

In this chapter [4] we are going to prove two things. First, that it is not lawful for a Catholic to impugn the apparition. Second, that on undertaking to examine the catalogue that the editors [of the Aditamentos] give us of those who do not favor the apparition, that author did not show himself a Catholic, much less a good Catholic, who, purposely writing the life of Venerable Zumárraga, first bishop and archbishop of Mexico, in the work that he published in 1881, completely left out everything that referred to the apparition. . . . So then, to speak objectively, the author of the biographical study of Venerable Zumárraga did not write as a Catholic writer when he said nothing about the apparition of the Virgin at Tepeyac. . . . Nor let it be said that in order not to impugn the apparition, the author judged it suitable to keep silence. That is precisely where the evil is: not to have submitted himself to the judgment of the Church, on the pretext of a lack, supposedly, of contemporary data. . . . Did the author perhaps think that what is theologically true could be historically or philosophically false?[85]

Antícoli's *Defensa* brought great discouragement to García Icazbalceta because of its virulent and personal tone. In 1890 he wrote to Nicolás León that "I call the book [the biography of Zumárraga] unfortunate, because having written it in defense of the bishop and in honor of the Church, it was poorly received because I was silent about that thing,[86] and they immediately denounced me as a heretic to the archbishop, and so I achieved a goal contrary to the one I set for myself."[87] Later he wrote to León, "Father Antícoli has just published in Puebla another pamphlet about *that thing* (anonymous, according to his custom). Now in it he attacks me *by name*. He says some good and peevish things about me and declares that I have fallen under I don't know how many censures for not having spoken in the Zumárraga work."[88] A month later, he wrote to León,

I began to read the book and gradually put it down, worn out by such great foolishness, stupidity, and insolence. With defenders like that no cause can be good. I have limited myself to complaining to Fathers [Aquilés] Gerste and [Marcelino de] Civezza. We shall see what they answer. Here I will not say a word, no matter what they may say to me. . . . Having learned my lesson from the *success* of the Zumárraga work, which saddened the bishops, I will not expose myself to saddening them again, and I have resolutely written finis to every publication of a kind like the previous ones, although I still have excellent material.[89]

García Icazbalceta claimed that the abuse would cause him to give up all historical studies, although there were undoubtedly other personal reasons that entered into that resolution.[90] This was a loss for both the Mexican nation and the Mexican Church. Antícoli's conduct throughout the controversy can most charitably be described as reprehensible.

Not long before his death, García Icazbalceta wrote,

As for what concerns Father Antícoli, I no longer give it any thought, and the best thing is not to touch this business again, because nothing that may be said to them is going to convince them and would only serve to have them act more foolishly. After having taken the resolution not to publish anything more about our history, I find that I am very rested, and I marvel at how I have forgotten some works that occupied me for so many years. I almost don't remember them nor do I have any fondness for them. This has come not only from the attack of the anonymous [author] but from seeing the futility of my efforts. I do not see that they have served to correct even one of the thousand errors that blemish our history, nor is there anyone who pays attention to those things.

Nicolás León believed that Gerste, as a Jesuit, did not take action, but that Civezza, the Franciscan, did.[91] There seems no doubt that Antícoli was denounced to Rome.[92] Antícoli himself feared such an eventuality and in 1893 wrote to Vera,

From what you have told me, that my books have been denounced to the Congregation of Rites, I will tell you with total fraternal confidence that I was already fearing those steps and that perhaps for my sins the Lord would permit something disagreeable for me. But if they take something from an isolated expression or from some terms, taken not in context but in the abstract, it could that happen that a "donec corrigitur" [until corrected][93] could be forthcoming, something they might be able to attribute to the substance of the fact and not to my mistakes, that is, to certain expressions of mine. Unless haste is made to inform Rome as to who they are, etc., and the opportunity that they could have to have triumphed against the apparition, if they are not made to see this entire matter in the same way that good Mexicans see it, I repeat, the Lord may permit this embarrassment.[94]

Rome took particular exception to this book on the magisterium. The assistant to the Jesuit superior general wrote on July 17, 1893, "I do not like good Father Antícoli's book or its style or personal attacks or the eagerness to want to prove theologically the fact of the apparition."[95] Antagonism toward Antícoli carried over to the Jesuit order in Mexico. In December 1895 Agreda y Sánchez wrote to Paso y Troncoso,

The members [of the Society of Jesus] who for some years have been coming from Europe behave badly here, since one in his writings insults, after the manner of a fishwife, those who do not think as he does. He and others meddle in what does not concern them and they sow tares.[96] Others on frivolous pretexts grab for themselves what belongs to others. Naturally one notices a great difference between these and the former ones we knew, sons of this country . . . some very much deserving respect for their virtue and learning.[97]

Unfortunately, the controversy had not yet reached its peak.

The Height of the Storm

Despite the approval of the mass and office, the controversy continued unabated. Although a work written in slovenly Latin seemed hardly destined to have wide circulation, the *Exquisitio historica* continued to engender controversy. In 1892 Vera, a dedicated apparitionist, published a massive volume called *Contestación histórico-crítica,* a rebuttal of both the *Información* and the *Exquisitio.* The book was more than seven hundred pages long, a large part of which dealt with the silence of so many authors and authorities. There was a lengthy discussion of the Montúfar–Bustamante inquiry. With regard to the *Exquisitio*, Vera quoted numerous paragraphs in the original Latin, followed by his Spanish translation, and concluding with a refutation.[98]

Reaction to this work varied according to the beliefs of the person passing judgment. Antícoli wrote, "It cannot be denied that the author has won a most brilliant victory over the anonymous Latin and the anonymous authors of the *Aditamentos* and *Notas* to the *Información* undertaken in 1556 against the scandalous objector to the apparitions. But he not only refutes them, he also routs them, he crushes them even to the point of being forgers, rationalists, and smacking of Protestantism and religious liberalism, because they are completely unaware of the authority of the Apostolic See on this point."[99] Jesús Galindo y Villa, on the other hand, was equally strong in his negative opinion. "I have read the voluminous volume, and . . . I still regret the loss of time that I invested in reading that work. . . . Such a defense of the apparition left me more than ever confirmed in my opinions."[100] Agreda y Sánchez was even more blunt. "The book of the bishop of Cuernavaca is a voluminous trifle, full of sophisms, historical inexactitudes, false suppositions, in sum, as much as is possible for falsifying the truth."[101]

García Icazbalceta commented, "I do not know the latest book of Father Vera except from the outside: certainly its size is frightening."[102] Later that same year, he wrote, "At last Father Vera has given me his latest book, which, like you, I have read in bits and pieces. I do not find anything new in it except the text of the *Exquisitio*, which I did not know. What do you think of it? There are also in Father Vera's refutations some rather strong passages. The best that both sides could do is to be quiet, since such a polemic can lead to no good."[103] By that time, of course, the eminent historian was aware that the *Exquisitio* was a translation of his letter, though he consistently denied knowledge of the Latin work.[104] Regarding the *Exquisitio*, Nicolás León wrote, "All this anti-Guadalupan scandal was brought about by Canon Andrade with the collaboration of Agreda [y Sánchez], [Paso y] Troncoso, Pastor [Antonio] Icaza, and in this miserable affair they dirtied as many persons, dead or alive, as they could. On the other side, and following similar procedures, the same thing was done by Vera, Antícoli, Carrillo y Ancona, [Luis] Duarte, Plancarte, and others of the second rank."[105]

Andrade kept up his anti-Guadalupan campaign. Under the pseudonym Eutimio Pérez he published a short book attacking the apparitionists.[106] After the appearance of Vera's *Contestación*, Andrade extracted the Spanish translation of the *Exquisitio* that had been included in it and published it in 1893 under the title, *Exquisitio historica: Anónimo escrito en Latín sobre la Aparición de la B. V. M. de Guadalupe* (Historical Inquiry: An Anonymous Work Written in Latin about the Appearance of the Blessed Virgin Mary of Guadalupe).[107] As an additional riposte, the title page stated that it was "Translated into Spanish by Fortino Hipólito Vera." Though the real publisher was again Albino Feria, the name given on the title page was Talonia, the maiden name of Vera's mother. Vera, needless to say, was not pleased by this rather crude joke, which seemed to make him the author of the book. He wrote a letter of protest against this fraudulent use of his translation that was published in *El Tiempo* (January 1, 1894) and other Catholic newspapers in Mexico.

Two years later, at the time when the image was to be crowned, another edition of the Spanish translation of the *Exquisitio* was published by a Protestant group, the Alianza Evangélica.[108] It was a brief version of García Icazbalceta's letter and at times was a paraphrase.[109] In addition, the booklet contained a great deal of virulent anti-Catholic propaganda, including an attack on images (based on the Ten Commandments) by José M. Cárdenas.[110] It also contained a lengthy attack on the coronation, claiming that Antonio Plancarte had trampled on the rights of the *cabildo* by undertaking the restoration of the church, and that Archbishop Labastida had sent a letter to each of the canons ordering them to conform.[111] The use that would be made by non-Catholics and anticlericals of the anti-apparitionist arguments would continue to be a source of great embarrassment and irritation to Mexican Catholics.

García Icazbalceta eventually learned the whole story of how the Latin translation of his letter and the Spanish translation of the Latin had come into being. It is said that he made inquiries among those to whom he had lent the letter or copies of it, but all protested, truthfully, that they had kept it confidential. He is said to have guessed the truth when he remembered that Andrade and Paso y Troncoso lived in the same building, and to have extracted the truth from Andrade.

Agreda y Sánchez urged him to publish the original, saying that it was better that it be known in its integral form rather than in a partial state. García Icazbalceta refused, foreseeing the obloquy that would be his. After the great historian's death in 1894, Agreda y Sánchez renewed his efforts to have the letter published. In December 1895 he wrote to the Spanish historian Justo Zaragoza that there was a widespread desire in Mexico to have the letter published by the Royal Academy of History in Spain because that organization's prestige would deliver "a good blow to the scoundrels here who with supreme impudence continued to mock the public."[112] Unfortunately for him, Zaragoza died within six months. Agreda y Sánchez then turned to José María Vigil, director of the Biblioteca Nacional de México, with the proposal that the publication be sponsored by the Museo Nacional. The matter eventually went to President Porfirio Díaz. The latter gave his consent but on the odd condition that no bibliographical data appear on the title page.

García Icazbalceta's letter was finally published in 1896 by the press of the Museo Nacional. It appeared in an edition of five hundred copies, with no indication of its provenance, though it did specify García Icazbalceta as the author. Vigil wrote a history of the letter that formed an introduction to the text. It was the first time that García Icazbalceta's name had been publicly affixed to the letter. Some apparitionists, however, remained convinced that the letter was a forgery. In August and September 1896 *El Universal* ran a series of interviews with Francisco Sosa, Jesús Galindo y Villa, and Agreda y Sánchez, proving that the letter was authentic.[113]

The liberal and anticlerical newspapers were quick to reprint the letter: *El Universal* on June 24, 1896, *El Monitor Republicano* on June 23, 26, 27, *La Patria* on August 25 and 26, and then *El Siglo XIX* on August 29. At almost the same time, the Methodist Episcopal Church of Mexico distributed a leaflet advertising the letter and making it available at a low price. The leaflet, which was distributed in large numbers at various Catholic churches, stated that "this small work was written by order of the Most Illustrious Señor Archbishop Don Pelagio Antonio de Labastida y Dávalos by the sincere and illustrious historian and bibliographer Señor Joaquín García Icazbalceta, and [it] overwhelms all the defenses written to date about such an important matter."[114]

On July 29, 1896, the collegiate chapter of Guadalupe sent to Archbishop Alarcón a protest against the publication of García Icazbalceta's letter in *El Universal*. The canons began by pointing out their obligation to defend a tradition "both consoling and well founded" and that they believed themselves wounded by the article.[115] Specifically, they protested the publication of a letter "that is said to be from Señor García Icazbalceta" and that was published only for the purpose of scandalizing those who read it.[116] "You know well, Most Illustrious Sir, who has published this letter, that it was translated into Latin and sent to Rome for the purpose of preventing the granting of the new office of Our Lady of Guadalupe, and that despite the fact that the Promotor of the Faith, by reason of his office, took from that letter thirty or more objections, none of them remained without a satisfactory solution, since not withstanding all this, the authoritative voice of the Holy Father approved the ancient and constant tradition."[117] "We believe that in religious matters no Catholic will give greater credit to the letter in *El Universal* than to the voice of the Sovereign Pontiff."[118]

Another strong reaction to the publication and distribution of García Icazbalceta's letter came from the archdiocesan curia of Mexico, which warned Catholics to avoid the document and accused the authors of the leaflet of falsehood. "This little work is nothing else than the letter that a few days ago was published in *El Universal*, and which has been the reason why the archdiocesan chapter and that of the Famous and National Collegiate Church of Guadalupe have protested against that letter, a letter that had caused the most profound disgust in all the illustrious archbishops and bishops of the Republic. The Most Illustrious Señor Archbishop also ordered us to remind all Catholics of his prohibition against treating of or discussing, even in private, the apparition of the Virgin of Guadalupe."[119] To forbid Catholics to discuss the matter even in private was an extraordinary act of ecclesiastical jurisdiction, even for an archbishop.

The Church in Mexico closed ranks against this attack on a beloved tradition. Montes de Oca wrote, "The responsibility for the storm raised in the Church of Mexico falls solely on those who without any right or mission brought to light a document that ought to have remained unpublished."[120] Cuevas was of a similar opinion. "Don Joaquín García Icazbalceta kept his letter on the apparition of the Virgin of Guadalupe locked up and guarded, without the intention of publishing it, among other things, because there was still room for preparation and correction. A genuine act of petty theft removed this document and brought it to public light."[121] There are two considerations here. The first is the violation of García Icazbalceta's right to privacy by Andrade in making a secret copy of the letter. While Benjamin Franklin's axiom that three may keep a secret if two are dead is often true, it was the great historian himself who let others see it, although all of his friends and confidants honored his wish. The letter became public by a stealthy and a dishonorable, not to say unethical, act. On the other hand, one sees also the excessive preoccupation of ecclesiastics with not shocking the faithful, a canard all too frequently used to hide uncomfortable truths.

In 1896, the Fifth Mexican Provincial Council met in Mexico City. The bishops of the council published the following statement:

The marvelous apparition, without being a dogma of faith . . . is an ancient, constant, and universal tradition in the Mexican nation, clothed with such characteristics and supported by such foundations that not only do they authorize any Catholic to believe it, but also do not even permit him to contradict it without greater or lesser rashness. . . . For a Catholic, the criterion of the pastors of Mexico who have transmitted this event for more than three centuries is of the greatest weight, and consequently to cast doubt on it would be to inflict a great injury on the very respectable integrity, knowledge, and virtue of such venerable prelates.

"In a spirit of expiation," the bishops decreed that on the first anniversary of the coronation there were to be special celebrations throughout the dioceses of the province.[122] A shorter version of this statement was incorporated into one of the decrees of the council.[123] The council also included December 12 among the holy days of obligation and decreed that every church in Mexico should have an altar, or at least an image, of Our Lady of Guadalupe.[124] Finally, taking the case of Sánchez Camacho as its starting point, it declared, "Lest anyone in this [ecclesiastical] province, whether out of imprudence or rashness or audacity or scandal and impiety should ever be rebuked by the Apostolic See or his way of acting and speaking against the miracle or apparitions of the Most Blessed Virgin Mary of Guadalupe be censured, we absolutely forbid that anyone should presume to speak, write or teach anything to the contrary."[125] Thus, while declaring that Guadalupe was not a dogma that all Catholics were bound to believe, the bishops both in the council and outside of it issued a clear gag order.

On September 23, 1896, *El Universal* ran a lengthy editorial that was extremely critical of the conciliar decree. The same paper published a lengthy critique of the bishops' letter on October 27.[126] "It would be an impractical and vain undertaking to refute all the errors of a clergy as ignorant and fanatical as that of Mexico, but when the bishops themselves fall into them and publish them in a document adorned with the pompous title of *edict*, which appears as if it had been issued by a council, the errors should not be allowed to pass without comment."[127] The article was lengthy and repetitious, but also highlighted the inner contradiction of the bishops' "decree." If Guadalupe was not a dogma of faith, then Catholics should be free to accept or reject it. Yet any denial or discussion was forbidden.

The controversy continued to be fought out in the press. The Catholic papers, such as *El Tiempo* and *La Voz de México*, defended the apparition tradition, while *El Universal, La Patria, El Monitor Republicano, El Siglo XIX, El Diario del Hogar*, and other liberal journals attacked it. Among the Guadalupan writers were Victoriano Agüeros (founder and editor of *El Tiempo*), Trinidad Sánchez Santos (editor of *La Voz de México*), the priest Melesio de Jesús Vázquez (pastor of the Sagrario Metropolitano and secretary to Archbishop Alarcón), Juan Luis Tercero, Canon Agustín de la Rosa, the priest Gabino Chávez, S.J., and J. S. Val (the priest Laureano Veres Acevedo, S.J.). On the opposing side were Sánchez Camacho, Vicente de P. Andrade, Antonio Icaza, Fernando Espinosa y Agreda (under the pen name of Savonarola), Eugenio Zubieta, Juan Antonio Mateos, José P. Rivera, Agreda y Sánchez, Francisco Sosa, Jesús Galindo y Villa, and Félix Ramos y Duarte. The opponents included priests and Catholics as well as liberals and anticlericals. Juan B. Iguíniz, who was hostile to the anti-apparitionists, said that they campaigned "with complete bad faith."[128] Though never a formal grouping, their focal point tended to be the Biblioteca Nacional de México, whose librarian was Agreda y Sánchez. Others in this informal coterie (which Iguíniz claimed worked in secret) were Sánchez y Agreda's nephew, Fernando Espinosa y Agreda, together with Francisco del Paso y Troncoso and Luis González Obregón. *El Universal* was their principal outlet. Andrade and Icaza worked on their own, though the former had contacts with the group.

García Icazbalceta had one staunch defender in Bishop Montes de Oca. Seemingly a man of blunt speech who did not suffer fools gladly, he was described by a journalist in the following terms: "The excellent priest does not find himself very welcome among his colleagues, who usually tremble likes leaves on a tree when Don Ignacio, armed with his bruising satire and his fearsome learning, lets fly his steel-piercing darts at any of those pastors *in literatura simplices et vituperabiles vitae* [guileless in learning and blameworthy in life]."[129] The author went on to say that "It is well known that the ecclesiastics of Mexico are divided into apparitionists and anti-apparitionists," and included Montes de Oca among the latter. "He was contaminated by the theories of García Icazbalceta, to whom he offered the protection of his bishop's mantle if someone had the infamy to attack the memory of the noted historian."[130] The article dealt with a sermon that Montes de Oca had given at a memorial mass for popes who had favored the Guadalupan tradition. He apparently claimed that Pope Benedict XIV's supposed quotation from Psalm 147, "Non fecit taliter omni nationi" (He has not done the like for any other nation), was actually an ironic joke, suggesting that Rome and Jerusalem were nothing in comparison to Mexico City. Apparently the sermon contained some anti-Jesuit statements, though he did not mention any Jesuits by name.

The bishop, however, may have equivocated in public. Antícoli cited his sermon of December 12, 1891, on the occasion of the dedication of the seminary of Our Lady of Guadalupe in Villa de Reyes, in the diocese of San Luis Potosí: "But in a century like the sixteenth in which a living faith and a sincere piety were the masters of our fatherland, documents were in no way necessary; since posterity would receive by word of mouth the universal and constant tradition of the most singular favor that the Mother of God deigned to do for Mexicans."[131]

After García Icazbalceta's death in 1894, Montes de Oca delivered a eulogy to the assembly of the Saint Vincent de Paul Society in San Luis Potosí.[132] Referring to the attacks on the famed historian, he said in an oblique reference to Antícoli that "the devil disguised himself as an angel of light, he clothed himself with a religious habit, and attacked him in the way that envy attacks, with savagery, with acrimony, with implacable cruelty. What he had published was misinterpreted and what *he had not written* was thrown in his face, his intentions were slandered, and wrong conclusions were attributed to him."[133] According to Montes de Oca, at the request of a bishop, "he removed a chapter, an entire chapter, from the work he loved best of all his works, a chapter that had cost him long years of study and sleepless nights."[134] Though Montes de Oca did not specify what this chapter was, it seems likely that it was a chapter on Guadalupe that had been intended for García Icazbalceta's biography of Zumárraga and that had been removed at the request of Bishop Verea y González.[135] Referring to the attacks on his friend, Montes de Oca declared, "On seeing that those who were most enraged against him were the ministers of that Church of which he was an obedient and submissive son and which he craved to defend, he laid down his learned pen forever. . . . To the unjust and totally uncharitable attacks of which he was the victim we owe the fact that most important works on the Church in Mexico have remained unfinished and that documents of supreme interest lie in the dust."[136]

The Coronation

While all this was taking place, the process of refurbishing La Colegiata in anticipation of the coronation went on at a slow pace. One reason for this was the lack of adequate financial resources for an undertaking that continued to grow in scope. Plancarte suffered a setback with the death of his uncle, the archbishop, in 1891. Though the new archbishop, Alarcón, confirmed Plancarte in his role as fundraiser and head of the reconstruction, in other ways Plancarte lost favor. Up to that time, he had received all the donations for the refurbishing and paid all the bills. The new archbishop allowed the canons of La Colegiata to receive the donations. He also assented to their request to return the image to the church even while the construction was going on. Both these things were done without previous notice to Plancarte. Upset, he wrote to the archbishop that "the head of the Mexican Church has taken away from me his moral support. . . . He does not share with me any financial help and takes away the means of obtaining it. . . . He puts the work into the hands of those who have persecuted it."[137] The archbishop did not answer this, nor an ultimatum that Plancarte gave him either to restore his authority or to consider his work terminated by July 29, 1892. When Plancarte began to settle accounts with the artisans and terminate the restoration, Alarcón yielded to his demands.

At the beginning of 1895 the bishop of Puebla, Francisco Melitón Vargas y Gutiérrez, was in Mexico City, leading a procession to Guadalupe.[138] On February 12, he asked Archbishop Alarcón why the refurbishing of La Colegiata was going so slowly. The archbishop answered that among other reasons was the lack of resources. Vargas asked him to set the date of the coronation definitively for October 12 of that year and promised to contribute to the restoration and to ask other bishops to do the same. On February 13, the archbishop urged Plancarte to try to have the work finished by September 15.[139] He apparently was successful in doing so.[140] On October 1, 1895, Archbishop Alarcón blessed the sanctuary and consecrated the main altar of the refurbished church. This was the opening act of the festivities for the coronation.

On September 22, just a few weeks before the coronation, Alarcón issued an edict. It had been rumored that certain "dissident sects" were planning to distribute anti-Guadalupan writings at that time. If any of these fell into the hands of the faithful, they were immediately to turn them in to their pastors. "At the same time we warn the faithful to abstain from disputing about the truth of the Apparition." Allying himself with Antícoli, he added that it should be considered "very much above all human criticism."[141]

The program for the coronation was drawn up by Bishop Camacho García of Querétaro.[142] It was somewhat extravagant, beginning with a novena of masses to be celebrated in all cathedral and parish churches. The day before the coronation, all Catholic men, women, and children were to fast. On the day of the coronation a solemn mass was to be celebrated in all cathedrals and parish churches in the nation. At 10:00 a.m. on that day, the same churches were to peal their bells to proclaim that the coronation had taken place, and all the faithful were to recite a prayer to the Virgin at that time. At the same time, all the churches were to have a solemn *Te Deum* sung, and priests were to add an additional prayer of thanksgiving to the opening prayer of the Mass, called the collect. To his credit, however, the bishop did include an exhortation that the faithful were to celebrate the occasion by giving alms to the poor, visiting the sick and the imprisoned, and performing similar works of mercy. The program, however, said nothing about who was to be invited, but invitations were sent to all the bishops in the Americas, at the expense of the Mexican Church.[143]

Apparently, Camacho García was also responsible for the plan of ceremonies of the actual coronation.[144] At 4:00 p.m. on October 11 the archbishop was to sing Pontifical Vespers, followed by the litanies and other prayers prescribed by the ritual. On the following day, at 8:00 a.m., the archbishop would begin Nones, and when it was finished would proceed to the reception and blessing of the crown.[145] The crown was to be carried in procession by the attending archbishops and bishops. After this came the Pontifical Solemn Mass and then the coronation, concluding with the *Te Deum*, after which there would be a second Pontifical Mass of thanksgiving for the coronation. During the *Te Deum*, the faithful who attended the first mass were to leave in order to make room for those who would attend the second. In the afternoon, after second Vespers, the panegyric was to be preached by Carrillo y Ancona.

On the eve of the coronation, Plancarte's enemies denounced him to the civil justice as having stolen the jewels from the crown and substituted paste ones. They also tried to have him arrested so that he would not participate in the coronation. However, Porfirio Díaz intervened by ordering an accelerated investigation that cleared him. It was also at this time that Plancarte had to obtain an *acta notarial* stating that he had not caused the erasure of the crown.

The ceremony of coronation took place as planned. It was a major national event, with pilgrimages arriving from all parts of the republic. At the entrance to La Colegiata, Archbishop Alarcón blessed the two crowns. Then the archbishop sat on a faldstool before the main altar, while Antonio Plancarte, who has been appointed abbot of the Collegiate chapter, knelt before him and recited an oath taken by all the members of the Collegiate chapter: "From this day forward we will make no attempt in any way by word, writing, or deed, against the apparition of the Blessed Virgin on the hill of Tepeyac and with all our strength we will seek to preserve this same crown on the brow of the same Venerable

Image."[146] After that, each of the canons swore acceptance of the oath with his right hand on the gospels.[147] A solemn pontifical mass was then celebrated, during the offertory of which the choir sang two Latin poems composed by Pope Leo XIII for the occasion.[148] Following a procession, Archbishop Alarcón and Archbishop José Ignacio Arciga of Michoacán, the only one present of the three bishops who had originally requested the coronation, placed the crown above the image. It was estimated that ten thousand people crowded the square outside the church.[149]

Also present were twenty-eight Indians, one from each of the bishoprics of the country. Their presence was the idea of Bishop Ramón Ibarra y González of Chilapa, who thought that it would be good to have some Indians from Cuauhtitlán, Juan Diego's home village, present at the ceremony. Antonio Plancarte approved the idea and had Santiago Béguerisse, a French pharmacist in Puebla and a devotee of Guadalupe, organize a pilgrimage of natives from the various dioceses.[150] In view of the fact that the original message of Guadalupe was directed to the indigenous peoples, this seems rather like tokenism.

At the last minute, Camacho García, who was scheduled to give the sermon at the coronation mass, was unable to attend because of a serious illness. He sent a written version to Archbishop Alarcón. It was read to the attending archbishops and bishops so that if anyone of them wanted to give the sermon, either totally original or based on Camacho García's, they could do so. They all agreed that no one could do so in such a short space of time, and so it fell to Antonio Plancarte to read it.[151] In the sermon, Camacho García sounded many familiar notes, including the special election of the Mexican people. "It is an oath of vassalage dutifully made to such a worthy Queen, because when she gathered us together here in Mexico as her people, she constituted herself Empress and Patron of all America. . . . Let us go on to see, my brothers, how this solemn coronation that we celebrate is an oath of vassalage that we are duty bound to make to such a great Empress and Queen, because by favoring us with prodigies of her Apparition and her Image of Guadalupe, he has chosen and sanctified in Mexico all America, all the West Indies as her privileged empire."[152] He also repeated a number of familiar stories, including that of Pope Benedict XIV having quoted Psalm 147, the identification of Tepeyac with the cult of Tonantzin, the testimony of Bernal Díaz del Castillo, and the miraculous preservation of the image.[153]

Concomitant with the coronation was the publication of a commemorative book, the *Album de la coronación de la Sma. Virgen de Guadalupe*, whose editor was Victoriano Agüeros. In discussing the question of historicity, it stated: "The Church's approval, although it does not raise belief in the miracle to a truth of faith, does imprint the final and most

respected seal of certainty on that belief which is philosophically demonstrated beforehand by the multiple logical criteria of history, tradition,
monuments, and especially the subsequent facts, the effects produced,
which can be explained only by the preexistence of a sufficient and adequate cause."[154] The *Album* also fostered a legend about Zumárraga's
having had an interpreter for his interviews with Juan Diego. "Tradition
has preserved for us the notice that the interpreter who participated in the
conversations of the Most Illustrious Señor Zumárraga with Juan Diego,
since the latter did not know the Castilian language and the former did
not know Nahuatl or Mexican, was the canon Juan González."[155] In
1896 Agustín Rivera wrote a refutation of this claim.[156] It continues,
however, to endure.

The controversy did not subside with the coronation. In fact, some of
the most difficult days for the various participants lay ahead of them.

"NEW LAW OF WEIGHTS AND MEASURES"
El Universal, September 20, 1896

Historical truth outweighs private interests. On the left, Bishop Eduardo Sánchez Camacho of Tamaulipas, with his miter askew, holds a placard with the opening and closing phrases of García Icazbalceta's letter on Guadalupe. With him are Bishop Joaquín Arcadio Pagaza of Veracruz (Jalapa), José María Agreda y Sánchez, and Bishop Ignacio Montes de Oca of San Luis Potosí. Perched on top of the scale is a figure that appears to be García Icazbalceta. On the right side, seated in the upended crown of Guadalupe, are Antonio Plancarte y Labastida, losing his bishop's miter, Bishop José María Armas Rosales of Tulancingo, Bishop Ramón Ibarra y González of Chilapa, Archbishop Próspero María Alarcón of Mexico, and Bishop Rafael Sabás Camacho of Querétaro. Plancarte is shown with a brush and bucket "for erasing the crown" on the image. On the right is Archbishop Nicola Averardi, the apostolic visitor to Mexico, who is holding a baby labeled *Voz de México*, the name of a leading Catholic journal.

"New Law of Weights and Measures" was originally published in *El Universal*, September 20, 1896. It has been reprinted by kind permission of the Biblioteca Miguel Lerdo de Tejada, Mexico City. Photo by Kevin Terraciano.

CHAPTER FOUR

The Visitation of Archbishop Averardi

❖

The Guadalupan controversy was beginning to recede into the background in 1896, when Nicola Averardi, titular archbishop of Tarsus, arrived to make a special apostolic visitation of the church in Mexico at the orders of the Vatican Secretary of State, Cardinal Mariano Rampolla. This was part of a diplomatic initiative launched by Pope Leo XIII at the beginning of his pontificate to pursue a rapprochement with powers that had been hostile to the Church or the papacy. The president of Mexico, Porfirio Díaz, wanted his nation to play a more active role on the international diplomatic stage. He also wanted to project an image of stability and peace, and Rome wanted more control over the church in Mexico. All of this was soon given the global name of "policy of conciliation."[1]

For all these reasons, the Vatican decided to send an extraordinary envoy to make a general visitation of the church in Mexico. This person was Averardi, who arrived on March 23, 1896. Public opinion was divided in its reaction to this visitation. In general, the Catholic media welcomed it, at least in the beginning, while the anticlerical media feared any warming of relations with the Holy See. One Catholic paper noted ironically, "Attila at the gates of Rome caused less panic than the news of the appointment of Monsignor Averardi, the envoy of His Holiness, has caused in two or three liberal papers."[2] There was even the possibility that diplomatic relations with the Vatican might be restored. Averardi's instructions, however, were concerned only with the internal affairs of the church.

Nicola Averardi (1843–1924) was born in San Egidio, in the diocese of Montalto in Italy.[3] He pursued part of his ecclesiastical studies in his home diocese and finished them in Rome, where he earned doctorates in theology and canon and civil law. After serving in secondary capacities at the nunciatures in Lisbon, Madrid, and Paris, he returned to Rome, where he held various offices in the Roman Curia. In 1895 he was named titular bishop of Tarsus and in the following year was sent to Mexico. It was not to be a happy experience. The initial impressions he made were not good, and he was widely regarded as being imprudent in his public statements. Francisco Plancarte y Navarrete, not an admirer of the delegate, considered him reckless in his pronouncements and referred to him as a man "whom nobody could shut up."[4]

The divisions within the Mexican Church carried over into many areas, but the effects of the Guadalupan controversy were to be found in the ensuing turmoil. Averardi's instructions said nothing about the controversy but did include investigation of two persons involved in it: Eduardo Sánchez Camacho and Antonio Plancarte y Labastida.

The Fall of Bishop Sánchez Camacho

For Eduardo Sánchez Camacho, the second bishop of Tamaulipas, the Averardi visitation brought nothing but misfortune. The bishop was an outspoken anti-apparitionist, and during his lifetime it was widely believed that he had been forced to resign his diocese because of his public denial of the apparitions and opposition to the coronation. A close examination of the papers of the Averardi visitation shows that there were other factors at work and that the Guadalupan question played little or no part in it.

On March 27, 1895, a year before Averardi's arrival in Mexico, the Holy See had received a letter from four priests of the diocese of Tamaulipas, accusing the bishop of drunkenness, greed, suspect relations with women, and neglect of the government of his diocese. According to this denunciation, Sánchez Camacho was often drunk, and because of this there were serious disorders in diocesan administration and his dealings with the clergy. They claimed that he had increased parish levies so much that some of the faithful no longer received the sacraments.[5] Many of these accusations were included in a special instruction given to Averardi, titled "Accusations against the Bishop of Tamaulipas." As an example of the bishop's poor relations with his priests, the instruction noted that at one time he had suspended more than twenty of them without any trial. He was also accused of imposing ecclesiastical penalties too easily, especially interdict and excommunication, and, it was said, he had even excommunicated a nine-year-old boy. The instruction noted that the accusation of immorality was "generic" and needed proof.[6]

On his arrival in Mexico, Averardi sent a formal circular in Latin to all the bishops of the republic, informing them of his commission and the reasons for his mission. The copy sent to Sánchez Camacho was dated March 26, 1896. The bishop of Tamaulipas responded with an equally formal Latin letter on April 5.[7] Averardi was pleased with this conciliatory response, but the cordial relations would not endure.

Averardi's initial inquiries confirmed many of the accusations made against the bishop. When Sánchez Camacho first arrived in Victoria, the state capital, after his appointment as bishop, he brought with him from Guadalajara two young women, stating that he was going to employ them as schoolteachers. They lived in his residence for a long time, and his carelessness in their regard gave rise to a number of sinister suspicions. Some persons in Victoria also told Averardi that Sánchez Camacho spent large sums of church money on wines and liquor. Others stated that he never forgave or forewent fees, even in cases of extreme need. As a result, many poor people abstained from getting married or having their children baptized until they were at the point of death. The bishop claimed to be poor, though it was well known that he owned a ranch and had extensive holdings in real estate. Still others considered him unorthodox, telling Averardi that *"the first enemy of the Catholic religion and of the pope, against whom he is eager to speak evil continuously and publicly, is their bishop."*[8] A Catholic lawyer, who had been a good friend of the bishop's, told Averardi that Sánchez Camacho stopped visiting him after his wife's death, telling him bluntly that he no longer had any reason to visit. Averardi admitted that he did not give total credence to these accusations, because "of all the other countries in North America this is the one that is most known for lies and slanders."[9]

On May 28, 1896, Averardi wrote Sánchez Camacho, asking him to come to Mexico City for a personal interview. Acknowledging that it was he who should go to Tamaulipas, Averardi alleged the numerous and difficult matters that he was dealing with.[10] On the May 31, Sánchez Camacho declined the invitation, citing his age (he was almost sixty), his delicate health, the persecutions he had been suffering, the lack of money (he had just spent 2,000 pesos on his cathedral), and lack of appropriate clothing.[11] In that same letter, he enclosed his resignation as bishop, "in order that your Excellency may work with complete liberty and without the obstacle that my unworthy person could pose."[12] The reasons given by Sánchez Camacho for not going to Mexico City are not convincing. Why did he submit his resignation at this time? It is difficult to say, especially in view of the volatility of his actions over the next few months. Romero de Solís hypothesizes that Sánchez Camacho feared a possible ecclesiastical trial, and that if he went to Mexico City his resignation might be demanded of him. There had been rumors in Tamaulipas that he would resign.[13]

Though Averardi may have been surprised by the resignation, he could only have been happy about what seemed to be a swift and peaceful resolution to the problem. He could scarcely conceal his pleasure and carefully avoided saying anything that could cause Sánchez Camacho to reconsider his decision. Thus, he did not ask for any further details on the reasons that led to it.[14] Averardi acknowledged receipt of the resignation and forwarded it to Rome, with the recommendation that it be accepted and that Sánchez Camacho never be allowed to resume the government of the diocese.[15] The bishop continued, however, to govern the diocese in the interim, and he still had some surprises in store. On August 26, 1896, he sent a letter to all the pastors of his diocese in which he ordered them to obey civil laws. These included not to wear clerical insignia in public, not to speak or preach against civil laws, not to perform marriages without previous civil registration and the presentation of proof thereof, and not to perform baptisms until the births were civilly registered.[16] As his critics pointed out, this went far beyond what even anticlerical governments had required.

On September 16, 1896, at the height of the crisis with Sánchez Camacho, Averardi included in a report to Rampolla a piece of paper dated August 21 and identified as "The Bishop of Tamaulipas and the Apparition and Coronation of the Virgen."[17] The document contained observations by Sánchez Camacho. It is not certain whether these comments were intended for publication, or were the draft of a letter, or were merely personal. They were occasioned by an unidentified *opúsculo* that had appeared two days earlier.[18] This may have been an article by Trinidad Sánchez Santos published in *La Voz de México* and mentioned below. It is also possible that it was the letter that Carrillo y Ancona wrote to Archbishop Alarcón on August 12, 1896, and that was published in pamphlet form under the title "Don Joaquín García Icazbalceta y la historia guadalupana."[19] The occasion for this letter was the publication of García Icazbalceta's letter by anti-Catholic newspapers. The bishop said of García Icazbalceta's letter that the great historian did not want to write it, did not want to publish it, and did not want it seen. It was written before the rebuke of Sánchez Camacho and before the Holy See granted the new office and permitted the coronation. According to Carrillo y Ancona, García Icazbalceta most certainly would not have permitted its publication after those events. Nor, in spite of his historical approach, would he have rejected the possibility of a miracle, nor "the authority of the Church to resolve the question, once the matter had been studied deeply by it."[20] "And what would Señor Icazbalceta say, if he were still alive, that his very letter of 1883, examined in Rome by mandate of the Holy See, and each and every one of his historical conclusions taken from it with care like so many other objections against the miracle of Guadalupe, have been satisfactorily resolved?" Referring to García Icazbalceta's letter to him in 1888, the bishop answered, "Is it not evident that Señor Icazbalceta would say to the venerable chapter of Guadalupe the same words cited above: this is sufficient for me to believe?"[21] That was not true, since García Icazbalceta retained his disbelief in the apparitions to the end of his life.

Carrillo y Ancona's letter reproduced the rebuke sent to Sánchez Camacho by the Roman Inquisition. Certainly, in dredging up the story of the rebuke, Carrillo y Ancona was going out of his way to embarrass the bishop of Tamaulipas. Even Averardi found fault with his boorishness. "I do not know if that good bishop, knowing the character of this man and his supreme pride, was very prudent in reproducing after many years a document containing the aforesaid rebuke."[22] Whatever the situation, the *opúsculo* seems to have provoked Sánchez Camacho to his most extreme step.

On August 23, 1896, he wrote a letter to the newspaper *El Universal* that sent shock waves throughout Mexico.[23] He began by citing the refutation of García Icazbalceta by Trinidad Sánchez Santos in *La Voz de México* (August 15).[24] All that the author did, however, was to point out some historical errors in the great historian's letter. He had also demeaned his reputation as an historian, calling him a "compiler." While respecting Sánchez Santos for his learning, Sánchez Camacho did not consider him the equal of García Icazbalceta. Who, after all, was exempt from making errors? He has just read in *El Tiempo* (August 19) a letter from Melesio de J. Vázquez, comparing Guadalupe to the dogma of the Immaculate Conception. "Such a comparison seems blasphemous to me."[25] In *El Tiempo* of August 20 was published the letter of Carrillo y Ancona of Yucatán, written "in the moderate style that that gentleman always uses."[26] This was probably the letter that Carillo sent to Alarcón concerning García Icazbalceta's views on Guadalupe. It was intended to refute García Icazbalceta. According to Sánchez Camacho, he did the contrary, destroying his own reasons and corroborating those of García Icazbalceta. He made the same mistake as Vázquez, confusing Guadalupe with a dogma of faith. "Guadalupan belief is not of Catholic faith nor obligatory for anyone."[27] Carrillo y Ancona asserted his own belief in Guadalupe, "and I believe that this belief or faith is sincere, because the pure, or almost pure, blood that runs in the veins of this gentleman carries with it faith in whatever is believed to be religious or marvelous."[28] Carrillo y Ancona claimed that García Icazbalceta wrote his letter before he knew of the Inquisition's rebuke of Sánchez Camacho, and that when he learned of it, he wrote to the bishop of Yucatán that he would not go contrary to the dictates of the rebuke. Carrillo y Ancona quoted from García Icazbalceta's letter to him about the rebuke.[29] Sánchez Camacho responded that what García Icazbalceta said was conditional and expressed out of courtesy. "I respect Señor Carrillo for his prudence (I do not know his moral virtues and it could be that he was like any one of us), as a geographer, as a writer and somewhat as an historian, but as a logician, as a theologian, and as a canonist, I do not think that there is anything special."[30]

Sánchez Camacho noted that Vázquez and company had been frightened by the prospect of scandal, but Jesus Christ had caused scandal. His scandals were in favor of the truth, however, and he paid no attention to them in his lifetime. Although it pained Sánchez Camacho to praise himself, in looking over his life and career, "I had received nothing but praise from everyone as a model in the fulfillment of my duty and as a man of honor and virtue."[31] He claimed, with exaggeration, that it was only when he talked about Guadalupe that he began to receive criticism. "Now worse is going to happen to me because I no longer have the character of an active bishop. I am certain that if those persons who defend in good or bad faith the apparition of Tepeyac could crucify me, burn me or kill me in any way, they would do it *full of charity*; I do not know if it will reach that point, but one man matters little in comparison with social interests."[32]

He went on to explain his retraction. The Inquisition demanded that he either retract or remove the scandal he had caused. This meant that he either had to resign his diocese, as the Inquisition suggested,[33] or he could do what he did, that is, retract his manner of working and speaking against the apparitions until conditions had improved, leaving him free in the meanwhile to think what he wanted. The first alternative would have made him appear to be a rebel who preferred his own judgment, or it could have opened a schism. He said that when he made his retraction, he asked the pope to take him from his diocese, a request he repeated in 1890. At that time, he had a modest personal income to live on, but he later spent it all on the repair of the Cathedral.

Scarcely had Averardi arrived in Mexico, according to Sánchez Camacho, when he heard that the envoy brought instructions to remove Sánchez Camacho from his bishopric. He was indignant that Averardi would not allow him the use of the Cathedral and the bishop's throne that he purchased with his own funds. "And notwithstanding that judgment of mine, which I think is correct, I formed my final resolution to hand over this diocese to the one who gave it to me and to separate myself from

Rome and its ilk, to live alone and forgotten in a corner or ravine of the sierra in order to dedicate myself to cultivating the land, to the business and raising of livestock, in order to take care of my needs."[34] He went on, "I have received from Rome nothing but rebukes without cause, warnings without motives, disdain and financial exactions. I have asked for many things for the good of this church, and it has not answered me. I sent it my first synod (its acts), and it did not want to accept them, solely because in it the institutions and laws of my country are reconciled and effectively have been reconciled here during my administration with the canons of the Church."[35]

I have received from the bishops of Mexico nothing but contempt and slander. I wrote to Alarcón, Arciga, and Barón[36] to ask them for a donation to finish my cathedral and they did not answer, perhaps because they did not receive my letter, but I doubt it. Gillow, in a useless provincial council, whose acts, they say, were written by a foreigner, denied the existence of my diocesan synods, which are the only ones that resolve some of our administrative difficulties; that gentleman is of a very limited intelligence, except for finances, and we should therefore excuse him.[37]

Even *El Imparcial*, a semi-official Porfirian newspaper usually sympathetic to Sánchez Camacho, considered this letter to be overwrought (September 12, 1896).[38] Adding to the uproar was the fact that it appeared so soon after the publication of García Icazbalceta's anti-Guadalupan letter.

On September 5, Averardi wrote his reaction to Sánchez Camacho.

I have scarcely been able to persuade myself that it was dictated by Your Excellency, having seen the courteous terms and benevolent sentences with which you answered the letter in which I announced my arrival in the capital of this republic. . . . It caused me much pain that Your Excellency could not have acceded to my desire [to come to Mexico City]. It was very grievous to me that the desired interview was frustrated. Nothing, therefore, of vexations, no threats nor hint of them on my part; fraternal love, deference, and a will solely to clarify some things were my only feelings. . . . I beg you, therefore, by the heart of Our Lord Jesus Christ, to do all you can to recover the calmness of your spirit and to abandon the attitude that you have taken in a moment, perhaps, of excitement.[39]

Sánchez Camacho replied in brusque form five days later. Calling the visitor's letter "injurious," he spoke of himself in the third person,

I say that Eduardo Sánchez Camacho thinks about what he is going to say in the press with months of anticipation and that you injure me by supposing that the attitude I have taken has been in a moment of excitement. I reaffirm everything said in my [letter] of the 23rd of last month published in *El Universal*. . . . I deny your right to communicate with me and to make observations to me, because I have clearly said that I do not belong to Rome nor its bishops, but that I am a simple Mexican citizen under the aegis of its laws and the protection of its political and civil authorities, the only ones that your servant recognizes.[40]

On September 15, Averardi cabled Rampolla the news of Sánchez Camacho's rupture with Rome and said that Sánchez Camacho was thought to be insane. Averardi said that he would provide for the interim administration of the diocese and asked for further instructions.[41]

Averardi now realized that it could appear that his tactics had brought about the apostasy of the bishop of Tamaulipas, and he hastened to justify himself to Rome. On September 16 he sent a self-serving report to Rampolla.[42] He told the cardinal that he found it difficult to believe that the bishop of Tamaulipas was of sound mind. The scandal caused by the letter was undeniable and caused great pain to the bishops of Mexico. Those, however, who knew Sánchez Camacho were not surprised. Even as a priest in Guadalajara he had showed signs of his "strangeness and of his satanic pride."[43] The bishop of Guadalajara (Loza y Pardavé), his protector and benefactor who brought him with him from Sonora when he was made archbishop of Guadalajara, felt remorse. It was said that Sánchez Camacho was a member of the masons before being made a bishop. That did not surprise Averardi, since Porfirio Díaz had mentioned it to him. Díaz also told Averardi that Sánchez Camacho had told him that he did not consider that he ever was a priest or bishop since he was ordained not out of a vocation but because of the desire of his parents. Averardi, who had an habitual tendency to justify himself to Rampolla, said that Sánchez Camacho had no reason to blame him since he always acted with respect and deference toward him. The delegate claimed that even the enemies of the church did not take Sánchez Camacho seriously and considered him to be mentally disturbed. A doctor who had taken care of Sánchez Camacho two years before had doubted his mental soundness and predicted madness because of his delusions of persecution. This lamentable event would not disturb the religious peace, as Averardi had been assured by Díaz, who told him that if he, Díaz, used any rigor against Sánchez Camacho, it would redound to the harm of the church. The president had told the state governor to keep an eye on the bishop and to see that he did not disturb the public peace.

Later, Averardi would claim, "My only consolation is the testimony of my conscience that I have acted not with energy but with the greatest prudence, charity, and even friendship."[44] He wrote to Montes de Oca, "No one in the world who wants to judge in conformity with the dictates of his conscience and without a malign spirit could ever affirm that I have ever given that unfortunate person any pretext whatever to cause such a grave scandal."[45] Shortly after this, Sánchez Camacho returned to Victoria and assured his vicar general that nothing had been settled. The vicar general wrote this to Archbishop Jacinto López, the metropolitan, and at the same time assured him that the priests of Tamaulipas were "firm in their principles, firm in their faith, and also firm in the devotion, love, and veneration toward the Most Holy Virgin of Guadalupe."[46]

On October 3, Sánchez Camacho relinquished the administration of his diocese and retired to Quinta del Olvido (Villa of Forgetfulness), where he devoted himself to study and writing. Some bishops, including Fray José María de Jesús Portugal y Serratos, O.F.M., of Sinaloa, and Montes de Oca of San Luis Potosí, sought to mediate with him. Their efforts proved futile. The bishops of Mexico were unanimous in their denunciations of their fallen colleague and the scandal he provoked. On October 15, they sent a joint letter to Pope Leo XIII affirming their love and obedience to the Holy See.[47] Despite his professed desire to live in isolation and obscurity, Sánchez Camacho would appear again on the national scene to bedevil the Church in Mexico.

Sánchez Camacho was a troublesome and volatile personality who alternated between submission and rebellion. He saw all issues as personal ones. There is a remarkable difference between his reaction to the Roman rebuke of 1888 and that to the *opúsculo* of 1896. It was claimed that he had purchased his villa with diocesan funds since he came from a poor background.[48] In contrast, he wrote to the bishops at the Fifth Mexican Provincial Council, "Use the goods of the Church in primary education for our Indians and disinherited poor and teach them a better life . . . in works of beneficence, in hospitals, in poorhouses, in asylums."[49] In a pamphlet published a year after his break with Rome, he wrote, "Not to want for the people priests who do not show themselves practical ministers of a religion that is holy and eminently progressive. To love the laws of my country and order that they be respected. Not to believe in apparitions nor lying superstitions that dishonor the Christian religion. To be in disagreement with the other bishops with regard to these points, conduct that has earned me the name of disruptive and a disturber of the peace with my brothers."[50] He had a genuine hostility to Rome and the papacy, accompanied by an exaggerated nationalism. The laws of Mexico replaced the canon law of the church. "For me the true representative of God is the laws of my country and the government that is founded on them."[51] The other bishops saw themselves in a state of permanent conflict, or at least alienation, from the secular government of Mexico. As Romero de Solís observed, if Sánchez Camacho had known about Porfirio Díaz's opinion of him, he might have changed his mind.[52]

In all this, the Guadalupe controversy played only a tangential role. It has been hypothesized that the Guadalupan question was a smoke screen for getting rid of the bishop without divulging his moral failures.[53] That is possible, though there is no substantial evidence for it. Sánchez Camacho wanted to present himself as a martyr to truth who was oppressed by an oppressive and obscurantist church. In part, he succeeded, at least temporarily. The existing documentation, however, reveals a different story. The bishop of Tamaulipas brought about his own downfall by his mistakes and personal failings.

There is no doubt that the whole affair had a negative effect on Averardi and his career. The Holy See had been seriously concerned about the scandal and uproar caused by Sánchez Camacho's apostasy and the visitor's handling of an incendiary situation. There were those in the Vatican who considered his mission a failure. The affair of the bishop of Tamaulipas was not the only one that damaged Averardi's career. There was also the case of Antonio Plancarte.

The Rise and Fall of Antonio Plancarte

On February 18, 1892, the fifteenth abbot of Guadalupe, José María Feliciano Juan Nepomuceno Nicolás Melo y Sotomayor, died, and the office was vacant for three years. In March 1895, as a way of rewarding Antonio Plancarte for his part in the coronation, the archbishops of Oaxaca and Durango, and then the bishops of Querétaro, Zacatecas, León, Tulancingo, Chihuahua, Cuernavaca, and Tehuantepec, wrote to Archbishop Alarcón asking him to request the Holy See to name Plancarte abbot of Guadalupe and a bishop. Plancarte himself maintained that in addition to the restoration of the church at Guadalupe, the principal reason was that for eight years he had been the object of attack by the liberal and anti-Catholic press.[54] He claimed that he had tried to resist the honors but that others had convinced him that they would be for the honor and glory of God.

Alarcón did as requested and sent the petition, together with a laudatory letter of support. Alarcón was very flattering about Plancarte, calling him zealous and hard working, especially in the restoration of the Colegiata. Archbishop Gillow of Antequera (Oaxaca) said the same at a later date, and he added that Plancarte was the only one of his class at the Academy for Noble Ecclesiastics who had not received honors, because he always wanted to lead a simple life of an apostolic missionary.[55] Both said that Plancarte would reform the Chapter and return it to its original constitution, so that it would no longer oppose the archbishops of Mexico and give scandal to the people of Mexico.[56] It is unclear what this cryptic statement meant, though it may refer to the opposition to the coronation and restoration.

The requests left Mexico on May 28, 1895. On June 5, an unsigned telegram arrived from Rome for one of the canons of the Colegiata, Manuel García Coray, with news of the appointment.[57] In an audience of June 25, 1895, Leo XIII named Plancarte abbot of Guadalupe and titular bishop of Constancia.[58] On June 27, Alarcón received a letter from Rampolla that Leo XIII had approved the requests. Plancarte's possession of the office of abbot was set for September 8. His consecration was set for October 2.

Plancarte had hoped that he and his nephew, Francisco Plancarte y Navarrete, bishop-elect of Campeche, would be consecrated at the same ceremony. Rampolla wrote to Alarcón that the nephew should be consecrated on October 2, but made no mention of the uncle. On September 3, Alarcón cabled Rome to ask what was going on. At the same time, Plancarte received a letter from the rector of the Colegio Pío Latino-americano, saying that the process of naming him bishop had been suspended, and guessed that someone had sent some contrary information. On September 3, 1895, Rampolla wrote to Alarcón that on that very day the pope had approved that the process for Plancarte's bishopric be completed, and so Rampolla told Alarcón to go ahead without delay. However, both Plancarte and Alarcón decided that they should wait for the papal brief of appointment. Plancarte took possession of the office of abbot and made plans to go on the retreat that was required prior to consecration as a bishop.[59]

Plancarte was never to become a bishop. In Rome, confidential information had been received that was unfavorable to him with regard to his years in Jacona that seemed to justify postponing the canonical process. He had enemies in abundance in Mexico, including members of the hierarchy. Bishop Portugal y Serratos of Sinaloa had wanted to be named abbot of Guadalupe and sharply criticized Plancarte's reforms of the *cabildo*, calling them "*extranjerismos*" (foreignisms), and his attempts to remove abuses in the liturgy, music, and the administration of pious legacies. José Ignacio Arciga y Ruiz de Chávez, archbishop of Michoacán, was the patron of Cázares and supported him against Plancarte.[60] Andrade continued to be one of Plancarte's fiercest enemies and rallied the chapter against him. In fact, Plancarte believed that the chapter had sent a letter to the Holy See asking that the appointment be withdrawn because Plancarte had been expelled from the diocese of Zamora.[61]

Plancarte had begun his episcopal ordination retreat on October 2, 1895, when a cablegram from Rome suspended his appointment. Not without reason, Plancarte blamed this on his enemies. It is not clear how widely known the suspension was in Mexico. The bishops of Tehuantepec, Querétaro, and Tulancingo telegraphed Rome that Plancarte was innocent of the accusations, calling them calumny.[62] Alarcón telegraphed that Plancarte was worthy of being a bishop and asked for immediate dispatch of the brief, calling the delay the cause of "gravissimi pregiudizi" (very serious prejudices). The unanimous response of the Mexican bishops made the accusations seem to be nothing more than the results of bad faith and jealousy. Then the curia received a letter from Bishop Cázares, and it was he who was principally responsible for stopping the appointment. One of the main issues was the incident of Concepción Calderón and Plancarte's suspect relations with her. Cázares called Plancarte "obedientiae ignarus, sui judicii tenax, verbo et opere non prudens, et facilis nimis in concitandis difficultatibus et odiis" (ignorant of obedience, obstinate in his own judgment, imprudent in word and action, and much too easy in arousing difficulties and hatreds). Rome decided that a further investigation into Plancarte's conduct was needed, to be carried out with great delicacy and prudence. Cázares, however, was not in a strong position, since it could lawfully be asked why he had not rebuked Plancarte or taken action when the suspect incidents first occurred. On November 5, 1895, Plancarte asked Rampolla to accept his resignation as abbot of Guadalupe and to leave his appointment as bishop permanently suspended.[63]

Averardi wrote to Rampolla that no sooner had he arrived in Mexico City on March 23, 1896, when he began discreetly to inquire of trustworthy persons about Plancarte. His friends, especially those educated at the Collegio Pío Latinoamericano in Rome, depicted him as a man of piety, zeal, and generosity, and worthy of the highest dignities. Averardi believed that Plancarte's defects had been exaggerated, especially by the liberal press, which attacked him with the lowest and most vile slanders. Convinced that he would not learn the truth in Mexico City, Averardi decided to go to Zamora. He talked mostly with Cázares, who confirmed everything that he had written about the flight of the young lady, Concepción Calderón, and the sentence that he had given against Plancarte. The bishop said that he had written or said nothing out of emotion or jealousy, as some persons had judged, but only out of a sense of justice and truth and to avoid further scandal if Plancarte was made a bishop. With regard to Plancarte's moral conduct, the bishop claimed that while Plancarte was director of the girls' school, he abused the innocence of the girls, permitting himself acts with them that were the most unlawful and immoral, which discretion forbade Averardi from mentioning to Rampolla. The bishop learned them from a woman who had left the school, and so Averardi did not know if they were said out of jealousy or some other motive or how much they should be trusted. He talked to Concepción Calderón, who did not want to give testimony because of her abhorrence of any judicial process. She also had no wish to do anything that would hurt Plancarte. Cázares defended his role, saying he was something of a bystander. He had not taken the part of the denouncers.[64]

With great prudence, or so he claimed, Averardi questioned the father and brother (a priest) of the young girl. At first they were unwilling to answer because they did not want to harm anyone or dredge up unhappy matters, but on his insistence they admitted in confidence that when Plancarte was director of the school they were not edified by his excessive intimacy with the girls. Other persons in the city confirmed this. With regard to the accusation that he had profited by the money received for the restoration of the church of Guadalupe, he was acquitted of this by the unanimous written testimony of the canons of the Colegiata. He said almost by way of indirection that many bishops who were friends of Plancarte knew that Averardi recommended Plancarte to Rampolla. So he thought it good to make them understand with delicacy and in general terms some of the difficulties involved in satisfying their wish. Two of them understood the difficulty, and advised Plancarte to resign the bishopric so that the rumors and comments about him would cease.

Plancarte was gradually learning what the accusations were and who made them. One was that he had been "solus cum sola" with the Calderón girl after a festival. In a letter to his nephew Francisco, he said that Cázares had told both him and his uncle "that he had nothing against my moral conduct. If he lied at that time, it would cost him dear that he had not rebuked me, punished me, nor said anything to my father and lawful superior, Señor Labastida."[65] His nephew wrote him that there were two accusations: one about his moral conduct that came from Zamora and Cázares; the other was the erasure of the crown. "We have not been able to learn with certainty where it came from but we suspect, because of many clues, from the land of salt."[66] In a footnote, Tapia Méndez said that the latter reference was to "The Bishop of Colima [*sic*] the most illustrious Señor Don Fortino Hipólito Vera, who had been recommended by Father Plancarte to be named a bishop."[67] It hardly seems possible that Vera, a devoted *guadalupano* who was bishop of Cuernavaca, not Colima, would have undermined Plancarte. On the other hand, he had been a canon of Guadalupe, was not a *romano*, and may well have resented Plancarte's innovations.

When Averardi arrived to begin his visitation, Plancarte asked him to begin a formal canonical inquiry in order to clear his name, but Averardi said that he did not have the authority to do so. Also, replied the visitor, the process would take too long and would revive ill will. Plancarte, however, pressed his request. On February 16, 1896, he wrote to his friend Enrique Angelini in Rome, "You say that in Averardi I will find a father and friend: I prefer in this case a sincere and inflexible judge. . . . There in

eternity we will find justice, since I expect nothing from men."[68] There
was fear of the scandal that would be caused by the revelation of the
names of his enemies, including the bishop of Zamora. This response may
have been misleading, since Averardi's instructions from Cardinal
Rampolla included the investigation of the Plancarte case. Plancarte had
enemies in the upper reaches of the Mexican government, and at a time
when both the Vatican and Díaz were working toward a rapprochement,
there was a fear that an inquiry would upset a delicate situation.[69] On
May 2, 1896, Montes de Oca had a three-hour interview with Averardi
during which they ironed out the terms of Plancarte's resignation of his
bishopric.[70] Plancarte, in turn, said that he would leave his case to the justice and mercy of God and sent a formal letter of resignation as bishop of
Constancia to Averardi on May 7, 1896.[71]

Plancarte's defenders kept up their campaign on his behalf after
Averardi's arrival in March 1896. Francisco Orozco y Jiménez wrote a
long, flowery letter in Latin in the name of all the professors at the
Pontifical University of Mexico that called Plancarte "worthy of all
praise and commendation."[72] With regard to the accusations against him,
these had not yet become public, but there was good reason to be suspicious of them.[73] Leopoldo Ruiz y Flores, a canon of La Colegiata, later
archbishop of Linares, wrote that "if the Señor Abbot saw himself finally
at death's door, it was due to the bitterness that was occasioned by the
unhappy outcome of his promotion to the episcopate."[74] He told the visitor that while his letter of July 27 had been very flattering, it had not
been enough to restore Plancarte's honor. At that time, Ruiz was censor-
ing Plancarte's mail to intercept anything that might upset him.

Averardi thought that the resignation was the best way out and
referred to the request from the archbishops and bishops that Rampolla
send Plancarte a letter to praise him for his act of humility and abnega-
tion. Rampolla presented a report on the situation to the pope, who,
"appreciating the virtuous sentiments of the priest Plancarte, as well as
his devout attachment to his august person and to the Holy See, directs
Your Excellency to be pleased to signify to him his gratitude for the zeal
with which he works in the works of the ministry of beneficence, in the
restoration of the church of San Felipe the martyr, and in confirmation of
his affection blesses him."[75] Averardi did so, in a letter of July 27, 1896.[76]
He believed that a process or trial would vindicate Plancarte but that his
enemies would continue to persecute him.[77] On that same day, Averardi
informed Plancarte that Leo XIII had accepted his resignation as bishop.
Ruiz y Flores was in Rome in 1898 and learned that the Holy See, with
the approval of some Mexican bishops, wanted to appoint Plancarte
bishop of Yucatán, and that Rampolla wrote to Averardi that in his

capacity as visitor apostolic he should make the request to Rome. On April 4, 1898, Averardi informed Plancarte of this "under the seal." Plancarte was of two minds about it, but he died before anything could be done.[78]

Matters were not helped when Plancarte's nephew, Francisco Plancarte y Navarrete, the bishop of Campeche, returned from a trip to Rome around September 1896. He claimed that a Vatican official, Msgr. Castagnis, the pro-Secretary of the Congregation for Extraordinary Ecclesiastical Affairs, had told him the content of all the reports that Averardi had sent to Rampolla.[79] Averardi hastened to justify himself to Rampolla: "To these reports, if Your Eminence wishes, I could add others that certainly would not be in favor of him or of his friends, whose number, to tell the truth, is rather limited, since he is not generally liked or well regarded because of his contemptible character and his great pride."[80] Averardi also took the opportunity to vent his frustrations at his mission and to enlist Rampolla's sympathy.

It pains me to find myself in a country where there is no one whom I can trust. Here there is nothing but factions, and each one despises the other in low fashion and everyone tries to deceive and compromise me. The intelligence of this people is developed only for lies and slander. Accustomed to habitual revolution, they are not satisfied with peace or civil and ecclesiastical laws. If for some time now there has been peace, that is due to the iron hand of the current president [Díaz], who has known well that this people wants to be governed only by brute force. I will say only that the cause of the wicked laws of this country has been in part also the undisciplined clergy, which has sought to be disturbers of the public peace, being by nature and education hostile to any authority whatever.[81]

Averardi added that the bishops, with few exceptions, and the clergy in general were opposed to his mission and used every means to frustrate it. "Permit me, Your Eminence, to say with all sincerity of my soul that I am depressed in spirit and body. God alone knows how much I suffer! With tears in my eyes I beg and implore you to take pity on me. Free me quickly from the pains that, I swear, I have never suffered so greatly in my life."[82] Rampolla replied that the Holy See had been accurately informed of events in Mexico and the truth of Averardi's reports. His sympathy for Averardi's plight, however, was somewhat perfunctory.[83]

Plancarte originally wanted to resign as abbot of Guadalupe as well as bishop, but there is no evidence that he did so. On the contrary, there are indications of continued difficulties between him and the canons, and it is probable that he was resented as an outsider. After the coronation, he set about reorganizing the services at the Basilica. This aroused tensions between the conservatives and the *romanos*. Plancarte wanted to remove the secular music that had crept into the services over the years and reform the liturgy on Roman models.[84] The inscription on his statue in the Old Basilica says that he "brought about the reform of the music and sacred chant in this basilica," with the approval of the Congregation of Rites, November 5, 1895.[85] Again, Plancarte's Romanità may have played a role. He had enemies in the Chapter, and clearly it was not an easy situation. In mid-1896 he suffered a severe illness, serious enough to cause fear for his life.[86] When he recovered, the canons of Guadalupe and other partisans of his cause wanted to have a thanksgiving ceremony at Guadalupe. Averardi now found himself in a rather awkward position. Apparently, he did not want to give a sermon at the function because it would give it an official nature.[87] The function was eventually postponed, with the pretext that the original date coincided with a national holiday. None of the existing correspondence gives a clear picture of what this was about. Averardi wrote, "I am not upset, but definitely offended by the not very sincere conduct of some persons with regard to this sort of affair, but for my part I tell you frankly that it was an act of ingratitude, since I have always treated everyone with the most sincere friendliness and deference; an act disrespectful toward the Holy See, and, in my opinion, compromising for the person whom they were seeking to benefit."[88]

Later Lives

The controversy followed García Icazbalceta to and beyond the grave. In his last years, he suffered from what seems to have been chronic depression. "The persistent rumors and the severe censures caused by the essay [the letter to the archbishop of Mexico] were a constant source of worry and sorrow to him in his declining years."[89] Henry Raup Wagner wrote, "I cannot but feel that the last years of his life were embittered by the attacks made on him on account of his letter of 1883 to Archbishop Labastida about the Virgin of Guadalupe. To question this peculiarly Mexican legend savored of heresy."[90] He was also deeply concerned about his daughter's health. On the evening of November 26, 1894, after visiting her in her sick room, he suffered a stroke and died. His body was not discovered until some time later. To some, the fact that his death occurred so suddenly and without the opportunity for preparation or the last rites was a sign of divine displeasure. Bishop Camacho García of Querétaro wrote to Vera, "Did you see how Icazbalceta died in a notably bad way?"[91] It is only reasonable to suspect that the emotional intensity of the controversy and the biting personal attacks made on him contributed to his sudden death. At his death, he was still a Spanish citizen.[92] He was buried from the church of San Cosme, of which, coincidentally,

Vicente de P. Andrade had once been pastor. His body rests in the chapel of Nuestra Señora de Valvanera in that church, together with those of his wife and parents. On his tombstone is carved his lifelong motto, *Otium sine litteris mors est* (Leisure without learning is death).

The stress of the different controversies also took its toll on the health of Antonio Plancarte y Labastida. In the early part of 1898 he declined notably, and by April he was dying, apparently of stomach cancer. When he was close to death, he wanted the canons of Guadalupe to administer the last rites. Two canons answered the call, Aristeo Aguilar and, astoundingly, Vicente de P. Andrade. The former gave him viaticum and Extreme Unction. Plancarte died on the morning of April 26, 1898, at the age of fifty-seven. Andrade, the *inimicus homo*, was present when he died and sent his obituary to *El Tiempo*.[93] The obituary said nothing about his having been appointed bishop.

Averardi offered to celebrate the pontifical funeral mass, an offer accepted by Andrade in the name of the Collegiate chapter. The account of the funeral in *El Tiempo*, however, says that the mass was celebrated by Camacho of Querétaro, assisted by Montes de Oca. Averardi read the *responsio* or commendation of the body.[94] Archbishop Alarcón also agreed to attend, though there is no evidence that he actually did so.[95] Plancarte was buried in the Panteón Español, where his uncle was also buried, but his remains were transferred to the Asilo de la Soledad in Tacuba on January 26, 1909. In 1996 the Daughters of Mary Immaculate of Guadalupe sent materials to Rome seeking the canonization of Plancarte. The matter apparently was stalled by the problem of the scandals associated with his various undertakings. In a telephone interview with the newspaper *Reforma*, the postulator of his cause, Sister Ana María Sada Lambretón, expressed confidence that the difficulties would be overcome.[96]

José María Cázares Martínez ruled the diocese of Zamora for more than thirty years. He resigned because of infirmities in 1908 and died on March 31 of the following year. He is buried in the Cathedral of his see city.

In 1897 Esteban Antícoli finally published his two-volume history of Guadalupe.[97] He died on November 7, 1899, with his eyes fixed on an image of Our Lady of Guadalupe.

Averardi returned to Rome in 1900 and was never again employed by the Vatican in an important diplomatic post. According to Plancarte y Navarrete, the pope was not happy with him and received him coolly on his return to Rome.[98] He appears to have spent the rest of his life as a relatively unimportant curial bureaucrat.

As for Sánchez Camacho, the later years of his life seem to have been passed in peaceful obscurity. It has been asserted, however, that he died an unhappy alcoholic. After his resignation, the former bishop became tangentially involved in efforts to establish a schismatic Mexican national church.[99] In 1899 the Anglicans attempted to recruit them to their side but failed. In July of that same year he wrote a letter of congratulations to a group of Benedictines in Cleveland, Ohio, who under the leadership of Edward Durkin had left the Catholic Church. In 1900 the schismatic "patriarch" Joaquín Pérez Budar invited him to become head of an independent church. Sánchez Camacho responded that at the time of his departure, he would have liked to separate the Mexican Church from Rome, but that it proved impossible. He offered to help Pérez, but appended a long list of conditions. Most of these dealt with the reform of the church as the former bishop envisioned it. Thus, for example, he said that the precepts of the church should be simple usages until such time as they were reformed; archbishops would have a preeminence of honor only, not jurisdiction; those priests who had a single concubine and lived peacefully would be allowed to continue to do so but would not be allowed to rise in the hierarchy; impediments to marriage would be those established by civil law. Overall, Sánchez Camacho's recommendations would have delivered the rule of the Mexican Church over to the local bishop and the state. There was room for only limited input by the laity, restricted to "enlightened people" (*el pueblo ilustrado*) in most cases. Paradoxically, the idea of a national church was anathema to Díaz, who feared the impact on the peace and stability of the country.[100] It is also strange that Sánchez Camacho would show such devotion to a government that at bottom was a repressive and exploitive dictatorship, one that marginalized the very Indians whom he wanted the bishops to help. Sánchez Camacho died in the city of Victoria on December 24, 1920, and was buried in the civic pantheon, having lived through some of the most turbulent years in Mexican history.

Vicente de P. Andrade encountered many difficulties within the Vincentian community. In an eerie replication of tensions within religious orders in the sixteenth and seventeenth centuries, the Vincentians were divided between Spaniards and native Mexicans. The target of the Spanish party's hostility was Andrade and, to a lesser extent, his friend, Antonio Icaza. Andrade's own erratic and rather devious personality did not help matters. Because of the hostility, Andrade began living outside his community. His acceptance of the post of pastor of the parish of San Cosme on October 31, 1880, though done at the insistence of Archbishop Labastida y Dávalos, created a crisis with his superiors, and on September 17 he was released from the community. On January 2, 1883, he was incardinated into the archdiocese of Mexico.[101] He became pastor of San Miguel in 1883, then of the *sagrario metropolitano* in 1885, a *prebendado* of the Collegiate chapter of Guadalupe on July 29, 1887, and a canon on September 27, 1891. In all these places, he was noted for his devotion and help to the poor. His friend and associate, Antonio Icaza, left the Vincentians in October 1883, and after two years in the diocese of Tabasco, whose bishop was his former provincial, Agustín Torres, he was incardinated into the archdiocese of Mexico in January 1884.[102]

In later life Andrade devoted himself to historical and bibliographical studies, of which the most important was the monumental *Ensayo bibliográfico mexicano del siglo XVII*. An outspoken anti-apparitionist, he wrote *Estudio histórico sobre la leyenda guadalupana*.[103] His brilliant but volatile personality, together with his anti-apparitionist stance, kept him from advancing further in his ecclesiastical career.[104] Though he was the senior canon of Guadalupe, he never became abbot. In August 1915 Andrade was struck by an automobile as he descended from a streetcar near the National Palace. He died on August 17, 1915, at the Hospital de Jesús in Mexico City, just as Mexico was being plunged into a long and bloody civil war.[105] One of his last acts was to help a poor woman in need. The entire Collegiate chapter of the Basilica of Guadalupe came to administer viaticum to him.[106] In his will, Andrade left a house to the Vincentian community, "in order to demonstrate my devotion and gratitude to the said Congregation, to which I owed my intellectual and spiritual education and to which I belonged for seventeen years."[107] He was buried in the Panteón de Dolores, where his family had a crypt.

During his lifetime, Ignacio Montes de Oca held four episcopal titles: first bishop of Tamaulipas, ninth bishop of Monterrey (Linares), fourth bishop of San Luis Potosí, and titular archbishop of Cesárea del Ponto.[108] He was widely recognized for his scholarship and linguistic abilities. He died in New York City, while on a return voyage from Europe, on August 18, 1921.

Fortino Hipólito Vera was named the first bishop of Cuernavaca in 1894. He was consecrated at the Church of the Capuchinas at Guadalupe (La Colegiata was under repair). He was the author of several books, in addition to the *Tesoro guadalupano* and the *Contestación*, including two works on the Mexican church councils, especially the Third Mexican Provincial Council of 1585.[109] None, however, was distinguished for any original scholarship. He was a bishop for only four years, dying on September 22, 1898.

Francisco Plancarte y Navarrete, nephew of Antonio Plancarte and grand-nephew of Archbishop Labistida y Dávalos, was the first bishop of

Campeche, the second bishop of Cuernavaca (succeeding Vera), and archbishop of Monterrey. He gained great renown as an archeologist and historian, and died in Mexico, of complications of diabetes, on July 2, 1920.

By the beginning of the twentieth century the virulent controversies over Guadalupe had subsided. There followed a period of calm, uneasy though it was.

CHAPTER FIVE

An Uneasy Calm

❖

The Guadalupan controversy subsided for almost a century after 1896, and although numerous apologetic and controversial works were published, they lacked the intensity that characterized the previous phase of the dispute. In general, works on either side of the question were less strident in tone and tended more toward the devotional or analytical. Paradoxically, while there was a certain level of peace on the Guadalupan front, Mexico went through some of the most turbulent decades in its history.[1] In September 1910, the Díaz regime celebrated the dictator's eightieth birthday and the centenary of Hidalgo's uprising. The euphoria of the celebration masked serious inequalities in Mexican society and the stresses that soon plunged the nation into revolution. In October, from his exile in San Antonio, Texas, Francisco I. Madero published his *Plan de San Luis Potosí*, which called for the overthrow of Díaz. Sporadic revolts broke out in various regions, led by local leaders, but the real center of resistance was Chihuahua. The fall of Ciudad Juárez to the northern rebels in May 1911 spelled the end of the Porfiriato. As he departed for exile in France, Díaz is reputed to have said, "Madero has unleashed a tiger; let us see if he can control it." Madero was overwhelmingly elected president of Mexico in October.

The Revolution was not over; it had just begun. Madero was an ineffectual leader — a sparrow in a sky full of hawks is how Díaz is supposed to have described him — who saw the Revolution in terms of political rather than social change. He was essentially a nineteenth-century liberal capitalist who believed that the Mexican people did not want bread so much as the opportunity to earn bread. He quickly alienated some of the revolutionary leaders, including Pascual Orozco in the North and

Emiliano Zapata in the South, both of whom demanded broader social and land reform. Zapata took as his symbol the Virgin of Guadalupe, with the slogan "Tierra y libertad" (Land and liberty). In 1913, Madero was overthrown and murdered by the forces of General Victoriano Huerta, and Mexico was plunged into a long and bloody civil war. Though Huerta did not pursue an overtly counterrevolutionary course, he quickly faced revolts in a number of places. In the North, Venustiano Carranza, supported by Francisco (Pancho) Villa and Alvaro Obregón, rejected the new government. In the South, Zapata rebelled against Huerta without having a formal alliance with the Northerners. The new president's problems were compounded by deteriorating relations with the United States, culminating in that country's occupation of Veracruz in 1914. In July of that year, Huerta resigned and went into exile. He died at Fort Bliss, Texas, in January 1916, of natural causes.

Huerta's fall did not bring peace. The victors soon fell out: Carranza and Obregón, Villa, and Zapata now fought a three-way civil war. In 1915, the Carrancistas began to prevail. In 1916, a convention was called at Querétaro that drew up a new instrument of government, the Constitution of 1917. The convention was under the control of radicals, who did not necessarily reflect the thought of the country at large. One potentially divisive aspect of the new Constitution was its rabid anticlericalism, which went far beyond the reform of the previous century. Marriage became a civil contract, religious organizations had no legal identity or status, public worship outside of churches was banned, state legislatures could determine the number of priests allowed to work in their jurisdictions, no foreign priests were allowed to minister in the country, and the wearing of religious garb in public was prohibited.

Carranza became president of Mexico in 1917 after a special election. No champion of social reform, the new president did not enforce the Constitution. He did, however, rid himself of two implacable enemies. Zapata was assassinated in 1919, and Villa accepted retirement and a government pension (1920), only to be assassinated in 1923. In 1920, when Carranza attempted to name his successor as president, Alvaro Obregón, aided by Adolfo de la Huerta and Plutarco Elías Calles, raised the banner of revolt. In May, Carranza fled from Mexico City but was assassinated in a small village on the way to Veracruz.

With Obregón's election as president in 1920 a relative peace descended on Mexico. In general, the new president followed moderate policies. Still, there was another revolt in 1923 when it was feared that Calles, more radical than Obregón, would become the next president. The uprising was suppressed, and Calles did become president in 1924.

He soon became known as *el jefe máximo* and his regime as the *maximato*. A strong anticlerical, Calles enforced the religious provisions of the Constitution of 1917. In response to his repression, the bishops of Mexico put the country under an interdict, that is, they stopped all religious services in the country (1926). The "strike" lasted three years, during which Calles became more hostile and repressive. The result was an uprising by Catholics that came to be known as the Cristero revolt or Cristiada. Though the government forces gradually gained the upper hand, they could not put down the revolt entirely. In 1928, Obregón was again elected president and showed signs of seeking an accommodation with the church. Unfortunately for Mexico, he was assassinated by an unbalanced young Catholic (July 17, 1928). From 1928 to 1934, Calles ruled Mexico through a series of puppet presidents. During that time, the Cristero rebellion was settled with the help of the American ambassador, Dwight Morrow. These years also saw a shift to the right and a move away from the social gains of the Revolution.

In 1934, Calles selected as president a man he thought would be another puppet: Lázaro Cárdenas. It was a classic example of miscalculation. Cárdenas was serious about implementing land reform and about removing Calles as an influence in Mexican politics. By 1936, he was secure enough to send the *jefe máximo* into exile in the United States. Cárdenas was left free to pursue a program of reform, especially in education and the redistribution of land, and economic nationalism. Forbidden by law to succeed himself, Cárdenas threw his support in 1940 to Manuel Avila Camacho, the conservative, rather colorless secretary of war. For the next twenty-eight years, the Revolution became more institutionalized, industrialization spread, and a steady, if unevenly distributed, economic progress was made. Beneath a relatively placid façade, however, tensions remained: poverty, social inequality, corruption in the ruling Institutional Revolutionary Party (PRI), an exploding population, increased urbanization, especially in Mexico City, and the authoritarian nature of the regime.

The situation reached crisis proportions in 1968, the year in which Mexico was to host the Olympic Games. Mexico City was shaken by student protests, which culminated in a rally at the Plaza de las Tres Culturas in Tlatelolco. The rally was dispersed by police and army units, a riot ensued, and some three or four hundred persons, including women and children, were killed. An implicit social contract had been broken, and though the PRI held on to power for another quarter century, its dominance would not last. With the election of Vicente Fox in 2000 the Revolutionary Party's rule came to an end and Mexico was launched into an uncertain future.

Guadalupe in a Revolutionary Age

The controversy over the historicity of Guadalupe had subsided by the time of Madero's revolution, and the turbulence of the ensuing years deflected attention from the question. A new trend in this period was the growing interest on the part of anthropologists who undertook scholarly studies of Guadalupe and its impact on Mexican life and culture. All, however, was not peaceful for Guadalupe during this unstable period. On November 14, 1921, a bomb exploded near the image in the Basilica. Though there was some damage, the image and its covering were unhurt, a fact that believers attributed to divine intervention. For many years, a twisted candelabra was kept on display as a reminder of this heavenly protection. Guadalupe also played a role in the Cristero revolt, though it was secondary to that of Christ the King.[2]

In the century following the coronation, the Guadalupe devotion received increasing recognition by the Vatican. In 1904, at the request of Archbishop Alarcón, La Colegiata was elevated to the status of a basilica. In 1910, Pope Pius X proclaimed Guadalupe the patroness of all Latin America, and twenty-five years later, Pius XII extended that patronage to the Philippines. In 1945, Pius XII proclaimed her Queen of Mexico and Empress of the Americas. Several popes were devotees of Guadalupe, especially John Paul II, the first pope personally to visit the sanctuary.[3] In addition, the Basilica was extensively refurbished from 1936 to 1938. The fourth centenary of the apparitions was observed in 1931, and the fiftieth anniversary of the coronation in 1945.

In this period, Guadalupan anniversaries were often marked by the publication of commemorative works, usually in the form of an "album." The first of these was published in 1895 on the occasion of the coronation itself and was the work of Victoriano Agüeros. Though the silver anniversary of the coronation in 1920 was celebrated with great festivities, no album was published on that occasion. In preparation for the fourth centenary of the apparitions, the Mexican Jesuit historian Mariano Cuevas published the *Album histórico guadalupano del IV centenario* (Guadalupan Historical Album of the Fourth Centenary). It follows a chronological format, dividing the history of Guadalupe into decades. It is strongly in favor of the traditional apparition account but is marred by Cuevas's flaws as an historian. In 1938, Antonio Pompa y Pompa also commemorated the fourth centenary with the *Album del IV centenario guadalupano* (Album of the Fourth Guadalupan Centenary). The book includes material on the tradition, the *patronato*, the coronation, and the sanctuary.

In 1973, to celebrate the seventy-fifth anniversary of the coronation, Father Lauro López Beltrán edited and had published the *Album del LXXV aniversario de la coronación guadalupana* (Album of the Seventy-fifth Anniversary of the Guadalupan Coronation). It is an exceedingly large book, well put together and handsomely formatted. It contains detailed histories of the coronation, the anniversaries, and other aspects of the Guadalupe devotion. In 1981, to commemorate the 450th anniversary of the apparitions, there appeared the *Album conmemorativo del 450 aniversario de las apariciones de Nuestra Señora de Guadalupe* (Album Commemorating the 450th Anniversary of the Appearances of Our Lady of Guadalupe). The editors were María Teresa Cervantes de Conde (an art historian), Ernesto de la Torre Villar, and Ramiro Navarro de Anda. It contains a generous amount of material, including a Spanish version of the *Nican mopohua* and a history of the coronation. It follows the usual format of giving a history of the cultus, the sources, and Guadalupe's connection with Mexican identity. It also contains essays by the Jesuit Luis Medina Ascensio, the Franciscan Fidel de Jesús Chauvet, and, interestingly in light of later events, Guillermo Schulenburg Prado, the abbot of Guadalupe, who wrote, "In fact, our entire historic past is profoundly bound to the image and the words of Saint Mary of Guadalupe. She is the delicately persuasive evangelizer, the forger of our nationality, and she who has been with us in the most difficult moments of our slow human maturation, whose most precious privilege is to be authentic and true freedom."[4]

During this period, García Icazbalceta's letter continued to generate rebuttals. In 1931, an offprint of the Catholic journal *Mensajero del Sagrado Corazón de Jesús* contained two essays: "Juicio crítico sobre la carta de Don Joaquín García Icazbalceta" (Critical Judgment on the Letter of Don Joaquín García Icazbalceta), by the Jesuit Eduardo Iglesias, and "Fuentes históricas de la 'Carta acerca del origen de Nuestra Señora de Guadalupe de Méjico'" (Historical Sources of the "Letter Concerning the Origin of Our Lady of Guadalupe of Mexico"), by Jesús García Gutiérrez. The latter work concludes that García Icazbalceta had merely reproduced arguments by Muñoz, Mier, and Bartolache that had already been refuted by 1883, and that to use the letter as an argument against the apparitions was a sign of either supine ignorance or a refined bad faith.[5] In 1944, García Icazbalceta's grandson, Luis García Pimentel y Elguero, published a short book, privately printed, titled *Don Joaquín García Icazbalceta como Católico* (Don Joaquín García Icazbalceta as a Catholic). It is a compilation of testimonies and eulogies of his grandfather, including that of Montes de Oca. Among the apparitionists whose tributes were included are Primo Feliciano Velázquez, Fortino Hipólito Vera, and Eulogio Gillow. Finally, in 1952, the *Investigación histórica y documental sobre la aparición de la Virgen de Guadalupe de Mexico* reprinted García Icazbalceta's letter, the *aditamentos*, the letter of Sánchez Camacho, and the *Información* of 1556.

The impact of the great historian's letter continued to linger. As late as 1954, Emilio Valton, in an *homenaje*, wrote with a tone of sadness,

The year 1883 was, for the memory of Icazbalceta, a date of sad remembrance, because that was when he wrote to the archbishop Don Pelagio Antonio de Labastida y Dávalos and by command of the said most illustrious prelate, his famous "Letter on the Origin of the image of Our Lady of Guadalupe," which remained for several years reserved to some friends under a cloak of discretion. But in 1896 it was published surreptitiously and provoked among Guadalupan historians a frenzy of protest that is easy to understand. Undoubtedly there were deep feelings on each side. Nevertheless, we judge that in such a case, if the rigorous criterion of Icazbalceta as historian should be considered very debatable, the rectitude of his intentions, as an illustrious and sincere Catholic, has always remained safe from any sinister suspicion.[6]

Of the later defenders of the apparition, Mariano Cuevas (1879– 1949) was especially important because of his influence as one of the major historians in Mexico.[7] He was the author of numerous works, both on Mexican history in general and on Guadalupe in particular.[8] Cuevas identified Mexican nationalism with Catholicism, an agenda that led him to be somewhat cavalier in his use of sources. At times he showed little critical sense and a great deal of tendentiousness, at least in his writings about Guadalupe. He found Guadalupan references where none were immediately obvious, and he was not above altering the wording of some in order to prove his case.[9] He was also very personal in his criticisms of anti-apparitionists, and in 1931 wrote with his accustomed lack of grace (and accuracy):

In the same way we discard a good part of the Catholic anti-apparitionists because we know them well: they were, generally speaking, men of average careers, average learning, and average intelligence; those who credited themselves that by speaking interminably in a bookstore or office of a man of letters, they increased their learning or the reputation they had. Of the same four prestigious ones who are still left standing, two were only discoverers or, better, fences for documents; historians they were not, nor even critics. . . . There are no surviving or noteworthy anti-apparitionists now. The only two men of worth who in times past seemed to march in the opposing ranks, keep silence because of their fine education and proximity to the final judgment. Their dignity on the other hand does not permit them to serve as instruments for a cause that they now saw as coming from a foreign sectarianism against the glory, peace, and unity of our fatherland.[10]

One of the most scholarly and authoritative of the apparitionists was Primo Feliciano Velázquez. In 1926 he published an excellent translation of and commentary on Luis Laso de la Vega's *Huei tlamahuiçoltica*. This was the only time that the entire book, not just the *Nican mopohua*, was translated into Spanish, and the first reprint of the entire book since 1649. In 1931 he published one of the best analyses of the sources of the Guadalupe tradition by an apparitionist, *La aparición de Santa María de Guadalupe*. It is a balanced work, one of the most scholarly to come from the pro-apparitionists school. It is still widely used by defenders of the apparitions.

During this time also there appeared a number of works of lesser importance but ones that are still cited. The priest Jesús García Gutiérrez wrote numerous devotional works but only one that can be classified as history, that is, the *Primer siglo guadalupano* (First Century of Guadalupe). As the title indicates, it is a survey of supposed documentation prior to the publication of Sánchez's book, but it contains little that is new. The same can be said for the Jesuit José Bravo Ugarte, whose *Cuestiones históricas guadalupanas* (Historical Questions about Guadalupe) contributes little.

More substantive contributions to Guadalupan studies were made by the noted Jesuit historian Ernest Burrus. A recognized scholar (who proved that it is possible to be such without a doctorate), he concentrated more on publishing critical editions of major works, such as those of Alonso de la Veracruz, Francisco Alegre, or Adolphe Bandolier, than original compositions. A man of encyclopedic learning, he was a widely respected and beloved figure. He was also, however, an uncritical *guadalupano*, and this sometimes required him to resort to rather convoluted reasoning.[11] In the 1970s and 1980s he produced a number of works, many of which were published by the Center for Applied Research in the Apostolate (CARA) as part of a series on Studies of Popular Devotion.[12] Of special value was the Guadalupan bibliography he compiled in collaboration with Gloria Grajales, and which has been cited several times in this work. As will be noted in Chapter 6, he was a witness in the first archdiocesan inquiry into the beatification of Juan Diego. His lack of critical sense in approaching the question of Guadalupe was a disappointment to many of his friends and admirers.

A noteworthy defender of the traditional account was the famed Nahuatl scholar Angel María Garibay, who wrote a number of articles on the indigenous *anales* and an article on Guadalupe for the *New Catholic Encyclopedia*.[13] In the latter, he claimed that an eighteenth-century model sermon in Nahuatl about the apparitions known as the *Inin huei tlamahuiçoltzin* (This Is the Great Miracle) was actually contemporary with the

event. According to Garibay, the author was the priest Juan González
who in 1531 was supposedly acting as Zumárraga's interpreter with the
Indians. In this hypothesis, it was not a sermon but a brief account drawn
up by a person who was present at the conversations between Zumárraga
and Juan Diego. Garibay's theory has been accepted, in whole or in part,
by a large number of historians.[14] However, it has been refuted by others,
especially Edmundo O'Gorman.[15]

The Exaltation of the Nican mopohua

The last quarter of the twentieth century saw a renewed interest in the
Nican mopohua, especially in the form of translations. As mentioned earlier, Velázquez produced a good translation of the *Huei tlamahuiçoltica* in
1926, together with a linguistic commentary, but after that, interest
lagged for almost half a century. Then, in 1978, Mario Rojas Sánchez
produced a new Spanish translation. In that same year, a translation by
Garibay was published posthumously in *Histórica*, the journal of the
Centro de Estudios Guadalupanos in Mexico City. Clodomiro Siller
reproduced Garibay's translation with some modifications in 1984. This
was quickly followed by translations and editions by Guillermo Ortiz de
Montellano, Jesús Galera Madrid, and Luis Guerrero Rosado. Richard
Nebel also included a transcription and translation in the published version of his doctoral dissertation. In his *Enciclopedia guadalupana*, the
Spanish Jesuit Xavier Escalada reprinted, in parallel columns, the translations of Becerra Tanco, Boturini Benaduci, Velázquez, Garibay, Rojas
Sánchez, and Ortiz de Montellano. The *Nican mopohua* was translated
into English in a poetic format by Martinus Cawley, a Trappist monk at
the monastery of Our Lady of Guadalupe in Lafayette, Oregon. The most
accurate translation and technical analysis, not only of the *Nican mopohua* but also of the entire *Huei tlamahuiçoltica*, is that of Lisa Sousa,
Stafford Poole, and James Lockhart, published in 1999. It is the only one
to translate the entire work into English.

In the year 2000 the celebrated Mexican historian and *nahuatlato*,
Miguel León-Portilla, published his own translation and commentary.
Surprisingly, he attributes authorship to Antonio Valeriano, an attribution that is arguable at best. León-Portilla believed that the use of
the term *achtopa*, meaning "first" or "recently," to date the apparitions
shows that Laso de la Vega was copying from an earlier manuscript, a
claim also made by Burrus. He also dated the incomplete copy of the
Nican mopohua in the *Monumentos guadalupanos* in the New York
Public Library to the mid–sixteenth century, perhaps to Valeriano him-

self. Contrary to Sousa, Poole, and Lockhart, he thinks that the *Nican mopohua* served as the source for Miguel Sánchez, rather than vice versa.[16] One purpose for his translation was a desire to highlight the link to pre-Hispanic language and thought. For him, the style of the *Nican mopohua* has similarities with the *tecpatlahtolli*, or noble speech, of the Mexica. He found statements in the *Cantares mexicanos* that paralleled those of Laso de la Vega. For example: "Cacahuani in intozqui, iuhquin quinahnanquilia tepetl" (Their voices were swelling and fading, as if the hill were answering them), and "iuhquin tepetl quinahnanquillia" (as if the hill were answering them).[17] There was also the importance of the mountain, Tepeyac: "The mountain, *tepetl*, in native thought was the sacred reality where the god dwelt who with his water caused germination and gave life to everything that bloomed on the earth."[18] In discussing Juan Diego's self-image, he says, "All the words with which Juan Diego describes himself as a poor man we find in various of the *huehuetlahtolli*, testimonies of the ancient word."[19] His conclusion was that the *Nican mopohua* is a melding of ancient Nahua thought with the Christian message, Catholicism clothed in a native garment.

One result of this renewed interest was the sacralization and elevation of the *Nican mopohua* to the point that some have considered it to be a Mexican gospel. Indeed, as Brading has pointed out, its status was raised almost to that of divine inspiration.[20] Xavier Escalada wrote, "We believe that the mysterious action of God was not only active in the apparitions to Juan Diego and in the imprinting of the image but that also it assisted Valeriano so that he could transmit, in writing, with the necessary truth, the narration of this history of salvific character."[21] Siller, who considers the account to be very ancient, calls the language classical Nahuatl, which he extravagantly describes as "a plain, direct, smooth, precise, elegant, sonorous, beautiful, profound, highly meaningful, and even sublime language."[22] He considers the language of the *Nican mopohua* to be highly symbolic, with meanings that go beyond the words. One example is the word *xochitl*, "flower," which he somewhat hyperbolically states came to mean truth, beauty, authenticity, and philosophy.[23] Virgil Elizondo carries this idea even further. The story of Guadalupe "is nothing less than an original American Gospel."[24] "The story of her appearances and compassion is sacred narrative as remembered by the victim-survivors of the conquest who were equally the first born of the new creation."[25] "The meaning resides not just in the words but also in how many times they are used and how they are arranged."[26] Hence, for him, every word, every sentence has cosmic meaning, not just as a narrative but as a sacred narrative. "The symbolic meaning of the images created by the words is all-important. Each detail had special signification for the Nahuatl [*sic*] peoples."[27] Archbishop Norberto Rivera Carrera, in his pastoral of June 2, 1996, addressed the Virgin in strongly hyperbolic terms. Brading sees in this another example of the exaltation of the *Nican mopohua*: "The manner in which he appropriated the voice of Juan Diego confirmed the *Nican mopohua* as an inspired text which could be cited alongside holy scripture."[28] In commenting on Guerrero Rosado's edition of Laso de la Vega's work, Brading observes, "Although Guerrero derided Sánchez and Mier as creole nationalists, his close reading of the *Nican mopohua* drove him to remark that the colloquies between Juan Diego and the Virgin were as beautiful and moving as any found in holy scripture. That the Indian had been able to remember and record Mary's precise words suggested that his memory had been assisted and inspired by a 'master artist.'"[29] And later, "In these comments Guerrero clearly identified the *Nican mopohua* as a divinely inspired text, a Mexican gospel, which marked the foundation of a new nation."[30] Yet Brading's comments are somewhat exaggerated. Elizondo is the one that comes closest to doing this, and the whole thing seems restricted to a rather small group of enthusiasts.

Documentary Sources

Similarly, there was a renewed interest in important documentation in the history of the Guadalupe tradition, which led to the publication of two important and useful works. The first of these is the *Testimonios históricos guadalupanos*, edited by Torre Villar and Navarro de Anda, which brings together in one volume almost all pertinent writings on the subject of Guadalupe. Though edited from an apparitionist perspective and despite a few omissions, it is an invaluable resource for researchers. The other work is *Las informaciones jurídicas de 1666 y el beato indio Juan Diego* (The Juridic Inquiries of 1666 and Blessed Indian Juan Diego), a facsimile and transcription of the capitular inquiry of 1666, edited by Ana María Sada Lambretón, a nun of the community founded by Antonio Plancarte and postulator for his cause. This, too, makes available to the serious student of Guadalupe one of the most important documents in the history of the question.

The capitular inquiry was reproduced again in *La Virgen de Guadalupe y Juan Diego en las informaciones jurídicas de 1666* (The Virgin of Guadalupe and Juan Diego in the Juridic Inquiries of 1666), edited by Eduardo Chávez Sánchez and published at the time of the canonization of Juan Diego. Unlike the other edition, this one contains a transcription of the text, a notable help since the facsimile is so faint as to be at times almost illegible. This edition also contains essays by Alfonso Alcalá Alvarado, Raúl Soto Vázquez, José Luis Guerrero Rosado, and Peter Gumpel, all of whom had been involved in the canonization process. Despite the impressive credentials attributed to these contributors, their essays contain little that is new. Guerrero Rosado and Gumpel, in particular, spend several pages refuting a letter that Stafford Poole had sent to Rome in an effort to delay the canonization.[31]

Differing Approaches

An entirely different view of Guadalupe, and one of the most influential recent works about it, is Edmundo O'Gorman's *Destierro de sombras* (Banishing of Shadows), published in 1986. It is a rather strange work that combined penetrating analyses and careful research with imaginative flights of fancy that have little basis in reality. According to O'Gorman, Guadalupe was originally an Indian devotion that was appropriated by the Spaniards. His thesis is that Alonso de Montúfar, the second archbishop of Mexico (1551–72), was the key figure in the development of the Guadalupe devotion. O'Gorman dates the foundation of the chapel at Tepeyac to 1556, though he says that the present image had been placed there in 1555 or 1556. He attempts to show that the name Guadalupe was imposed on the shrine and the image in 1556, thus removing its Indian character and making it a Spanish devotion. It was thus a way of legitimizing the Virgin for Spaniards. The *Nican mopohua*, which O'Gorman dates to 1556, was an attempt to reclaim its original character as a means of exalting and affirming the Indian. One difficulty with this thesis is that the *Nican mopohua* was composed in 1648 and published in 1649. The archbishop was the person responsible for the placing of the image — surreptitiously, claims O'Gorman.

In 1981, what many consider a major contribution to the field, Francisco de la Maza's *El guadalupanismo mexicano*, appeared. After briefly surveying the history of the tradition, de la Maza concluded that it lacked any historical basis and was a legend. His book has been influential and highly praised, and is frequently cited, but it is of limited value. Aside from some research into *criollo* sermons and Guadalupan poetry, it contains little that is original. The absence of any scholarly apparatus, including bibliography and footnotes even for direct quotations, makes it frustrating for the serious reader.

In his prize-winning study "The Virgin of Guadalupe: An Inquiry into the Social History of Marian Devotion," William Taylor examined

Guadalupe in the wider context of Marian devotion in the late colonial
and early national periods. He rightly saw Guadalupe as a predominantly
criollo devotion, "more popular among creole clergymen of the mid-17th
century than among Indian villagers."[32] It was these clergymen who con-
sciously sought to propagate the devotion among the Indians in the latter
half of the eighteenth century. Taylor found evidence for this in judicial
records, in which "from the late 1750s and 1760s on, concerted efforts by
curates in rural Indian parishes of central Mexico to establish or increase
popular veneration of the image of the Mexican Guadalupe appear."[33]
The priests who appeared in these records as devotees of Guadalupe had
been trained in Mexico City, had published sermons on the Virgin of
Guadalupe, and had listed sermons at Tepeyac in their professional
résumés. "Even at the end of the colonial period the prophetic appeal to
an Indian past in the Guadalupe cultus was promoted mainly by creole
intellectuals."[34] Taylor is cautious about connecting the Mexican
Guadalupe with any pre-Hispanic devotion. "Too little is known at present about the cultus of Tonantzin to elaborate on this relationship."[35]

The Historical/Documentary Approach

Between 1993 and 1995 two important works, both of an anti-apparitionist nature, appeared. These were the works of Xavier Noguez and
Stafford Poole.

Noguez's *Documentos guadalupanos* is a survey and analysis of the
earliest documentation on the shrine and devotion at Guadalupe. He concludes that these did not support the Guadalupan tradition. He deals primarily with the history of the sources, not their symbolic meaning.
Unfortunately, the format or arrangement of the book is a bit confusing,
and in the contents there is both repetition and overlapping. It remains,
however, a major contribution.

In 1995 appeared *Our Lady of Guadalupe: The Origins and Sources
of a Mexican National Symbol* by the American priest-historian Stafford
Poole. In his introduction, Poole surveys some of the contemporary interpretations of Guadalupe, especially by anthropologists, and gives a critique of each.[36] His book reviews the history of the apparition accounts
and evaluates the sources from an historical point of view. The author
sees Guadalupe as the symbol of *criollismo*, dating from the middle of the
seventeenth century. For Poole, neither Juan Diego nor the apparitions
had an historical basis, and the entire story is judged to be a pious fiction,
the work of Miguel Sánchez and Luis Laso de la Vega.

Reactions to Poole's work varied according to the discipline or specialty of the person reacting. In general, historians were approving. More negative opinions were voiced by anthropologists and theologians. These were not so much hostile as dismissive, that is, they felt that the historical reality or unreality of the Guadalupan apparitions is irrelevant. Theologians, in particular, asserted that there is a level of truth beyond history that is more important.

Many of the reviews, however, raised important questions, some of which had wider meaning than just for Guadalupe. What, for example, is the relationship of history to faith or national identity? Can a sign exist independently of the historical, or supposedly historical, fact that gave rise to it? What part in all this was played by oral tradition or the manifold ways that natives negotiated their religious and cultural institutions? How does one know the existence of an oral tradition or evaluate it? And, shades of Esteban Antícoli, can a miracle be subject to historical analysis?

The Jesuit Allan Figueroa Deck wrote that "it would be a mistake to take Poole's work as definitive. Historical analysis is but a part of a larger hermeneutical task. The Guadalupe event is a *mythos* of enormous and ever-increasing importance, which must be studied in an interdisciplinary manner from the perspectives of anthropology, semiotics and theology. For Catholics of the Americas, for whom this devotion is paramount, no ultimately satisfactory assessment of the Guadalupe phenomenon can be made outside the framework of faith."[37]

One such question was posed by John Gledhill:

Beyond the lack of textual evidence for an indigenous tradition, Poole's argument revolves around the lack of an indigenous practice focused on the shrine. This is, however, negative evidence, and it might have been wise to complement it with a more positive analysis of how indigenous peoples were drawn into identifying with the symbol. . . . The image of the natives as disinterested bystanders at Tepeyac may be consistent with the evidence on use of the shrine itself, but wider evidence suggests that we should think more about how the colonized appropriate the symbols of the colonizers and about what kind of dialogues took place between them if we are to understand the popular cultures that sustained the peasant activism of the 19th century.[38]

Thomas Ascheman put it even more forcefully:

Part of the trouble begins with a methodological position staked out in the introduction. Poole contends that the appropriate interpretation of Guadalupe as a symbol is dependent on whether the apparition accounts report factual events or whether they are "legend and pious inventions." Absurdity. . . . No historian could ever prove conclusively that the woman was in fact Mary, nor is history equipped to evaluate the "reality" claims of such a vision. Poole would be on safer ground to limit the scope of his work to ascertaining the cultural-historical contexts in which the principal elements of the tradition are developed. For instance, it would be a tremendous help to have a clear understanding of whether the apparition account is primarily a product of 16th century indigenous oral tradition or whether it is the invention of mid-17th century *criollo* nature. . . . One is left with the impression that Poole is unequipped to take an oral tradition seriously. He seems to be bewitched by the maxim, "If it isn't written down, it never happened," or at least, "Whoever writes it down first is the author."[39]

Richard Nebel voiced a similar concern, but then pointed to a fundamental difficulty: "To a certain extent we can excuse this lack because there are still no important researches with regard to the process of indigenous acculturation toward the Spanish Guadalupe world."[40] Therein lies the conundrum. How does one know the existence of an oral tradition, particularly if there is no documentary evidence? Even given its existence, how does one judge its validity? The fact is that in the case of Guadalupe there is just not enough evidence for any of these things.

As for the question whether a sign of symbol can exist apart from an underlying reality, Richard Salvucci answered very directly: "Of course it can. There is a world of difference between the Christ of Christianity and the historical Jesus . . . but that difference is of scant importance to a believer, assuming that the typical Christian knows or cares about the distinction."[41] In a letter to Professor Salvucci (February 12, 1997), Poole admitted to having been of two minds about this, but "I find myself returning to my original thesis: if the sign does not rest on an objective reality, then I believe that it is devalued, if not rendered entirely worthless. . . . I agree that the Christ of history and the Christ of faith are different, but I do not think that they are disconnected. We see the one through the prism of the other."

In 1996 Father José Luis Guerrero Rosado published a work on the *Nican mopohua* that was mentioned previously.[42] While it was still in press, Poole's book appeared. Guerrero, who apparently had an amenable publisher, added a lengthy appendix that rebutted Poole's work chapter by chapter, though mentioning his name only once.[43] In explaining the history of Guadalupe, Guerrero borrowed from the methodology of contemporary Catholic scripture scholars. In his view, a great religious event took place in 1531, an event whose precise nature is now unclear or unknown, but one that led to the mass conversion of millions of Indians. This event came to be formulated in the Guadalupe story, the form in which it has been handed down to later generations. The difficulty with this hypothesis is that there is no conclusive evidence of the conversion of millions of Indians in 1531 or any other year, other than the exaggerated claims of some of the early missionary friars. Guerrero also accepted and propagated the idea, found earlier in the *Positio* of the beatification, that Juan Diego was descended from the royal family of Texcoco and was not the humble *macehualtzintli* he called himself.

Typical of the approach of many modern-day authors is that of Margarita Zires in a recent article.[44] She embraces the idea of "guided syncretism" on the part of the missionary friars, especially the Franciscans, and consequently the identification of Guadalupe with the Mexica goddess Tonantzin. She does, however, admit the difficulty in attempting to define or describe clearly the various gods of the Nahuas. She also accepts that such syncretism was often unconscious. She states erroneously that Sahagún claimed that Archbishop Montúfar had permitted preachers to speak of Tonantzin when speaking of the Virgin Mary.[45] She also depends heavily on O'Gorman, especially his belief that Montúfar was the author of the apparition devotion and was responsible for the surreptitious change of images in the shrine. She also accepts O'Gorman's thesis that Guadalupe was appropriated by the creoles for their own purposes — a thesis that can be sustained only after 1648. She follows Lafaye in mistakenly stating that the feast of Guadalupe was celebrated on Tepeyac on September 10 and that the dates were changed around 1600.

A magisterial work is that of the Mexican priest Francisco Miranda Godínez, *Dos cultos fundantes* (Two Foundational Cultuses), published in 2001. The two foundational devotions are Remedios and Guadalupe, both at the center of Mexican identity. Like O'Gorman, Miranda sees Archbishop Montúfar as the true founder of the Guadalupan cultus, although without the story of the apparitions. However, he also says that there was an *ermita* at Tepeyac before that of Montúfar and that it had been established by the Franciscans in the earliest years of the mission enterprise.[46] He says that it is possible that the original image in the shrine had been a statue. He seems also to have accepted Valeriano as the author of the *Nican mopohua*. A valuable part of the book are the documentary appendices which, among other things, contain a full transcription of the Montúfar–Bustamante interrogatory.

D. L. Brading's book *Mexican Phoenix* had been long awaited in scholarly circles, both because of Brading's stature as an historian and because of abundant advance publicity. It finally appeared in August 2001 and seems destined to be highly influential. As the author explains in his introduction, the purpose of the book is "to illumine the sudden efflorescence and the adamantine resilience of the tradition of Our Lady of Guadalupe."[47] From there he traces the convoluted history of the tradition, beginning with the role played by sacred images in early Christianity. He views the theological significance of such images as deriving more from the Eastern than from the Western Church. He investigates the role of images in Spanish religious devotion at the height of empire. In dealing with Miguel Sánchez and his book, Brading is vastly more laudatory than most other commentators. He calls it "a book brimming with devotion in which religion and patriotism were inextricably meshed, and where audacious claims were sustained by deep learning."[48] Sánchez "must count among the most original, learned and audacious of Mexican theologians."[49] Even Sánchez's contemporaries found his book difficult to read, one of the reasons for Mateo de la Cruz's abridged edition of 1660.

One of Brading's most important contributions is his careful study of Guadalupan sermons from the seventeenth and eighteenth centuries. He is clearly impressed by those preachers who "appear to have embarked on a vertiginous ascent, scaling the heavens in a series of metaphors which challenged the very limits of orthodoxy."[50] These included equating Mary's presence in the image with Christ's presence in the Eucharist and seeing Guadalupe as "a living, perpetual sacrament."[51] Others, however, might see in them the extravagant outpouring of an exhausted theology.

Another valuable contribution is Brading's narration of the Guadalupan controversy resulting from Joaquín García Icazbalceta's letter to the archbishop of Mexico. There was at the time of publication no other account of this unhappy series of events in English or, for that matter, in any language. His account of the current controversy, especially that over the beatification and canonization of Juan Diego, is less detailed, a fact that is understandable in view of the meagerness of available sources.

In one sense, *Mexican Phoenix* is not a history of the sources of the apparition tradition. Thus, for example, Brading's treatment of the capitular inquiry of 1665–66 is very brief, omitting the limited nature of its scope and the anachronisms and inconsistencies that weaken the credibility of the witnesses. He casts his net over a wider field, and as a result his book is more comprehensive than the works of Lafaye, Noguez, or Poole. Also, he deals skillfully with theological and religious matters, terra incognita for most contemporary historians. Still, his work is open to criticism on several grounds. Despite the author's declaration in the introduction, it is difficult to know what the actual thrust of the book is. It is not a historical survey of the origin and development of the apparition tradition, a subject adequately covered in other recent works, yet he cannot avoid delving into these questions. These, however, are not presented in any lineal or organized way. It is not strictly a theological or sociological interpretation. It combines elements of both, and the combination is at times awkward. The book is often repetitious, and at times moves from one topic to another and back again. He does not mention the important testimony of Antonio Freire, the vicar of Guadalupe (1570) until page 323, when dealing with the Mexican Jesuit historian Mariano Cuevas, though this testimony was first published by Luis García Pimentel in 1897. The book was poorly copyedited and contains an unacceptable number of typographical and other errors.[52] There are also inaccuracies in the translations, especially those from the Nahuatl.

The author makes a fundamental error by not clearly distinguishing Guadalupe before Sánchez's book from Guadalupe after that. Though the shrine, image, and devotion existed from the mid–sixteenth century, it was not until 1648 that the story of Juan Diego and the apparitions became associated with them. "By the time Sánchez wrote his celebrated work the cult of Our Lady of Guadalupe was well established and obviously gathering momentum."[53] Perhaps, but that cult had nothing to do with the apparitions or Juan Diego. The distinction of Guadalupe as a pre- and post-Sánchez phenomenon is essential to any understanding of its history.

The most problematical part of the book is the final chapter, "Epiphany and Revelation." The author makes the assertion, odd for an historian, that the current controversy "derives from a nineteenth-century concern with 'historicity' and is animated on both sides of the debate by a latter-day positivism which impels apparitionists to insist on 'the Guadalupan Fact,' and their opponents to hint at forgery and condemn error."[54] He turns to Eastern Orthodox theology to establish not just a comparison but an equivalence between holy images and scripture as a means of transmitting divine revelation. "It follows from this equivalence of image and scripture that the great iconographers were as much inspired by the Holy Spirit as were the evangelists,"[55] a conclusion that is difficult to accept. From this, and the Second Vatican Council's declarations on the role of the Holy Spirit in the Church, he concludes that the image of Guadalupe "must number among the most potent expressions of the Holy Spirit in the long history of the Catholic Church."[56] Following out this equivalence of image/scripture, Brading admits the possibility of a human artist for the image, but adds, "Such an origin in no way derogates from the character of the Guadalupe as a pre-eminent manifestation of the Holy Spirit's inspiration."[57] Ultimately, Brading appears to side with those who would divorce theology from history and who would take theology into the realm of the subjective. In an earlier chapter, when discussing Richard Nebel's book *Santa María Tonantzin: Continuidad y transformación religiosa en México*, he observes, "For Nebel, the truths of theology soared far above any concern with mere historicity."[58] Yet, in the final chapter, Brading seems to do the same thing.

In 2002, when the controversy over the canonization of Juan Diego was at its height (see Chapter 6), Cardinal Norberto Rivera Carrera, archbishop of Mexico, published a book titled *Juan Diego: El águila que habla* (Juan Diego: The Eagle Who Speaks). It contains a brief survey of the process of his canonization and a summary defense of the apparitions and historicity of Juan Diego. It also reprints in full an article in the Vatican newspaper *L'Osservatore Romano* by Fidel González Fernández defending the historicity of Juan Diego. The rest of the book is mostly devotional reading. On the whole, the archbishop's book adds little or nothing to ongoing discussion of Guadalupe.

The Theological Approach

As was mentioned above, theologians tended to be dismissive of Poole's book, primarily on the basis that whether the apparitions ever occurred or not is inconsequential. That is how they were viewed by the feminist theologian Jeanette Rodriguez in *Our Lady of Guadalupe: Faith and Empowerment among Mexican-American Women*, a work published in 1994.[59] As the title indicates, the work sought to study Guadalupe's impact on a rather small sampling of Mexican American women. The author was heavily influenced by Virgilio Elizondo, and hence like his works (see below) hers rests on a fragile historical base. Typical is the assertion, "Virgilio Elizondo contends that only a divine intervention could have turned around the devastation caused by the conquest."[60] Rodriguez is unconcerned about the historical reality of Guadalupe: "The question as to whether the apparition did in fact occur is inconsequential: for those who believe, no explanation is necessary; for those who do not believe, no explanation will satisfy."[61] It is precisely an attitude like this that separates Guadalupe from objective reality and opens the way for the most extravagant and fanciful interpretations of the event. One is left free to spin out the most outlandish theories without feeling any need to prove them.

The German Catholic theologian Richard Nebel went deeply into both the national and theological meaning of Guadalupe in his 1995 book, *Santa María Tonantzin, Virgen de Guadalupe: Continuidad y transformación religiosa en México* (Saint Mary Tonantzin, Virgin of Guadalupe: Religious Continuity and Transformation in Mexico). As the title indicates, Nebel sees Guadalupe as the Christianized form of the Aztec mother goddess Tonantzin, and hence as a symbol both of the continuity of the pagan past with the Catholic present and the transformation of that past into the Mexico of the present day. "Venerated originally in the first place by the Indians, Our Lady of Guadalupe soon also captivated the mestizos. Already in the second half of the sixteenth century the creoles began to prefer this virgin to that of the same name in Extremadura, whose cultus, as is well known, the conquistadores and colonizers had introduced in continuity with their history in Spain, but which, together with the image, had been transformed by the Guadalupan event and had been interpreted in very diverse ways by the distinct ethnic sectors of the population and by the distinct classes of society."[62]

It is difficult at times to know exactly what Nebel believes. He gives an adequate survey of the historical problems attached to Guadalupe and seems to favor the anti-apparitionists' cause. Yet at the end he also appears to embrace the commonly accepted interpretations of Guadalupe. He reads cosmic meaning into the *Nican mopohua* while failing to locate it in its historical context. He interprets the Guadalupe event from the perspectives of history, literature (especially the *Nican mopohua*), and theology.

Like many contemporary Catholic theologians, Nebel is dismissive of history. "What we do want to do is to emphasize as a notable fact that the veneration of this image has inspired a cultus of such great scope as is the cultus of the Virgin of Guadalupe and Mexico, and therefore the question of whether the image was created by human hands or is of divine origin is totally irrelevant."[63] He maintains that there are two errors of interpretation that have given rise to arguments, not just between apparitionists and anti-apparitionists but within the ranks of the apparitionists themselves. The first consists in disregarding the pictorial nature of religious narrative, meaning that what is meant by religious metaphors cannot be expressed in a non-metaphorical way. The result is that it is impossible to determine exactly the extent to which the religious concepts of the *Nican mopohua* can be understood. This means that there will always be a certain vagueness or lack of definition. The second error lies in thinking that religious faith in the apparitions is capable of rational demonstration. He continues:

Whatever may be the results of the attempts to prove or to establish faith in the *Nican mopohua*, it would be absolutely inevitable to renounce any historical evidence. . . . To accept the religious faith in the Guadalupan event is not an act of knowing; no "rational" bases accompany it. . . . For this reason, when the anti-apparitionists demand foundations and the apparitionists make efforts to give them, both do equal violence to the religious character of the belief. Their controversy, then, is a sham battle that bypasses their true difference. This consists not so much in the fact that some believe something determined and the others in the opposite but rather that it is at the point where, while some believe something, the others for the most part believe not in something different, but in nothing at all.[64]

This borders on the unintelligible.

Father Martinus Cawley, also a translator of the *Nican mopohua*, approached the development of Guadalupe in terms similar to those of Guerrero Rosado:

Guadalupe is not a thing of the past, but the on-going experience of devotees, whose trust in Providence is kindled and reinforced by mutual support and who understand their prayers to be heard and answered by Our Lady, present in person among them, with the image and the shrine for sacrament and living out with them a covenant, which finds its best verbal expression in the Promises and its best dramatic expression in the gift of the roses and of the image. . . . From the very beginning of Guadalupe, the "reality" has lain in the pilgrims' own experience, their shared trust that Our Lady is graciously present and is answering their day-to-day petitions. There is a shared discernment that these answers imply a covenant, whose terms are best expressed in the traditional text of Our Lady's request for the shrine to be built and in her Promises to respond to her clients there. . . . First comes the experience of trust and of prayers answered, and then the explanation of this in terms of Our Lady's intervention.[65]

The thrust of the argument is that objective reality is not an issue. Rather, the truth is to be found in the shared experience of the faithful, which finds expression in the story of the apparitions. Cawley has reversed the proper order of things: for him, the prayer experience comes first, followed by the formulation of the event as an explanation or justification for it.

In 1997, Virgil Elizondo, a priest of the archdiocese of San Antonio and one of the founders of the Mexican American Cultural Center there, published *Guadalupe: Mother of the New Creation*. He had already published several works, mostly of a devotional or inspirational nature, about Guadalupe. This book was highly praised and by 2001 had gone through five printings. Elizondo is one of the principal proponents of a particular approach to the Guadalupan question that sees the Spanish conquest as the total, bloody destruction of everything native ("Nothing of meaning or value was left; there was no reason to live"[66]), the indigenous peoples as passive victims, and the message of Guadalupe as the one thing that gave them hope, recognition as human beings, and regeneration ("Everything good and meaningful had been destroyed and replaced by a cruel and totally incomprehensible reality"[67]). He goes on to say:

Whatever was not in accordance with the imagery and ways of the Euro-Christian worldview, especially in matters of religion, had to be destroyed. The Europeans came with a preconceived horror of anything linked to other religions and proceeded with a fanatic zeal to destroy as diabolical everything of the indigenous religions, which meant the brutal destruction of the deepest roots of Indian existence and the collective soul of native peoples. This mentality would constrain and poison the missioners and keep them from entering into any type of real dialogue with the native peoples while at the same time deepening the collective trauma of the conquest.[68]

Such an exaggerated assertion ignores not only the reality of sixteenth-century New Spain but the more accommodating approach of the church in other parts of the world — for example, the approach of the Jesuits in

China. It is a claim that Elizondo drives home with mind-numbing repetition.

In his book, Elizondo includes his translation into English of Siller's Spanish translation of the original Nahuatl of the *Nican mopohua.* Elizondo also adds comments and observations based on Siller's notes. Whatever the source, these notes tend to see symbolism in specific words and expressions, but they also contain some egregious errors. Thus, for example, Elizondo translates *ermita* as hermitage, and says that it "could refer to a home for homeless, an orphanage, a hospice — all would have a special meaning for a people who had been totally displaced and left homeless by the conquest."[69] In actual fact, it referred to a chapel of ease, one that did not have a full-time canonical pastor. With regard to Juan Diego's fear that the bishop had not believed him, Elizondo observes, "In the presence of those in power, the poor understand very well that they are not credible."[70] He thus misses a central theme of the apparition genre, that is, the initial disbelief of those in authority.[71] "My owner" is his translation of *netecuiyoè,* whereas it really means "my lady" (lady being the feminine equivalent of lord) or "my patron."

Equally wrong are his comments on Juan Diego's deprecatory self-descriptions. Thus, "I am a piece of rope," Elizondo says, is a reference to "the rope that was tied around the Indians' necks as they were chained and pulled around for forced labor."[72] Rather, it meant the *mecapalli,* a rope or cord that secured a pack to a porter's back and wound around the forehead for a better grip. It should be kept in mind that prior to the conquest the natives did not have draft animals and so all carrying was done by humans, a situation that continued into the Spanish period. Similarly, Juan Diego calls himself "a small ladder" (Elizondo: "The Indians were 'stepped on' in the process by which others climbed the ladder of social and economic mobility. They were often used as beasts of burden"[73]). What Elizondo translates as "the excrement of my people" actually reads "I am a tail, a wing," all of which lead Elizondo to conclude, "The worst part of domination is that the oppressed begin to believe what those in authority say: that they are subhuman, inferior, incapable of dignified tasks, and a burden to society."[74] What Elizondo misses in all this is that these were conventions of polite Nahuatl speech to express that one belongs to the lower class. An essential part of the apparition genre is that the person who receives the vision or revelation belongs to the poor or marginalized in society. Similarly, when Juan Diego says to the Virgin, "Forgive me, I will cause pain to your countenance and to your heart; I will displease you and fall under your wrath, my lady and my owner," Elizondo's comment is, "This is a perfect example of the soul-crushing victimization of the victims of society. They are made to feel guilty for their situation of misery and deserving of disgust and punishment."[75] Again, he fails to see that these were the formalities of traditional Nahuatl speech.[76]

Elizondo's admiration for the Guadalupe tradition and devotion knows no bounds, and he is every bit as hyperbolic as the preachers of the seventeenth century. "I do not know of any other event since Pentecost that has had such a revolutionary, profound, lasting, far-reaching, healing, and liberating impact on Christianity."[77] And, "Thus, liturgically, for us in the Americas, December 12 is as important a feast as December 25 and Easter Sunday are for the Christians of the Old World."[78] Such exaggerated assertions cannot be taken seriously.

The Anthropological Approach

As has been mentioned, the twentieth century saw a growth of interest in the Guadalupe phenomenon on the part of anthropologists. This led to interesting and valuable insights, although the results of these labors were sometimes uneven.[79]

Eric Wolf's article on *guadalupanismo*, "The Virgin of Guadalupe: A Mexican National Symbol," is often cited favorably, though for the most part it repeats what can be found elsewhere. Given Wolf's stature as an anthropologist who sought a rapprochement with historians, and given the depth of his knowledge of Mesoamerican culture, the article is surprisingly thin.

In 1974, one of the most influential of modern studies appeared, Jacques Lafaye's *Quetzalcoatl and Guadalupe: The Formation of Mexican National Consciousness, 1531–1813*. It was highly praised in most quarters, though Peggy Liss gave it a negative review in 1977.[80] The author used a multidisciplinary approach to show the roots and evolution of Mexican nationalism and self-identity, though he did not accept the authenticity of the apparition legend. Lafaye sees Mexican national consciousness as arising from the Hispanization of Quezaltcoatl and the Indianization of Guadalupe. The two met in the center, in a syncretic process that created the modern Mexican nation. Some of Lafaye's jargon and anthropological thought are vague and imprecise. The principal difficulty, however, is that his analysis of Guadalupe rests on an inadequate historical foundation.

A unique approach to the Guadalupe question is that of Serge Gruzinski in his 2001 book, *Images at War*. In a kaleidoscope that takes the reader from the Spanish conquest to the movie *Blade Runner*, the author seeks to investigate the place of images and their use and misuse over almost five centuries. It is a daring approach, but one that ultimately confuses more than it enlightens, in part because of his use of jargon. The first challenge for the reader is negotiating Gruzinski's prose. At times he seems incapable of writing a simple, coherent, declarative sentence. What is one to make of words like "hierogamies" (175), or clauses like, "the rejection of all painting which, like baroque art, would transcend groups and classes while exuding the pomp and circumstance of a misleading unanimism" (221), or "a plasticity of polymorphous medieval piety" (38)?

Some of the difficulties of the language may be the fault of the translation, which borders on the amateurish. The translator seems oblivious to the technical meaning of many words. Thus, we find "Tarasque" for Tarascan (68), "Augustines" for Augustinians (77, 79, 82, 107, 217), "Duns Scott" for Duns Scotus (80), "Naturals" for natives (*naturels*, 101, 178), "diocese churches" for diocesan churches (*les églises diocésaines*, 106), "holiday" for holy day (122), "Catholicity" for Catholicism (124), "Nimègue" for Nijmegen (154), and the use of the French *imaginaire* throughout, without any attempt at definition or translation. Almost beyond belief are "St. Jack" for Saint James (*saint Jacques*, 179) and "Hierome" for Jerome (*Jérôme*, 179). "Having become a ferment of devotion and appeasement, the cult at Tepeyac became associated by its thurifers [*sic*][81] with a cleansing of mores, with the cessation of games and 'illicit pleasures'" (106), is a statement that defies understanding. A description of one Nahuatl drama says that "a procession led the Holy Communion on the grounds of the show" (89), apparently a reference to a Eucharistic procession (*le saint sacrement*); either the author or the translator was ignorant of the distinction between monks and friars. Another example: "The Mexica 'idols' were emptied of their power and then relegated to the nothingness of matter, except when the seduction of form, allied to the fascination of gold, spared them from destruction by condemning them to the aesthetization of collections, and thus to another form of neutralization" (41). It is astounding and disappointing that a major university press could publish a work with what appears to have been the total lack of any copyediting or correcting process.

Another, more serious problem with the book is its blithe disregard of the historical basis or foundation of the Guadalupe story and devotion. Some statements do not jibe with history: "as much as television, this miraculous effigy is still a magnet that draws multitudes, and her cult remains a phenomenon of the masses that no one would dare to question, upon pain of iconoclasm" (4). The fact is that the image has been questioned ever since the seventeenth century, and often quite vehemently. Later, Gruzinski says that the Spanish crown "tried to impose a language — Castilian" (5), a statement that is patently inaccurate. Gruzinski also thinks that Alva Ixtlilxochitl was the author of the *Nican mopohua* (119).

Sometimes he gives up on facts and appeals to the imagination: "One can imagine repeated scenes of mysterious bundles circulating from one pueblo to another . . . ," or "How can one imagine and describe the intensity of the gaze that clung to these inhabited shapes . . . ?" (54, 55). "Hidden behind the great names one must imagine a crowd of Spanish, Italian, and mestizo students . . ." (113). Or to speculation: "It is probable that officials within the archbishop's palace, without openly accrediting a miraculous basis for it . . . tried to make people forget that a native painter, Marcos, was its author" (117). "It is also probable that the information was oral, painted, and written all at the same time" (118).

In both the theological and anthropological approaches, the perils of interpreting Guadalupe without a sufficient regard for the historical basis are clear. Whether one is dismissive of the history, like Rodriguez and Elizondo, or inaccurate in dealing with it, like Lafaye and Gruzinski, the result is a conglomeration of fanciful theories, outlandish speculation, or just plain error that does nothing to advance our understanding of the preeminent devotion of Mexican Catholicism.

The Inspection and Restoration of the Image

Though it is sometimes asserted that the image has been subjected to scientific examination, that is not true. There were inspections by teams of painters in 1666, 1751, and 1787, but nothing in modern times comparable to that of the Shroud of Turin.[82] The closest thing to a scientific examination occurred in 1982, when the image was moved from the old Basilica to the new.[83] At that time, it was decided that a new case should be made for it. This provided a unique opportunity to examine the *tilma* at close range. It also required taking precise measurements of the image. Some of the more important results of this inspection, none of which was made public at the time, are outlined below.

The most important conclusion was that the image had suffered serious deterioration over the years. "We were also able to confirm by a minute examination the state of deterioration found on the pictorial surface of the Tilma."[84] The cloth was flaccid and showed deformations at the corners because of insufficient tension. The image had been damaged by abrasion, stains from dampness, and drops of water (perhaps holy water) and wax. It also had a black-colored film caused by soot, which was most noticeable in the upper part. The wooden frame to which the *tilma* was attached showed signs of worm damage, though it was impossible to say if that was still happening. The *tilma* showed signs of having been trimmed, leading to the conclusion that it was once larger than at present. The cloth had been cut to fit the wooden frame, both around the edges and at the bottom. In addition, the left side had been trimmed, apparently in haste, perhaps with the object of preserving pieces as relics.[85]

The image had a sizing of white color which in some cases seeped through the cloth and was visible in the back. On the basis of the initial examination by microscope, it was concluded that the cloth of the image was linen with a mixture of canvas. The technique used seemed to be tempera of different variations: gouache (*aguazo*), wax tempera, tempera with resins or oils (*temple labrado*). The image shows signs of "corrections" (*arrepentimientos*) in different places: the sunburst, the gold ornamentation on the mantle and the tunic, the angel, are all additions or changes.

Experts in art preservation were consulted and a number of recommendations were made for steps to prevent further deterioration. The date set for doing these things was November 4, 1982. Those participating were Guillermo Schulenburg Prado, the abbot of Guadalupe; the archpriest Carlos Warnholtz Bustillos; the *sacristán mayor* Father Abel Escalona; the architects Javier García Lascuráin, Fray Gabriel Chávez de la Mora, and Oscar Jiménez Gerard; and Señores José Sol Rosales (expert in conservation and restoration of works of art), Emeterio Guadarrama (professional photographer), Jorge Guadarrama (coordinator and conserver), and their two assistants, Félix Vértiz and Félix González.

It is important to remember that this report was in the hands of Archbishops Corripio y Ahumada and Rivera Carrera during the course of the beatification of Juan Diego. At a date that he cannot now remember with certainty, Schulenburg hand-delivered the report to Msgr. Giovanni Battista Re, at that time the relator general of the cause of Juan Diego.[86] Both authorities were fully aware of the doubts surrounding the miraculous nature of the *tilma*, but the reports were never mentioned or referred to in the course of the beatification and canonization.

The "Códice 1548"

In August 1995, Father Xavier Escalada, a Spanish Jesuit living in Mexico, announced the discovery of what became known as the Códice 1548, also sometimes called the Códice Escalada.[87] He claimed to have found the document in a private library, whose owner remained anonymous by his own choice. If authentic, the document would obviously be of the greatest importance. "There is no document as old nor as clear for proving the historicity of Guadalupe as this codex which we have called 1548."[88] He also asserted, "We have given the codex to experts to be examined, and they have all agreed in indicating that it is authentic."[89] He did not specify, however, who those experts were. Later, in an appendix to the *Enciclopedia guadalupana*, of which he was editor, Escalada went into more detail about the scientific examination of the codex.

The codex is a picture on leather, 20 × 13.3 centimeters, somewhat wrinkled, with a yellowish patina, so that photographs or reproductions of it in newspapers and books are almost totally indecipherable. The lines are traced with a color between sepia and black, which has degenerated into a rust color in some places. At the top is written the date 1548, in hyphenated form: 154-8. It contains representations of two of the apparitions: a large one of the fourth apparition at the foot of the hill, and a small one of first apparition at the summit of the hill. In one corner is the glyph of the judge Antonio Valeriano, the alleged author of the *Nican mopohua*, and the signature of Bernardino de Sahagún, the great sixteenth-century Franciscan ethnographer.[90] There are also inscriptions in Nahuatl, which have been transcribed by the noted *nahuatlato* Rafael Tena. One is "Zano ipan inin 15031 [*sic*] zihu[itl in] Cuauhtlactoatzin omonexti[tzino] in totlazonantzin sihuapilli Gadalupe Mexico," which can be translated as "Likewise in this year 15031 our precious mother, the noble lady of Guadalupe, appeared to Cuauhtlactoatzin in Mexico." Cuauhtlactoatzin was the native name attributed to Juan Diego by Carlos de Sigüenza y Góngora in a work composed in 1689.[91] The second inscription is "Omomoquili cuauhtlactoatzin" (Cuauhtlactoatzin died), the verb being in the applicative reverential form.[92] Both quotations have somewhat eccentric spelling as well as erasures.

According to Escalada's later account, in May 1995 a group of experts gathered together to evaluate the codex.[93] This included Mario Rojas Sánchez, a Nahuatl expert who had published his own translation of the *Nican mopohua*; the historian Salvador Sotomayor; Ana Rita Valero de García Lascuráin (who was associated with the Basilica archives); the chemical engineer Manuel Betancourt; and Father Escalada. It was decided that various specialized agencies and persons would be consulted. These were El Taller, a center for restoration of antiquities; the Centro de Estudios Guadalupanos; and specialists in the study of codices: Dr. Víctor M. Castillo [*sic* for Castaño?], Dr. Miguel León-Portilla, Dra. Josefina Muriel, Dr. Guy Stresser Peán, Rafael Tena, and Dr. Marc Thouvenot.

The first point to be investigated was the signature of Sahagún. Charles Dibble, professor emeritus of the University of Utah at Salt Lake City and a noted authority on Sahagún, was asked to verify the signature. In a letter of June 23, 1996, he wrote, "I believe it to be the signature of Fray Bernardino de Sahagún. I base my conclusion on the indications of three crosses; the form of the 'Fray', the 'de' and the 'b'." He added, however, "In my opinion the signature is not the same as, that is not contemporaneous with the 1548 date of the *códice*. I would assign the signature to the 50's or the 60's."[94] Further verification was sought from the Procuradurías de Justicia, both that of the national government and that of the Federal District. Both groups replied that they did not do such work themselves but made use of the Gerencia de Seguridad e Investigación y Fotografía of the Banco de México.[95] The technicians began by comparing reproductions of known signatures with that on the codex. Despite the wide variations in the known signatures and that on the codex, the conclusion was reached that "the signature in question, attributed to Fray Bernardino de Sahagún, which appears in the 'Códice 1548,' was done in his handwriting, therefore it is authentic."[96]

Further scientific investigation of the codex was entrusted to the Instituto de Física of the National and Autonomous University of Mexico (UNAM), together with the restoration department of the Museo de Churubusco.[97] The Instituto presented its plan for the study of the codex on January 30, 1996. The codex was photographed in a variety of ways and X-rayed.[98] The study concluded that "the inks used in the preparation of the codex are not of a synthetic variety but of animal, vegetable, or mineral origin." These inks and the means used to make them were deemed "compatible with the materials used and the techniques of manufacture peculiar to the realization of this type of document during the sixteenth century in Mexico. In agreement with the experimental technique employed, it can be said with certainty that no element was found that could suggest the years after that century as a date when the document was prepared."[99] The final conclusion was that there was sufficient evidence "to presume the authenticity of the *Códice 1548* as a document created in the sixteenth century."[100] All of these inspections were done by persons chosen by Escalada and his associates. The Codex has never been subject to a truly open investigation.

Until 1995, the existence of the codex had not even been suspected. It was not mentioned in any survey or catalogue of Guadalupan documents, such as the *Catálogo del Museo Indiano* of Boturini Benaduci,[101] nor by other authors such as Becerra Tanco, Francisco de Florencia, Sigüenza y Góngora, or Beristáin de Souza. That a document of such surpassing importance should have remained unknown until the late twentieth century strains credulity. That its existence was publicized only two months before the publication of the *Enciclopedia guadalupana* and at a time when the campaign to canonize Juan Diego was underway places it in the category of "too good to be true." In 1995, nothing was known about the provenance of the document, other than that it was discovered among some papers in a private library, that its owners did not realize its value, and that they wished to remain anonymous. As a result, it was impossible to learn anything about its history or the nature and date of the papers among which it was found.

In contrast with this scientific evidence is the fact that the codex contains numerous anachronisms and inconsistencies. The date "154-8" at the top of the codex is not in a sixteenth-century hand and is written in an ink different from that of the rest of the document. The signature of Antonio Valeriano is preceded by the word "juez," a position that he did not receive until 1573. The Nahuatl glyph for his name that precedes the signature is taken from the Codex Aubin in the Bibliothèque Nationale de France. Sahagún is not known to have signed native codices, and the presence of his signature is inconsistent with his known opposition to Guadalupe.[102] The picture appears to be a copy of the frontispiece of Luis de Becerra Tanco's *Felicidad de México*, republished in Seville in 1685, the only depiction of Guadalupe prior to the nineteenth century that shows the image without a crown. Juan Diego's supposed native name (which was never used in any Nahuatl document) would more likely have been spelled Quauhtlactoatzin. In 1548, the glottal stop in the name, represented by a "c," would probably not have been written. Finally, the phrase "zanno ipan xihuitl" (likewise in that year) that begins the statement of Juan Diego's death was a standard usage in Nahuatl chronicles for beginning an entry under a particular year. In other words, the sentence has been taken out of context from one of the indigenous chronicles.

In May 2002, Escalada broke his silence about the provenance of the document in an article in the newspaper *Reforma*.[103] According to his account, Antonio Vera Olvera, a devotee of Guadalupe from Querétaro who died in 1994, was in the habit of visiting the Sunday market at La Lagunilla to look for rare books. In 1968 he purchased a book on the *tilma* and found the *códice* inserted in it. He showed it only to his family. When his son was asked why his father had not made the document public, he replied, "He was a believer and did not question anything about the miracle of Tepeyac." It was one of Vera Olvera's daughters who made it known to Escalada. Eventually, the family decided to donate it to Archbishop Norbert Rivera Carrera on condition that it never be sold.

On the same day that the donation was made known, Víctor M. Castaño, the physicist who directed the 1997 examination of the material and inks of the *códice*, gave a different interpretation of the results.[104] According to him, the conditions imposed by Father Escalada, namely, that the *códice* not be damaged in any way, hindered a thorough investigation. "We were very limited, it was like playing soccer with your legs tied and your eyes bandaged. The studies that we did are not definitively conclusive or exact, only indications." Carbon-14 dating was ruled out, both because it would have required the destruction of almost half the document but also because the range of error (100 to 150 years) was not useful in a document that was relatively recent. For similar reasons, there was no analysis by thermoluminescence or neutron activation, both of which would have permitted a more definitive dating of the inks. The tests that were used were microscopic and photographic analyses with the use of different filters, ultraviolet light, X-rays, and the PIXE method of infrared rays. In his original report of January 30, 1997, Castaño declared that "there exists sufficient evidence to presume the authenticity of the Códice 1548 as a document created in the sixteenth century." In 2002, however, he added that his affirmation did not come from "scientific certainty," but from clues or indications. "The probability that the document is from the sixteenth century is 60 or 70 percent, but there is a long stretch from that to saying that it is authentic with the historical implications." He added that the studies of the *códice*, "which was presented by the postulators of Juan Diego's canonization as an 'irrefutable' proof of his historicity — do not rule out the possibility that it may have been produced at a later period, using ancient support material and with inks similar to those used in the sixteenth century."

The same article in *Reforma* carried opinions by two well-known scholars about the *códice*. Xavier Noguez was quoted as saying, "What strikes me is that a document whose contents are supposedly very important offers such a poor manufacture without a uniform style."[105] By that he meant that the document mingled realistic scenes of the apparitions with the representations that were traditional in codices, such as the glyph of Antonio Valeriano. He pointed out that the picture of the apparitions was copied from an engraving published in 1669 in a pamphlet by Antonio Castro called *Poeticum viridiarium*. "Escalada has said that it is the opposite, that Castro saw this document in order to make his engraving, but if this had been the case . . . how to explain that this artist would not have mentioned such an important document if already since 1666 there was a concern to demonstrate the historicity of Juan Diego?"[106]

Rafael Tena agreed. He pointed out that the quotations in Nahuatl were taken from seventeenth-century annals and that the document could not antedate 1573, the year in which Antonio Valeriano became a judge. "I would say that it is false in the sense that it is not from the sixteenth century. . . . I think that it is a private document that someone made for his personal use at the end of the nineteenth century or the beginning of the twentieth in order to provide an answer to the rationalistic objections raised against the apparitions."[107]

According to the article, one element that most bothered specialists was the date 154-8. Father Ignacio Pérez Alonso, S.J., director of the Jesuit historical archive, believed that the numbers did not correspond to those of the sixteenth century. "The numerals are not from that period: the eight is not correct, neither is the five, the one is, and I have my doubts about the four."[108] Luis Avila Blancas, director of the archive of the Mexico City Cathedral, said flatly, "The numerals are modern."[109]

In sum, the Codex 1548 appears to be a rather clumsy forgery, and probably dates from a period when the whole question of Guadalupe was already being disputed. As will be seen in Chapter 8, it became one of the key pieces of evidence for the canonization of Juan Diego.

The *Enciclopedia guadalupana* has been mentioned several times already. It is flawed by a total lack of historical objectivity, or, better, any sense of history at all. Every article is slanted in one direction, with the result that what could have been a valuable resource turned into empty apologetics.

Discoveries in the American Southeast

Escalada appeared to have unusual access to the Mexican newspaper *Excelsior*, in which he published numerous articles in the years 2000–2001. On January 15, 2000, he lamented the "unnecessary" contention over Guadalupe.[110] In his interpretation, "unnecessary" referred to the fact that the proofs for the existence of Guadalupe and Juan Diego were so clear that only base motives could lead to their denial. "There seems to predominate the eagerness for a cult of personality, the preponderance of the 'self,' which is so opposed to the humble simplicity of Guadalupe." Opponents, he said, rejected these proofs "without more proof than the capricious superficiality with which they deal with this subject, important and delicate for the faith of our people." Again, there is the imputation of motivation that has marred the apparitionist response throughout the controversy. On August 3, 2001, Escalada wrote of "Juan Diego's partic-ipation in the most transcendental and most joyous event in all the history of this unique country that we call Mexico."[111]

Escalada continued his hunt for new proofs of the authenticity of the apparition account, which he also published in various issues of *Excelsior*. In July 2000, he announced that archeological digs at various sites in the United States which had once been under Spanish rule had uncovered evidence of devotion to the Guadalupe of Tepeyac. One of these was a medal of the Immaculate Conception found at the U.S.

Marine base at Parris Island, South Carolina, which Escalada identified as Our Lady of Guadalupe and dated prior to 1587.[112] Yet the image, as reproduced in the press, could just as easily be the statue in the *coro* at the shrine in Extremadura. Another medal, which came from the Spanish mission of Santa Catalina that was abandoned in 1680, is more clearly that of the Mexican Guadalupe.[113] The image closely resembled the frontispiece of Becerra Tanco's *Felicidad de Mexico*, even to the anachronism of Juan Diego's beard. This really has no probative value relative to the antiquity of the Guadalupan cultus. A third discovery was a copper plaque or breast ornament from northeast Georgia, which probably dated from before 1560.[114] It was found on the body of a young girl in her grave. The breastplate shows a native in Nahua dress, with one arm outstretched and the other holding what appear to be flowers. He faces a woman, also in native dress, who has one finger pointed upward and is also holding flowers in her left hand. On the right of the plaque is a seated animal that could be either a dog or pig. According to Escalada, the animal represented the demon in the first stage of flight. He also said that the woman was depicted as giving instructions to Juan Diego, although the image contained no speech signs. Escalada quoted an archeologist, John Belmont, as theorizing, "It is my opinion that a Mexican, seeing that the important natives used collars which were in fact pagan religious idols, decided to make his own collars, products of the proper Christian image. Most recent artists of the apparitions clothe Our Lady as she appeared in her image but they clothe Juan Diego with the clothing and hair style of a indigenous peasant. This artist, without knowledge of the image, clothed her with her Aztec blouse."[115] In actual fact, the plaque, as reproduced in the press, bears little or no resemblance to Guadalupe.

In another interview, Escalada claimed that the *tilma* had been secretly removed from the Basilica in 1926, at the height of the church-state conflict in Mexico.[116] According to him, it stayed for three years in the home of a certain Luis Murguía. During that time, a copy painted by the artist Rafael Aguirre was substituted.[117] Perhaps Escalada's most bizarre assertion about Guadalupe is his claim that the image appeared on Juan Diego's *tilma* horizontally, not vertically.[118] His reasoning is that the mantle was too long and so had to be worn horizontally. The Virgin's image thus appeared horizontally, and either Zumárraga or other church authorities trimmed it to its present size.

The uneasy calm came to an abrupt end in the mid-1990s with the campaign for the canonization of Juan Diego and some attendant dramatic events. At the heart of the renewed controversy was the question of Juan Diego's historical existence.

CHAPTER SIX

The Beatification of Juan Diego

❖

It was not books or codices that renewed the Guadalupe controversy, but two interrelated events: the campaign for the beatification and canonization of Juan Diego and the abbot of Guadalupe's denial of his historical existence.

Beatification is a preliminary step toward canonization and is more limited in scope. It is a declaration by the pope that a person has practiced virtue or suffered martyrdom and that public cultus can be paid to him or her. "This is expressed usually in the use of a special eucharistic liturgy (Mass) and liturgical prayer, but is always limited to a particular diocese, region, nation, or institute of consecrated life."[1] Beatification does not automatically mean that canonization will follow. What canonization adds is a formal declaration that the saint is in heaven and that the cultus is permitted throughout the universal church.[2] Ordinarily, only a saint can be the titular patron of a church.

It is difficult to reconstruct with precision the process for the beatification and canonization of Juan Diego. For the most part, both were carried out in secrecy and relatively little has become public knowledge. There is no way of knowing what deliberations took place in the Vatican or what maneuvers were used to bring the process to a successful conclusion. The few works that have dealt with the question have often been incomplete or contradictory.[3] What follows is the story as far as it is publicly known.

The Process of Beatification

Cases of beatification and canonization belong to the Congregation for the Causes of the Saints. Originally, such cases had been under the Congregation of Rites, but in 1969 Pope Paul VI divided the Congregation into two dicasteries. The newly created Congregation for the Causes of Saints then took charge of everything dealing with beatification and canonization and the honoring of the saints. A cardinal prefect, assisted by a secretary, is the presiding officer of the Congregation. He acts as liaison with the bishops who are introducing causes. He also participates in the discussions of the cases and has a vote in the meeting of the cardinal and bishop members of the Congregation. After that meeting, he draws up a report for the pope on how the cardinals and bishops voted.

In 1983 Pope John Paul II totally revised the procedures.[4] The process of beatification and canonization is inaugurated at the local level, by the diocese or archdiocese in which the candidate died, and in the beginning is the responsibility of the local bishop or archbishop. The petitioner, who can be anyone, appoints a postulator of the cause, with the consent of the bishop. The postulator seeks all information about the life and holiness of the candidate and is in overall charge of the preliminary process.[5] This first phase also includes the collection and scrutiny of all writings by the candidate, whether published or unpublished, a step that rather obviously was not part of Juan Diego's process. The second step is consultation with other bishops, laypersons, and the Holy See about proceeding with the cause. The third step is the establishment of a formal inquiry

The idea of canonizing Juan Diego was not new. In 1888, at the very height of the Guadalupan controversy in Mexico, the poet José Joaquín Terrazas had proposed it. A Frenchman, Santiago Béguerisse, wrote to some of the Mexican bishops and clergy urging the introduction of the cause. He received replies from Vera of Cuernavaca, Plancarte y Labastida, and Ignacio Díaz y Macedo (first bishop of Tepic). Benito Pardiñas, pastor of the church of San Juan de los Lagos in Jalisco, asked the Second Catholic Congress of Mexico to solicit the cause.[6] In 1931, Father Lauro López Beltrán founded a journal, called *Juan Diego*, in which he lobbied for the canonization.[7] Nothing came of these efforts, but the idea had been put forward. On April 12, 1939, the bishop of Huejutla, José de Jesús Manríquez y Zárate, in exile in San Antonio, Texas, wrote a pastoral letter exhorting people to work for the cause.[8] "It is hardly possible to explain the lamentable oblivion in which we have held Juan for more than four centuries."[9] In the following year, apparently at López Beltrán's urging, the archbishop of Mexico, Luis María Martínez Rodríguez, established a commission to work for the beatification.[10] It included Father Jesús García Gutiérrez, Jesuit Father José Bravo Ugarte, and Don Juan Bautista Iguínez. They produced a study that was rejected by the Holy See because it did not conform to its juridical norms.[11] In 1950, Manríquez y Zárate, in Rome for the declaration of the dogma of the Assumption, had an interview with Cardinal Nicola Canali and sought to interest him in the cause. Canali was already familiar with it, since in 1949 López Beltrán had given him a series of documents concerning Juan Diego.[12] The cardinal became an advocate of the cause. Back in Mexico, Manríquez y Zárate interested Archbishop Martínez in resuming the cause.[13] In 1951, the archbishop named an eminent historian (not identified) to organize the documentation for forwarding to Rome. These efforts seem not to have been effective.

In 1974, on the occasion of what was believed to be the fifth centenary of Juan Diego's birth, bishops in Mexico and Latin America proposed his canonization as the model of a Catholic layperson. During his first visit to Mexico (1979), Pope John Paul II spoke of Juan Diego as an historic person and one who was fundamental in the evangelization of Mexico. After the papal visit, Archbishop Ernesto Corripio Ahumada of Mexico City held a number of meetings with Jesuit Father Luis de Medina Ascensio, Monsignor Enrique Roberto Salazar Salazar, and others, to advance the cause.[14] On October 25, 1979, he appointed Salazar Salazar as the local postulator. In November, Salazar Salazar departed for Rome in order to ascertain what steps needed to be taken.[15]

In November, Corripio Ahumada had a meeting with Franciscan Father Agostino Amore, chief of the department of history of the Congregation for the Causes of the Saints, who gave him a copy of the norms to be followed. Salazar Salazar informed Amore of some of the difficulties involved in the cause — for example, the lack of any remains after four hundred years (though proof of his burial would be sufficient), and the lack of any documents for Juan Diego's baptism or marriage.[16] Amore replied that since Juan Diego had died before the Council of Trent there was no need for documents concerning his death and burial, but that evidence would have to be found for his baptism and marriage. Amore also insisted that they prove with sufficient documentation his existence, his virtues, and his reputation for sanctity. Each document was to be authenticated by a notary, together with an attestation signed by three expert historians. This constituted the first step, which was called *in solidum*.[17]

As a result of these discussions, the first task was to search out the largest possible number of sixteenth-century documents that made mention of Juan Diego and the Guadalupe tradition. A commission was established to work on this, and it labored from January 31, 1980, to May 29, 1981.[18] Its members were Medina Ascensio, Father Manuel Rangel Camacho of the diocese of León, and Professor Ramón Sánchez Flores, who was described as a specialist in the documents of sixteenth- and seventeenth-century New Spain.[19] On June 26, 1981, Salazar Salazar submitted the preliminary *acta* of the "Causa Histórica del Siervo de Dios Juan Diego" (Historical Cause of the Servant of God Juan Diego) to the

Congregation for the Causes of the Saints.[20] On June 15 of the same year the Mexican bishops' conference petitioned the pope for Juan Diego's canonization.[21]

Salazar Salazar now encountered the delays that were often character-istic of the Roman Curia. He returned to Rome in January 1982, but just when he appeared to be making progress, Amore died. The process lan-guished, and an anonymous hand inserted a note in the *acta*: "The Virgin of Guadalupe is a myth."[22] Salazar Salazar brought letters requesting the beatification, including one from the mother of Mexico's President José López Portillo. His reception was not a favorable one. He was told to see the cardinal prefect of the Congregation for the Causes of the Saints. He told the cardinal, "This has to go forward, because even the masons are interested in this cause."[23] The cardinal introduced Salazar to Monsignor Giovanni Papa, who in turn introduced him to another, unnamed monsi-gnor. The latter told Salazar Salazar, "Look, this business of Juan Diego, there is nothing. This business of the Virgin of Guadalupe was a myth which the missionaries used for the evangelization of Mexico, and Juan Diego did not exist."[24] Salazar Salazar had to go through a long process of convincing people, until a certain Monsignor Sandro Corradini involved himself in the cause. The monsignor requested an image of Juan Diego with a halo, in order to open the way to beatification "by way of immemorial cultus." By demonstrating that Juan Diego had been re-garded as a saint from earliest times, the proponents of the cause would not have to prove that Juan Diego practiced heroic virtue, nor would there be any need for miracles.

On July 8, 1982, the Congregation informed Archbishop Corripio Ahumada that it had accepted the cause, but that the documentation should be completed in an exhaustive way, including archaeology, iconog-raphy, hieroglyphology, and linguistics.[25] A new commission was formed for this purpose. The members were Licenciado Alberto Fragoso Cas-tañares, Father Mario Rojas Sánchez, Professor Saturnino Téllez Reyes, Father Francisco Ruiz of the diocese of Toluca, and Licenciado José Ignacio Conde y Díaz Rubín, described as an expert on sixteenth-century colonial art.[26] They finished their work in April 1983. Among the find-ings that they presented as evidence was a sixteenth-century portrait on wood of Juan Diego dressed as a Franciscan and pictured with a halo, the work of an anonymous native painter. The halo would have been evi-dence of an early cultus. An alabaster sculpture, a native work of the six-teenth or early seventeenth century, showed Juan Diego as a Franciscan and with the staff of a missionary. There was an eighteenth-century paint-ing that bore the label "Verdadero retrato del siervo de dios Juan Diego" (True portrait of the servant of God Juan Diego). A notable feature of this so-called "true portrait" is that Juan Diego is portrayed with European features and a beard, something uncharacteristic of sixteenth-century Nahuas. Later, at the time of Juan Diego's canonization, this portrait became a source of controversy. The archeological remains of what was claimed to be Juan Diego's house in Tlayacac were also presented.[27] Next to it were the remains of a church dating from the first half of the sixteenth century. There was also an archeological study of the first *ermita*, or chapel, at Tepeyac, which supposedly housed the burial place of Juan Diego. Numerous native codices that supposedly made reference to Juan Diego were cited, as were different indications of popular piety. Despite the questionable nature of much of this evidence, it was submitted as part of the process.

The tribunal finished its work on March 23, 1986, and the cause, together with all its documentation, was sent to Rome. In the course of the process, the secretary of the Congregation for the Causes of the Saints is assisted by a college of relators, which is headed by a relator general.[28] The latter also presides over meetings of the historical consultors. The task of the individual relators is to study the evidence, sometimes in collaboration with outside experts, and to prepare a *positio* on virtues or martyrdom, a compendium of testimonies and proofs. They also prepare written explanations of an historical nature that may be requested by the consultors. They can be present at the meeting of the theological consultors, but without the right to vote. One of the relators is selected for the specific task of preparing the *Positio* on miracles, something that was not necessary in the case of Juan Diego.

In October 1983, Monsignor Giovanni Papa, the relator general of the Congregation for the Causes of the Saints, assumed the overall direction of the cause.[29] He considered it time to initiate the diocesan cause and granted the coveted "Nihil Obstat ad causam introducendam" (No obstacle stands in the way of introducing the cause). This meant that the Holy See could find no reason why the cause should not proceed at the diocesan level. Though Papa was helpful in this instance, his later insistence on solid evidence would slow the cause considerably. Because at this stage the postulator must reside in Rome, the archbishop appointed Franciscan Father Antonio Cairoli as postulator, with Salazar Salazar as vice-postulator.[30]

The next step was the establishment of a diocesan inquiry and the naming of the various officials who would participate in it. This involved the establishment of a tribunal to hear all witnesses, both those ex officio and those called by the vice-postulator. On January 7, 1984, the archbishop issued an edict for the opening of the process. Salazar Salazar appeared before an archdiocesan court presided over by the archbishop and formally requested the initiation of the process (February 11, 1984). The judge, by reason of office (*juez ordinario*), was the archbishop, who was represented by a delegate. The promotor of justice was the Carmelite Father Luis Avila Blancas. The archdiocesan tribunal had thus been established.

On that same day, the tribunal had the first of ninety-eight meetings. As required by law, it drew up an interrogatory which, among other things, dealt with *de cultu* and *de non cultu*. The norms laid down by Pope Urban VIII in 1642 regarding canonization decreed that there could be no public cultus or honoring of the candidates prior to beatification. The case of Juan Diego, however, antedated those norms, and so it was possible to advance his cause by demonstrating an "immemorial cultus" as evidence that his sanctity had been recognized from the beginning. Special care was taken that the witnesses should explain their sources. The principal ones cited were the *Nican mopohua*, the *Nican motecpana*, and the *Informaciones* of 1666. In their testimonies the witnesses followed a rigid formula, standard in such tribunals, of evaluating the candidate in terms of the theological and moral virtues, a practice that does not offer much insight into the future saint's actual life and attitudes.

The first witnesses were Father Ernest J. Burrus, S.J., of the Jesuit Historical Institute, who testified about the original of the *Nican mopohua*; Jesuit Father José del Castillo, who had been responsible for the cause of the Tlaxcalan martyrs; López Beltrán, a well-known author and advocate of the Guadalupe devotion; Professor Antonio Pompa y Pompa, a well-known historian and the editor of *Album del IV centenario guadalupano*; Father José Luis Guerrero Rosado, author of the analysis of the *Nican mopohua* mentioned in Chapter 5; Father Alfonso Alcalá Alvarado, of the Missionaries of the Holy Spirit, doctor in church history from the Gregorian University in Rome, and well-known teacher and author on Guadalupan themes; Father Mario Rojas Sánchez, a *nahua-tlato* and translator of the version of the *Nican mopohua* used in the *Positio*; and Licenciado Alberto Fragoso Castañares, chronicler of Cuauhtitlán. Later there were some witnesses ex officio: Señor Vicente Ibarra, gardener of the Basilica; Señor Francisco Benítez Reyes, tourist guide at the Basilica; Dr. Juan Homero Hernández Illescas, physician, university professor, and expert on the stars on the Virgin's robe; Father Manuel Rangel Camacho, of the diocese of León, historian, who had been a member of the first commission that was formed for the purpose of seeking out documents about Juan Diego; and Luis Medina Ascensio. There was also an accountant, Jorge Alberto Ochoa Schulenburg, an employee of the Basilica; Señorita Carolina Ignorosa Alvarez, a neighbor of the Basilica; Señora Mariana Enríquez Vidal de Rodríguez, also a neighbor of Basilica, as were her ancestors; and Professor Joel Romero Salinas, member of the National Academy of History and Geography of Mexico.[31] Of these witnesses, only Burrus and Pompa y Pompa were recognized authorities on Mexican history.

An important session of the tribunal was held on November 7, 1984, because of the presence of the bishops' delegate, Monsignor Vicente Torres Bolaños. In accord with the decree of Urban VIII, he gave a verdict that at least since the second half of the sixteenth century until the present there had been no public cultus to Juan Diego (the first half of the century would come under "immemorial cultus"). The ninety-eighth and last session of the tribunal met on March 23, 1986.[32]

When the diocesan process is complete, it is sent in duplicate to the Congregation. On receiving all the acts and documents from the local bishop, the Congregation first reviews them to make sure that they are in accord with all the rules of law. If it so finds, it chooses a relator who, together with an outside collaborator, prepares the *Positio*. The *Positio* ordinarily is threefold, dealing with virtues, martyrdom, and/or miracles. In the case of ancient causes, such as that of Juan Diego, the relator and his associate are supposed to ascertain if there is sufficient information. In addition to the relator, there is also a promotor of the faith, or prelate theologian.[33] He presides over the meetings of the theologians, with the right to vote, and prepares the report on the meeting. He is also present at the meeting of the cardinals and bishops of the Congregation, but without the right to vote. The *Positio* is submitted to a meeting of historical scholars, and if they approve them, then to the theological consultors. The votes of the theologians together with the opinion of the promotor of the faith are submitted to the cardinals and bishops. In turn, their vote is submitted to the pope, who has the final say in these matters.

Salazar Salazar was commissioned to carry the original *acta* of the tribunal and a copy to Rome. The Congregation for the Causes of the Saints, whose prefect at that time was Cardinal Pietro Palazzini, began consideration of the *acta* on April 7, 1986.[34] At the same time, the relator general, Monsignor Papa, began an informal process of looking into native culture and knowledge of the *Nican mopohua*. His outside collaborator was Father Guerrero Rosado.

On October 7, 1986, Salazar Salazar returned to Rome to see the postulator, Father Cairoli, and with him to work out some of the business of the process. On this occasion he was accompanied by Romero Salinas, who was given the title of outside consultor in order to be involved in drawing up the *Positio*. One of his duties was to arrange documents and sources chronologically. On October 10, 1986, they gave to Papa a copy of Romero Salinas's appointment as consultor, a copy of his book

Precisiones históricas, and a video on Juan Diego that had been on Mexican TV.

The cause now met its first measured opposition. Some persons, both clergy and lay, were opposed to the beatification of Juan Diego.[35] The day of December 4, 1986, was, in the words of Romero Salinas, a day of bitter surprises.[36] The consultors went to their normal meeting with Papa. The latter gave Romero Salinas a letter, addressed to Cardinal Palazzini, dated November 18, 1986, on the official stationery of the Basilica of Guadalupe and signed by Monseñor Guillermo Schulenburg Prado, the abbot of the Basilica. In the letter, Schulenburg presented observations (*animadversión*) by Canon José Martín Rivera, archivist of the Cathedral chapter of the archdiocese of Mexico. This letter would prove to be the biggest obstacle to the beatification because of the objections and difficulties that it raised.

On handing the letter to Romero Salinas, Papa said, "Professor, until this is resolved favorably, we have finished, take the letter to Mexico to Cardinal Corripio Ahumada in order that he may respond."[37] Papa's attitude was to not continue the cause, even informally, until the doubts had been resolved and he could be sure that there were no secret motives involved. On January 9, 1987, however, Cardinal Palazzini recognized the validity of the process. With this, the formulation of the *Positio*, which had been suspended by the Schulenburg/Rivera letter, could be undertaken with canonical formality. The emphasis of the *Positio* would be on the immemorial cultus, without failing to show Juan Diego's virtues. Papa decided that, as much as possible, Juan Diego's life should be separated from the Guadalupan apparitions. Another decision was to study all the objections against the tradition that had been made over the course of years. No deadline was given for the completion of the *Positio*. As part of the preparation, various archives in Rome, including those of the Franciscans and Jesuits, were consulted. Papa, however, stuck to his position that there would be no formal preparation of the *Positio* until the points in the Schulenburg/Rivera letter had been resolved.

Archbishop Corripio Ahumada entrusted Alcalá Alvarado with a careful study and critical review of that letter, and also determined that Romero Salinas would forward a letter of support based on the points raised by Papa. In the meantime, in Rome, Guerrero Rosado attended the meetings, in an informal capacity, in order to explain aspects of Nahua culture related to the *Nican mopohua*. In April 1987, the response to the Schulenburg/Rivera *animadversión* was completed and sent to Rome. A topic of specific interest would be the *Informaciones* of the capitular inquiry of 1666, whose purpose had been to secure a special feast day for December 12.[38] They were also used to secure the new office and mass for

Guadalupe (March 6, 1894). At the same time, they were used to respond to García Icazbalceta's letter to the archbishop of Mexico, which supported its thesis with the famed Montúfar–Bustamante dispute of 1556.[39] The intention was that those elements showed the life, virtues, reputation for sanctity, and immemorial cultus of Juan Diego.

At this stage, Romero Salinas found the documentation of the religious profession, in Corpus Christi, of María Micaela Gerónima de Escalona y Rojas, considered to be the great-great-great-great-great-granddaughter of Juan Diego. This document had been thought lost, and was so declared by Dr. Josefina Muriel in her book *Las indias caciques de Corpus Christi* (Female Indian Chieftains of Corpus Christi). On the basis of this document, Licenciado Horacio Sentíes found different wills that led him to formulate a genealogy for Juan Diego and also to declare him a member of the royal house of Texcoco. He also located the will of the first vicar of the *ermita*, Father Antonio Freire, who left an important legacy for the embellishment of the *ermita*.[40] The claim that Juan Diego had a descendant contradicted the assertion in the *Nican mopohua* that Juan Diego and his wife had been lifelong celibates.[41] Similarly, the attribution of royalty contradicted unvarying description of him as a *macehualli*, or *macehualtzintli*, a commoner.[42] This, however, was an idea that began to grow in popularity.

In May 1988 Salazar Salazar and Romero Salinas went to Rome to inform Cairoli and Papa about the state of the work that had been entrusted to them, which seemed to be well advanced. Papa, however, still demanded a rigorous study of the discrepancies concerning Juan Diego. He asked that in the preparation of the *Positio* consideration be given to the observations of Martín Rivera presented by Abbot Schulenburg. He also thought that they should analyze the book *Destierro de sombras* (The Banishing of Shadows) by Edmundo O'Gorman. The period from July 1988 to February 1989 was spent in analyzing the *animadversión*.[43] A general introduction was prepared, which identified Juan Diego as a "Chichimeca" and presented testimonies by his contemporaries. Chichimeca was a global term used in both pre- and post-conquest times to describe the more primitive Indian tribes that periodically invaded the central valley of Mexico. How or why the authors came to identify Juan Diego as a Chichimeca is not clear, since there is no basis, documentary or otherwise, for it. It also contradicted the assertion that he had been descended from royalty.

Enough work had been done so that the definitive redaction of the *Positio* could be begun. For this purpose, Salazar Salazar and Romero Salinas departed for Rome on February 26, 1989. Salazar Salazar informed Cairoli and Papa of the conclusion of the preliminary work and his intention of staying in Rome as long as necessary for drawing up the *Positio*. On March 9, 1989, Salazar Salazar returned to Mexico, and on that same day Cairoli, in the offices of the Congregation, spoke with Papa asking his favor for the cause of Juan Diego, "whose preliminary documents he considered to be exceptionally well worked out."

On March 10, the cause suffered another setback when Cairoli died. Papa thought that it would be possible to continue the cause without a postulator as long as Salazar Salazar satisfactorily carried out the duties of vice-postulator from Mexico. On May 12, however, Papa decided it was time to name a postulator. He informed Salazar Salazar, who consulted with the archbishop. The latter suggested asking the postulator for the cause of Escrivá de Balaguer, the founder of Opus Dei, and Father Paolo Molinari, procurator general of the Jesuits. On June 5, it was learned that it was impossible for the postulator of Escrivá y Balaguer to accept the cause. On March 6, an interview was held with Molinari that turned into a three-hour discussion of the cause of Juan Diego. Molinari needed not only the documentation of the process but also the approval of the Jesuit superior general, Father Peter Hans Kolvenbach. The documentation was given to him two days later. "The analysis would have to be precise, Father Molinari does not take on a business in order to lose it, he could not gamble with his enormous prestige."[44] On June 13, Molinari formally accepted the cause. "Tell his eminence Cardinal Corripio that it will be an honor to defend the cause of the envoy of Our Lady of Guadalupe."[45] On June 22, 1989, Corripio Ahumada named Molinari the postulator. From then on, Romero Salinas would work closely with Molinari and the latter's "alter ego" and secretary, Jesuit Father Peter Gumpel. On June 30, the documentary corpus of the *Positio* was given to Papa, who wrote to Corripio to tell him of the conclusion of the work and ask him to convoke a meeting of historians to comment on it.

This meeting was held on October 9, 1989. Among the twenty-one notables who attended were Schulenburg, Rojas Sánchez, Guerrero Rosado, Pompa y Pompa, and Romero Salinas. After a brief introduction, the archbishop asked those in attendance for their opinions. "No opinion was presented contrary to the physical existence of the Servant of God and in a positive way it went deeper into his reputation, virtues, and cultus."[46] The key question was why Schulenburg said nothing about the doubts concerning Juan Diego's existence. In his memoirs, he said that he did not know the purpose of the meeting when he attended it, specifically, that it was part of the diocesan process, and hence came unprepared.[47] At the forty-fourth Plenary Assembly of the Mexican Bishops' Conference in Durango, held on November 6–10, the bishops unanimously voted to send a letter to the pope asking for the beatification of Juan Diego. It was dated November 17, 1989, and signed in the name of all the bishops of Mexico by the archbishops of Monterrey, Guadalajara, and Tlalnepantla, and the bishop of Querétaro. On December 3, Adolfo Suárez Rivera, the archbishop of Monterrey and president of the conference, sent a lengthy letter to Cardinal Felici, the prefect of the Congregation for the Causes of the Saints, in which on behalf of the bishops he asked for the beatification. He surveyed the issues involved and concluded that the case for immemorial cultus and reputation for sanctity was clear. One of his proofs for this was the capitular inquiry of 1666.[48]

One fundamental question about the preparation of the *Positio* involved the approach that should be used. In general, it would deal with the immemorial cultus, but it would also be necessary to include a consideration of Juan Diego's practice of virtue. Papa refused to accept immemorial cultus for the *Positio*, even though the entire document had been prepared on this basis, and so the title page of the printed *Positio* focused on Juan Diego's virtues, "*Positio* sobre virtudes." In this way, the *Positio* would have to be examined by historians. This involved a risk, because if the historians passed a positive judgment on the virtues and only on the virtues, the process would necessarily be lengthened and miracles would be required for beatification.

The next step in the process was to submit the *Positio* to an examination by historical consultors.[49] If approved, it would then be submitted to the theological consultors: "Consultors are to be drawn from various parts of the world to deal with the causes of saints. Some are to be experts in historical matters and others in theology, particularly in spiritual theology."[50] On December 21, the printed *Positio* was given to the Congregation for distribution to the historical experts, whose meeting was scheduled for January 30, 1990. Romero Salinas went to Rome again on January 26, 1990, to work with Molinari.

The historians met in the meeting room of the Congregation on January 30. The meeting was presided over by a new relator general, Father Ambrogio Eszer, a Dominican, replacing Papa, who had reached retirement age.[51] There were three collaborators, Monsignor Sandro Corradini, who in the beginning of the cause thought that immemorial cultus was the way to go; Monsignor Leonard Flisikowski, an expert (*adetto*) of the Secretariat of State, and Don Nicola Lanzi. The historians who attended with a right to vote were:

Father Domingo Fernández, Carmelite, rector of the Instituto Teresiano;

Father Fabriciano Ferrero Centero, Redemptorist, president of the Redemptorist Historical Institute;

Father Alessandro Galuzzi, superior general of the Minims and professor of church history at the Pontifical Lateran University;

Father Conrado Gneo, Capuchin, dean of the professors of theology at the Lateran University and a consultor for the Congregation for the Causes of the Saints;

Father Fidel González Fernández, Comboni missionary, professor of church history at the Urbaniana University; and

Father Atanasio Matanic, Franciscan, professor at the Ateneo Antoniano, who was also a consultor to the Congregation.

It is immediately clear that this group was not competent to judge anything as complex as the history of Guadalupe. None of those participating was an authority on Mexican history, indigenous culture, or popular religion. As was to be apparent in the Congress of Theologians (mentioned below), this was a closed process. No dissenting voices were called or given serious consideration. With Papa out of the picture, the process could follow its predetermined course.

Not surprisingly, the vote was affirmative. There was a not a single negative vote on any of the questions presented for judgment by the relator general. The historians believed that there was a solid historical basis for the holiness, immemorial cultus, and heroic virtues of Juan Diego. Yet, at the same time, they found some difficulties. One of those who voted believed that the *Positio* seemed clearly oriented toward the immemorial cultus and that the cause should be studied under that heading rather than by virtues, as the title page of the *Positio* indicated. Some also believed that the presentation had certain methodological deficiencies, perhaps because of haste in preparation. In accord with the norms of the law, the historians could also present any doubts they had. Only two did so. Within a week, the voting was printed, Romero Salinas answered the doubts, and Monsignor Papa [*sic*] had reviewed the details and conclusions and signed it, on February 5, 1990.[52] On February 8, the work was given to the Congregation, in time for distribution to the Theological Congress, fixed for March 9, thanks to the work of Molinari. He had also arranged through Felici that the *Positio* would combine the two approaches, that is, "sobre fama de santidad, virtudes, y culto por tiempo inmemorial" (on the reputation for holiness, virtues, and immemorial cultus).

The Theological Congress met on March 9, 1990. The president was the promotor of the faith, Monsignor Antonio Petti, whose task it was to preside over the meeting, with the right to vote and to prepare the final report.[53] Eight theological consultors, whose names were not made public, had the right to vote. The relator general, Father Eszer, was present without the right to vote. All the votes were affirmative. There was absolutely no doubt, they said, about the immemorial cultus, and they also found enough in the documentation to support the heroic virtues. In addition, they all found that the question of cultus was perfectly consistent with the norms of Urban VIII. The consultors' recognition of the immemorial cultus removed any need for miracles. "For some of the consultors the work analyzed [the *Positio*] could have had a greater methodological vigor; for others, the investigation into archives should have been more complete; for others there was an unnecessary abundance of data and documents."[54]

Molinari had the theological votes printed and given to the Congregation for distribution to the members of the commission that would communicate the results of all the deliberations to the pope. This commission of bishops and cardinals met in secret session on April 3, 1990. Father Gumpel communicated the results in the absence of Molinari. "Those present unanimously judged as proven both the holiness of life and the cultus paid to Juan Diego since time immemorial."[55]

On April 8, Archbishop Corripio Ahumada asked the pope that the glorification of Juan Diego be by way of canonization. The pope refused. On April 9, 1990, he issued a decree recognizing the holiness of life and the cultus given to Juan Diego from time immemorial.[56] On May 6, 1990, in the Basilica of Guadalupe, at the same ceremony in which the three child martyrs of Tlaxcala and Father José María Yermo y Parres were beatified, the Holy Father granted to Juan Diego the privilege of ratification of cultus, which meant that he declared him blessed since the moment of his death.[57] Archbishop Corripio Ahumada read the decree that recognized the virtues and immemorial cultus of Juan Diego, which was issued by the secretary of state, Cardinal Agostino Casaroli, and not by the Congregation for the Causes of Saints.[58] The decree said that the events of Tepeyac were of great importance in the evangelization of America. It also admitted that there are few known facts about his life.[59] Juan Diego's feast day was set for December 9, the day on which, according to tradition, the Virgin first spoke to him. For Romero Salinas, as for many previous *guadalupanos*, the beatification vindicated the story of the apparitions. "His Holiness John Paul II with the decree of beatification of Juan Diego validated the tradition of Guadalupe."[60]

The decree did not formally beatify Juan Diego. It simply declared that a liturgical cultus to Juan Diego "as blessed" was granted.[61] The "Ordinary Congregation of cardinals and bishops . . . judged unanimously as proven both the holiness of life and the cultus paid to Juan Diego since time immemorial."[62] It also established his feast on December 9, and declared it a holy day of obligation in Mexico, but optional in the rest of Latin America. Though the statements in the decree seemed clear, there was much about the beatification ceremony that was ambiguous. Witnesses said that the pope did not say a word in public about Juan Diego in his homily. Yet the text of his homily that appeared in the *Acta*

Apostolicae Sedis did contain such references. The *Acta*, however, like the *Congressional Record*, contains the final, official version of events, not what actually happened. A Vatican bureaucrat called it a beatification in a minor key (*en tono menor*). Others called it *aequipolenter*, an "equivalent beatification." At his first audience on his return to Rome, the pope said only that he had recognized the cultus of Juan Diego.

The next step was to promote the canonization of Juan Diego. Before that could be done, however, a number of dramatic events intervened.

The Crisis of Abbot Schulenburg

Guillermo Schulenburg Prado was born in Mexico City on June 12, 1916.[63] His father, Mateo von der Schulenburg, was a German mining engineer, his mother, Carmen Prado de von der Schulenburg a native of Mexico. His father had come to Mexico during the First World War as an expert metallurgist, but his travels through Mexico caused him to contract a fever, of which he died when his son was quite young. In 1930 Guillermo Schulenburg entered the conciliar seminary of the archdiocese of Mexico, where he studied humanities and philosophy. He was sent to Rome to the Colegio Pío Latinoamericano, and earned a licentiate in theology and a bachelor's degree in canon law from the Gregorian University. He returned to Mexico during the Second World War and taught at the conciliar seminary, of which he eventually became rector. On March 16, 1963, Pope John XXIII appointed him secular abbot of the Collegiate chapter of Guadalupe, a position he held for thirty-three years. On July 17 of that same year the pope named him to the honorary but prestigious post of prothonotary apostolic. Schulenburg admitted that prior to his appointment to Guadalupe he did not have a deep knowledge or appreciation of the tradition and devotion. However, he dedicated himself to learning all that he could, though throughout his years as abbot he avoided any involvement in or statement about the historical question.

In 1995 Schulenburg wrote a Presentación for the Spanish edition of Richard Nebel's doctoral dissertation, *Santa María Tonantzin, Virgen de Guadalupe*. He did not go into the question of Juan Diego's historical existence, and in general was rather circumspect in what he wrote. He did note, however, that "it is not a question of a dogma of faith but of a pious belief deeply rooted in the people of Mexico."[64] Regarding the *Nican mopohua*, he stated that the author was unknown, but accepted the idea that the work was based on a preexisting tradition that may have dated from the last part of the sixteenth century.

This introduction did not attract any undue attention. What caused a storm of protest and inaugurated a major new phase of the controversy was an interview that Schulenburg gave in 1995 for an obscure Catholic journal called *Ixtus,* on the occasion of the centenary of the coronation.[65] Somewhat surprising, in view of the ensuing furor, was that the tone of the interview was deeply devotional and a major part of it was devoted to the spiritual and national significance of Guadalupe.

> She has a great significance in the evangelization of our country and was the one who forged our nationality. Therefore we have sought to express our service of love, fidelity, devotion, obedience to her, queen of heaven and of men, by means of a royal coronation, because she is the mother of the king, who is Christ, and she has taught us the way to him, just as Christ has shown us the way to the Father. In this way our devotion to Mary, in addition to having a mariological, theological, spiritual meaning, has a Christocentric meaning, because Christ is the one who is at the center, who is our great intercessor, and we use Mary in order to reach him.[66]

Schulenburg regarded Guadalupe as a great work of syncretism and hence one that had a special indigenous significance. The Virgin's message was one of vindication of the dignity of the natives, and the dialogues of the *Nican mopohua* expressed love, understanding, and acceptance. The intense devotion of Mexicans toward the Virgin of Guadalupe, however, was independent of the historical fact. He denied that the photographs taken by Callahan and Smith proved that the image was supernatural, as some had claimed.[67] Rather, he considered it to be an ordinary picture but one that produced a magnetic effect on viewers. "But this does not reveal its precise origin. We must make a distinction. The scientific and critical historian is one thing, the devout lover of the Virgin is another. But, by any hypothesis, the Virgin Mary is the permanent miracle. I don't meddle in the discussion of the historical problem, because throughout our history you are going to find very qualified apparitionists and anti-apparitionists. For me that is a secondary problem."[68]

The two interviewers, Javier Sicilia, a journalist and poet, and Ricardo Newman, a painter, pursued him on the historical fact. Schulenburg gave a somewhat irrelevant answer. The interviewer then asked, "Doesn't the *Nican mopohua* narrate an historical fact? If not, don't you think there would be some deceit?"[69] Schulenburg continued to insist on a distinction between faith and the historical fact. "Theologically and biblically, what is an apparition? It is an interior phenomenon that by a special grace of God causes a man to see what no one sees and hear what no one hears. He is the only witness of his own experience."[70] What, then, of Juan Diego? "He is a symbol, not a reality."[71] This led to the question of the beatification. "That beatification is a recognition of cultus. It is not the recognition of the physical and real existence of the person. For the same reason it is not properly speaking a beatification. . . . Juan Diego is a tradition. . . . In summary there is no way of discovering his existence. All the historical documents that exist have been investigated."[72] Schulenburg also opposed recognizing Juan Diego's cultus, since the proper object of devotion was the Virgin Mary. "Have you seen anyone light candles to Juan Diego before that beatification, which is called equivalent?"[73]

Asked why, under the circumstances, the beatification had taken place, Schulenburg went into detail:

Because the archbishop of Mexico, with a team of four or five priests, presented the cause before the Congregation for the Saints, they insisted on this cause, they studied it, and the person immediately responsible in the process of study, said, "Look, treat this as cultus *in memoriam*. Prove that there has been a cultus for many years and handle it in that way. Do not try to prove the historical existence of the person because you are going to run into many difficulties," that is, difficulties of a documentary nature. But the archbishop of Mexico persisted and asked the pope for the beatification of Juan Diego. The pope said, "Good, let them study it." They did so. The Congregation gave the results of their study to the pope . . . and he recognized the cultus. In this decision is the Holy Father infallible? He was not speaking *ex cathedra*, as when he defines a dogma of faith, because this is not a dogma of faith. The fact of an equivalent beatification does not compromise the pope's authority. *If he should canonize Juan Diego, then it would be most serious, because in that case theologians would have to study whether the pope can or cannot be in error in a canonization.*[74]

The last sentence highlights the principal reason that later impelled Schulenburg to oppose the canonization of Juan Diego. The canonization of a person whose existence was so doubtful presented theological difficulties to many persons. Schulenburg would later assert that the interview was "improvised," without his having had any notes or paper before him.[75]

As provocative as some of the statements seemed, the interview attracted no attention until the following year. Although some press reports stated that it was republished in an Italian journal, *Trenta Giorni*, and then in translation in the Spanish version, *30 Días* (May 25, 1996), that is not accurate. What appeared in both journals was an article by Andrea Tornelli, Vatican correspondent for *Il Giornale* of Rome, which quoted from the interview but also exaggerated and distorted its meaning.[76] Under an inflammatory headline, "For Modern Ecclesiastics Miracles Are Impossible," Tornelli began by stating that "the abbot rector of the greatest Marian sanctuary in America says to the 'enlightened' faithful that the apparition of 1531 is not an historical fact and that the visionary, recently beatified, never existed."[77] This news, he continued, had crossed the ocean and provoked chaos in even the most secret rooms of the Vatican. The article accused Schulenburg of having for years articulated a theory that the apparitions were the result of a syncretism involving the faith of the Spanish missionaries and native religious traditions. After quoting more from the article, Tornelli continued, "The prelate, then, has no doubts. The visionary is a person of fantasy, the elaboration *a posteriori* of an old tradition. That image of Mary . . . is no more than a fable."[78] He also gave a brief résumé of the proofs of the apparition, including the *Nican mopohua.* Toward the end, he quoted Bishop Cipriano Calderón Polo, vice-president of the Pontifical Commission for Latin America: "It is an isolated theory, different from that of the rest of historians. Perhaps he holds it because he believes that this is the way to reach modern men."[79]

On that same day, an article on the interview appeared in *Reforma.* It caused an uproar throughout Mexico, together with demands that Schulenburg resign. Enrique Salazar Salazar made a public call for the abbot's resignation, and the Mexican bishops asked Rome to retire him, particularly in view of the fact that, at eighty, he was far beyond retirement age.[80] "Schulenburg must be removed from his position," Salazar Salazar was quoted as saying. "For the good of the Mexican people and the Catholic Church, we must see to it that he leaves his position. Because of his advanced age, he does not think about what he says."[81] Schulenburg, however, insisted that he had been appointed abbot for life by Pope John XXIII.

The ensuing controversy was reported in journals and wire services throughout the world.[82] A taxi driver in Mexico was quoted as saying, "The Virgin of Guadalupe is the patron saint of all America; everyone believes in her and it doesn't make any difference what the abbot may say; nothing will cause believers to lose their faith. I hope that God will forgive him because the people won't."[83] One person commented that in Mexico even the Communists were *guadalupanos.* The *National Catholic Reporter* reported, "Public outrage flared. Schulenburg was called 'a traitor to the church,' crowds shouted 'Viva Juan Diego,' and the archbishop of Mexico City said during Mass that the incident 'has wounded all Mexicans.'"[84] Within days of the appearance of the interview, Luis Guerrero Rosado published a rebuttal in a pamphlet titled *¿Existió Juan Diego?* (Did Juan Diego Exist?).[85] "We, the immense majority of Mexican Catholics, not only love our **Most Holy Mother** in her invocation of **Guadalupe,** but we are fully convinced of the objectively historical truth of her intervention in the birth of our mestizo fatherland, as well as the real existence of Juan Diego."[86] He gave a brief survey of the process of beatification to show its historical accuracy. He described the beatification as something special, in that the recognition of the cultus meant that Juan Diego had been among the blessed from the day of his death. Finally, the pamphlet reproduced Schulenburg's interview in full.

Archbishop Corripio Ahumada of Mexico City at first attempted to calm things. "What I would say is that it is best for everyone to be quiet, and let him think what he wants and that each one should seek to base his beliefs on the knowledge that he may have about the truth of the matter."[87] In contrast, the spokesman for the archdiocese, Héctor Fernández Rousselón, was less accommodating. "Any declaration by a minister of worship that casts doubt on the miracle of Tepeyac harms the Catholic Church. . . . Anything that goes against Juan Diego and the Most Holy Virgin of Guadalupe affects all of us, because it is part of our very own identity."[88] At first, Schulenburg tried to backtrack on the interview. "I take the liberty of protesting vehemently against the absolute falsity of the interview attributed to me in the magazine *30 Giorni* published in Italy."[89] He did not, however, retract his belief that Juan Diego never existed and was merely a symbol of evangelization.

According to newspaper reports, there was more than religion or historical truth behind the furor. An editorial in *Proceso*, a leading Mexican newsweekly, declared, "Our historic banner, the symbol of so many popular causes, the Virgin of Guadalupe, has been imprisoned in the middle of a sordid ecclesiastical struggle for political and economic power."[90] Enrique Dussel, a well-known historian and liberation theologian, was even more blunt. "The Virgin of Guadalupe is being used in a struggle for power. Groups within the hierarchy are pulling from both sides trying to win economic advantage. Neither side cares for the people of Mexico. Neither group is concerned about the true condition of our people. It makes no difference who wins."[91] One newspaper reported, "Church observers here said it is possible that Monsignor Schulenburg, who drives a Mercedes and is not a favorite of Mexico City Archbishop Norberto Rivera, could be the target of internal church politics. One observer suggested that the monsignor's opponents were doing 'a hatchet job' on him because he favors splitting Mexico City's huge archdiocese into two parts, with his cathedral at the center of one part. The archbishop opposes the division."[92] The reference was to the fact that Schulenburg and Girolamo Prigione, the papal nuncio, advocated the erection of a new diocese, to be called La Villa, that would for all practical purposes encompass the Basilica and its environs. This plan was energetically opposed by the archbishop of Mexico and the other Mexican bishops.[93]

Some of the attacks were bitingly personal. Under a banner headline, "The Abbot Has Enriched Himself at the Expense of the Basilica," the Spanish-language section of the *San José Mercury News* reprinted

Proceso's assertions that Schulenburg had made a personal fortune from the Basilica's revenues and had a residence in Bosque de Lomas, one the most exclusive areas of Mexico City, valued at fifteen million pesos, and one in Cuernavaca said to be worth a million pesos, together with expensive automobiles and valuables.[94] It is not clear what connection this had with the historical existence of Juan Diego. The abbot defended himself, saying, "In more than thirty-three years of evangelical labor I have never benefited from the church [the Basilica] in a personal way. . . . The entire structure and infrastructure of the Basilica is for the benefit of the people of God."[95]

On that same day, Archbishop Rivera Carrera issued a strong pastoral letter on Our Lady of Guadalupe. He strenuously defended the historicity of the apparitions, citing the *Nican mopohua* fourteen times. His sensibilities as a devotee and a Mexican had been hurt, but not his "faith as a Catholic, because in no way do I consider myself insulted or aggrieved because other brothers of mine have made use of their right to disagree on a point in which we all enjoy full freedom of conscience to believe or not to believe." He did, however, proclaim his belief that the Virgin Mary was "queen and mother of our mestizo fatherland." He expressed his sympathy for those who did not share this security. His reasons for this belief were "the tradition, the documents, and the deeds that adorn and constitute our history." Without Guadalupe, the history of Mexico was incomprehensible. She alone was able to reconcile and unite the Spaniards and the Indians. "How would our Indian ancestors have been able to accept Christ if she had not complemented for them what the missionaries preached to them . . . ? These testimonies are now reinforced better than ever since, for some years, many of the best talents in the Church, strict professionals in history and theology, have examined them, discussed them, evaluated them and approved them for the process of Juan Diego's canonization, and because, on that basis, the Holy Father personally endorsed it." The tone of the letter was personal and emotional, and included an apostrophe to the Virgin in his own words. In it, his tone also became less irenic: "Thank you also because these events have unmasked those who would want to see us divided, without faith and without hope, without national symbols, and on the way to being absorbed by other cultures and other powers."[96] As was mentioned above, he contributed to the growing idea of the divine inspiration of the *Nican mopohua*.

On June 2, 1996, the priest Prisciliano Hernández Chávez published an article in the *Observador* in Querétaro, in which he called for Schulenburg's resignation.[97] "The sanest thing for you, Señor Abad, for Mexico, and the world, would be to request to be relieved of your charge

before the archbishop of Mexico and the Holy Father John Paul II do so."
Like so many others, Hernández Chávez overstepped the bounds of pro-
priety. "It could be that like Saul you may kiss the ground and be transformed into a Saint Paul . . . although at your eighty years it will be better to prepare yourself with humility for the judgment of God."[98] He also
summarized the assumptions behind so many of the apparitionist arguments. "It is true that it is not a dogma of faith but it is rash to reject a
gift of God, especially of this nature, as evident as a flower, as elevated as
a star, so much life of our life that without GUADALUPE we would cease
to be Mexicans. . . . The enemies of Catholic unity and of our national
identity know that if they tear Saint Mary of Guadalupe from its heart we
will lose our shield and defense."[99]

A key question in all this was why Tornelli's article was published in
Mexico at the time that it was. Almost four years later, Javier Sicilia, one
of the original interviewers, published his version of events.[100] He was
moved to do this, he said, by the uproar that followed Tornelli's publication of a private letter of Schulenburg and three other priests to the
Vatican that had been leaked to him (on this, see the next chapter).
Another reason was that a *noticiario*, Joaquín López Dóriga, had quoted
words that he claimed were Schulenburg's. The interview, he said, was
contained on two tapes, one of which he had and Cardinal Rivera
Carrera the other. Sicilia called on López Dóriga and Cardinal Rivera to
clarify the question "that compromises not only the honesty and credibility of both but the integrity of the editorial policies of *Ixtus* which are
alien to scandal, yellow journalism, and the idiocy of our times."[101] He
pointed out that the original interview had passed unnoticed. "Almost a
year later (1996), using the more polemical fragments of that interview,
Andrea Tornelli . . . published a report that unleashed a terrible indigna-
tion in Rome and a lynching campaign in Mexico. . . . Who gave Tornelli
that interview that no one had paid any attention to a year before?"[102]
Sicilia said that he had heard the answer from a high church functionary,
who said that it was Cardinal Rivera because he wanted to take over the
Basilica and its money.

It was at this point that López Dóriga, in a radio broadcast, quoted
certain assertions of Schulenburg that he said came from the original
interview in *Ixtus*. After Sicilia had called him to demand that he stop
attributing these words to *Ixtus*, López Dóriga did so. On June 1, 1996,
the cardinal had an interview with Sicilia and Newman, together with
Tomás Reynoso (a member of the publication board of *Ixtus*). He asked
them to sign a letter to the effect that the interview in *Ixtus* had been
taped and reproduced faithfully in the journal and that it had not been
altered or manipulated. He gave as his reason his concern that the whole

affair be fully documented and to avoid confusion and harm to the church. After a "prickly" conversation, in which the two original interviewers reproached the cardinal for the way in which the entire matter had been handled, they signed. The cardinal insisted that they give him copies of the tapes. Again, his reason was that the archdiocese and the Holy See would have documentation about what was actually said. Sicilia gave him the copies over the protests of Newman, saying that he did so out of respect for the cardinal's office. He placed one condition, "Give me here, in front of witnesses, your word that those tapes will never leave the archdiocese or the Holy See and that they will not be used in a bad way in the media." The cardinal promised.[103]

Sicilia asked why the scandal was being revived in 2002. He accused the cardinal of being the one who had turned the tapes over to López Dóriga. He also believed that a network of churchmen and others in Mexico were involved in this, including the Legionnaires of Christ, who were promoting the possibility of Rivera Carrera as pope. He believed that the motive was to destroy Schulenburg's credibility. Another motive would be the appropriation of what the Indian means for church and society. This would mean perpetuating the picture of the Indian as silent, passive, retrograde — a paternalistic approach in which the Indian is always manipulated. He concluded by once again asking López Dóriga and Rivera Carrera to take responsibility for what happened to the tapes.

On July 8, 1996, Schulenburg submitted his resignation, which was accepted on July 25, though it was not made public until September 6.[104] He was the last abbot of Guadalupe. On December 12, 1998, a papal directive changed the structure of the Chapter. The administration of the Basilica passed to a committee of bishops headed by the archbishop of Mexico, and the positions of the canons of the Chapter became purely honorary and liturgical.[105] The Catholic Church in Mexico, however, had not heard the last of Schulenburg.

CHAPTER SEVEN

History versus Juan Diego

❖

The abbot emeritus had opposed the beatification of Juan Diego and had written to that effect to Rome. He now continued his campaign, this time against the canonization, which was pursued very actively by Norberto Rivera Carrera, who became archbishop of Mexico in 1995. In addition to all the historical questions involved, Schulenburg's opposition arose from his belief that the canonization of Juan Diego would seriously harm the Church's credibility, especially in view of the opinion held by some theologians that the pope is infallible when he canonizes saints. As he said in the original interview, "If he should canonize Juan Diego, then it would be most serious, because in that case theologians would have to study whether the pope can or cannot be in error in a canonization."[1]

On November 17, 1997, Monsignor Schulenburg invited a number of scholars and historians, both priests and laypersons, to meet at his office in Mexico City. The first part of the meeting was devoted to an analysis of the so-called Codex 1548, the second part to the concerns that the participants felt about the canonization. These were: (1) that the canonization process was moving far too rapidly and that more time was needed to analyze the historical difficulties involved; (2) that if a canonization was an infallible or at least authoritative act of the Roman Pontiff, the canonization of a person of dubious existence would create a crisis of conscience for those who accepted this position; (3) that there was danger that the credibility of the church would be seriously compromised; (4) that the focus of devotion at Tepeyac was the Virgin Mary, not Juan Diego. It was decided that the group would write a common letter to the cardinal secretary of state with a copy to the Congregation for the Causes of the Saints, and each person would write an individual one to the same parties. Father Stafford Poole, one of the participants, sent his letters on December 24 and 27, 1997. He also sent a copy of his book on the history of Guadalupe. The joint letter was sent in March 1998.

Ordinarily, all that would have been needed for canonization was a miracle after the beatification.[2] At the beginning of 1998, however, with the bishops of Mexico pushing the cause, the Congregation for the Causes of the Saints decided to study the historical questions in greater detail.[3] On January 23, it appointed an unnamed relator to study the state of the question from the point of view of history. On May 15, 1998, he presented all the documentation relative to the beatification and the historical problems. He was critical of Poole's book and claimed that its conclusions "lacked all reasonably persuasive proofs, since he frequently made use of the documents with a preconceived thesis and rapid and categorical judgments."[4] Poole was not informed of these criticisms, much less allowed an opportunity to answer them. Still, the Congregation recognized the necessity for a thorough scientific investigation, and for that purpose appointed an ad hoc commission of historians to review the documentation and pursue the investigation in archives and libraries, for the purpose of clarifying doubts and arriving at a conclusion.

It is quite clear that the commission was stacked in favor of the canonization. The coordinating president was Fidel González Fernández, professor of church history at the Gregorian and Urbaniana Universities in Rome and a devoted *guadalupano*.[5] Some thirty persons actively participated in the work of the commission, especially Eduardo Chávez Sánchez, José Luis Guerrero Rosado, Xavier Escalada, S.J., and Mario Rojas. All of these were well-known *guadalupanos*. Others consulted were Josefina Muriel, Miguel León-Portilla (for the *Nican mopohua*), and Alfonso Alcalá Alvarado. The results of their labors were incorporated into twenty-four thematic sections that were presented by González Fernández in an extraordinary meeting of the Congregation for the Causes of the Saints on October 28, 1998. He first summarized the various positions that had been taken with regard to the apparitions and Juan Diego, and then surveyed the sources, under the headings of indigenous, mixed Spanish–indigenous, and Spanish. The most important sources were the *Nican mopohua* and the so-called Codex Escalada.[6] González Fernández admitted the lack of any testimonies prior to 1548 (his date for the *Nican mopohua*). As in other studies, he presented the native sources uncritically, without noting the questions of dating and authorship that affected so many of them. This report, dated November 1, 1998, was unanimously accepted and approved in that session, with the prefect of the Congregation presiding. It is quite clear that this so-called historical commission was anything but an objective search for the facts. Yet this meeting came to be regarded among supporters of the canonization as a crucial one for the progress of the cause.

On October 5, 1998, Poole received a phone call from Schulenburg, bringing him up to date on communications with Rome. He and the group had sent to Rome copies of three books: Nebel's, Noguez's, and Poole's. Schulenburg said that González Fernández had been sent from Rome to Mexico to investigate the question. He had taken a group of devotees to the Basilica for a private and secret viewing of the image. This was done without the knowledge of Canon Warnholtz, the archpriest. González Fernández was now one of the principal agents for the canonization. Poole agreed to sign a joint letter to Rome, pointing out the errors and deficiencies of the *Positio*. At Schulenburg's suggestion, on October 19, 1998, he sent a copy of *The Story of Guadalupe* (a critical edition and translation of the *Nican mopohua*) to Archbishop Giovanni Battista Re of the Secretariat of State. On Friday, December 4, 1998, Schulenburg called Poole to tell him that all the books had arrived in Rome but that some persons there had been busy refuting them, especially Poole's. The former prefect of the Congregation for the Causes of the Saints had died, and his replacement was a Portuguese bishop, José Saraiva Martins, of the Claretian community, who had formerly been on the Congregation for the Doctrine of the Faith and the Congregation for Education. Schulenburg was planning to send him a personal letter about the entire matter.[7]

It was the hope of the Mexican hierarchy that the canonization of Juan Diego would take place on the occasion of the pope's visit to Mexico in January 1999. That did not happen. On August 24, 1999, Archbishop Rivera Carrera gave a press conference in which he announced that the canonization would take place on May 21, 2000.[8] The Vatican, however, did not make any public statement to support this, at least in relation to Juan Diego. As it turned out, this was the day of canonization for twenty-seven Mexican saints, though Juan Diego was not one of them. Shortly before the pope began a prayer, a cry of "Juan Diego" arose in Saint Peter's, indicating the people's desire for his canonization.[9] The pope responded by introducing the prayer with the words, "At this time I return in heart to the hill of Tepeyac," followed by cries from the assembly. The fact was, however, that contrary to earlier hopes and expectations, Juan Diego was not included among these saints.

On August 27, Schulenburg called Poole to tell him about a book being published in Rome by three authors. The book that Schulenburg referred to was *El encuentro de la Virgen de Guadalupe y Juan Diego* (The Encounter of the Virgin of Guadalupe and Juan Diego), written by González Fernández, Chávez Sánchez, and Guerrero Rosado. References in newspapers and journals indicated that it had been written at the direction of the Vatican, which was requiring a thorough rebuttal of the anti-apparitionist position. It was actively promoted by apparitionist groups and quickly became quite popular. Schulenburg seemed resigned to the success of the canonization, saying that it was difficult to swim against the current.

The book was more a polemic than serious history. The scholarship was on an elementary level, and the authors seemed unaware of current research into the life and history of colonial Mexico, especially that based on Nahuatl-language sources. Written entirely from the apparitionist perspective, it gave no credit for good faith or objectivity to critics. The tone was adversarial, and all critics of the apparition tradition were accused of partiality, prejudice, and preconceptions. The fact that the authors themselves were guilty of these same faults was studiously ignored. Thus, in the pages dealing with the work of Richard Nebel, his conclusions were preceded by the phrase, "He feels himself authorized."[10] Regarding his skepticism about the authorship of the *Nican mopohua*, the authors said, "and he deals with this in an ideological way."[11] In that same context, they spoke of "arbitrary speculations, easily manipulable by another kind of interests."[12] For some unknown reason, they made no mention of Xavier Noguez's book on the sources of Guadalupe.

Some of their sharpest barbs were reserved for the author of this study. Thus, they spoke of Poole's "polemical work" and said that "it starts more from a preconception or a thesis of an ideological character. . . . The page that Stafford Poole devotes to the testimony of Bernal Díaz del Castillo gives us a clear example of how prejudice serves to obscure an historical testimony, denying the evidence of the document. . . . Stafford Poole, under a prejudice, as in his anti-Guadalupan arguments, seeks to minimize this evidence [of Cervantes de Salazar]." Discussing the omission of the apparitions in the report of Antonio Freire, they said, "Poole's supposition about Freire, which corresponds with that of Icazbalceta, is another of the frequent, gratuitous conclusions in his book."[13] Even when this author agreed with them, they implied that it was only because he was impelled to do so against his will by the force of the evidence. "Stafford Poole himself finds himself obliged to recognize the facts."[14]

Like Esteban Antícoli in the nineteenth century, the authors saw the beatification and canonization as Rome's decision in favor of the historicity of Juan Diego. "The Holy See never beatifies or canonizes a symbol but persons, real persons; human beings who faced problems like any man, with capacities and limitations, like any other human being."[15] And again, "The judgment rendered by the Holy See deserves our absolute confidence and on the basis of it one can be sure that the beatification of

Juan Diego was totally real, that there was no question of a symbol but of a person as real as any one of us and that his process did not suffer from any irregularity."[16] The book never addresses the serious problems concerning Juan Diego, and is content to repeat arguments that date back to Antícoli. Again, it is testimony to the closed and partial nature of the entire process that those authors who are criticized in the book were never invited by Rome to give a rebuttal. This they had to do on their own.

Schulenburg's opposition to the canonization again brought down on him the wrath of Mexican churchmen and laity alike when it became known that he had cosigned, with Warnholtz and Esteban Martínez de la Serna, a letter to Rome in an attempt to prevent or delay the canonization (September 27, 1999).[17] The three pointed out the scandal that would result from canonizing a person whose historical existence was doubtful at best, and argued that the pope would be made to look ridiculous. Like all correspondence with the Roman Curia, this was intended to be confidential. However, it was leaked to Andrea Tornelli. Schulenburg believed that the leak was the work of Archbishop Rivera Carrera, but others thought that it might have been Guerrero Rosado or Oscar Sánchez Barba, the promotor of Mexican causes at the Vatican. Once again, the press was filled with attacks on the abbot emeritus.

In an interview, published on December 3, 1999, with a correspondent for the Los Angeles Spanish-language newspaper *La Opinión*, Salazar Salazar, by this time the director of the Centro de Estudios Guadalupanos, launched a vitriolic attack against Schulenburg. He accused him of discriminatory ideas because he was disparaging everything Mexican: "He is dumb, stupid, and stubborn [Es un tonto, necio y terco], who thinks that anything that comes from Mexicans is worthless."[18] Salazar Salazar claimed that he had told Schulenburg to his face, echoing arguments used by Esteban Antícoli, "You are a perjurer because when you came to the Basilica you promised to defend the devotion to the apparition of the Virgin of Guadalupe, and you are a heretic because you are against what the pope is teaching."[19] Salazar Salazar had a rather broad definition of heretic, since Guadalupe has never been defined as an article of faith. Guerrero Rosado was quoted as saying that "all the anti-apparitionists' arguments have been tinged with racism," an idea that was echoed by Humberto Ramos, at that time the associate director of Hispanic ministry for the archdiocese of Los Angeles.[20] Bishop Onésimo Cepeda Silva of Ecatepec was quoted as asserting, in a statement of breathtaking insensitivity, that the root of the difficulty lay in Schulenburg's age, with the implication that he must be at least partly senile.[21] "Logically, all older people become a bit erratic, and their thinking loses some of its lucidity."

On December 6, Archbishop Rivera Carrera declared that in accord with the ordinary magisterium of the church, Schulenburg was excommunicating himself by casting doubt on the *hecho guadalupano*.[22]

On December 22, 1999, Poole wrote a letter to Cardinal Angelo Sodano, the Vatican secretary of state, in support of the Schulenburg–Warnholtz–Martínez de la Serna letter of the previous September. In addition, he protested in strong terms the campaign of vilification against Monsignor Schulenburg, pointing out that in writing to the Holy See the former abbot was doing only what he, or any Catholic, had a clear right to do. Poole deplored in a special way the published comments of Enrique Salazar Salazar, Luis Guerrero Rosado, and Bishop Cepeda Silva. Poole received no answer to this letter.

As the Feast of Our Lady of Guadalupe approached in December 1999, the media campaign intensified. The papal nuncio, Archbishop Justo Mullor García, a Spaniard, involved himself rather undiplomatically in the controversy. In an interview with a reporter for *Reforma* on December 8, 1999, he came down firmly on the side of the archbishop and the apparitionists. "I believe that a person who lives as he [Schulenburg] does has no right to make those accusations. May he be converted, may he ask forgiveness. God will forgive him and if he chooses me as a confessor, in my confessional I will also forgive him."[23] On the other hand, the nuncio believed that the evil was not so great, since so few people believed the abbot emeritus. "It is absurd that people like Señor Schulenburg and his friends can suspect that the pope can canonize anyone without having absolute certainty of his historicity and his holiness. It is the history of the entire church that they are placing in doubt." He added, in a statement that bordered on the slanderous, "For that reason there is a suspicion that ecclesiastics who live a life more lay than ecclesial — since they may have other motives for these things — can go from personal vanity to other hidden interests." He also claimed that with the publication of *El encuentro*, the Holy See was totally certain of the historicity of Juan Diego and that fact overthrew "the dreams" of some "very small groups." With regard to the money collected at the Basilica, "One of the nicest things that a servant [that is, Mullor himself] has done on arriving here is to put in order the accounts of Guadalupe with a council of administration, with audits, so that no one else in the future can benefit from that money, which is the money of the poor, the poorest in Mexico." That statement did not go unchallenged. In that same issue of *Reforma*, Monsignor Antonio Macedo Tenllado, the administrator of the Basilica and former chancellor of the archdiocese of Mexico, responded that the nuncio had nothing to do with putting the accounts in order. Macedo had been doing that since his appointment on October 31, 1996.

On the day after this interview appeared in the press, Mullor and Schulenburg had a meeting at the nunciature, during which the nuncio tried to persuade him of the truth of the apparitions.[24] An article in the periodical *Contenido* pointed out that the "diplomatic representative of a foreign state decided to invade the jurisdiction of the Mexican Catholic Church and ordered an audit of the Basilica of Guadalupe, implicitly accusing the ex-abbot of having made a fortune by stealing for decades the alms of the poor."[25] On February 11, 2000, the Vatican announced that Archbishop Mullor had been transferred to Rome to be president of the Pontifical Ecclesiastical Academy. There was speculation that this was because of his support of Bishop Samuel Ruiz García of Chiapas.[26] It is quite possible, however, that his public and clumsy meddling in the internal affairs of the Mexican Church may also have played a role in his removal after having spent only a brief time in his post (April 1997–February 2000). His successor, Leonardo Sandri, an Argentine, had an even shorter term: less than a year before being transferred to Rome.

Even a politician became involved in the controversy. Vicente Fox, the presidential candidate of the PAN–Partido Verde coalition, in a statement quoted in *Reforma* on December 9, 1999, said that Schulenburg had behaved "very mistakenly." "What does he gain with his historical rigor? I think that it is to go against the current, to go against an entire people, to go against the historical rigor used by the Catholic Church in order in propose the canonization of Juan Diego. That is a canonization that involved very much preliminary work, and with a stroke of the pen he wants to throw it out."[27]

On the Feast of Guadalupe, December 12, 1999, Cardinal Rivera Carrera presided at the principal mass at the Basilica. He was joined by the nuncio and the former archbishop, Corripio Ahumada. In his homily, Rivera said, "The first thing I want to reiterate with all the force of my personal and ecclesial conviction is that, together with our Holy Father John Paul II and together with the immense majority of all of you, my Mexican brothers and sisters, I am totally convinced, as is the Holy Father, not only of the moving beauty of this account [of the apparition] but also that it deals with an objective and historic event."[28] If not, he said, then he and the pope were "cheats" (*embusteros*). On that same day, *Reforma* quoted Xavier Escalada as saying that denial of the apparitions and authenticity of the *tilma* was "the greatest nonsense" that could be committed. In the same issue, the parish priest Alberto Athié, vice-president of Caritas, declared that if the Indian Marcos painted the image, then "that Indian Marcos is the greatest man in all the history of humanity." He added, "If it is true, our error has been twofold: first, in not recognizing in this man the super genius of history, and secondly, because we would have to consider him the true father of all Mexicans."[29]

Up to this time, the pro-canonization forces had monopolized the media, which they manipulated with great skill. In December 1999, for the first time, the voice of the opposition began to be heard. On December 12, *Reforma* ran three interviews with priests who took the opposing side. Father Manuel Olimón Nolasco, *catedrático* of the Pontifical University of Mexico and president of the National Commission on Sacred Art, criticized the book *El encuentro* as not being a serious study or bringing forth anything new. He also asserted that the book presented documents of doubtful provenance. He pointed out that Escalada had not allowed professional historians to see the Codex. "For some years we asked for the document and he never gave it to us." He also noted that none of the three authors of the *El encuentro* was an expert on native codices or history. He added that it would be inopportune to canonize Juan Diego, because of the weaknesses in the historical investigation that had been carried out, and because of the scandal surrounding the matter. He decried the hostility toward Schulenburg which was being inflamed by churchmen. "If they lynch him in the street, the people who lynch him will say that they are doing right. It is very irresponsible that we, within the church, are fomenting this. This seems to me to be very serious and in this we are the ones who have to ask forgiveness and not him." He was concerned that the matter was being treated as a dogma of faith and that anything that was said contrary to it or which did not correspond to a particular line bordered on heresy. Saying that he was disgusted by the irresponsible attacks on Schulenburg, he pointed out that all that the abbot emeritus had done was to ask that the matter continue to be studied. He accused Guerrero Rosado of being the person who photocopied the September letter, and Oscar Sánchez Barba, the postulator of the cause, of being the person who leaked it.

Another critique of the book *El encuentro* was launched by Father Francisco Miranda Godínez, a well-known historian and professor at the Colegio de Michoacán, in an article that appeared in the journal *Efemérides Mexicana*, a publication of the Pontifical University of Mexico.[30] The proponents of the canonization had pointed to the *El encuentro* as positive proof of the existence of Juan Diego. "The editor of the work made a methodological presentation attached to the strictest canons of historical criticism which, unfortunately, were not respected in the work itself." Father Miranda said that the authors were guilty of a prejudice that contaminated the entire work.

The third interview, with the Dominican Gonzalo Balderas, took a different approach. Balderas was the coordinator of the team of theologians of the Conferencia de Institutos Religiosos de México and professor at the Colegio Iberoamericano. Calling the debate over Juan Diego secondary, he said, "What concerns me as a Christian, as a Catholic, as a religious, is that the same interest is not shown in the Indians of today." Expressing confidence that the scandal that had been provoked would serve to cause the Mexican hierarchy to enter a process of conversion, he declared, "It is not that Schulenburg should ask forgiveness from the people. After this scandal, it is necessary to ask forgiveness of the people on behalf of the Catholic hierarchy. May the church evangelize in the spirit of Saint Mary of Guadalupe, may it be a church that places itself in the world of the poor." Some days after the archbishop of Mexico had asserted that Schulenburg was separating himself from the church, Balderas said that no one could be excommunicated for doubting the existence of Juan Diego. "Although the Guadalupe event is very important, it is not a dogma to which every Catholic is obliged."

For all the controversy that was engendered, the opponents of the canonization were circumspect, even conservative, in their denial of the historicity of Juan Diego and the apparitions. Schulenburg consistently viewed Juan Diego and the Virgin of Guadalupe as symbols used in the early evangelization of the natives. In an interview with the *Mexico City News* on December 11, 1999, Warnholtz said, "We never said anything about this to people before, and we never intended to hurt anyone." He called the Guadalupe tradition a "tender, beautiful and very Indian story. . . . We don't have any doubts about the tradition, but where is the proof? Where are Juan Diego's remains? Where is his tomb?" As for the image, "People say it is supernatural. But I've seen it and it is a painting. We agree, though, that it is mystical because it remains so well preserved." Of the group seeking to delay the canonization, only Poole denied the total reality of Guadalupe and called it a seventeenth-century pious fiction.

The Schulenburg–Warnholtz–Martínez de la Serna letter of September 1999 did retard the progress of the cause. The apparitionist forces now seemed to accept that the canonization would not take place on May 21, 2000, but they attributed that to Rome's desire for more exhaustive studies, not to any weakness in the cause itself. In April 2000, Schulenburg notified Poole of the group's intention of sending another letter to Rome, including one to the Congregation for the Doctrine of the Faith.

One of the more bizarre developments at this time was the reinterpretation of the person of Juan Diego, not as a peasant or commoner (*macehualli*) but as a native leader (*principal*) of his village, and then as a member of the nobility and even of royalty. Though mention of this could be found earlier, the first major formulation came from the Internet. In early May 2000, there was an announcement of a website devoted to Juan Diego, and specifically of a new movie about him that was being planned.[31] The announcement was made in a letter from

Guerrero Rosado. Stating that he had worked for many years at the request of the Holy See on the commission studying the cause of Juan Diego, he then made the following astonishing statements:

The Commission has made some startling discoveries about the true identity of Juan Diego. He is so much more than the humble Indian we thought him to be.
  His name was Cuauhtlatoatzin.
  He was a royal prince, a fearless military general, a philosopher, a poet and had several wives, as was the custom of his people in sixteenth-century Mexico. He gave all this up to become a Christian and an ambassador of Christ not only for the Mexican peoples but for the whole world.
  It is my opinion that Juan Diego will soon become known as one of the greatest saints in the history of the Church. He will be recognized as something of a Patriarch, along the lines of Abraham and Moses.[32]

The source of much of this information, Guerrero Rosado added, was a new book by Christine Jones of the University of Montreal. The book was not for general sale, but a copy could be received by making a contribution of $100 or more to the movie. Guerrero Rosado did not try to reconcile the fact that Juan Diego had had many wives with the clear statement in the *Nican mopohua* that he had been a lifelong celibate.
  The aforementioned website provided more of this exaggerated information:

The King of Texcoco agreed to fight with Cortés, and sent an army led by one of his eight sons to fight their neighbors. This prince, known as the Tlacateccatl, was an able and honored general in the king's army. Like his brothers and contemporaries, he had several concubines.
  Upon the defeat of the Aztecs, this Prince, through his encounter with Franciscan missionaries, gave up his royal heritage and became a catechumen at the mission at Tlateloco [*sic*]. He adopted the name of Juan Diego.

The website also said that Juan Diego's royal status made him a more convincing messenger for the Virgin: "Juan Diego's royal background more convincingly explains why, when he claimed to have had a vision of the Virgin Mary, his story was so readily accepted by the entire Aztec nation. He was still regarded as a Prince, and his word carried significant weight among his people." There is no evidence of this in any of the early documentation. In fact, it runs directly contrary to the information found in the *Nican mopohua*, according to which Juan Diego pleaded with the Virgin, "I greatly implore you, my patron, noble Lady, my daughter, entrust one of the high nobles, who are recognized respected, and honored, to carry and take your message, so that he will be believed. For I am a poor ordinary man, I carry burdens with the tumpline and carrying frame, I am one of the common people, one who is governed. Where you are sending me is not my usual place."[33] The Virgin, of course, refused, precisely because her message was aimed at the humble masses. Assertions like those on the website miss the central point of all apparition stories, that is, that the Virgin appears to the poor, marginalized, and helpless in society. She is their protector. The website also reported that the actor Martin Sheen would play the role of Bishop-elect Zumárraga in the movie.

Later that year, an announcement appeared on the Vatican website saying that the Centro de Estudios Guadalupanos in Mexico, in conjunction with personnel from the Instituto Nacional de Antropología e Historia, had presented the pope with a book, *The Virgin's Messenger*, which had been written by a team from both institutions. According to the press release, Asunción García Samper, the head of the team, had "reconstructed the Blessed's [Juan Diego's] family tree, going as far back as one hundred years after Christ, and including nine hundred relatives. Juan Diego, the book said, had come from a noble Indian family; he was a grandson of Nezahualcoyotl and highly respected in Mexico-Tenochtitlan."[34] It is scarcely conceivable that any documentation, or even oral tradition, could have survived that long. If these statements were true, they would constitute a revolution in Mesoamerican studies.

On May 14, 2000, another joint letter was sent to the Congregation for the Doctrine of the Faith.[35] For the most part, it repeated what the other letters had said and provided background for the entire controversy over the canonization. As for the book *El Encuentro*, the letter said, "We have read this book with care; fundamentally it repeats everything that was said in the *Positio*; the latter, unfortunately, makes use of arguments whose scholarly value is dubious and which, according to the historians whom we have mentioned, in no way brings to bear the elements necessary for creating the moral certainty of the person whose canonization is sought."[36] Unlike some earlier correspondence, this letter addressed the question of the nature of the image:

On the one hand we have a critical judgment that is serious and trustworthy because of the competence of the persons who did it, that our image of Guadalupe is a picture of a European character that dates more or less to the middle of the sixteenth century. We are sending to Your Excellency a copy of the said judgment, the result of a full and direct examination of the picture, a very private examination made by us but which was witnessed by the abbot, the archpriest, and the *sacristán mayor*[37] of the Basilica in the year 1982. Everything seems to indicate that our image of the Most Holy Virgin of Guadalupe which is in the Basilica is a human pictorial work and therefore it is not of supernatural origin.

On the other hand — we have an obligation in conscience to say so — the authors of the aforementioned book, beginning on page 200, speak of a direct examination of the image carried out on the night of July 30, 1998, and initiated by Father Fidel González Fernández, historical consultor of the Holy See, so they say, and sent by the Congregation for the Causes of the Saints. In actual fact, they viewed the image solely through the acrylic which is part of the case in which it is kept, without their being able to examine it directly, in spite of the fact that they affirm the opposite in their book. This examination was very superficial, and in reality they did not ask for any serious judgment from the expert persons who had been called to this meeting.[38]

The letter also included a defense of the historians who have questioned Juan Diego's existence, especially Noguez and Poole, who "possesses a solid reputation in the academic world of North America. . . . The majority of these authors are Catholics who are orthodox in the faith and in no way rationalist historians."[39] The letter writers concluded by expressing the hope that the letter would be kept confidential and not leaked.

On that same day, May 9, Poole received copies of two historical studies of the Guadalupe question. The first was titled "La cuestión de Guadalupe vista desde España" (The Question of Guadalupe Viewed from Spain), by the Claretian Father Eutimio Sastre Santos, who had been deeply involved in the canonization process. It used a highly scholastic approach to history. The author seemed to believe that the current controversy was entirely the work of the same "trio" of Mexican ecclesiastics who had authored the letter of September 27, 1999, and he falsely asserted that they had exploited the media in order to disseminate their ideas.[40] Father Sastre also mentioned the historical problem of García Icazbalceta's having failed to mention the account of Antonio Freire.[41] To support his claim that documentation for Guadalupe does exist, Sastre cited the Grajales and Burrus bibliography, and Burrus's assertion that if there were no documentary proofs in García Icazbalceta's time, the same could not be said of the 1980s. Sastre Santos echoed a frequent refrain among *guadalupanos*, that is, that modern-day critics had added nothing new to the argument and were merely following Muñoz and García Icazbalceta, whose criticisms had long before been totally refuted. "Nevertheless, today, in December of 1999, the trio of Mexican ecclesiastics, whose historical publications are not known, continue to interpret the old song of the duo: Muñoz and García Icazbalceta. And it is out of tune."[42] This comment about the historical credentials of the three ecclesiastics could, with equal justice, have been made about the authors of *El Encuentro*.

Like other apparitionists, Sastre Santos is guilty of outlandish speculations and implied accusations:

Who leaked to the communications media the letter that the three Mexican ecclesiastics sent to the Holy See and dated at Mexico, D.F., on 27 September 1999? I doubt that the perpetrator was its recipient, the Secretariat of State. What profit was there in publishing a confidential letter? And why does even a Catholic publication divulge without the least criticism the current lies (believe me, reader) and the historical absurdities of the letter and ignore the response in the work *El encuentro de la Virgen de Guadalupe y Juan Diego*? I don't even try to guess the reason. Who gains, and what by orchestrating this entire campaign of disinformation against the Virgin of Guadalupe? Certainly not Holy Church, either in Mexico or all of Latin America. Neither does historical criticism. Even less, shame and a sense of honor.

The three Mexican ecclesiastics appear to be front men. But for whom? An historian of the Indies would say that the devil is in the middle. And in a nice way he would exonerate the ecclesiastical trio of every charge and even three dozens of them. In truth, I insist that nothing in this business seems to be motivated by zeal for the House of God and historical criticism.[43]

Sastre Santos's approach was rather theoretical, and he went into much unnecessary detail. In fact, his entire book is pedantic, verbose, and exhibits an unnecessary display of erudition. He sees two fundamentals in the evangelization of the Indians. The first is the role of the Virgin Mary, which he explains with a rather exaggerated Mariology.[44] The other is the fight against the devil and the idols of the New World.[45] He also rejects the idea that Guadalupe was a conscious substitute for Tonantzin. Like the authors of *El encuentro*, he devotes more space than necessary to the history of the conquest and its background. He attributes the growth of *criollismo* to the declining strength and fervor of the regular orders, especially as manifested in the *peninsular/criollo* conflicts within the mendicants: "*Criollismo* did not need Guadalupe nor to wait till the end of the seventeenth century to burst forth and develop."[46] He accepts the idea that after Guadalupe there was a great increase in conversions and in the growth of the Native church. "Difficult beginnings, the missionaries found the Indians to be cold. After the encounter the faith grew, and the Church needed juntas and councils . . . a growth so precocious that the Council of Trent (1545–1563) considered the Church in the Indies to be capable of receiving the common law."[47]

For his written sources, Sastre Santos went through the list of last wills, such as those of Francisco Verdugo Quetzalmamalitzin and Bartolomé López, and even including the suspect will of Gregoria Martín.[48] Among other documents, he included the confused poem of Luis Angel Betancurt.[49] For all his long discourses on the rules of history, Sastre Santos shows little mastery of the Guadalupan sources. In fact, his interpretation of them, aside from saying nothing new and repeating what is to be found in *El encuentro*, is quite superficial. The same is also true of his treatment of liturgical sources.[50] As with his interpretation of Bernal Díaz and Miles Philips, he believes that any reference to Guadalupe is a confirmation of the apparition story.[51]

Among unwritten documents, he cites the *tilma* as the most important. "If the *tilma* is a picture by the Indian Marcos and the account of the apparition a miracle tale of the seventeenth-century, where did the cultus of the sixteenth century come from? And a 'man of talent,' such as García Icazbalceta, fell into the 'inexplicable mistake' in an historian of advancing 'conjectures'; the Virgin of Guadalupe is the transformation of the Aztec goddess Tonantzin who in the years from 1528 to 1531 also appeared at Tepeyac."[52] Like so many others, Sastre Santos makes the mistake of not distinguishing between the *ermita*/devotion and the apparitions.

Sastre Santos then turns to the archeological evidence. "There exists a program of excavations at the sanctuary and the house of Juan Diego. The first archeological evidence declares Juan Diego to have been an Indian property owner and, therefore, a 'señor,' not a *macegual* [commoner, or peasant]. Tradition makes him a noble, 'poor in spirit.' Let us trust that archeological studies at Tepeyac, already begun, can give us an answer."[53] Again, making Juan Diego a nobleman misses the whole point of the story, and contradicts the *Nican mopohua*. Sastre Santos also puts his faith in the so-called Codex Escalada. So it is with his entire study, which does nothing to confront the strong objections that exist as to the sources used, and which merely repeats what may be found in *El encuentro* and other pro-apparitionist works. Like *El encuentro*, this work, too, is bloated and pedantic.

The other work that Poole received was aimed directly at him. It was titled "Breves observaciones sobre la ciencia de la historia y su método con algunas referencias al libro de Stafford Poole C.M., *Our Lady of Guadalupe . . .*" (Brief Observations on the Science of History and Its Methods, with Some References to the Book of Stafford Poole, C.M., *Our Lady of Guadalupe . . .*). Though the copy Poole received carried no author's name, it was the work of Alfonso Alcalá Alvarado. The apparent purpose of Alcalá's critique was to counteract the impact of Poole's book at the Vatican: "The fundamental thesis of the author [Poole] consists in denying the historical value of the *Nican mopohua*. With this he denies at the same time the historicity of the apparitions of the Virgin Mary, even more than he also rejects the historical value of the tradition. In this way his entire work is marred and in addition to showing a slanted vision of the documents without giving them the necessary stress that historical methodology demands, he remains trapped in the anti-apparitionist outlines of the argument from silence, faithfully following the footsteps of Muñoz and Icazbalceta."[54] Alcalá Alvarado, of course, is mistaken when he says that the denial of the *Nican mopohua* was Poole's fundamental thesis. He also misunderstands, or deliberately ignores, Poole's fine-tuning of the idea of an argument from silence: "Thus, all the studies of the anti-apparitionists seek to know, not if the apparitions really occurred but they only seek to know how the legend originated, how the cultus originated, etc. Poole is no exception."[55]

With regard to the argument from silence, Alcalá Alvarado declares, "It would require first that the author cited [whose silence Poole had noted] had the obligation of mentioning the fact. Just not mentioning something is not an omission or denial."[56] That is true, but Alcalá Alvarado ignores the fact that Poole's book also gives good reasons why a particular author should have or would have been expected to say something—for example, Zumárraga in his will, or the Franciscans of Cuauhtitlán, and Las Casas. Alcalá Alvarado calls "strange" Poole's conclusion that the story of Guadalupe was unknown to the Spaniards and *criollos* of Mexico City before 1648, but he ignores evidence such as the introduction of Laso de la Vega, or the comments of Antonio de Lara, Francisco de Siles, and Antonio de Robles, all of whom bore witness to the fact that, in 1648, the story of the apparitions was something new.[57]

A good part of Alcalá Alvarado's observations are devoted to the historical value of the *Nican mopohua*, about which he makes a rather astonishing statement: "Therefore Poole has no recourse but to maintain that the author of the *Nican mopohua* is the bachelor Laso de la Vega . . . [thereby] falling back on a strange intervention of native helpers skilled in classic Nahuatl who would have corrected Laso's text. . . . I understand that this is a bright idea of Poole's. In my ignorance I had never before heard of this idea."[58] On the contrary, the use of native assistants was a common practice among ecclesiastics, and in some cases the names of these helpers are known. Alcalá Alvarado also says, "Poole has a pejorative opinion of tradition as is indicated by the very title of chapter 8, "It Is a Tradition. Seek No Further."[59] If Alcalá Alvarado had read the chapter carefully, he would have noticed that Poole was not downgrading the importance of tradition, but emphasizing its probative force for ecclesiastics of the seventeenth century. This probative force was so strong that the aphorism "Traditio est, nihil amplius quaeras" (It is a tradition; seek no further) summarizes it totally and dates far back in church history.

Again, it should be emphasized that these two works were submitted to the Congregation as evidence in favor of canonization, without Poole, or any other opponent of the cause, being told of them or being allowed an opportunity to respond to them. The process continued to be as closed as before.

By the middle of the year 2000, it began to appear that the canonization process had slowed, perhaps stalled. Under the headline "Prudencia Vaticana," an article in *Reforma* for May 22 stated that the pope had decided not to canonize Juan Diego along with the others saints that year in order to avoid more scandal. A Vatican official was quoted as saying, "The investigation is valid, but there is no hurry." Guerrero Rosado noted, "This takes away a little of the nationalistic pleasure that the canonization had awakened in us, but Rome does not wish to take sides at a moment of polemic, and we who have faith know that God does things for a reason. . . . Schulenburg's objections are not valid, but the scandal that arose in the media meant that for the moment it would not be convenient to raise Juan Diego to the altars." In contrast, another Vatican official, Archbishop Arturo Szymansky Ramírez, former archbishop of San Luis Potosí, announced in a press conference, "The case of Juan Diego is very advanced, perhaps at the end of the year we may have some news."[60] Despite these mixed signals, it appeared that the cause was in temporary abeyance.

There had been a somewhat unfounded hope in apparitionist circles that the canonization would take place on October 12, 2000, or at least some time before the end of the year. Archbishop Sandoval Iñiguez of Guadalajara expressed that hope during a visit to Rome.[61] In an interview with *El Universal* on September 20, 2000, Archbishop Szymansky Ramírez said that it would be very difficult for the canonization to take place in the last months of 2000.[62] As the person responsible for pursuing the causes of Mexicans for beatification and canonization, the archbishop said that there was no news about Juan Diego. He also refused to speculate as to whether the promotion of Leonardo Sandri to Rome would help the cause. At a farewell for Sandri (who after a very short stay as nuncio was assuming a position in the Secretariat of State), in response to a talk by the archbishop of Guadalajara in which the latter urged the canonization of Juan Diego, Sandri pledged to fight for it with all his might. Three days later, *Excelsior* carried an article in which the Vatican spokesman, Joaquín Navarro Valls, likewise said that the date of October 12 was impossible and that not even a tentative date had been set. "No, I do not have it in the calendar."[63] The same article cited sources in the Congregation for the Causes of the Saints as saying that the essentials of the cause had been concluded in a positive way and that Juan Diego's existence and virtues had been proved.

On June 24, 2001, Father Olimón Nolasco wrote a letter to *Reforma*. He began by saying that his position was based on intellectual and moral honesty and not a desire to play devil's advocate. He had made this clear in an "amplio documento" that was in the hands of Monsignor Bertone, secretary of the Congregation for the Doctrine of the Faith, and Monsignor Bertello, the papal nuncio in Mexico. He said that a previous article in the paper (June 20) was correct in stating that he did not believe that there was sufficient historical evidence for the canonization. In the beatification, the existence of a cult was proven "with pictures and sculptures that not even remotely led to those conclusions. . . . It was enough for Juan Diego to be dressed as a Franciscan to prove his holiness because 'the friars were considered to be saints.'" These "proofs," however, did convince the Roman historical consultants.

My concern is that the credibility of the church shine forth in this case. For that purpose, nothing better than to follow the recommendation of Cardinal Re, when he was the substitute in the Vatican's Secretariat of State, that the historical questions to be clarified should be discussed in full in academic circles. And these are most appropriate in Mexico, where *guadalupanismo* has been studied so much and there is a more respectful and open environment for this study than among Roman experts for whom Mexico is one question among many. I do not believe that the best approach is haste and pressure on Rome and that for "fear of scandalizing" the people it would be necessary to suffer it rather than continue considering them minors in matters of tradition and faith.[64]

The proponents of the canonization, however, were still optimistic. On June 26, 2001, Chávez Sánchez, who had been appointed postulator of the cause in May 2001, had a telephone interview with *Reforma*, during which he stated that "the cause of Juan Diego before the Congregation for the Causes of the Saints follows its normal course, overcoming obstacles."[65] Giving the interview on instructions from the Congregation, Chávez Sánchez, who was also acting as prefect of studies at the Pontificio Colegio Mexicano in Rome, said that the canonization "is well on its way . . . although it cannot be known how much more time will be required or what new challenges could be confronted." He also considered the existence of Juan Diego to be definitively proven. At the beginning of 1998, he had been sent by the archdiocese of Mexico to become part of the commission that was studying the documentary proofs for the existence of Juan Diego. "There are not only manuscripts and codices, but also at the archeological level there exists, for example, the probable home of Juan Diego and to one side is a chapel that was constructed immediately after his death. There are remnants of the house where he was born in Cuauhtitlán and the house he lived in at the time of the apparitions in Tulpetlac."[66]

In July and August of 2001 Monsignor Schulenburg became intensely interested in David Brading's forthcoming book, *Mexican Phoenix*. Schulenburg hoped that its publication would slow any momentum in the campaign for canonization. On August 20, 2001, the Brading book was sent to Rome with a covering letter signed by Olimón Nolasco, Martínez de la Serna, Warnholtz Bustillos, Tena, Poole, Miranda Godínez, and Schulenburg. On October 4, Schulenburg phoned Poole to talk more about Brading's work. The former abbot seemed a little concerned about Brading's position, which, it must be admitted, is difficult to discern at times. He was relieved to be assured that Brading did not believe in the historical existence of Juan Diego as the *vidente*. Schulenburg also said that Chávez Sánchez continued to give interviews, the latest in *El Financiero*, claiming that the cause was going well and that all obstacles had been overcome. The Mexican cardinals were also pressing the case in their visits to Rome, saying that the delay was an insult to the Mexican people.

Pressure in favor of the canonization was coming from other quarters. The rector and canons of the Basilica of Guadalupe wrote to Cardinal Sodano, "We are fully convinced of the historicity of Blessed Juan Diego. . . . For that reason our voice is now directed to His Holiness to ask him humbly for the prompt canonization of Blessed Juan Diego."[67] On October 12, 2001, the bishops of Mexico declared, "The truth of the apparitions of the Most Holy Virgin to Juan Diego on the hill of Tepeyac has been, since the dawn of evangelization until the present, a constant tradition and a deeply-rooted conviction among us Mexican Catholics and not a gratuitous one, but founded on documents of the time, rigorous official investigations in the following century, with persons who had lived side by side with those who were witnesses and participants in the construction of the first *ermita*. . . . We also consider it our duty to make clear that the historicity of the apparitions necessarily includes recognizing that of the seer/spokesman of the Virgin Mary. . . . We express our confidence that his canonization will not be delayed and for that purpose we lift up our prayer."[68]

On October 30, 2001, the Mexican television news program, *El Noticiero*, reported that the Vatican had approved the canonization of Juan Diego and that it would take place some time in 2002.[69] In an interview, Cardinal Rivera Carrera said that the medical and theological commissions of the Congregation for the Causes of the Saints had approved a miracle, one of the prerequisites for canonization. He declared that the process was "going very well," though he gave no date for the canonization. The report went on to say that the pope had been invited to visit Mexico after World Youth Day in Toronto, and that the canonization might take place at that time. There was, however, no corroborative declaration forthcoming from the Vatican. On November 12, Schulenburg called Poole to express his concern over the cardinal's interview. Apparently, the cardinals of the Congregation for the Causes of the Saints were to meet in December 2001. The abbot emeritus wondered what competence they had for deciding an historical fact. If they approved the canonization, they would be turning an *hecho histórico* into an *hecho dog-*

mático. He believed that the person supporting the cause in Rome was the former nuncio, Sandri. Whatever went to the secretary of state ended up with Sandri. Schulenburg believed that Sandri was responsible for blocking a monsignorate for Olimón Nolasco because he did not believe in the apparitions. Schulenburg asked Poole if there were any other North American historians who might write to Rome about the issues involved, especially since it always seemed to be the same persons who were writing to Rome. Poole promised to seek out such an historian.

Shortly thereafter Poole contacted Professor Louise Burkhart, professor of Anthropology and at that time director of the Institute for Mesoamerican Studies at New York University at Albany, asking if she would be willing to send a letter to Rome. Burkhart was a recognized authority on Marian devotion among the Indians and the author of several groundbreaking studies on the Christianization of the Nahuas.[70] On November 1, she replied, "I never intended to step so directly into the controversy, but I've already published my interpretations of all this, so it's not really anything new."[71] In a later communication, she added, "On Juan Diego, well, you know that I'm in your camp even though what the Church does really isn't any of my business. . . . But the reality is more interesting than the legend. Has anyone ever tried to promote Cristóbal of Tlaxcala, the 'child martyr,' as a candidate for, at least, beatification? At least he really existed."[72] Professor Burkhart's letter covered the issues very well. One of her most important points was that if the Guadalupan events had really occurred in 1531, the subsequent history of Marian devotion among the natives would have been entirely different. It would have been genuinely Mexican rather than just borrowings and translations from Europe.

At the end of October 2001, the various news media and wire services carried a declaration by Cardinal Rivera Carrera that the way had been cleared for the canonization. On December 4, Schulenburg, Warnholtz, and Martínez de la Serna, joined by Olimón Nolasco, sent another letter to the Secretariat of State and to Cardinal Sodano, reiterating that the Vatican "is committing a grave error because his existence has not been demonstrated."[73] The letter went on, "We do not wish to provoke useless scandal, we simply wish to avoid diminishing the Church's credibility." Once again, a letter that should have remained confidential was leaked to the press, and the person who made it public was the same Andrea Tornelli (or Tornielli, as his name was given in the newspaper) who had published the letter of September 27, 1999. According to an interview that Tornelli gave to *Reforma*, the most recent letter had caused "not a little commotion." Tornelli predicted that the letter "will have no result," especially because the decision had already been made, and it was only a matter of waiting for the date to be fixed in the next consistory to be celebrated in the Vatican. Tornelli asked, "If Schulenburg has never believed either in the sanctuary or in Juan Diego, why did he not resign twenty years ago?" He also added the irrelevant comment, "It seems to me that he has lived very well, thanks to the sanctuary." He claimed that the signatories brought forth no new information to substantiate their claims, and he cited a lengthy essay by Fidel González Fernández in the *Osservatore Romano* (December 20, 2001). In that essay, González cites the Codex Escalada as evidence. Tornelli also referred to the book *El encuentro* as proof. He said that the Holy See had approved the canonization only after the most rigorous historical examination. The author of the article, however, added, "It must be said, nevertheless, that the promulgation of the canonization of Juan Diego, like that of the founder of Opus Dei, José María Escrivá de Balaguer, has caused a bit of unease in certain ecclesiastical circles that for some years have hoped for the beatification of Monsignor Romero, archbishop of San Salvador, assassinated on the 24th of March 1980."[74]

Guerrero Rosado also anticipated the pope's signing of the decree.[75] Such a decree would open the way to the canonization. The article indicated, however, that "Juan Diego's progress toward the altars has not been easy. It has had to pass through a series of steps which, in turn, encountered obstacles in the declarations concerning his non-existence by the former abbot of Guadalupe, Guillermo Schulenburg." Guerrero Rosado added, "Even with battles and contrary declarations, Juan Diego goes on pointing out the problems and solutions. The detractors are shown that they were mistaken. I suppose that Schulenburg by now ought to realize this." The same article quoted Salazar Salazar as saying that the beatification in 1990 was *aequipolenter*, that is, that it was equivalent to a beatification. "At that time we were told that we could put him on the altars, have a date for his feast day, with cultus, and celebrate a mass in his honor." Salazar Salazar reiterated that Juan Diego had been the nephew of Nezahualcoyotl, that his native name was Cuauhtlatohuac [*sic*], that he was born around 1474 in Cuauhtitlán, but that he had lived his first years in the barrio of San José Milla and then gone to Tlacpac (Santa Cruz el Alto). The latter information, of course, comes from the spurious will of Gregoria Martín.[76]

What actually happened on December 20 was that the pope signed a decree that recognized a miracle for canonization and opened the way for it some time in 2002.[77] Cardinal Saraiva Martins, the prefect of the Congregation for the Causes of the Saints, described Juan Diego as a "Mexican Indian of the sixteenth century, husband and father of a family. His fame is linked to the Virgin of Guadalupe, who appeared to him in 1531. The unexpected meeting with the Mother of God empowered his journey of faith, which began in adult life, and led him to leave his home and dedicate himself to the upkeep of the first Guadalupe chapel." Apparently, the cardinal was unaware of the tradition of Juan Diego's lifelong celibacy. Vatican sources also indicated that in late February or early March the pope would set the date for the canonization.[78]

Another dispatch from Rome gave an account of the miracle approved by the pope.

The miracle, which occurred on May 6, 1990, at the very moment the Holy Father was proclaiming Juan Diego blessed, changed the life of drug addict Juan José Barragán Silva. Barragán, then in his 20s, had been using marijuana for five years. That day, exasperated and under the drug's influence, he stabbed himself with a knife in his mother's presence, and went to a balcony to throw himself over. His mother tried to hold him by the legs, but he managed to free himself and plunged head first to the ground. He then was rushed to the intensive care unit of Durango Hospital in Mexico City. J. H. Hernández Illescas, regarded internationally as one of the best specialists in the field of neurology, and two other specialists described the case as "unheard of, amazing, and inconceivable." Other medical experts who were consulted could not explain the case, given the height of the balcony (10 meters), the youth's weight (70 kilos or 154 pounds), and the angle of impact (70 degrees). Suddenly and inexplicably, three days after the fall, Barragán was completely cured. Subsequent examinations confirmed that he had no neurological or psychic effects, and the doctors concluded that his cure was "scientifically inexplicable." Medical experts say the youth should have died in the fall, or at least been left seriously handicapped. Esperanza, the youth's mother, said that when her son was falling she entrusted him to God and the Virgin of Guadalupe. Invoking Juan Diego, she implored: "Give me a proof . . . save this son of mine! And you, my Mother, listen to Juan Diego."[79]

This is one version of the miracle. Another was that after the young man was taken to the hospital, Doctor Juan Homero Hernández Illescas told his mother that she should pray to Juan Diego for her son's recovery. It should be noted that this same Doctor Hernández Illescas was a witness in the archdiocesan tribunal for Juan Diego's beatification in 1984, when he was described as a physician, university professor, and expert on the stars on the Virgin's robe. He is currently a member of the Centro de Estudios Guadalupanos in Mexico City.

According to Chávez Sánchez, the archdiocese of Mexico began investigating the cure in November 1990.[80] He said that more than fifteen medical specialists analyzed the cure and agreed that there was no rational explanation for it. The Congregation for the Causes of the Saints confirmed the archdiocesan process on November 11, 1994. On February 26, 1998, five medical experts appointed by the Holy See to analyze the cure unanimously approved it as inexplicable by medical science. On May

11, 2001, a commission of theological consultors also unanimously approved the miracle.[81]

The news of the pope's action was reported in media throughout the world, with at least one reporting that the canonization had already taken place. Diego Monroy Ponce, rector of the Basilica, declared, "Not a thousand Guillermo Schulenburgs can prevent the process of the canonization of Juan Diego."[82] He said, however, that there was no resentment against either Schulenburg or those who had questioned Juan Diego's existence. "This goes beyond believing or not believing, the mother is the mother and she unites us." He also made the point that the canonization was a good occasion for society to look at the situation of the Indians "who at the present time suffer the violation of respect for their human dignity." There were two steps, he said, that were still wanting in the canonization: consultation by the pope with the College of Cardinals, and the consistory. Eduardo Chávez Sánchez declared that "the canonization means that God is with us in order to reconstitute our dignity. . . . We are a great people but what is lacking is belief that we are."[83]

While the announcement brought joy to the advocates of canonization, it produced only dismay and shock among Catholic scholars. One Mexican historian wrote to Poole:

I cannot say what my feelings are when seeing Cardinal Rivera using every chance he gets in the media to proclaim the "now confirmed and indisputable historicity" of Juan Diego, and I cannot help feeling sad when I see good, simple people being interviewed in the streets by ignorant journalists and [they] say they're immensely happy because "they" (I suppose they mean the Vatican) have "finally realized" that blessed Juan Diego was a saint. Father, in this I must ask for your opinion not only as a scholar, but also as a Church man. What happens once that Rome has officially approved canonization? Are we supposed to remain silent upon our doubts? Are we expected as historians to stop searching for the truth?[84]

On the same day that the pope signed the approval of the miracle, the official Vatican newspaper, *L'Osservatore Romano*, carried a lengthy article titled "The Virgin of Guadalupe of Mexico and the Indian Juan Diego: Myth, Symbol, or History," apparently authored by Fidel González Fernández.[85] The article was filled with references and citations to different sources, with a special reliance on the *El encuentro* and the Codex Escalada. Superficially, it seemed very authoritative, though most of the proofs it offered would not stand up to serious scrutiny. One outlandish claim was that the Codex contained the "death certificate" of Juan Diego. It also accepted the existence of descendants to Juan Diego, despite the early tradition of his lifelong virginity. Other records for which claims were made have not yet become available to scholars. One example: "A Franciscan convent was built at Cuauhtitlán whose parish registers from

1587 contain numerous entries with the name 'Juan Diego,' a name seldom used elsewhere and here repeated in honour of the visionary." Interestingly, the article made no mention of Miguel Sánchez and his 1648 publication of the apparition story.

On January 21, 2002, Guerrero Rosado was interviewed on Radio Fórmula by the journalist Joaquín López Dóriga. He declared that "if the ex-abbot [*sic*] insists on denying the dogma of Juan Diego, he could be excommunicated because he would be doubting God himself."[86] Here again we see the tendency of defenders of the apparition and Juan Diego to elevate to the level of defined doctrine something that had no basis in reality.

> The ultimate testimony, the definitive one, is no less than that of God. . . . The matter has been examined and super-examined from the human point of view. Reports pro and con have been reviewed. The conclusion was reached that matters were favorable. Nevertheless, the Church even in this way does not decide with an unqualified yes, but it appeals to the most absolutely trustworthy witness, God himself, in the form of a miracle. That in the judgment of the Church it remains clearly demonstrated that it is supernatural and that it is done in favor of canonizing the person who intercedes for him. That has now been done. The matter has been examined for years. There is no turning back.[87]

Olimón Nolasco believed, given the absolute certainty that the matter had been closed on both the historical and theological levels, that no attention would be paid to the sixty-four-page manuscript he sent to the Congregation for the Doctrine of the Faith in July 2001 (another version of that manuscript, titled *La búsqueda de Juan Diego* [The Search for Juan Diego], was published in May 2002). Olimón Nolasco explained, "In the same way, in Rome, the last word has been considered to be [that of] Fidel González's long article published in the *Osservatore Romano*, which has many arguable aspects with regard to the sources, and does not succeed, although it claims to, in proving their convergence in order to establish historicity beyond doubt."[88] Nolasco quoted Modesto Suárez, "The canonization of Juan Diego ought to be a reason for pride for Mexicans, always and when it is done on the basis of historical proofs. Not to do so will thus weaken the figure of the new saint and open the way for the manipulation of his image."[89]

The presumption was that the pope would accept President Vicente Fox's invitation to visit Mexico after World Youth Day in Toronto in July 2002, and would take the opportunity to canonize Juan Diego in the Basilica, even though a Vatican spokesman denied it. Two weeks later, the situation changed. On January 21, Cardinal Rivera Carrera announced that plans were under way for the pope's "possible" visit to Mexico to canonize Juan Diego: "The archbishop primate told the press Sunday that there are two things that could impede the Holy Father's visit: a deterioration of his health or a delay in the canonization. The cardinal said he was confident the pope would make the trip. He also said the Holy Father himself has expressed his determination and desire to visit Mexico for the sole purpose of canonizing Juan Diego, the Indian who witnessed the apparitions of the Virgin of Guadalupe."[90]

In January 2002, Cardinal Roger Etchagaray arrived in Mexico as an envoy from the Vatican, ostensibly to arrange the pope's visit. The cardinal, however, "preferred not to confirm that he would come," saying only that the pope was thinking about the visit. He refused to guarantee that any visit would imply the canonization of Juan Diego because "the process is not yet finished, and it is necessary to see how this final step will develop."[91] Shortly after this interview, Cardinal Rivera Carrera confirmed that the pope had accepted the invitation. On January 24, *Vida Nueva*, the Spanish-language newspaper of the archdiocese of Los Angeles, announced, "The founder of Opus Dei and Juan Diego will become saints in 2002." The accompanying article, however, added the qualification "if the pope ratifies, as is foreseen, the respective decrees of canonization." The pope is "the only one who has the authority to conclude the processes and designate the eventual dates of the celebrations." The article also indicated that Juan Diego had been the focal point of controversy because of doubts over his historical existence. "The Vatican, nevertheless, considers that the 'historical aspect' of the existence of the Indian Juan Diego, to whom the faithful of Mexico attribute numerous miracles, is 'clearly' proved, so that it has gone forward with the canonization." It then added a rather puzzling statement. "His defenders hold to documents such as the chronicle of the period written by Fray Jerónimo de Mendieta, in which he [Mendieta] gives an account of the apparitions of the Virgin to an illiterate native who had scarcely received from the missionaries the rudiments of the Catholic religion." It is unclear what apparition the article is referring to, but Mendieta said nothing about Guadalupe.[92]

At this time, when the date for the canonization had not yet been set, John Allen wrote a summary of the question for the *National Catholic Reporter*.[93] "John Paul II's reforms of the saint-making process, shortening the waiting period and cutting the number of required miracles, have fueled his extraordinary run of beatifications and canonizations: 1,282 and 456, respectively, more than all previous popes combined. With the recent approval of a miracle clearing the way for canonization of Juan Diego, however, some critics say the pope is preparing to waive the most basic requirement of all: historical existence." The article went on to give a good survey of the problems involved and quoted Brading, Chávez Sánchez, and Poole.

A break in the ranks of the proponents of the canonization appeared in early 2002 when Salazar Salazar accused Cardinal Rivera and Diego Monroy, the rector of the Basilica, of trying to sideline him after twenty-two years of service.[94] He had been named postulator in 1979 by Cardinal Corripio y Ahumada and, he claimed, he had not received a single centavo in his work to promote the beatification and canonization. He differed with Chávez Sánchez and Guerrero Rosado in their claim that Juan Diego had been a virgin. Rather, he said, Juan Diego had had nine children by a lawful wife and his descendants were still to be found in Mexico. He said that he had invited Guerrero to be a witness in the *postulaciones*. "I have his answering note: he asked to go to Rome for four years in order to work. And he didn't do a thing." As for Chávez Sánchez, Salazar Salazar said that seven months previously Chávez Sánchez had come to see him to give him the results of his investigation. With these, Chávez Sánchez was able to push for the canonization in Rome. "He knew nothing. I taught him. Doctor Omero [Illescas] and I gave him a résumé of the miracle, we gave him photographs that we had taken. They named him postulator and that was good." Salazar Salazar added, however, "They are working, God bless it, but it is not good for them to say, 'Get out now that I am here.' Not even a thank you. They haven't said anything to me." He said that when he asked to see the cardinal or Monroy, he was always told that it was not possible. He was not sure whether he would even be invited to the canonization mass or whether he would have to watch it at home on television.

In early 2002, newspaper articles and interviews in Mexico City tended to be more favorable to Schulenburg and the opponents of the canonization. Luis Reyes de la Maza described the abbot emeritus's letter of December 4 as "worthy of praise and admiration," and spoke of the right to speak one's opinion as the "inalienable right of every human being in a free country."[95] Somewhat inconsistently, the author added that "the former abbot and the scholars, on the other hand, are in no way denying the miraculous apparitions of the Virgin of Guadalupe . . . but they have only cast doubt on the existence of Juan Diego." Reyes de la Maza expressed his own belief in the reality of Juan Diego. What Schulenburg was opposing, he said, was the fuss about a man "whose existence is lost in the mists of some documents that appeared 130 years after the supposed events." He compared Schulenburg's attitude to that of a politician who denies the leader of his party without denying the party. "To hurl anathemas and even petitions of excommunication for Schulenburg is to go back to the times of obscurantism, when it was demanded of Galileo or a [Miguel] Servetus that they retract their ideas valiantly expressed."

Another article, by Ricardo Becerra, carried the provocative headline, "Long Live Schulenburg."[96] "Schulenburg belongs to a strange breed because of which he looks illustrious: those Catholics who do not want to base their faith on deceit, salesmanship, legends, and mythology. . . . For my part, that is precisely what seems to be inadmissible in the Church: that need to nourish itself on the basis of myths, to make an ideological profit out of ignorance, to leap Olympic-style over the historical evidence, if that is within their power. It does not matter what Schulenburg or the evidence may say, on July 29 [*sic*] the pope is coming to cap his own evangelizing work: he is coming to proclaim as a saint a nonexistent person."

Olimón Nolasco continued his campaign to the very end. In a newspaper interview, he argued "that adding Juan Diego's name to the church's hallowed roster of saints might make millions of Catholics feel good, but his candidacy does not meet the church's rigorous standard of documentation for those it canonizes."[97] He also cast doubt on the miracle of Juan José Barragán because, he said, Hernández Illescas was not an impartial witness. "The doctor wanted to believe that his patient was miraculously cured because of his strong devotion to the Virgin of Guadalupe." Olimón Nolasco stated his belief that Mexicans, both in Mexico and the United States, constituted a strong political force that the church wanted to please. In that same article, Guerrero Rosado was quoted as repeating his belief that the opposition was motivated by racism. "They can't understand how an Indian, who was nothing, could ever have been chosen by God." As proof of Juan Diego's existence, Guerrero Rosado cited the mass conversion of Indians in the early sixteenth century. Indian cultural beliefs, he said, should have made such "conversion to an unknown religion virtually impossible." This, of course, is directly contrary to the Nahuas' well-known penchant for welcoming other gods into their pantheon and easily incorporating the religious beliefs of others. Guerrero Rosado also cited the *Nican mopohua,* "written in the Aztec and Toltec [*sic*] language Nahuatl," noting that "critics have dismissed it as unreliable because it is written in Nahuatl," a claim that is patently untrue.

In a separate interview, Guerrero Rosado also claimed that had it not been for Schulenburg's opposition, Juan Diego would have been canonized without having had to pass through the stage of beatification. He blamed Schulenburg for delaying the cause for at least ten years. But, he added, "Now there is no problem. As far as Rome is concerned, everything has been resolved. The date could be deferred but it [the canonization] has already been approved."[98]

Olimón Nolasco told another interviewer that the danger in the canonization was that the Vatican would eventually have to "de-canonize" Juan Diego, as it had done with Saint George and others. "If a myth or a symbol gets canonized, which is exactly what Pope Paul VI tried to avoid some forty years ago, it would return us to the canonization methods of the Middle Ages."[99] Salazar Salazar, however, speaking to the same reporter, hinted at sinister, even racist motives behind the complaints of anti-apparitionists. He claimed that during the time he worked at the Basilica, Schulenburg had "bragged about his German heritage and refused to accept 'Indian documents' that back[ed] up the story. 'He thought the Indians were below him, that he was more important because he is German. . . . Oh, I'm German,' he would say."[100]

A different accusation of racism was leveled against the proponents of the canonization, specifically in the official portrait of Juan Diego that was circulated by the archdiocese of Mexico. Labeled a "verdadero retrato" (authentic portrait), it had been painted in the eighteenth century by the noted Mexican artist Miguel Cabrera. It depicted Juan Diego with strongly European features and a beard. Francisco Ortiz Pedraza, director of Antropología Física of the Instituto Nacional de Antropología e Historia in Mexico City, considered the portrait racist. "It seems to me that instead of looking like Juan Diego, it looks more like Hernán Cortés. There is racism in this image because it is claimed that he does not have the features of an Indian but has a more mestizo character, weighted more toward the Spaniard." An anthropologist, María Elena Salas, contrasted the portrait with what is known of indigenous physical characteristics, saying that Juan Diego would not have had a beard, would have been shorter, would have had straight, not wavy hair, and that his eyes would have been oval rather than round. The archdiocese had said that the portrait is the oldest known and is the most faithful to what tradition says about Juan Diego. "It may be the oldest picture," replied the anthropologist Elio Masferrer, "but it was done two hundred years after the apparition, and it is not known if it reflects an oral tradition of what Juan Diego was like or the ideologies of the time."[101]

One week before the scheduled meeting of the cardinals of the Congregation for the Causes of the Saints, opponents made a last-ditch effort to stop the canonization. Through the agency of his nephew in San Antonio, Monsignor Schulenburg asked Poole to send personal letters and copies of the article from the *National Catholic Reporter* to Cardinal Martini in Milan and Cardinal Ruini, the vicar of Rome. He also sent e-mail to major newspapers in Italy and the United States. It was, however, too late.

On February 26, 2002, at a solemn liturgy, the pope announced that he would canonize Juan Diego on July 30. The date was later changed to July 31. The Mexican Church set the location of canonization at Ecatepec/Texcoco, anticipating one of the largest outdoor masses in history.[102] Early predictions were that as many of five million people might attend. Bishop Cepeda Silva carried out an intense media campaign to have the ceremony in his diocese, and spoke of "passing round the hat" to collect the tens of millions of dollars needed for the project, including millions of raincoats to protect attendees from the seasonal rainstorms.[103] According to press reports, Rivera Carrera endorsed a plan to pave 2,500 acres of a dried-up lake bed.[104] Eventually, the realization dawned that the logistics involved in such a celebration were insuperable. There were also ecological concerns. The Vatican finally announced that the site did not correspond to the needs of the pope's visit, and the mass was transferred to the Basilica at Guadalupe.

In an interview after the cardinals' decision, Rivera Carrera asserted, "Recent documents confirm not only the existence of Juan Diego but also his fame of holiness."[105] When asked if anyone could still doubt the existence of Juan Diego, he replied, "No one of sound judgment can doubt the existence of Juan Diego because it is proved by a lot of information — for example, a document regarding an investigation carried out in 1666 among people who knew Juan Diego or lived at the same time. These people confirmed that Juan Diego existed and was known for his outstanding holiness. Another decisive element is the recent discovery of the original Codex Escalada of which up to now there existed only copies." The archbishop did not explain where these copies were to be found or why they had not been known before 1995.

Despite the fact that the canonization had been approved and a date set, the controversy did not subside but rather became more heated. In early 2002, British scholars began to be involved. Fernando Cervantes, a highly respected historian at the University of Bristol, wrote an article on the subject for *The Tablet*, an authoritative Catholic journal in Britain.[106] "Writing as a Mexican, a Catholic, and a devotee of Our Lady of Guadalupe, I can only share in the general enthusiasm. But I am dismayed at the decision to go ahead with the canonisation because it seems to ride roughshod over some incontrovertible evidence which, as an historian, I cannot ignore."[107] Cervantes said he had examined the evidence adduced for the authenticity of the apparitions, and that "any attempt to root that account in an earlier local tradition necessarily relies on speculation backed by flimsy evidence or, in the worst of cases, on plain fraud."[108] He referred to the Codex 1548 as "dubious."

This is why the controversies over Juan Diego's historical existence have served only to obscure the fundamental theological truth of the Guadalupe tradition. It is sadly ironic that the decision to go ahead with the canonisation risks falling into the very same trap, that of turning the story into a matter of historical, not spiritual, significance. The decision can only add valuable grist to the mill of the sceptics by implying that what is at stake is a matter of factual rather than spiritual truth. Paradoxically, the persistent and no doubt well-intentioned attempts to prove the existence of Juan Diego, despite the clear absence of reliable evidence, reveal a lack of faith in the devotion as it has developed over the past five centuries.[109]

He concluded, "By the Congregation's own scientific standards, Juan Diego fails to meet the requirement of historicity. It might well be that new evidence has emerged; but if this is not the case, and if the current *Positio* repeats the flimsy and distorted arguments used to support the 1990 beatification, the Vatican risks doing great damage: both to the credibility of the canonisation process and to the true nature of the Guadalupe devotion itself."[110]

Brading joined the discussion with a letter to the same journal, raising the issue that had so bothered Schulenburg: "The forthcoming canonisation of the Mexican Indian, Juan Diego, will constitute an unprecedented and disconcerting exercise of papal infallibility."[111] Like Cervantes, he was critical of the procedures that had been followed. "The Congregation for the Causes of Saints has thus chosen not to apply the normal rules governing historical evidence and apparently failed to acknowledge that the story of Juan Diego and the Virgin Mary is a sublime parable, a foundation myth, a Mexican gospel, a private revelation." He then went on to give an apt and concise summary of the entire historical question: "To canonise Juan Diego makes as much sense, and as little, as to canonise the Good Samaritan." He concluded by returning to his original question, "Should not theologians reflect on the implications of this case for the doctrine of papal infallibility in the canonisation of saints?" Brading's argument was remarkably similar to what Schulenburg had originally expressed in his interview in *Ixtus*. Brading's question brought an immediate response. Sir Michael Dummet of Oxford wrote, "If canonisation were an infallible act, what would be the content of the truth so guaranteed? That the person canonised had been martyred for the faith, or had displayed heroic virtue? Or that his or her soul is now in heaven? Canonisation is in fact a liturgical authorisation of the celebration of the feast of the new saint, the inclusion of his or her name in a litany, etc. Any tendency to represent it as an infallible declaration is a doctrinally indefensible instance of creeping infallibility."[112] Richard McBrien, a well-known theologian at Notre Dame University, also wrote to demonstrate that canonizations were not acts of infallibility and that the Church had never taught that.[113]

At about the same time, the Mexican magazine *Nexos* ran a series of articles under the heading "La cruzada por Juan Diego" (The Crusade for

Juan Diego).[114] The authors were Brading, González de Alba, Antonio Annino, and Olimón Nolasco. Brading's contributions were adapted from his book *Mexican Phoenix*, as was a chronology of Guadalupan history drawn up by the editors. In a somewhat polemical article, González de Alba gave a brief survey of the Guadalupe controversy and then sought to deconstruct the "miracle" of young Barragán.[115] Relying on the assurance of an unnamed neurologist with thirty years of experience, he wrote "The patients could get well, with or without divine intention, because ten of every 100 skull fractures heal spontaneously."[116] He then stated, "The doctor [Illescas] bet and won. He lost nothing: if the patient had died, it would not have been a proof against the existence of Juan Diego; if chance and the good health of the young man cured him, he then had the miracle for the canonization. That is the logic that produced 'miracles.'"[117] González de Alba then gave an indirect defense of the abbot emeritus of Guadalupe. "The media's harassment has, once again, turned against Abbot Guillermo Schulenburg. No television program, no newspaper shows us the homes of Archbishop Norberto Rivera, nor tells us how many automobiles he has. No one wants to remember when he injured a bothersome reporter with a blow of a walking stick. Between a flood of violence and sex, the television programs beat their breasts, bring out file footage of the pope before the Virgin, and depict the life-term abbot of the Basilica as the villain in a television serial."[118]

The most interesting article was Olimón Nolasco's.[119] One of his concerns was "the authoritarianism latent in certain areas of Mexican culture" despite the declarations of the Second Vatican Council. He then when on to quote two authorities. The first was Bernardo Barranco, who wrote: "It is clear that behind [a] false polemic is not the existence of Juan Diego but the appropriation of what the Indian represents for church and society. There are commercial and political interests in the media for the symbolic representation of Juan Diego . . . the one who is born excluded . . . who never says 'no' and will always speak in diminutives. . . . On the other side, there is the native as the subject of rights and a true social actor, whose dignity begins with respect for his cultural and religious identity."[120] The other quotation was from Carlos Martínez Assad: "The problem to clear up is . . . why the haste for canonization if for believers the bureaucratic procedure is unnecessary and in the imaging the apparition is indissolubly linked to the Virgin who grants grace to the Mexican Indian. Perhaps the rehabilitation of the ancient peoples of Mexico may come, according to the church, through the cause of Juan Diego. But what is not explained is why, to achieve it, Schulenburg had to be pointed out as if the Inquisition were on the point of burning him at the stake."[121]

With regard to the leaked letter of December 4, 2001, Olimón Nolasco quoted Javier Lozano Barragán:

Their position is absolutely false. Because [Juan Diego's] existence is absolutely proven. Those gentlemen keep on in the same way, even though they have no reason to. They have already come here to Rome and were at the Congregation for the Doctrine of the Faith, and there they were told to present their arguments to the Congregation for the Saints. They did nothing in this regard, but this Congregation set up a special team that studied the case in depth and gave its report. . . . For the rest, the Inquisition no longer exists.[122]

Olimón Nolasco also pointed out that in October 2002 he had gone to Rome to present in person the case against canonization. He was received by two priests at the Congregation for the Doctrine of the Faith on October 13. They suggested that he speak with Gumpel and González Fernández. The occurrence of the interview and what had been discussed had been leaked to Lozano Barragán in Rome, who mentioned it in two articles, one in *Novedades*, the other in *Excelsior*, both published on January 23, 2002. "What was said by Lozano could not have been known, except that my conversation in the ambit of the secrecy of the processes that guarantee the freedom to approach the Holy See in the most serious cases was revealed in writing or verbally."[123]

In January 2002, Poole contacted the editors of the influential Jesuit magazine *America* to see if they would be interested in publishing an article on the canonization. When they answered affirmatively, he prepared an article, "History vs. Juan Diego," which was accepted for publication.[124] However, on April 8, 2002, he received an e-mail from the editor saying that there had been a change of mind. The editors believed that in view of the current atmosphere in the church it would not be wise to publish an article that was critical of the Vatican, especially where the question of infallibility might be involved. But they had contacted the editors of *Commonweal*, a respected Catholic lay journal, who had agreed to publish the article. In his reply to the Jesuit editor, Father Poole said that their decision said more about the atmosphere in the church than did his article, which eventually appeared in *Commonweal* (June 14, 2002) under the title "Did Juan Diego Exist?"

The canonization of Juan Diego finally took place in the Basilica of Guadalupe on July 30, 2002. Thousands of people thronged the streets to follow the pope's journey to the Basilica, and their enthusiasm was genuine and moving. Millions more watched on television. The ceremony itself incorporated many indigenous elements, both because of Juan Diego's ethnicity and as a sign of inclusiveness. There is no doubt that the canonization touched a chord in the hearts of millions of Mexicans. There was, however, one significant absence. The subject of Juan Diego's miracle, Juan José Barragán Silva, was nowhere to be seen.[125] One might have expected that he not only would have been invited to attend the ceremony, but that he also might have been asked to participate — for example, by bringing up the gifts to the pope. There was no word of explanation for his absence, and so it will remain another one of the many mysteries surrounding the canonization of Mexico's first Indian saint.

CHAPTER EIGHT

A Sign of Contradiction

❖

The Guadalupan controversy in Mexico has centered on questions of documentation, proof, and evidence for a devotion that from its beginning was identified with *criollismo* or incipient Mexican nationalism. The nineteenth- and twentieth-century stages of the controversy revealed a deep conceptual and religious division within the Mexican Church and nation. Any criticism of Guadalupe was seen as an attack on *mexicanidad*, as some defined it. Neither side gave the other credit for good faith. It has also caused a great deal of harm, both personal and institutional. One is truly unprepared for the level of invective and virulence to be found in the later stages of the controversy, including the present day.

From the publication of Miguel Sánchez's *Imagen de la Virgen Maria* in 1648, proponents of the apparition devotion had to face the problem of the lack of contemporary documentation in support of the account. Sánchez himself was the first to acknowledge this lack of written evidence, and Laso de la Vega, in his Nahuatl version of the story of the apparitions, confirmed it: "But a great deal has been left out [of this account], which time has erased and no one at all remembers any more, because the ancients did not take care to write it down when it happened."[1] The difficulties were implicit in subsequent sermons and histories, and can be deduced from the efforts at finding proof for the Guadalupan account.

The first recourse that apologists had was to the concept of tradition. In place of documentary evidence, they claimed that the story of the apparitions had been handed down from generation to generation until finally put into written form. It was a potent argument. It is this concept of tradition that explains the capitular inquiry of 1666, which was not, as sometimes claimed, an investigation into the historic truth or falsity of the apparitions and miraculous origin of the image. The historicity of both the apparitions and the image was fully accepted by the persons carrying out the inquiry. Their objective was to accumulate evidence that would persuade Rome to grant a proper mass and office. In the absence of written records, they appealed to tradition. The formulae followed by the witnesses, especially in their assertion that the event was public knowledge and that there had never been any contradiction of it, was a standard way of proving the existence of a tradition.[2] Luis Becerra Tanco followed this line of argumentation very closely, and developed his own list of witnesses who could testify to the existence of the tradition. This argument is still being used today.

Early in the history of Guadalupe, apologists fell back on a second argument, that of the image itself, which, in its beauty and perfection, as well as its preservation, bears witness to the truth of the apparitions. They pointed out how the image had survived in the humid and salty atmosphere of Tepeyac. It was this argument that led to the inspections of the image that took place in the seventeenth and eighteenth centuries. Usually, the persons who performed the inspections were painters or experts in the art of painting, along with ecclesiastics. The first two such inspections took place in conjunction with the capitular inquiry, that is, on March 11–13 and 28, 1666.[3] In the following century there was a renewed effort to secure the proper liturgical texts, which led to a second inspection of the image, beginning on April 30, 1751. In 1787, there was a third inspection, done at the initiative of José Ignacio Bartolache. This was carried out by five painters, including Miguel Cabrera, in the presence of the abbot of Guadalupe and one canon from the Collegiate chapter. This was the first inspection to note the retouchings on the *tilma*. On October 22, 1795, Conde y Oquendo and the painter José de Alcíbar conducted yet another examination, in part to refute what they considered errors by Bartolache. The only other serious inspection of the *tilma* by experts was that conducted in 1982, under the auspices of Abbot Schulenburg, when the image was moved from the old to the new Basilica. This inspection revealed both damage and deterioration, and steps were taken to preserve the *tilma* against the effects of time. The results of this inspection dealt a serious blow to the claim of the image's miraculous origin and survival. Both the archbishop of Mexico and the Vatican were aware of these findings at the time of Juan Diego's canonization.

The third argument that apologists used was that Rome's approval of the devotion, including the granting of proper offices and the beatification and canonization of Juan Diego, confirmed the historicity of the account. This argument has two aspects. The first is that the care taken by the church to verify the historical truth of the apparitions was sufficient basis for any Catholic to accept them. This was the stance taken by Esteban Antícoli, who claimed that the three approvals by the Holy See — the mass and office, the institution of December 12 as a holy day of obligation, and the confirmation of the oath of the *patronato* in 1754 — would not have been done without an historical foundation. The historical apparatus of the Vatican was deserving of trust. The authors of *El encuentro* followed Antícoli in this argument: "The Holy See never beatifies or canonizes a symbol, but persons, real persons, human beings who faced problems like any human being, with capacities and limitations like any other human being."[4] And again, "The judgment rendered by the Holy See deserves our absolute confidence, and on that basis one can be sure that the beatification of Juan Diego was totally real, that it was not a question of a symbol but of a person as real as the rest of us, and that his process did not suffer from any irregularity."[5] Chávez Sánchez asserted, "The work of the Congregation for the Causes of the Saints is in the highest degree professional, the greatest specialists in the material work there; those who carry out every process in a meticulous and detailed way leave no doubt unresolved, no question unanswered."[6] From the point of view of the advocates of canonization and the Congregation for the Causes of the Saints, this last statement is true. By their standards, the cause was moving forward just as it ought to. By more objective criteria, however, it suffered from great irregularities. The second aspect of argument went further, by asserting the church's authority to pass judgment on an historical fact, to declare it to be true or false, turning an historic fact (*hecho histórico*) into a dogmatic one (*hecho dogmático*). Thus, it became unlawful to question the apparitions or the existence of Juan Diego, despite the fact that neither of these was in any sense a dogma of the church. Papal authority was substituted for historical analysis.

Despite the plethora of clear statements that there was no documentary evidence in support of the apparition story, from an early date attempts have been made to prove the opposite. Out of this emerged the mysterious and now unknown *Relación* in Nahuatl of the seventeenth century, a document that was seen only by one or at most two persons but does not exist today. This account came to be identified with the *Nican mopohua*, and with the tangled story of the latter as a nearly contemporaneous account of the apparitions authored by Antonio Valeriano. The search for documentation also led to the acceptance of such dubious or clearly false documents as the wills of Cuauhtitlán.[7] In this search, *guadalupanos* have also cited the various wills or testaments that mentioned Guadalupe, even though these made no mention of the apparitions. In recent times, it has led to the acceptance of the so-called Códice

1548, or Codex Escalada, despite serious questions about that document's authenticity. It is probably no exaggeration to say that a great part of the controversy has been devoted to arguments over the probative force of various documents. Apologists for the apparition found themselves in the contradictory position of admitting that there were no corroborating documents and at the same time accepting some of them.

In view of all this, it is not surprising that the concept and practice of scientific history has generally been considered inimical to Guadalupe. At three different stages in the controversy — the eighteenth century, the last quarter of the nineteenth century, and the last two decades of the twentieth — the *guadalupanos* have felt that the devotion was threatened by the advance of rational, scientific historical criticism. This was one aspect of a general feeling that was shared by church authorities and others concerning history and scriptural studies.

In the eighteenth century, the threat came from the Enlightenment. A new school of Catholic historiography, represented by the Benedictines of Saint-Maur, the Jesuit Bollandists, and the Spanish Benedictine Benito Feijóo, sought to apply stricter historical standards to history. This was especially true with regard to popular devotions and practices. To those who continued to cling to the Baroque approach to history, this new approach represented a mockery of piety and an attack on religion itself. In the Guadalupan controversy, the major representative of the new approach was Juan Bautista Muñoz, whose name has been anathema to *guadalupanos* for more than two hundred years. In many ways, scientific history was considered an even greater threat in the late nineteenth century. Church leaders felt threatened by many aspects of contemporary thought, including that which was to be found within the church. The pontificate of Pius IX was marked by the triumph of ultramontanism and by an ecclesiology of the "fortress church" withstanding the onslaught of rationalism and irreligion. Scholarly endeavors, whether in theology, scripture, or history, were supposed to be subordinate to and dependent on the ordinary teaching authority of the church. This authority was at times notoriously non-historical and highly scholastic in its approach. Antícoli was an extreme example of this type of thinking.

It was against this background, as well as that of hostilities and tensions between church and state in Mexico, that the controversy was fought out at the end of the nineteenth century. In fact, Guadalupe seems to have been merely the surface manifestation of deeper divisions and animosities that existed within and between church and state at that time. Also in the background was a move toward a rapprochement between the Díaz regime and the Vatican. Thus, this phase of the story is convoluted in the extreme: the controversy over García Icazbalceta's letter, the petition for a new office and mass, the coronation, the controversies surrounding Antonio Plancarte, and the fall of Sánchez Camacho.

This stage of the controversy also coincided with changes in the Mexican church hierarchy. A new generation of bishops was emerging, many of them alumni of the Colegio Pío Latinoamericano, which was strongly under Rome's influence and generally ultramontane in its thinking. New dioceses were erected. The bishops conducted synods and provincial councils. Yet, at the same time, there were many problems within the Mexican Church. The level of the clergy does not seem to have been high. Bishops tended to come from similar backgrounds and to follow similar career patterns. They were sometimes related, as is witnessed by the numerous members of the Plancarte family or the Camacho García brothers. A position as abbot or canon of the chapter of Guadalupe was often a stepping-stone to higher office. The Vatican was concerned both about the level of the clergy and the seeming independence of the Cathedral chapters and the hierarchy. Sánchez Camacho was the most extreme of these problems. The Averardi *visita* was one outcome of this concern, but in the end it was a failure.

For Averardi, the visitation and his rather obvious missteps and failures spelled the end of his diplomatic career. Rome apparently held him responsible for provoking Sánchez Camacho. Averardi had a tendency toward self-pity and self-dramatization and sought to avoid blame as much as possible. He was up against a difficult situation in the local church, but he did not seem to have had the savoir-faire to handle it. He gave the impression at times of relying more on Díaz, or getting more support from him, than from the bishops. He had a low opinion of Mexicans and the Mexican Church, of which he painted a dismal picture. He was impulsive in some of his actions, and his relationships with the bishops were uneven.

In all probability Sánchez Camacho was mentally unbalanced, alcoholic, and unstable. He could swing from amiable submission to spiteful rebellion. All of this raises the question of how he managed to become a priest, much less a bishop — and what role Montes de Oca or Loza de Pardavé played in his advancement. His was a problem that should have been handled at the local level. No one anticipated that he would formally break with the church, resulting in an enormous scandal throughout Mexico.

Antonio Plancarte Labastida is often considered the "martyr" of the coronation process, but he was not without blame.[8] He seems to have had an elastic conscience, or at least to have been careless, in his handling of money and in his relationships with young girls. He certainly had a gift for making enemies. His own bishop harbored a deep dislike of him, as

did the diocesan curia of Zamora. It cannot be said that the Vatican handled his case well, especially in the last-minute cancellation of his ordination as bishop. At the present time there is a move to beatify and canonize Plancarte. It is to be hoped that careful historical studies will be made
before such an event. He is a figure who needs to be studied without ran-
cor or partisanship.

If there was a true "martyr" in the second stage of the controversy, it
was Joaquín García Icazbalceta. The unjustified opprobrium that was
heaped on him, first because of his silence about Guadalupe and then because of his letter, brought him deep discouragement. That it also turned
him away from further historical studies was a tragedy for the church in
Mexico and for the Mexican nation itself. He was a man caught in the
middle. One cannot help but wonder if the intense emotional pressure of
the controversy did not contribute to his sudden and untimely death.

One cannot think of García Icazbalceta's difficulties without turning a
harsh glance on Esteban Antícoli. The man was clearly a fanatic. He was
also reckless and cruel. He approached the question of Guadalupe from
a narrowly nationalistic and theological focus. He had an exaggerated
concept of papal and episcopal power, and his ecclesiology reduced the
church to an absolutist and authoritarian regime. In general, his conduct
was reprehensible and cannot be justified.[9] It scarcely seems credible that
Antícoli could have done what he did without at least the tacit approval
of his local superiors or the support of the Mexican bishops, despite the
disapproval expressed in Rome. Similarly, it is difficult to extenuate the
actions and attitudes of some of these bishops, such as Sabás Camacho or
Verea y González. On the basis of his own writings, there is reason to suspect that Antícoli was a disturbed personality, a factor that would dimin-
ish his culpability. It would not do the same, however, for the bishops
who supported him and subsidized his publications, nor for his superiors,
who failed to moderate his extremism.

The more recent phase of the controversy is of a piece with the earlier
one. There are striking similarities in the arguments, the personal attacks,
and the maneuvers of the more recent actors. As in the nineteenth century,
there has been an unbecoming, even scandalous, spectacle of clerical name-
calling and slurs, all of which have been reported in the media. A Jesuit,
Father José Romero, was quoted as saying of the anti-apparitionists,
"Their names have passed into history like a black stain which no one
and nothing will be able to erase."[10] For many *guadalupanos* the historical truth of the apparitions and the devotion has reached the level of official Catholic dogma. García Icazbalceta, a conservative and devout
Catholic, nevertheless found himself accused of heresy merely for failing
to mention Guadalupe in his biography of Archbishop Zumárraga.

Antícoli said that anyone who denied the apparitions was objectively a heretic: "If such a one denies the competence of the Roman Pontiff in judging about the historical fact linked with the cultus, [then] the extent of the Church's magisterium is limited."[11] Sánchez Camacho accused Melesio de J. Vázquez of comparing Guadalupe to the dogma of the Immaculate Conception, and Bishop Carrillo y Ancona of confusing it with a dogma of the church. Salazar Salazar accused Schulenburg of heresy because his ideas were contrary to what the pope was teaching, despite the fact that the pope had never made a dogmatic statement about the authenticity of Guadalupe. Cardinal Rivera Carrera asserted publicly that by opposing the canonization and doubting Guadalupe Schulenburg was excommunicating himself from the church, a statement that was clearly untrue. Guerrero Rosado asserted that "any Catholic who does not believe in the existence of the Indian Juan Diego has until July 31 to publish or express it out loud. . . . From the canonization Mass onward, anyone who casts doubt on the authenticity of the saint will excommunicate himself."[12] That statement is patently ridiculous.

From the 1980s onward, certain assertions about Guadalupe have been formulated, canonized, and popularized. Many of them are particularly widespread among contemporary Catholic theologians and devotional writers. Though it is probably no exaggeration to say that today these are essential to the thought and argumentation of apparitionists, none of them stands up under serious historical scrutiny.

The first of these assertions is that the destruction caused by the Spanish conquest was total and complete; that the native peoples were left desolate and in despair; that their lands, customs, languages, and even proper names were stolen from them by the conquerors; and that hence the Spanish conquest was an act of physical and cultural genocide. As shown in an earlier chapter, Virgil Elizondo has been one of the foremost proponents of this view: "Virgilio Elizondo contends that only a divine intervention could have turned around the devastation caused by the conquest."[13] The experience of Mexican history is rooted in oppression, and localized religion is a response to this oppression. The modern Mexican male is the descendant of the prototypical violated native woman, *la chingada*, and this image has formed his whole mentality. Carlos Fuentes has given a good summary of this position.

In early December 1531, on Tepeyac Hill near Mexico City, a site previously dedicated to the worship of the Aztec goddess Tonantzin, the Virgin of Guadalupe appeared, bearing roses in winter and choosing a lowly *tameme*, or Indian bearer, Juan Diego, as the object of her love and recognition.[14] In one fabulous stroke, the Spanish authorities transformed the Indian people from children of violated women to children of the pure Virgin. From Babylon to Bethlehem, in one flash of political genius, whore became virgin and Malinche became Guadalupe. Nothing has proved as consoling, unifying, and worthy of fierce respect since then as the figure of the Virgin of Guadalupe in Mexico. . . . The conquered people now had a mother.[15]

La Malinche, Cortés's mistress and interpreter, becomes the symbol of the violated woman who betrays her people to the foreign invader. "It was through active volition on her part — sexual transgression — that she became the violated mother who then symbolically gave birth to her illegitimate child — the Mexican people. She was the beginning of the mestizo nation, its mother — she initiated it with the birth of her mestizo children. . . . Malinche thus emerges as an infamous emblem of female transgression and treachery."[16] On the other hand, contemporary research by serious and respected historians has shown that this image was not so simplistic nor the process so steady or ongoing. As Lockhart observed, "Absolutely unaltered survival and total displacement are equally rare in the history of cultural contact in central Mexico."[17]

In contrast, contemporary research, especially into native-language documents, has shown that both the Spanish conquest and the missionary enterprise took place sporadically and unevenly. The conquest was violent, bloody, and destructive in many areas, but there were parts of New Spain that never saw a conquistador and peoples whose first contact with Spaniards was with missionaries and tribute collectors. The progress of the missionary endeavor was uneven.[18] "The general impression is of an unhurried process tending ultimately toward universal baptism but not bringing about large attitudinal change at any one time."[19] In many parts of Mexico the natives never experienced the spiritual destitution so vividly described by apparitionists.

A second commonly accepted assertion is that Tepeyac was a pre-Hispanic site sacred to Tonantzin, mother-goddess of the Mexica (Aztecs). By an act of conscious syncretism (or, perhaps, by divine intervention), the Virgin of Guadalupe was substituted for Tonantzin. This provided a sense of continuity between the indigenous past and the post-conquest present. It also undid the total destruction caused by the Spanish conquest. It gave Mexicans a mother figure who was not *chingada* but simultaneously Virgin and Mother. Guadalupe united all ethnic and social groups into one people. It is the only principle of unity in an otherwise divided nation, *mexicanidad*. "Without Guadalupe we would cease to be Mexicans." Yet the evidence for this pre-Hispanic cult is weak, as is the evidence for any conscious syncretism.

A third assertion is that there was a mass conversion of the natives in the aftermath of the apparitions in 1531. Mexicans flocked to a new mother who consoled them in their desperate condition. "Am I, your mother, not here? Are you not under my protective shade, my shadow? Am I not your happiness? Are you not in the security of my lapfold, in my carrying gear?"[20] This is an essential element in much contemporary thinking. According to one theory, a great religious or spiritual event of uncertain nature took place in 1531, which led to the mass conversion of the natives and which was later formulated in the terms of the apparition narrative. The legend continues in full flower to the present day. "Also, we know that with the apparition of Mary on the hill of Tepeyac there began in all the former Aztec territory an exceptional movement of conversions that extended to all Central North America and reached even the distant archipelago of the Philippines."[21] This assertion was repeated by Fidel González Fernández even after the canonization; in an interview, he declared that millions of Indians converted to Christianity after the apparitions.[22] The flaw in this argumentation, of course, is that there is no evidence of any such mass conversion. Rather, the picture is one of a gradual and sporadic process of evangelization. Much of this thinking is based on the inflated claims made by the early missionary friars in their attempts to impress the Spanish crown with the success, and necessity, of their efforts in the New World. Despite the findings of contemporary research, this claim shows no signs of fading away.

A fourth claim is that even if Juan Diego and the apparitions never existed, he and Guadalupe nevertheless acted as symbols or instruments of evangelization in the early days of the missionary enterprise. Hence, the historical reality or unreality of Juan Diego and Guadalupe are irrelevant. The real truth is theological and personal, that is, what people believe and what difference it makes in their lives. Again, the difficulty with such an assertion is that it does not fit with the known evidence. At the very beginning of the "spiritual conquest," a conscious decision was made to evangelize the native peoples in their own languages. The result was the production of hundreds, perhaps thousands, of books, chronicles, sermonaries, confessional manuals, catechisms, and even sacred dramas written in the indigenous tongues, yet up until 1648 there was not a single mention of Juan Diego or the story of the apparitions. If, indeed, the Virgin Mary had appeared to Juan Diego at Tepeyac in 1531, the entire history of Marian devotion among the natives would have been different, something native rather than an importation and translation of a Spanish original.

The contemporary controversy over the beatification and canonization of Juan Diego raises a number of important issues, among which are the following:

There are serious doubts about the historical existence of Juan Diego. Although those opposing the canonization would have preferred to see it stopped altogether, they also sought to have the process slowed down until the question of Juan Diego's existence could be seriously studied by historians on both sides. The studies that were done in the process of beatification and canonization were not of a caliber to remove these doubts.

What is actually known about the life and person of Juan Diego? What are the sources? The information is scanty and contradictory. Miguel Sánchez said only that Juan Diego was a recently converted Indian.[23] Laso de la Vega went into more detail, saying that he was a commoner (*macehualli*), a lowly commoner (*macehuatzintli*) who was said to have been a homeowner (*chane*) or resident of Cuauhtitlán. His wife, whose name was María Lucía, died two years before the apparitions. According to Laso de la Vega, Juan Diego and his wife, upon hearing a sermon by Fray Toribio de Motolinía on how pleasing celibacy was to God, resolved to live in chastity for the rest of their lives. Yet, inconsistently, Laso de la Vega also affirmed that both were lifelong virgins. "His wife died a virgin. He too lived as a virgin; he never knew a woman."[24] Juan Diego was also said to have had an uncle named Juan Bernardino. Laso de la Vega also reported that Juan Diego lived out the last sixteen years of his life at the sanctuary of Tepeyac, where he led a life of penance and prayer. He died in 1548 at the age of seventy-four.[25] In contrast, Becerra Tanco asserted that Juan Diego was a native of Cuauhtitlán but resided in Tolpetlac. His wife was alive at the time of the apparitions and died two years after them. Their celibate marriage was a well-known fact. They began to observe celibacy after their baptism.[26] Witnesses at the capitular inquiry of 1666 testified that Juan Diego had lived in the barrio of Tlayac or Tlayacac (which today cannot be identified). His wife was María Lucía and his uncle Juan Bernardino. He was fifty-five or fifty-six at the time of the apparitions. He was a holy person whose prayers other Indians often sought, especially for good weather and good harvests. Florencia quoted the mysterious Nahuatl *Relación*, which said that Juan Diego's wife, whose name was given as María Luisa, died two years before the apparitions. They had no children because they had always observed celibacy. On the other hand, Florencia also believed that Juan Diego had descendants and gave a number of convoluted explanations as to how this was possible.[27] A now unknown will, cited by Boturini Benaduci, supported the assertion of a celibate marriage.[28] Clavigero, on the other hand, said that Juan Diego and his wife decided to live celibately after they were married. The wife, María Lucía, died in 1534, three years after the apparitions.[29] Juan Diego's native name was Cuauhtlahtoatzin, a claim that came very late in the history of Guadalupe.[30] The so-called will of Gregoria María, a most unreliable source, said that Juan Diego grew up in the barrio of San José Millán, but was married in Santa Cruz Tlapac. His wife, who died soon after the marriage, was named Malintzin. The apparitions took place soon after her death. Juan Diego was a young man at the time.[31] The major inconsistencies in these accounts are the nature of the celibate marriage, Juan Diego's age at the time of the apparitions, whether María Lucía (or María Luisa) died before or after the apparitions, and whether the couple had any issue. None of these inconsistencies was ever directly addressed by the Congregation for the Causes of the Saints.

In the twenty or so years prior to the canonization, even more outlandish and unsupportable claims about Juan Diego were made — or invented: that he was a Chichimeca, a leader (*principal*) of his village, that he was descended from the royal house of Texcoco, that he had had two wives before his conversion, that he had fought against the Spaniards, that he was a poet and philosopher, and that his numerous descendants are alive in Mexico today. The claim is also made that it was Juan Diego's high-born status that gave his message credence among the Indians. There is no proof for any of these assertions, all of which seem to have been made up out of whole cloth. Further, they miss the central point of all apparition stories — that Mary comes to the poor, the helpless, the marginalized in society.

The focus of the Guadalupe devotion is the Virgin Mary, not Juan Diego. Traditionally, the seer, or *vidente*, in an apparition account is not the object of cult. He/she is merely an intermediary for a heavenly message. This has changed in recent times, and the holiness of the visionary is now considered a guarantee of the authenticity of the message.

Some opponents of Juan Diego's canonization believed that it would be an infallible, or at least authoritative, act of the pope. This presents a problem of conscience for some, although there is no good reason for accepting this opinion, which owes more to the speculations of neoscholastic theologians than to authentic Catholic tradition.

The move toward canonization did not arise from the spontaneous devotion of the people but rather from the church hierarchy, who then enlisted the people in their cause. The people of Mexico enthusiastically embraced the cause of canonization, but it was not their initiative that gave rise to that cause.

The case of Juan Diego is not comparable to popular canonizations of the past, including those personages who were eventually removed from the calendar of saints, such as Saint Christopher or Saint George. In earlier times, there was no set process for canonizations, which were often the result of popular acclamation or haste (as in the cases of Francis of Assisi and Thomas Beckett, who were canonized within two to three years after their deaths). Some of these saints were later removed from the calendar, not "decanonized" as some claim, because of doubts about their historical existence. The case of Juan Diego is different. He is not a figure of tradition, myth, or legend, like some famous religious or civic personalities of the past. Comparisons are sometimes made with Alexander the Great, Buddha, Christ, and various saints around whom legends and stories grew up, without their ceasing to be historical figures. On the contrary Juan Diego is a pious fiction, a figure out of literature who has no more historic reality than Captain Ahab or Sherlock Holmes. Brading phrased it best when he compared canonizing Juan Diego to canonizing the Good Samaritan.

The haste in seeking the canonization of Juan Diego after his beatification was inappropriate. Normally there is a longer waiting period, which in previous times was at least twenty-five years. In Juan Diego's case, much could have been gained by more prudence and caution rather as opposed to the rapidity with which his elevation to sainthood was carried out.

The dubious nature of the "miracle" approved by the pope, which provided the basis for moving forward with Juan Diego's canonization, required far more serious consideration. The virtual disappearance of Juan José Barragán Silva raises further disturbing questions about the whole affair.

The flawed procedures followed in the process of both beatification and canonization reflect little credit on the Congregation for the Causes of the Saints. One fundamental defect was that the sponsoring parties had far too much control over the progress of the cause. They called only the witnesses they wanted, guaranteeing that only favorable voices were heard. Chávez Sánchez totally misstated the case when he wrote, "We all know the doubts and speculations that Monsignor Schulenburg and a group of persons have transmitted, although not in the normal way that should be followed in these cases."[32] Those opposed to the canonization had no recourse but to send private letters to the Vatican to express their opinions, and on two occasions such letters were leaked to the press. The result was an uproar in Mexico and the further demonizing of Schulenburg. These letters were seldom, if ever, acknowledged by the Congregation, and because of the secrecy of the process there was no way of knowing what their impact was.

Not unexpectedly, one of the paramount defenders of the Congregation and its consultors was the archbishop of Mexico, Norberto Carrera Rivera. In his pastoral letter of June 2, 1996, he gave thanks for the "doubts that, centuries later, you have permitted to rise about your coming to us, that let us corroborate even more firmly the historic truth of that gift of your love; thanks for the intrigues about your coronation a century ago that led Rome to study you and proclaim official its approval. . . . Thanks for the scrupulous care that Rome used in investigating it. . . . Thanks for the officials of the Congregation for the Saints who cared for, examined, objected, and demanded so much; thanks for the consultors, historians and theologians, who spent so many hours in revising everything done up to now; thanks for the commission of cardinals that gave its final approbation."[33]

Despite exaggerated claims like these, the reality was quite different. The procedures followed by the Congregation do not command the assent or respect of any serious-minded person. At no time was there any attempt at an honest and open dialogue about the substantive issues involved. In the initial process of beatification, Father Ernest Burrus, S.J., and Professor Antonio Pompa y Poma were the only persons called to testify who were experts on Mexican history — and both were devout *guadalupanos*. Criticisms were made of the books of Poole, Noguez, and Nebel, but without any opportunity for those authors to respond. At no time was there a roundtable or open forum in which the two sides could confront one another and discuss the issues involved. A serious and fundamental question remains: Why the secrecy? What would have been lost by a more open discussion? The Congregation for the Causes of the Saints seems to have ignored serious issues, such as the dubious nature of the miracle, the 1982 inspection of the image and the doubt that it cast on its supernatural origin, and the lack of any clear evidence for Juan Diego's existence. Equally reprehensible was its acceptance of evidence that was dubious at best, fraudulent at worst. The prime example is the Códice 1548, or Codex Escalada. The Vatican, however, takes a longer view. With patience, and a sufficient period of time, it believes the controversy will recede and be forgotten. One need only wait. There seems no doubt that this is also the hope of many of those who brought about the canonization.

The bishops of Mexico campaigned forcefully for the honors of the altar for the visionary of Tepeyac, but at the cost of historical truth. On the other hand, opponents of the cause believed that both the integrity of the canonization process and the credibility of the church were at stake. The Holy See seemed unwilling to be hurried into the final phase, but the pressure was very strong. In general, the behavior of Archbishop Rivera Carrera and his associates was unconscionable. They made no effort to enter into dialogue with Schulenburg and the others, and did nothing to calm the situation or dampen the controversy. On the contrary, they inflamed it. There seems no reason to doubt that the politics of the

Mexican Church were deeply involved in this most recent phase of the controversy, just as they were in the earliest stages. Though Monsignor Schulenburg's past actions and lifestyle may have contributed to the hostility against him, that did not justify the slanderous and outrageous accusations made against him. The reprisals and persecution inflicted on Schulenburg, Warnholtz Bustillos, Martínez de la Serna, and Olimón Nolasco reflected a mean and petty spirit on the part of Cardinal Rivera Carrera.[34]

The wider question is that of the church's attitude toward history and the freedom of historians to pursue their investigations without having to fear ecclesiastical intervention or personal attacks and recriminations. This was a paramount issue in the nineteenth century and continues to be so today. For many theologians today, historical truth resides at the bottom of a hierarchy that exalts theological truth and subjective feelings. The neoscholastic theology of the nineteenth and early twentieth centuries was gravely deficient precisely because of its lack of a scriptural and historical consciousness. It seems that some theologians are determined to repeat this mistake. The cost, as the canonization of Juan Diego has shown, can be very high.

The canonization of Juan Diego is an accomplished fact, and with it another chapter in the history of Our Lady of Guadalupe is closed. The issues in the controversy, however, are still with us. The canonization reflects little or no credit on those who brought it about. The procedures followed in Mexico and Rome were so slanted and one-sided as to be dishonest. One is tempted to use even stronger and more pejorative terms. The truth will never be known in full until the veil of secrecy surrounding the canonization is lifted. On the whole, it was a sad and tawdry spectacle that did little service to the church's mission and credibility.

Letter Concerning the Origin of the Image
of Our Lady of Guadalupe of Mexico,
Written by Don Joaquín García Icazbalceta
To the Most Illustrious Señor Archbishop Don Pelagio
Antonio de Labastida y Dávalos (October 1883)

[This translation is of the version published in 1896. Apparently, the autograph original or handwritten copies of the letter no longer exist. The boldface type appears in the original and was the author's way of expressing emphasis.[1]]

Most Illustrious Señor:

1. Your Excellency commands me to give my opinion about a manuscript that you have been pleased to send me, titled "Saint Mary of Guadalupe of Mexico, Patroness of Mexicans. The truth about the Apparition of the Virgin of Tepeyac and about her picture on the cloak of Juan Diego. For the Purpose of Extending, if it were possible, throughout the Entire World the Love and Cultus of Our Lady."

2. Your Excellency also wishes that I evaluate this work solely from the historical aspect. That is how it would have to be in any case, since, as I have not been trained in the ecclesiastical sciences, it would be rash for me to pass judgment on the writing with regard to its theological or canonical content.

3. I do not consider it necessary to make an analysis of it insofar as I do not intend to impugn it. I prefer to present to Your Excellency in a simple way what history says about the Apparition of Our Lady of Guadalupe to Juan Diego.

4. I want to make it clear that by reason of Your Excellency's superior and repeated command I am breaking my firm resolution never to write a sentence regarding this matter which I have carefully avoided in all my writings.

5. I presuppose that since Your Excellency asks me, you leave me in complete freedom to respond according to my conscience, since it is not

a question of a matter of faith; for it if were, Your Excellency would not ask my opinion nor would I be able to give it.

6. Doubts about the event of the Apparition, as it is referred to, did not originate with the dissertation of Don Juan B. Muñoz. They are quite old and sufficiently widespread, so it seems. This last point is proven by the many defenses that have had to be written, something that would not have been necessary if the matter had remained so clear from the beginning as to leave no room for doubt. As for the antiquity of the skepticism, Your Excellency can see among the books and papers that Señor Andrade gave you an autograph letter of Father Francisco Javier Lazcano, of the Society of Jesus, dated in Mexico City April 13, 1758, and addressed to Don Francisco Antonio de Aldama y Guevara, at that time residing in Madrid. He is responding to one from the latter, written May 10, 1757, in which there is mention of the challenge of a "foolish Hieronymite friar," about which Father Lazcano asks for more data. The bull of concession of the *patronato* was in 1754, so that less than three years after it was known, there was already a religious who verbally or in writing was not afraid to impugn what was approved in that bull. Doctor Uribe, in the last years of the last century, undoubtedly provoked by the sermon of Father Mier, although he does not mention it, had to rise to the defense of the miracle. The *Memoria* of Muñoz, written in 1794, remained buried in the archives of the Royal Academy of History until the year 1817.

7. In order to add today a new defense to the various ones that have already been written, it would be a good idea to keep in sight the many documents discovered after that published by Señor Tornel (since I do not want to give such a name to the anonymous virulent pamphlet published not long ago in Puebla[2]). It seems that the author of the manuscript has not been aware of these documents, since he does not cite them.

8. Neither did Muñoz know them nor was he able to know them, but all of them have done no more than confirm in an irrevocable way his proposition that "before the publication of the book of Father Miguel Sánchez, there is no mention of the Apparition of the Virgin of Guadalupe to Juan Diego."

9. We have already come upon the **negative argument**, so impugned by the defenders of the Apparition, undoubtedly because they know that there cannot be any other against a fact **that did not take place**. The reason is that it would be absurd to demand that contemporaries should have the gift of prophecy and guessing that in the future an event of their time would be invented, they should leave something written in anticipation that it was not certain nor would credit be given to those who related it.

10. The force of the negative argument consists principally in the fact that the silence should be **universal** and that the authors cited should have written of matters that demanded a mention of the event about which they were silent. Both circumstances come together in the documents prior to Father Sánchez; and there is even something more than negative arguments in them, as we are soon going to see.

11. That there are no inquiries or original acta of the Apparition is something acknowledged by all its historians and defenders, including Father Sánchez, and they explain their absence with more or less plausible reasons. Some persons have insisted that they really did exist and they try to prove it by telling how Archbishop Don Fray García de Mendoza (1602–1604) was reading **with great tenderness** the original acts and processes of the Apparition, all of which is based only on hearsay.[3] They also relate that Father Pedro Mezquia,[4] a Franciscan, saw and read in the convent of Vitoria "where Archbishop Zumárraga took the habit," the history of the Apparition of Our Lady of Guadalupe "according to and how it occurred" written by this prelate for the religious of that convent. . . . Father Mezquia left for Spain and offered to bring this most important document on his return; but he did not bring it, and when reproved for this, answered that he had not found it and that it was thought to have perished in a fire that the archive suffered, with which everyone remained satisfied without seeking to find out anything more. Your Excellency knows that Señor Zumárraga did not take the habit in the convent of Vitoria nor is there even any evidence that he ever lived there nor is there any notice of the convenient fire in the archive. Apart from that the lack of the original acts would not **in itself** be a decisive argument against the Apparition since it could well be that they were not drawn up or after being drawn up were lost; although to tell the truth, in dealing with an event so extraordinary and glorious for the history of Mexico, any kind of negligence is highly unlikely.

12. The first witness of the Apparition ought to be the Illustrious Señor Zumárraga to whom is attributed such a principal role in the occurrence and in the subsequent placings and transfers of the image. However, in his many writings that we know of there is not the slightest allusion to the event nor to the *ermitas*. The name of "Guadalupe" is not even found once. We have his doctrinal books, letters, opinions, a pastoral exhortation, two wills, and an inquiry into his good works. Of course we do not know everything that came from his pen nor is it reasonable to demand that much, but if he said absolutely nothing in the many that we have, it is a gratuitous supposition to affirm that in some other document, of those that have not yet been found, he spoke

of the occurrence. If Señor Zumárraga had been the privileged witness of such a great prodigy, he would not have been content with writing about it in only one document but would have proclaimed it everywhere, especially in Spain, where he went in the following year. He would have promoted the cultus with all his energy, dedicating to it a part of the income that he spent with such liberality. He would leave a bequest or remembrance to the sanctuary in his will. The witnesses in the inquiry into his good works would have said something. In the eloquent exhortation that he addressed to the religious so that they would hasten to help him in the conversion of the natives, the account of a prodigy that made clear the predilection with which the Mother of God saw those neophytes would serve his purpose in encouraging them. But nothing, absolutely nothing, anywhere. Neither in the various *doctrinas* that he printed is there any mention of the prodigy. Just the opposite, in the **Regla Cristiana** of 1547 (which, if not his, as seems sure, at least was compiled and ordered printed by him) these significant words are found: "Now the Redeemer of the world does not wish that miracles occur, because they are not necessary, since our holy faith is founded on so many thousands of miracles, such as we have in the Old and New Testaments."[5] How could he, who had been present at such a great miracle, say this? . . . It seems that the author of the new defense does not know the writings of Señor Zumárraga since he never cites them and only assures that if he said nothing in them, he said enough with his deeds, building the *ermita*, transferring the image, etc.[6] It must be said, once and for all, that all these constructions of the *ermita* and transferals of the image have no historical foundation whatever. The author still discusses the possibility that Señor Zumárraga made one of these processions at the end of 1533, though it is already a fact proven by trustworthy documents that he was at that time in Spain and that he returned to Mexico in October of 1534.

13. If we pass from Señor Zumárraga to his immediate successor, Señor Montúfar, to whom is attributed a principal role in the erections of *ermitas* and transferals of the image, we will find that in 1569 and 1570 he sent, by order of the *visitador* of the Council of the Indies, Don Juan de Ovando, a full description of his archdiocese (of which I have the **original**), in which is given an account of the churches of the city that were subject to the archbishop and there is no mention of the *ermita* of Guadalupe.[7] No matter how small it may have been, the splendor of its origin and the heavenly image that it contained definitely deserved a special mention, with the corresponding news of the miracle. When we question the first religious, we will find them equally silent. In 1541 Fray Toribio de Motolinía wrote his *History of the Indians of*

New Spain, in which he told about various heavenly favors granted to Indians, but the name of Guadalupe never appears in it. The same thing is true of the other manuscript of that work, which I possess, very different from the printed one. Very notable is the silence of the famous letter of the Most Illustrious Señor Garcés[8] to Pope Paul III in favor of the Indians, in which he also speaks of some favors that they had received from heaven. Neither is anything found in the letters of Venerable Gante, Señor Fuenleal, Don Antonio de Mendoza and many other bishops, viceroys, *oidores*, and personages which have lately been published in the **Cartas de Indias** and in the voluminous **Colección de Documentos inéditos del Archivo de Indias**.

14. Fray Bartolomé de las Casas was here in the years from 1538 to 1546. Undoubtedly he knew and had contact with Señor Zumárraga since both were present at the *junta* of 1546. From his mouth he could hear the account of the miracle. Even so in none of his many writings does he speak of it, and that would have been so useful for bolstering his energetic defense of the Indians. What effect would not have been produced in the Spanish Catholic monarchs by evidence that the Most Holy Virgin was taking the conquered race under her protection! What an argument against those who had come to doubt the rationality of the Indians and pictured them full of vices and incapable of the sacraments!

15. Fray Jerónimo de Mendieta came in 1552. He wrote his **Historia Eclesiástica Indiana** [Ecclesiastical History of the Indies] toward the end of the century, making use of his predecessors' papers. He was an ardent defender of the Indians. The same as Motolinía he recounted the favors that they were receiving from heaven and particularly in chapter 24 of book 4 he brings forth the appearance of the Virgin in 1576 to the Indian of Xochimilco, Miguel de San Jerónimo, who told it to the same Father Mendieta.[9] But he says nothing about Our Lady of Guadalupe, not in his letters, of which I have some that are unedited. There is still more, because he intentionally wrote the life of Señor Zumárraga in three chapters, and he was silent about the whole occurrence. For what future date was he keeping his account? Perhaps there will have been charitable souls who, because I published that work, mistakenly judge that I suppressed some passage. I ought to warn them for their peace of mind that the manuscript exists in the possession of Señor Don José María Andrade and that that same silent biography of Mendieta's was sent to the general of the order, Fray Francisco de Gonzaga, who printed it in a Latin translation in his work **De Origine Seraphicae Religionis** [On the origin of the Seraphic Religious Order, i.e., the Franciscans]. The general of the order did not notice that omission nor in 1587 did he say anything whatever about such a notable event.

16. In the other chronicles of that time, written by Spaniards or Indians, we will also look in vain for the history. Muñoz Camargo (1576), Father Valadés (1579), Father Durán (1580), Father Acosta (1590), Dávila Padilla (1596), Tezozomoc (1598), Ixtlixochitl [*sic*] (1600), Grijalva (1611), equally keep silence. Neither did Father Fray Gabriel de Talavera say anything who in 1597 published at Toledo a history of Our lady of Guadalupe of Extremadura, even though he makes mention of the sanctuary in Mexico. The Franciscan chronicler Daza in his **Crónica** of 1611, Fernández in his **Historia Eclesiástica de nuestros tiempos** [Ecclesiastical History of Our Times] (1611), and the chronicler Gil González Dávila in his **Teatro Eclesiástico de las Iglesias de Indias** [Ecclesiastical Theater of the Churches of the Indies] (1649) wrote the life of Señor Zumárraga and were silent about the history of the Apparition. Then Father Luzuriaga recounted it in the life of the same prelate, when he published his history of Our Lady of Aranzazu in 1686.

17. Let us now come to Father Sahagún. The author of the manuscript faithfully copied the famous text. The same is not true of the author of the Puebla dissertation who with bad faith shortened it, suppressing whatever contradicted his purpose. Your Excellency may make the comparison of both texts. For greater clarity what the writer from Puebla omitted is highlighted.

FATHER SAHAGÚN'S TEXT

Near the mountains are three or four places where they used to offer sacrifices, and they would come to them from very distant lands. One of these **is here in Mexico [City], where there is a hill that** is called Tepeyacac and the Spaniards call Tepeaquilla and now called Our Lady of Guadalupe. In this place they used to have a temple dedicated to the mother of the gods, whom they called Tonantzin, which means Our Mother. **In that place they would offer many sacrifices in honor of this goddess, and they would come there from very distant lands, from more than twenty leagues from all these regions of Mexico, and they would bring many offerings. Men, women, and children of both sexes would come to these festivals.**

TEXT OF PUEBLA

Near the mountains are three or four places where they used to offer sacrifices, and they would come to them from very distant lands. One of these is called Tepeyacac and the Spaniards call Tepeaquilla and now called Our Lady of Guadalupe. In this place they used to have a temple dedicated to the mother of the gods, whom they called Tonantzin, which means Our Mother. . . . Now that the church of Our Lady of Guadalupe has been built there, they also call her Tonantzin, taking their cue from the preachers who call Our Lady, the Mother of God, Tonantzin. . . . They now come to visit this Tonantzin from far away.

The gathering of people in those days
was great, and everyone would say
"Let us go to the feast of Tonantzin."
Now that the church of Our Lady of
Guadalupe has been built there, they
also call her Tonantzin, taking their
cue from the preachers who call Our
Lady, the Mother of God, Tonantzin.
What may be the basis for this use of
Tonantzin is not clear. However, we
know for certain that the original
use of the word means that ancient
Tonantzin. It is something that should
be remedied because the proper name
for the Mother of God, Our Lady is
not Tonantzin but Dios inantzin. This
appears to be an invention of the devil
to cover over idolatry under the ambi-
guity of this name Tonantzin. They
now come to visit this Tonantzin from
far away, as far as in former times.
They devotion itself is suspect because
everywhere there are many churches
to Our Lady, and they do not go to
them. They come from distant lands
to this Tonantzin, as they did in
former times.

This passage of Father Sahagún's is also found in the edition of Don
Carlos María de Bustamante and in that of Lord Kingsborough.

18. This is not the only place where Father Sahagún spoke of Our
Lady of Guadalupe. In a manuscript codex in quarto that is in the
National Library, labeled on the outside "Songs of the Mexicans and
other brief works," when it deals with the calendar it says, "The third
[idolatrous] dissimulation is taken from the very names of the idols
that were venerated in those towns, for the names with which they
are signified in Latin or Spanish are the same in meaning that the names
of these idols signified. For example, in the city of Mexico, on the hill
where Our Lady of Guadalupe is, they used to adore an idol of a goddess whom they called Tonantzin, that is, 'Our Mother,' and this same
name they give to Our Lady, and they understand it in reference to the
ancient one, not the modern one. There is another dissimulation similar
to this in Tlaxcala, in the church that they call Saint Ann."

19. Father Sahagún came in 1529, and he would have been well informed of the history of the Apparition, if this had occurred two years

later. No one dealt with the Indians like him: he could have known Juan Diego perfectly well and other persons who figured in the matter. In spite of everything he says with finality "the origin of that foundation is not known for sure." And by means of the two passages quoted it is seen with total clarity that the devotion of the Indians, which he considered as idolatrous, was displeasing to him, and that he wanted to see it prohibited. One of his bases is that the Indians thronged to that place **as they did in former times**, while they did not go to the other churches of Our Lady. On the supposition that the Apparition was real, Father Sahagún should not have been surprised that the Indians would prefer the place in which one of their own had been so singularly favored by the Most Holy Virgin. Looked at carefully, the testimony of Father Sahagún is now something more than negative.

20. At about the same time the king asked Don Martín Enríquez what was the origin of that sanctuary, and the viceroy answered on 25 September 1575 that around the years 1555 and 1556 there existed there an *ermita* with an image of Our Lady, which they called Guadalupe **because it was said that it resembled the one of the same name in Spain** and the devotion began to grow because a herdsman proclaimed that he had recovered his health by going to that *ermita*. We see, then, that the viceroy himself, who had so many ways of gathering information and reporting to the king, did not succeed in learning the origin of the *ermita*. He explains how the image got the name of Guadalupe and informs us that the devotion had grown because of the story of a miracle worked there. Soon we shall see confirmed by another authentic document that it was precisely about those years that the devotion to Our Lady of Guadalupe was made known and many miracles publicized. Since Muñoz inserted in his Memoria only the paragraph of Enríquez's letter that suited his purpose, there are those who presume to suppose that in the rest of the letter something more would be said, a completely gratuitous supposition, as has now been demonstrated with the whole document published in **Cartas de Indias**.

In addition we have a detailed account of the journey of the Franciscan commissary, Father Alonso Ponce, and in it is told how, having left from Mexico City on July 23, 1585, he passed a great irrigation channel "by a stone bridge next to which is a small village of Mexican Indians, and in it, close by a hill, an *ermita* or church of Our Lady of Guadalupe, to which the Spaniards of Mexico City go to keep vigil and hold novenas, and a cleric resides there who says mass for them. In that town the Indians, in the time of their paganism, used to have an idol called Ixpuchtli, which means virgin or maiden, and they came there as to a sanctuary from all over the land with their gifts and offerings. **The Father Commissary passed by there at a distance,**" etc. That the editor of the account, as someone new in the land, would mistake the name of the idol is not the least surprising, but it is, very much so, that if the tradition existed, as is affirmed, none of those in the company would have informed the Commissary that in that *ermita* was kept a miraculously painted image so that he might go to see it and venerate it, instead of **passing at a distance.**

21. The passages from Torquemada and Bernal Díaz in which mention is made of the church have provided apologists with material for long discussions. The undoubted fact is that neither of these authors mentions the Apparition. Here I ought to make an important observation. All the apologists, with only one exception, have fallen into the mistake, inexplicable in so many men of talent, and it has been that of constantly confusing the antiquity of the cultus with the truth of the Apparition and miraculous picture on Juan Diego's cloak. They have exhausted themselves in proving the first point (which no one denies, since it is evident from irrefutable documents), insisting that by means of that [the first point] the second stands proven, as if the least relationship existed between the two things. There are innumerable images inside our country and outside of it in which worship has been offered since time immemorial, without anyone's deducing from that fact that they are of miraculous nature. The most that has been done has been to attribute them to the evangelist Saint Luke. Only about Guadalupe (as I remember) is it said that has come down from heaven.

22. Father Fray Martín de León, a Dominican, published in 1611 his **Camino del Cielo** in the Mexican language, and on folio 96 he almost reproduces and makes his own, after so long a time, Sahagún's second text. This is what he says:

The third [dissimulation] is taken from the very names of the idols that were venerated in those towns, for the names with which they are signified in Latin or Spanish are the same in meaning that the names of these idols signified. For example, in the city of Mexico, on the hill where Our Lady of Guadalupe is, they used to adore an idol of a goddess whom they called Tonantzin, that is, "our mother," and this same name they give to Our Lady, and they always say that they are going to Tonantzin, or that they are celebrating a feast to Tonantzin, and many of them understand it in reference to the ancient one, not the modern one of today.

Like Sahagún he then speaks of the image of Saint Ann located in Tlaxcala and that of Saint John the Baptist in Tianquismanalco, **the most superstitious that there has been in all of New Spain.** It is worth noting that when these ancient missionaries deal with the hidden idolatries of

the Indians, they bring up the devotion to Our Lady of Guadalupe. This
is not easily reconciled with belief in the miracle.[10]

23. Fray Luis de Cisneros of the order of La Merced published in
1621 his **History** of Our Lady of Remedios. Chapter 4, book 1, is titled
**"On how most images of devotion of Our Lady have their hidden and
miraculous beginnings."** In it he speaks of various images in Europe and
Guatemala but he does not mention that of Guadalupe, it being the case
that he is dealing with images with **miraculous beginnings**. In a later
chapter he then speaks of it in these terms. "The most ancient [sanctu-
ary] is that of Guadalupe which is a league to the north of this city,
which is an image of great devotion and crowds almost since the day
the land was won. It has worked and does work many miracles. They
are building a notable church to it which by the order and care of the
archbishop is in a very good state." Nothing about an Apparition.

24. Among the books that Señor Andrade gave you, Your Excellency
has the sermon on the nativity of the Virgin Mary preached by Fray
Juan de Zepeda, Augustinian, in the *ermita* of Guadalupe outside the
walls of the City of Mexico, on the feast day of the same church. It was
printed by Juan Blanco de Alcázar in the year 1622 in quarto. There are
two notable things in this sermon. (1) The preacher says in his dedication that the Nativity (8 September) is the **patronal day of the ermita**.
(2) The other is that he does not say a word about the Apparition. The
first point is confirmed by an act of the Cathedral chapter, 29 August
1600. On that day they directed that Sunday, 10 September, the Feast
of the Nativity of Our Lady would be celebrated in the *ermita* of
Guadalupe because it was its **titular feast day**, and immediately the
cornerstone would be laid to begin the new church. From this it is
a clear deduction that at that time it still had not occurred to anyone
that the image was painted on the *tilma* of Juan Diego and that the
titular feast day was 8 September on which are celebrated those of all
the images that do not have a day set for their particular title, so that
ninety years after the supposed appearance no thought was yet given
to celebrating the twelfth of December.

25. In the same way Your Excellency should note that nothing is said
about the Apparition of the Virgin of Guadalupe in the three Mexican
Councils nor in the acts of the ecclesiastical and civil *cabildos*, prior to
Father Sánchez's book. The civil one did not make even one allusion to
that great happening or to the solemn transferals of the image, given the
fact that in its acts are references to even the most insignificant public
festivities.

26. Lastly, the Jesuit Father Cavo, who around 1800 wrote in Rome
his Tres Siglos de México, in the rigorous form of annals, on reaching

the year 1531 was silent about the event of the Apparition and went on.[11]

27. If we go from writings to the Indians' maps and pictures we will find that in none of the authentic ones that exist today is there anything of what is sought. As examples I will cite the codices Telleriano-Remense and Vaticanus, published by Kingsborough, and the annals or pictorial histories of Monsieur Aubin, which go to 1607. With regard to the pictures cited by the defenders I will say something later.

28. As Your Excellency knows, the silence of the documents before the publication of Father Sánchez's book is complete. There is no good reason to suppose that for more than a century so many serious and pious persons, separated by time and place, would have agreed to hide a fact that was so glorious for religion and the fatherland. The defenders of the Apparition want **all** the documents to be presented for such a long epoch in order to be convinced that the silence is universal, a claim that is not admissible because in that way history would never be written while waiting for documents that **could** have existed and that **could** be found. Those that we have bear sufficient witness to what those which perhaps **could** yet **be found** would contain. There is already some proof of that. Muñoz, in 1794, based his refutation principally on the silence of writers: in the ninety years since that time innumerable and most important documents have been found and not a single one of them has spoken but by their silence they have greatly added to the weight of Muñoz's argumentation.

29. In the same way the defenders maintain that the writings of some of the authors who favor them the least have been corrupted. I will cite only Sahagún and Torquemada. The former twice wrote the last book of his **History**, saying that in the first writing there were things that should not have been included and others were omitted that should not have been passed over. From this Bustamante and others drew the peculiar argument that just as in Book 12 there are those things that should not have been included and not omitted, the same thing must have happened in the other books and that among the things that should not have been omitted was the history of the Apparition. As if it were not a common occurrence that an author retouches what he writes, when he has obtained better data; and as if Sahagún had simply **passed over in silence** the history and had not left texts in which he clearly denied it, insofar as someone could deny it who did not guess that it was to be invented with the passage of time. Torquemada has been branded a liar, and it has also been claimed that his work is mutilated, precisely in what affects the case. In truth, he was not a liar, but something of a plagiarist, and because he did not carefully weave

together others' bits and pieces of which he made use he fell into the contradictions that he is accused of. To judge by what the defenders say, it seems only that God set about to destroy the written proofs of the wonder after having brought it about, permitting that the documents in which it was related should disappear down to the last one and others should remain or that from the very moment of the Apparition there was a universal agreement to be silent about it and erase its memory, since not only did the original documents disappear but all the mutilations of the authors were done precisely to the passages relative to the same happening.

30. I said at the beginning that in the documents of the period there was something more than negative arguments, and it is time to offer proof of that. Your Excellency has in his possession an **original** investigation, in fourteen written and three blank folios, made in 1556 by Señor Montúfar, the immediate successor of Señor Zumárraga. The case that brought about the investigation was the following. On the Feast of the Nativity of Our Lady, September 8, 1556, a solemn religious function was celebrated in the chapel of Saint Joseph, with the assistance of the clergy, viceroy, *audiencia*, and the principal citizens of the city. The sermon was entrusted to Fray Francisco de Bustamante, the Franciscan provincial, who enjoyed a reputation as a great speaker. After having spoken in a very fine way about the subject proper to the feast, he suddenly paused and with an outward show of fiery zeal he began to declaim against the **new** devotion which had risen **without any foundation** "in an *ermita* or house of Our Lady **that they have given the name** of Guadalupe," describing it as idolatrous and asserting that it would be much better to do away with it, because it was destroying what had been done by the missionaries, who had taught the Indians that the cultus of images did not stop with them but was directed to what they represented and that now to tell them that an image **painted by the Indian Marcos** was working miracles would be great confusion and would be to undo the good that was being planted because other devotions that there were had **greater beginnings** and the fact that this one had arisen **so much without foundation** amazed him, that he did not know what impact this devotion had, and that in the beginning it should have been ascertained who was the author of it and of the miracles that were recounted, in order to give him one hundred lashes and two hundred to anyone who thereafter recounted it; that in that place great offenses were committed against God; that he did not know where the alms collected at the *ermita* went, and that it would be better to give them to the needy poor or to apply them to the hospital for venereal diseases and that if that business was not stopped, he would never again preach to the Indians because it was wasted work.

He then accused the archbishop of having promulgated false miracles of the image. He exhorted him to remedy that disorder, since it was his concern as ecclesiastical judge; and finally he said that if the archbishop was negligent in carrying out his duty, the viceroy was here who as vice-patron for His majesty could and ought to intervene in it.

31. Señor Montúfar, who did not put up very well with nor was a friend of Franciscans, upset over that public rebuke on such an occasion and before such a gathering, and perhaps all the more for having been turned over to the secular arm, and began on the following day to institute an inquiry, the original of which Your Excellency has. Its purpose was, as appears in it, to learn if Father Bustamante had said anything for which he should be reprimanded. The questionnaire, with thirteen questions, had **as its only purpose** to leave a good record of what the preacher had said. Nine witnesses were called and the results of their declarations were that Father Bustamante preached what we have said. Some added that he was not the only one who thought that way but that other Franciscans followed him, all of whom were op-posed to the devotion and they even brought up against it texts from Holy Scripture in which it is commanded that God alone should be adored, that that *ermita*, they said, should not be called Guadalupe but Tepeaca or Tepeaquilla, that making a pilgrimage there was not to serve God but rather to offend him because of the bad example that was given to the natives, etc. The archbishop also tried to prove that in a sermon that he had preached a few days before he had said that in the Lateran Council it was ordered under pain of excommunication that no one should preach false or uncertain miracles and he "**had not preached any of the miracles that they say the said image of Our Lady had worked nor did he make any reference to them**, that he was under-taking the inquiry and according to what would be found to be certain and true, that would be preached or hidden, that the miracles which His Excellency preached about Our Lady of Guadalupe is the great devotion that this entire city **has had** toward this blessed image and the Indians also." The inquiry was suspended and remained unfinished. Nothing was done against Father Bustamante who, in spite of that sermon, was again elected provincial in 1560 and later commissary general.

32. Your Excellency has before you the **original** papers and can assure yourself both of their authenticity and of what I have extracted that is in them. No one, after reading the document, can still doubt that the Apparition of the Most Holy Virgin in the year 1531 and her mirac-ulous picture on the *tilma* of Juan Diego is an invention born much later. Of course this document coincides surprisingly with what nineteen years later Viceroy Enríquez wrote. The provincial said in 1556 that the

devotion was **new** and had no foundation but that it had arisen from dubious miracles which were related about the image. The viceroy did not assign a certain origin to it and gives us to understand that it began in 1555 or 1556 because a herdsman proclaimed that he had recovered his health when he went to the *ermita*. One of the witnesses in the inquiry, bachelor Salazar, had just confirmed that the foundation of the *ermita* did not come from any apparition or miracle because he said "that what he knows is that the foundation that this *ermita* had **from its beginning** was **the title of the Mother of God**. This caused the entire city to have devotion in going to pray and entrusting itself to her." The conclusion is that that title alone, the **Tonantzin** of which Sahagún speaks, was the one that gave rise to the cultus.

33. Father Bustamante said that the image was painted **by the Indian Marcos** and other testimony confirms the existence and talent of that painter, since Bernal Díaz, in chapter 91, mentions with praise the Indian artist Marcos de Aquino.

34. We have proved then, in an irrefutable way, that for the twenty-five years from the date assigned to the event and in the eyes of many contemporaries, Father Bustamante was on a most solemn occasion condemning the **new** devotion to Our Lady of Guadalupe. He was asking for severe punishment for the person who had raised it up with the publication of false miracles, and he made it known that the image was the work of an Indian, without one voice being raised to contradict him. Becerra Tanco wrote that no sooner was the last apparition to Señor Zumárraga verified than "everywhere the report of the miracle" was spread and a great crowd of people hastened to venerate the image. But why did not the archbishop, so many eyewitnesses, all the people destroy the preacher's charges by simply throwing in his face the divine origin of the image, sufficient to justify that devotion? How could they hear without scandal that the marvelous work of the angels was attributed to an Indian? How could the person who said such things in a pulpit not have been worried? How did the archbishop, who saw himself accused *coram populo* [before the people] of fomenting an idolatrous devotion and of preaching false miracles, attempt to bring to trial in a timid way such accusations instead of confounding the preacher with the proof of the great prodigy? If the original documents existed, it was enough to publish them since once printed they were not lacking. If they had already perished, that was the occasion for replacing them by a very easy investigation instead of leaving it for one hundred and ten years later. Nothing was done. Your Excellency should consider the effect that not just the entire sermon of Father Bustamante but just the proposition that the image was the work of an Indian would cause today; what an uproar would be raised among the many

who believe in the Apparition, the defenses that would be published (since they are written even without that motivation) and the bad moments that the preacher would be put through. Remember what happened to Father Mier simply because he said that the image was not painted on Juan Diego's *tilma* but on Saint Thomas's cloak. But twenty-five years after the event, that sermon did not cause scandal only because in it the archbishop was attacked in a disrespectful way and because in a certain way it resulted in diminishing the cultus of the Queen of Heaven.

35. The devotion of 1556, fervent like all new ones, was giving way even to the point of disappearing. The Licenciado Don Antonio de Robles has left us testimony of this in his **Diario de sucesos notables** (Journal of Notable Events], a private document in which beyond doubt the truth is found. Entering the death of Bachelor Miguel Sánchez, March 22, 1674, he says, "He wrote a learned book about the apparition, which seemingly has been the means by which devotion to this holy image has spread throughout all Christendom. It had been forgotten, even by the citizens of Mexico [City], until this venerable priest made it known, since there was in all Mexico [City] only one image of this sovereign lady, in the convent of Santo Domingo, and today there is not a convent or church where it is not venerated, and rare indeed is the religious house or cell where there is not a copy of it." So, in 1648 nobody knew about the Apparition, nobody yet knew the image. The devotion had disappeared completely.

36. But lo and behold Bachelor Sánchez publishes his book (the first in which is seen the history of the Apparition to Juan Diego) and everything changes as if by magic. Was it because in that book a glorious history, unknown until that moment, was recounted, with the support of authentic and irrefutable documents? No. Truth always opens a way for itself, and the author begins with this confession, "With determination, eagerness, and diligence I looked for documents and writings that dealt with the holy image and its miracle. **I did not find them,** although I went through the archives where they could have been kept. I appealed to the providential curiosity of the elderly, in which I found some **sufficient** for the truth." He goes on to say very much in passing that he compared those papers with the chronicles of the conquest which told him about ancient persons and finally that even when all that had been lacking, he would have written because he had tradition on his side.

37. On publishing such a strange story, he ought to have made evident with the greatest precision the sources from which he had taken it and not contented himself with such vague generalities, on his own authority qualifying some papers as **sufficient,** without saying what they

were or who was their author. He counted very much on the credulity
of his readers, and in that he was not deceived. In order to take advantage of it still more and to discredit completely his great weapon of
tradition, he had the crazy idea of publishing at the end of his book a
letter of praise from Licenciado Laso de la Vega, vicar of the *ermita* of
Guadalupe itself, in which the good vicar admits openly that **he and all
his predecessors** had been "**sleeping Adams,** possessing this second Eve
without knowing it"[12] and to him had fallen the good fortune to be the
"Adam who has awakened." In present-day language this means that
neither he nor all the vicars or chaplains of the *ermita* had known
anything about the miraculous origin of the image that they guarded,
until Father Sánchez had revealed it. The **Adam who has awakened,**
that is, Licenciado Laso de la Vega, took the matter so seriously that
in the following year, 1649, he published an account, his or someone
else's, in Mexican [Nahuatl], with which Father Sánchez's history ended
by circulating among the Indians.

38. The latter's book came out at an opportune moment for gaining
credit. The impressive credulity of the period, together with a wayward
piety, compelled belief from the beginning in how much it seemed to
redound to the glory of God, without noting, as many do not know
today, that honor is not given to the Highest Truth by falsehood and
error. The parchments of the Turpiana tower and the lead plates of
Sacromonte of Granada achieved such credit that a century was spent
in disputes before the Holy See condemned them.[13] The Jesuit Father
Ramón de la Higuera for a long time infected the history of Spain with
his false chronicles which were followed by those of Lupián Zapata,
Pellicer de Ossau, and others.[14] The purpose of those forgeries was to
fill out the incomplete episcopal lists of many Spanish sees, to prove
that Saint James and other disciples of the Apostles came to Spain, to
provide saints for various Spanish cities that did not have them, and, in
short, to enhance the glory of the church in Spain. Each one of those
who saw that hurried to make up their unknown bishop or their new
saint without there being any way of letting go of them. Cities formed
their individual histories on such bad foundations, which spread the
contagion. Not everyone was deceived, but no one dared to challenge
those clumsy inventions out of fear of the outcry that would be raised
against anyone who would combat such pious lies. The popular pressure was irresistible, and it cost much time and work to cleanse the civil
and ecclesiastical history of Spain of that trash. It was an age of mysti-
cism in which the public spirit was inclined to accept and support
whatever concerned supernatural communications or manifestations,
in the end, any form whatever of miracle. He who provides nature with
the invariable fulfillment of his laws was not enough. The need was

always for the exception to the rule and that the direct intervention of the Divinity would come to repeal, even in the most futile matters, what had been wisely established since the creation. Miracles were almost always to be worked by means of images, all of which were also of miraculous origin. Whence so many histories of them: in one case the images that two angels under the appearance of Indians left in the gateway of a convent, in another case, the one that was renewed all by itself; in another, one that became so heavy in the place where it wanted to remain that it was impossible to move it from there; in another, the one that left from Spain half finished and arrived here finished; or the one that returned several times to the place from which they had taken it, or the one that spoke, blinked, perspired, or at least, yawned. So determined was the liking for miracles that even obviously natural facts were considered and sworn to be marvels.

39. The book of Father Sánchez fell on a field so well prepared and thus bore fruit. It did not occur to anyone to ask him where he had taken such a strange story from, of which the chaplain of the *ermita* himself was ignorant; his book was simply approved like any other; the authorities did not call him to account, but by a procedure that was entirely contrary to what was natural and due, instead of demanding from him the evidence for that history and of the miracles that he recounted, every effort was turned toward providing it with the foundations that it did not have. To this wayward idea we owe the wretched inquiry of 1666.

40. In confirmation of Muñoz's assertion I have said that before the publication of Father Sánchez's book in 1648 no one had spoken of the Apparition. The defenders, knowing the urgent need to destroy such an assertion, have brought forward various earlier documents whose value should be examined. Señor Tornel (vol. 1, pp. 15 and 18) has listed them, dividing them into **probable** and **certain**. The **probable** are:

1°. The original acts drawn up by Señor Zumárraga.

2°. The letter that he wrote to the religious of his order residing in Spain.

3°. The history of the Apparition written by Father Mendieta and paraphrased by Don Fernando de Alva.

The **certain** are:

4°. The account of Don Antonio Valeriano.

5°. The song of Don Francisco Plácido, lord of Atzcatpotzalco [*sic*].

6°. The map mentioned by Doña Juana de la Concepción in the inquiry of 1666.

7°. The last will of a female relative of Juan Diego.

8°. Those of Juana Martín and Don Esteban Tomelín.

9°. That of Gregoria Morales.

10°. The account of Don Fernando de Alva Ixtlilxochitl.

11°. The papers from which bachelor Sánchez took his history of the Apparition.

12°. Some annals that Father Baltazar González saw in the possession of an Indian.

13°. The history of the Apparition in Mexican [Nahuatl] published in 1649 by bachelor Laso de la Vega.

14°. A history of the Apparition that until 1777 was kept in the University of Mexico, "whose antiquity goes back to times not very distant from the event."

15°. The chronicle of the university cited by Bartolache.

41. As is evident, the list of documents is rather long, but misfortune has not wanted any of them to be published (with the exception of number 13), nor is it even known that they exist anywhere. Although it would not be strange that some or even most would have been lost, that total disappearance is inexplicable. Individual defenders, those who, writing works that are sometimes rather bulky, did not reserve a corner for the documents on which they were relying, having spent so much ink and paper to mend an edifice which has openings on all sides. A collection of those most ancient and rare papers in a small notebook would be worth more than all defenses. But some have been lost, others stolen; the former were sold as old paper, those further back were burned; in the end, all have disappeared, and today none of them can be examined or subjected to criticism. The only thing that is known is that they existed because someone who saw them told another, and this person another and this last still another who told it to the one who is writing it down; and all the intermediaries were, of course, older, grave, and most truthful persons, to end up, after so many stages and adjustments, with the story of that letter of Señor Zumárraga that Father Mesquia saw and which was so conveniently burned.

42. With regard to numbers 1 and 2, that is, the original acts and that letter of Señor Zumárraga, I have said enough; and since they are given only as **probable**, I affirm that they never existed and go forward. The same classification of **probable** is attached to the history written by Father Mendieta (number 3); it would be more worthwhile to say openly that there never was such a history. The issue is an account by an uncertain author which Betancourt attributed dubiously to Father Mendieta or to Ixtlixochitl [*sic*]. Florencia, always inclined to additions

and embellishments, now says that Betancourt **affirmed** to him that
it was Mendieta's; Sigüenza comes along and is annoyed with Father
Florencia for having added that after he gave the approbation for the
Estrella del norte [The North Star]; this caused him to declare and even
swear that it was a question of the **paraphrased** translation of a Mexican original in the hand of Don Antonio Valeriano, made by Ixtlilxochitl. Cabrera attributes it to Fray Francisco Gómez, who arrived with
Señor Zumárraga. After all this I do not understand how Señor Tornel
could consider, even as **probable**, that history of Father Mendieta.

43. The first of the **certain** documents is the history of Don Antonio
Valeriano. Since Sigüenza swears that he had an account **in the hand** of
Don Antonio Valeriano, I will not express any doubt about it. But here
is the misfortune, because this key piece does not exist nor has any
modern person seen it nor has it ever been published so that we could
know what it said and how it said it. Father Florencia, who used it so
abundantly, intended to publish it at the end of his history and finally
he got out of this with the bare comment that because that book had
already turned out to be too bulky, he was not then publishing the
account. For that Conde y Oquendo upbraided him strongly and
rightly. Bad luck always. Sigüenza, in order to prove that Mendieta
could not have been the author of that account, says that in it were
some miraculous events and cases "that occurred years after the death
of the said religious." Father Mendieta died in May of 1604 and Don
Antonio Valeriano in August of 1605. So if it is a question of events
that occurred **years** after 1604 someone could not write them who died
in the following year of 1605, and Valeriano is not the author of that
document, although it would seem to have been written in his hand, or
rather, the document is inserted. To sum up, the account does not exist
nor can it be known except by the extract from it that Florencia gives,
in which there is certainly no lack of implausible details. The defenders
of the Apparition demand that in order to prove the negative argument
they should be presented with the ultimate possible and imaginable
document while they give in return documents that are doubtful,
obscure, and feeble, which cannot even be produced.

44. The song of Don Francisco Plácido (n° 5) is exactly the same case.
Florencia also offered to print it and also left it in the inkwell **because the
book was bulky**. Could he not have thrown away some part of the many
pages that it has in order to leave room for papers of such high importance? And if the person who had them refused to print them, why
complain that now no credit is given to what we know only by second-
hand knowledge and extracts that are not at all sure.[15] The song was
given to Father Florencia by Don Carlos de Sigüenza, who found it

among the writings of Chimalpahin. There are some who think that
there was no writer by that name.[16] Although I would not be that daring,
I think that the only circumstance of its having been sung on the day that
"from the residence of the Señor Bishop Zumárraga the sacred image
was taken to the *ermita* of Guadalupe," is enough to deny the authenticity of the hymn, since there was no such occasion for it to be sung.

45. Let us go on to the map in the Inquiry of 1666. Doña Juana de
la Concepción, an eighty-five year old Indian woman, declared that
because her father had been a man of great curiosity he wrote down
and placed in maps everything that happened in Mexico [City] and its
environs and that, **if she remembers correctly**, he had put the Apparition in them. And here comes the misfortune as always, because the old
man was robbed of those maps and the daughter could not give more
than that vague indication, so that I do not know what use it is.

46. The will of a female relative of Juan Diego (n° 7) appears to be
of greater appearance because in it is mentioned (according to Boturini,
the only one who saw it) an apparition in these terms: "On Saturday
appeared the much loved Lady Saint Mary and the beloved pastor of
Guadalupe was informed of it." The translation is Boturini's, since the
original was in Mexican [Nahuatl], for sure the word **teopixque** does
not correspond exclusively to that of pastor, as Señor Alcocer noted
very well, but signifies **father** or **priest** in general; but I cannot admit
that the indication refers to Señor Zumárraga "who was truly a father
and beloved of the Indians," as the same Señor Alcocer asserts, because
common sense is saying that Señor Zumárraga's high charge was not so
that the title of an *ermita* could be added to him. The bishop was called
Hueyteopixqui (greater or principal priest) according to Florencia.
What the text says purely and simply is that the Virgin appeared on
Saturday and the priest (chaplain or vicar) who was at the *ermita* of
Guadalupe, was advised of the event. What this means is that the
apparition that is dealt with is not the famous one of the Virgin to
Juan Diego, since according to all those who write about it, when it
happened there was no name of Guadalupe nor an *ermita* nor a priest
there to advise, but that everything came from that wonder. It deals
with one of so many miracles that from 1555 to 1556 were attributed
to the image; and this is confirmed by the curt manner of describing the
case without any special circumstances to distinguish it.

47. In agreement with this is another notice that the latest defenders
have not made use of, although they could have attributed great value
to it. Juan Suárez de Peralta in his **Noticias históricas de la Nueva
España** [Historical Notices of New Spain], written around 1589, says
that the Viceroy [Martín] Enríquez "arrived at Our Lady of Huadalupe

[*sic*] which is an image of great devotion which is about two leagues from Mexico. It has worked many miracles (it appeared among some rocks and the whole land flocks to this devotion) and from there he entered Mexico." We see that Suárez mentions that apparition with the same curtness as the will, inside a parenthesis, and without making a point of it. He does not call the image one that appeared but one of devotion. It is necessary to distinguish between any apparition whatever of the many that are told, that leave no trace of themselves nor go beyond the person favored, on whose word alone it is based, and the Apparition of the Virgin to Juan Diego, in front of witnesses, and remain permanently attested to in the image painted by a miracle. It must be repeated: what is in question is not whether the Virgin appeared to someone under the form of the image of Guadalupe now existing, but whether she appeared to Juan Diego in 1531 under the circumstances that are related and finally remained painted on his *tilma*; that is, if the image that we have is of heavenly origin.

48. There is a certain confusion in this matter of Indian wills. Señor Lorenzana saw those of Juana Martín and Don Esteban Tomelín (n° 8); he did not publish the first one **because the year had been changed**: in the other, executed in 1575, there is a legacy to Our Lady of Guadalupe. This has to be put aside because leaving a legacy to Our Lady of Guadalupe is not to bear witness to her apparition, and since in 1575 there was already a church, it is not the least bit significant that Don Esteban should leave a bequest or legacy nor does it prove anything. With regard to that of Juana Martín we know nothing: not even the date; there are those who think that it is the same one that Boturini attributed to a female relative of Juan Diego. Señor Alcocer says that the original was sent to Spain with the other papers of Don Fernando de Alva (Ixtlilxochitl). I do not know what basis he would have for this assertion. What is certain is that copies of the papers of Don Fernando remained in Mexico, but not one of the will. The ill fortune continues, destroying the papers of the defenders.

49. With regard to the will of Gregoria Morales, executed in 1559 (n° 9) Señor Alcocer says that he possessed a copy which contained the Apparition and that many consider this and that of Juana Martín to be one and the same. Why did he not publish the copy that he had in order that we might see how **the Apparition was contained** or if there is only a legacy of land, as in that of Tomelín. What credit do these unknown wills deserve when it is not even known if they are different ones or just one?

50. Mention is also made of an account by Don Fernando de Alva Ixtlilxochitl (n° 10) which according to the sworn declaration of

Sigüenza was only a paraphrased translation of the account attributed
to Valeriano. For that reason it cannot be considered a different document. The papers on which Father Sánchez based his history (nº 11) are
also offered in evidence. Nobody knows what they were, if there were
any. The malicious Bartolache says that "the bachelor Sánchez would
have done very well to have said what papers those were that he found
and where." And since he did not say, what do they prove? Who can
evaluate them now? The Indian annals that Father Baltazar González
of the Society of Jesus had seem to be of more weight, which went up
to 1642 and in the year that **concerns it** is the **miracle of Our Lady of
Guadalupe**. Those are Florencia's words. Why did he say **the miracle**
and not **the Apparition**? These vague clues about maps in which the
Apparition is entered do not inspire confidence because, as I said
before, they do not deal with **just any apparition** of the Virgin of
Guadalupe but with **the apparition** to Juan Diego and the miraculous
picture on the *tilma*. Among the many miracles which in the middle
of the century were attributed to the image, it is also sure that they
included some **apparitions,** like those mentioned by the female relative
of Juan Diego and Suárez de Peralta. Even when it may not be the case,
it is a custom that still endures to paint on the *retablos* of the miracle
the image of the saint who worked it, as if he would appear in the air
to his devotee, without, therefore, anyone's claiming that the apparition
was real, but is a manner of indicating who was the intercessor. A similar **retablo** painted on some Indian annals, without a text to announce
the subject, can be taken for a real apparition without being so.

51. It will strike anyone's attention that counted among the
documents **prior to** Father Sánchez's book is Laso de la Vega's Mexican
account which appeared in the following year (nº 13). The fact is that
without more basis than the elegance of the language and others equally
slight, it has been asserted that the Licenciado Laso is not its author but
that the true author is much older "and **most probably** is the same history or paraphrase of Don Antonio Valeriano." If that probability in the
superlative is accepted, the document is reduced to the other and is not
an additional one. But it would be quite strange that after Laso's declaration on 2 July that he had not known until then a word about such a
history, now on 9 January 1649 he would have the account presented
and approved. Did chance cause the account which had been hidden
for so long a time to appear within those six months? If Father Sánchez
already had it, why did he not mention such a precious document instead of contenting himself with vague comments? Here there is no
account whatever. After Laso's devotion was stirred by Sánchez's account, he wanted to make it known among the Indians and for that

purpose he shortened it and put it in the Mexican language. That is all.
If the language is good, for that purpose there were at that time great
masters of Mexican, and it is enough to remember the name of Father
Carochi, who in the year 1645 published his famous grammar.

52. Doctor Uribe (1777) speaks of a history of the Apparition in the
Mexican language "in the archive of the Royal University, whose antiquity, although not known precisely, is known to go back to times not
very distant from the Apparition, both because of the nature of the
writing, and because of its material, which is maguey fiber, which the
Indians used before the conquest." (n° 14) They continued to use it
much later, and I have documents from 1580 written on that paper. But
what did that account contain? What was its date? Where is it today?
There is no one to answer these questions. Why, I ask again, was not
even one of these documents published? There were doubts in Señor
Uribe's time since he wrote a defense. The chapter of La Colegiata was
not poor. What prevented it from bringing to light the documents that
the defender was citing, as was customary in every argument? Did not
Don Carlos Bustamante later have them finance the publication of book
12 of Sahagún, leading them to believe that it was an irrefutable document of the Apparition, even though it did not say a word about it? But
if the carelessness has been so great, why do they want us to accept as
good and conclusive what is not known? When we see the constant and
inexplicable persistence with which the defenders confuse the devotion
and the apparition, the fear is well founded that those unknown papers
speak only **of the devotion**, of bequests and alms, as happens in the
will of Tomelín and most probably in that of Gregoria Morales, which
nevertheless they offer as proofs of the Apparition.

53. Bartolache, more cautious, did not want to proceed as quickly as
his predecessors but having found a manuscript calendar in the university's library had his secretary certify exactly the two passages that he
extracted. The calendar is not original but a **copy** apparently made in
Tlaxcala, undoubtedly in comparatively modern times, since according
to Bartolache it covers events from 1454 until 1737 **inclusive**. The
passages quoted are one from the year 13 reeds, 1531, which translated
into Spanish says, "Juan Diego revealed the beloved Lady of Guadalupe
of Mexico: it was called Tepeyacac." The other is from 1548, 8 flint,
and says, "Juan Diego died, to whom the beloved Lady of Guadalupe of
Mexico appeared." The correspondence of the year is incorrect because
the sign for 1548 is **4 flint**, not 8. I do not know what arrangement the
calendar had. Ordinarily what was done was to put in the margin, as in
a column or on a board the year signs and in front of each one to write
whatever notable happened. If there was nothing, only the sign was left.

At least that is the arrangement of the Aubin picture and others. If Bartolache's calendar went **to** 1737, the copy was at least from that date, which is precisely that of the epidemic that was the cause or occasion for the oath of the patronage of Our Lady of Guadalupe. It was very easy at that time to add to the copy those passages, in front of the corresponding signs. At any rate it does violence that only in a calendar of a few folios, not an original but a copy, finished at a time when pious sentiment in favor of the image was at its height, such references are found and not in others that are authentic and known and which did not feel the influence of Father Sánchez's book, because they do not go up to his date.

54. Doubts about the existence or value of all those documents are intensified by the fact that in 1662 the canon Don Francisco Siles, great friend and admirer of Sánchez, brought it about that the Apostolic See was asked for the grant of a proper feast and prayer for the 12 of December, and instead of sending in support of the petition, as was natural, some authentic instruments that would assure a prompt and favorable settlement he included only requests from the *cabildos* and religious orders. At least those papers, which bachelor Sánchez described as **sufficient**, could have gone in support of his never-before-heard story. From Rome an announcement was made in response to the sending of a questionnaire by which the witnesses of the miracle were examined. Before it arrived, the canon prepared what was necessary to undertake the inquiry, which in fact was done at the end of 1665 and the beginning of 1666. The document was lost in Rome, and its text has never been published. We have only the extracts given by Florencia. These are the famous **Informaciones of 1666** which because of the number of witnesses and the status of many of them are considered to be the best proofs of the truth of the miracle.

55. The inquiry was made 130 years after the date assigned to the event, and it is clear that no eyewitnesses still survived. But conveniently, octogenarian and even older than centenarian Indians were found who reached back to parents and grandparents equally long-lived, so that two lifetimes were enough to go back to 1531 and further. The incomprehensible thing is that before 1648 no one knew of the Apparition; there was no writer who mentioned it, not even in passing: Father Bustamante preached a sermon that equivalently denied it: none of the elders of Cuauhtitlán, who were so well informed by their parents and grandparents, advised the chaplains of the *ermita* of the value of the treasure that they watched over: they knew nothing and were some "sleeping Adams": the cultus had declined to the point that there did not exist in the city of Mexico more than one copy of the Virgin of

Guadalupe; and in the middle of that general silence, Father Sánchez no sooner publishes his unsubstantiated book than the devotion again catches fire, corporations as respectable as the Cathedral chapter take part in promoting it; let the matter be taken to Rome for clarification; everywhere qualified witnesses appear who unanimously and under oath declared that they knew from a long time before what up to then no one, not even they, had known. The most superficial reading of the inquiry of Señor Montúfar, without any other proof, leaves an absolute inward conviction that the history was invented later; and nevertheless, after 110 years there are those who affirm that they had heard it from those who had gotten it from Juan Diego's very mouth. This would not bother me if it involved only the Indian witnesses, because they have always been inclined toward marvelous narratives and not well known for telling the truth; but when I see that serious priests and illustrious gentlemen affirm the same falsehood, I cannot but be confused, considering how far moral contagion and distortion of religious feeling can go. There is no reason to say that those witnesses undoubtedly came close to perjury but it is clear that they affirmed under oath what was not true. It is a common enough phenomenon among the elderly, and I have often observed it, even to the point of being persuaded that what they have imagined is true. It will undoubtedly be considered absurd and rash to reject a juridical instrument in this way, but the fact is that historical demonstration does not admit reply, and the affirmations of some twenty hearsay witnesses, however qualified they may be, carry no more weight than the terrible inquiry of 1556 and the mute but unanimous and dispassionate testimony of so many writers, and no less authoritative than those witnesses, and in whose forefront stands the Most Illustrious Señor Bishop Zumárraga.

56. Reports from painters and physicians are attached to the inquiries. The former affirmed that that picture exceeded human abilities and the latter that its preservation was miraculous. Against them there is the public declaration of Father Bustamante: he said from the pulpit that the image was the work of the Indian Marcos, and no one contradicted him. One could say to the physicians that very many papers of greater antiquity have been preserved in spite of the fact that they are more fragile than a canvas and that they circulate everywhere. The canons who in 1795 submitted a report against the sermon of Father Mier said that "the colors have grown dim, faded, and in one or another area the gold has come off, and the sacred canvas not a little damaged." In any case the preservation of the image would be a different miracle and not mentioned in that of the Apparition. It is also believed that the image of Our Lady of the Angels has been miracu-

lously preserved on an adobe wall, and no one has for this reason
attributed a divine origin to it.

57. The Holy See, acting with prudence, put off the affair and it
seems that the Mexican devotion again cooled a bit because the records
slept in Rome for some eighty years; the inquiry of 1666 was even lost.
It was necessary that an event as noteworthy as the epidemic of 1737
should come to revive fervor. The city wanted to take an oath to the
Most Holy Virgin of Guadalupe as its patron and for that purpose the
requests were renewed in Rome with the greatest pressure. The result
was the granting of the request, May 25, 1754.

58. In order to make an exact copy of the image and send it to Rome
in support of the new activities, another inspection by painters was
made on April 30, 1751; among them was the famous Don Miguel
Cabrera, who later published his report with the title of "Maravilla
americana." One can presuppose what a painter would say who was
already concerned with the general belief, with the result of the inspection of 1666, and with the presence of lofty personages who did not
leave him freedom nor would have tolerated the least hint that there
was in the image anything that was not supernatural and divine. Years
later and in different times, just because Bartolache published in the
Gaceta the announcement of his "Manifiesto satisfactorio," someone
did not fail to direct an anonymous work at him, treating him as a **Jew**
and threatening him with appropriate **punishments** for his **sin** in this
or the next life. And the charitable Conde y Oquendo desires "that the
fires of purgatory not be stoked for any unbeliever" (Bartolache was
only partly so); when the copy located in the **Pocito** would have just
fallen into pieces. So it is that Cabrera explained in the best way he
could, by converting the artistic defects that are noticeable in the picture
into artistic skills, and directing attention to the most obvious, which
is that the gold figures on the tunic and on the stars of the mantle are
located as on a flat surface instead of following the folds of the cloth.
Bartolache had a third inspection by painters carried out on January 25,
1787, in the presence of the Abbot and a canon of the collegiate church.
The declarations of these qualified men are sufficiently different from
what the former ones had entered. The rough *ayate* of maguey became
a fine mantle of the palm **iczotl**: they assured that it had sizing [under-
painting]; they denied some specific things noted by Cabrera and finally,
asked if, presupposing the rules of their profession and prescinding
from any personal feelings or commitment, they considered this holy
image to have been painted miraculously, they replied, "Yes, with
regard to the substantial and original that they see in our holy image,
but no with regard to certain retouchings and strokes which show

beyond doubt that they were executed at a later date **by presumptuous
hands.**" Great is the distance between Cabrera's enthusiasm and the
cold reticence of Bartolache's painters. I do not imagine that the former
would act in bad faith. The Indians' colors were very different from
ours, and therefore it is not strange that they should cause confusion
to the painters of the seventeenth and eighteenth centuries, to the point
of causing them to imagine that four different kinds of painting, different and even opposed to each other are gathered together on one
canvas alone: they did not yet know that kind of painting. This fact,
preconceived ideas, and the respect inspired by a gathering of serious
persons, explain quite well the reports of older experts. Since some of
these circumstances did not act with equal force on those of Bartolache,
they responded in a different way.

59. Let us come to tradition, which is the defenders' strongest
weapon and to such an extent that Sánchez would have dared to write
on that basis alone, even if he should lack everything else. **Traditio est,
nihil amplius quaeras** [It is a tradition, seek no further], everyone repeats. So be it, although I am not at all in agreement with the meaning
that it gives to such an absolute proposition. But first it is necessary to
know if the tradition exists and because of everything that has already
been pointed out one should be warned that there was none. Tradition
is **quod ubique, quod semper, quod ab omnibus traditum est** [what has
been handed down everywhere, always and by everyone]. In order to be
quod semper it would be necessary for it to have come without inter-
ruption from the days of the miracle to the date of Father Sánchez's
book (1648): after that there was no tradition since the event is mentioned in writing. Precisely in that critical period is when we do not
have it. There was none in 1556 when Father Bustamante preached his
sermon because if there had been one by that time, he would not have
said that he did or if he said it a **general** outcry would have been raised
against the presumptuous person who attributed the heavenly image to
an Indian's paintbrush. There was none in 1575 when Viceroy Enríquez
wrote his letter since he did not succeed in learning the origin of that
cultus; nor in 1622 when Father Zepeda preached his sermon. There
was none in the year 1646 [*sic*] because the chaplains of the sanctuary
or *ermita* themselves had not known it or did not know it until Father
Sánchez's book came to open their eyes. Where, among whom, then,
did the tradition go? Neither is it **quod ab amnibus** [*sic*] because none
of the distinguished writers of that time knew of it or at least none who
believed it worthy of attention. That was not a very remote and dark
time with ten centuries of the Middle Ages ahead of it; no invasion of
barbarians who destroyed everything came after it. There were printing

presses that multiplied the writings of the **negative argument;** there was
not **one** that gave **one** of the **positive** documents that are now offered
in proof. If in even one or two writers of those who were closest to the
event, no matter how untrustworthy they may otherwise have been, I
would find references to the tradition, I would then believe at least that
it circulated among the ordinary people and that it would be worth the
effort to assess it. However, I do not know how to label as **authentic,
juridical, and ecclesiastical tradition** that which is not found anywhere,
which Señor Montúfar and the chaplains of the *ermita* did not know;
which is not found included in any writing; which, rather, has proofs
against it, and which at the end of more than a century of silence appears for the first time to general amazement in the pages of Sánchez,
in order to be elevated immediately to great, general, and uninterrupted
in the declarations of the elders of 1666, who until that time had kept
a dead silence and let even the cultus of the image that appeared be
lost. If this is what is to be understood as **tradition,** there will not be
any fable that cannot be proved with it.

60. I do not want to spend time examining the authors after Sánchez's
book; they all drank from that fountain, adding, filing past, pondering,
and exaggerating more and more. They are second-hand authors who
published no new document. Among them Father Florencia stands out
because of the multitude of details that he mentioned, taken from nobody knows where, and some as unlikely as that of the celibacy that
Juan Diego observed in his marriage because he had heard a sermon by
Fray Toribio de Motolinia. How could the author of the account that
Florencia said he had seen have learned such intimate things, if he had
not heard Juan Diego's confession? The prolific Jesuit spent most of his
long life writing wondrous histories of Our Lady of Guadalupe, Our
Lady of Remedios, Our Lady of Loretto, the Holy Christ of Chalma,
Saint Theresa, Saint Michael of Tlaxcala, and the sanctuaries of Nueva
Galicia. He was truly typical of the era and had a thirst for miracles.
In his hands everything is wondrous and he closed his career leaving
"Zodiaco Mariano" unedited, which Father Oviedo, of the same Society,
revised and expanded in order to give to the press. A detestable book
that deserves more than others to be on the **Index** because of the multi-
tude of fables, false and ridiculous miracles with which it is packed, with
not a little irreverence toward God and his Most Holy Mother.

61. The improbabilities of the history of the Apparition as given by
Becerra Tanco, who is considered the most trustworthy author, deserve
some reservations.

62. Juan Diego was a recently converted Indian. That is what Tanco
says and other circumstances confirm it. In the first years the sacrament

of baptism was administered only to children and rarely to adults, when they gave extraordinary signs of their faith or were on the verge of death. It is true that the recent nature of the Indian's conversion was not in itself an obstacle to his receiving a special favor from heaven; but it seems that his religious instruction was scanty. As soon as he saw the splendor and heard the concert of the small birds on the hill, there occurs to him a pagan exclamation. "By chance have I been carried to the paradise of delights that **our elders** call the origin of our flesh, the garden of flowers or heavenly land, hidden to the eyes of men?" Soon after, in order not to encounter the Most Holy Virgin and avoid another meeting, he takes another route: this is not naiveté but an absolute ignorance of the religion he had embraced. What idea of the Most Holy Virgin did the good Juan Diego have, when with such a childish stratagem he thought he could excuse himself from being seen by the Sovereign Lady? The fault he committed consisted in not having gone to the appointment that she gave him the day before because he went to Tlatelolco in order to ask that the sacraments of Penance and Extreme Unction be administered to his uncle Juan Bernardino. Everyone knows, since Mendieta says so, that "in the beginning for **many years** Extreme Unction was not given to the Indians." Penance was a rare thing for them.

63. When the Indian wanted to go into the presence of the Lord Bishop, the servants prevented him and made him wait a long time. I would like to know what **servants** Señor Zumárraga had in 1531 and how it was that the Indians found it difficult to approach a prelate who always walked among them, to such an extent that some Spaniards took it ill.

64. The last time that Juan Diego presented himself to the Lord Bishop he brought the credentials of his mission, which were roses only, according to some, or those and other flowers according to others. Certainly the sign did not inspire belief. The marvelous aspect of this case is made to consist in the fact that the Indian would find the flowers in the winter season and that they would be on top of a barren hill. The first point has nothing special because the Indians were very fond of flowers and the collected them at any time. Today we see that there is no month of the year in which bunches of flowers are not sold in Mexico [City] at a very low price. He did not tell Señor Zumárraga about the second circumstance: he did not know where those flowers had been cut; they could well have come from a **chinampa**. So it is that it could cause them no surprise that the flowers should fall to the floor when the Indian opened his mantle nor was that sign of any use to accredit his mission.

65. However, at the same time that the flowers fell, the Most Holy Virgin appeared painted on the mantle. "[A]nd [the Lord Bishop] having venerated it **as something from heaven** untied the knot of the mantle from the Indian and carried it into his oratory." According to this Señor Zumárraga was quick to believe, and it is impossible to attribute to him a quality more foreign to his character, scrupulous and most severe as he was in the matter of miracles. Guadalupe authors discuss at length when the image was painted although all agree that when Juan Diego opened the *tilma* it already appeared painted. This was the great wonder; but it was not evident to Señor Zumárraga. If it should be said to him that for a moment, when it was let go, the mantle was blank and immediately the holy image appeared on it, the wonder would have been evident, and since it was done in his sight, Señor Zumárraga could not have had any doubt about it. For Juan Diego it would be such, since having left home with his mantle blank, he saw it suddenly painted without human intervention: but not for the Lord Bishop. He would have had to doubt, and with very good reasons, the origin of the picture. The Indian had offered with spirit to bring him the sign that he asked for and he came forth with some flowers that meant nothing: if he had worked some wonder in the presence of the Lord Bishop, like Moses before pharaoh, that would be something else. Immediately he shows an image painted on his *tilma*. Only by a special light from heaven could Señor Zumárraga have known instantly that that picture was from heaven: without that, the natural thing was to think that that Indian had done no more than procure the image for himself in some way in order to give weight with it to the poor credential of the flowers. Although we may not know for sure that there were already painters in Mexico by that date, neither do we have evidence to the contrary; and in any case, it was well worth the effort that in such a serious business the cautious Señor Zumárraga would have ascertained at great length where the picture came from, instead of kneeling in front of it as soon as he saw it, taking it immediately from the shoulders of the Indian with his own hands, and exposing for public cultus in his oratory. No bishop would proceed so quickly, much less such a serious man. Another circumstance ought to have increased his correct lack of belief: that the image was painted on a fine mantle of palm and not on a coarse **ayate** of maguey, which was the material that the **macehuales** or commoners, like Juan Diego, used on their **tilmas**. Where would he have gotten that cape so foreign to his humble condition?

66. The name of Guadalupe that the Most Holy Virgin gave herself when she appeared to Juan Bernardino has tormented authors and defenders. "The reason that the Virgin had for naming her image Guada-

lupe (writes Becerra Tanco) she did not say, and so it is not known, until God will be pleased to clarify this mystery." It is really extraordinary that the Virgin, when she appeared to an Indian in order to announce to him that in a special way she favored those of his race, should choose the already famous name of a Sanctuary in **Spain:** a name that none of her favored ones could pronounce because the Mexican alphabet lacks the letters **d** and **g.** So it was that it was necessary to torture the name in order to drag by the hair another which in the Mexican language would be similar to it and then to attribute to the habitual corruptions of the Spaniards the transformation into **Guadalupe.** From there Becerra Tanco conjectures that the Most Holy Virgin said **Tecuatlanopeuh,** that is, "she who had her origin on a rocky peak" or **Tecuantlaxopeuh,** "she who put to flight and drove away those who were eating us." There is a notable difference, in my opinion, between these words and Guadalupe: there is no need to invent nonsense. Among the conquistadors there were many Andalusians and Extremadurans, great devotees of the Spanish sanctuary, which is in the province of Extremadura. Before this the discoverers had already attached the name Guadalupe, which it still has although it is not now Spanish, to one of the lesser Antilles; and as Fray Gabriel de Talavera says (who in 1597 published his History of the Sanctuary of Spain) "the devotion and respect for the sanctuary took such deep root in those inhabitants that they immediately began to show signs of the good spirit with which they had received doctrine, raising churches and sanctuaries with much devotion with the title of Our Lady of Guadalupe, **especially in the city of Mexico in New Spain.**" Here we have a simple declaration of the origin of the name by an author who was writing in the very century of the Apparition and did not know of it. Those who migrate to distant lands have a tendency to repeat in them the names of their own and to find similarities, although they may not exist, between what there is in the new fatherland and what they left behind in the old one. So it was that Mexico received the name of New Spain because they said it was similar to the old one; and the extensive territories discovered and conquered by Nuño de Guzmán were called New Galicia because of a fancied resemblance to that small province of Spain. Spaniards thought they noticed that the image of the **Mother of God** venerated at Tepeyac resembled in some way that in the choir of the sanctuary of Extremadura, and that was enough for them to give it the same name. That is what Viceroy Enríquez says.

67. But if the history of the Apparition has no historical basis, where did it come from? Did Sánchez totally invent it? I do not think so. He found something that gave him a basis for his book. Perhaps an account

in Mexican came into his hands, to which he would add new circumstances in the way that grandiloquent writers are accustomed to do,
almost without being aware of it, but carried away by that zeal to
praise and embellish whatever matters fall into their hands. Sánchez
belonged to that guild, and his insufferable book gives good testimony
to it, which perhaps for that reason has never been reprinted, though
it was the capital piece of the process, and the printing presses having
sweated so much with the histories of Our Lady of Guadalupe. What
can be known through historical documents and what can be tracked
down through conjectures is the following.

68. As soon as the first religious arrived, they erected many chapels
and *ermitas* in different places, with the desire to destroy idolatry. They
preferred as locations for those small churches those places in which
previously major worship was paid to idols, and they even gave them
analogous titles. If in this they were right or wrong, this is not the place
to ascertain it: suffice it for us to know that that is how it happened,
and that one of those *ermitas* was that of Tepeyac, with the title of **the
mother of God**, without any specific dedication, as Sahagún indicates,
bachelor Salazar declares in the Inquiry of 1556. It was natural that it
would be in order to correspond to the name **Tonantzin** or Our Lady
Mother, that the idol adored there had. We do not know in what year
the *ermita* was built nor what image was placed in it: perhaps none
because they were very scarce at the time. A little later the Indians set
about making them, for which they could then count on the students
of Fray Pedro de Gante's school, "and so it is a very ordinary thing"
(says Torquemada) "for images that they had made of the mysteries
of our Redemption or figures of saints to whom they had the most
devotion to remain in each convent from time to time." Without doubt
one of these was that of Guadalupe, and finding it to be well painted,
devotional, and attractive as it really is, the religious sent it to the
ermita, taking elsewhere the one that was there, if there was one:
and when the Spaniards saw it they gave it that name, as I have said
previously. Around the years 1555 and 1556 the devotion began to
catch fire because of the miraculous cure claimed by the herdsman and
also the simple apparition (to that or another Indian) was recounted, of
which Juana Martín and Suárez de Peralta speak. At that time sacred
presentations of autos and mysteries, of which the Indians were very
fond, were in vogue and continued to be so for a long time after. Don
Antonio Valeriano, a learned Indian, *catedrático* in the college of Tlaltelolco [*sic*] had a sufficient talent for this kind of composition. He or
another made use of the account of the miracles of Our Lady of Guada-

lupe, and taking as a basis the Apparition that was mentioned, they added circumstances that gave form and liveliness to the piece, without the intention of having them taken as true, as dramatic authors are still accustomed to do. The history of the Apparition has a dramatic make-up that is noticeable at first sight. The dialogues between the Virgin and Juan Diego; the missions to the bishop; his rejections; the episode of Juan Bernardino's illness; the flight of Juan Diego by a different road; the flowers born miraculously on the hill, and finally, the unfolding with the apparition of the miraculous painting before the Lord Bishop, form a dramatic action. This would be the text or Mexican account that fell into the hands of Sánchez, who took it verbatim and presented it as true history. The spirit of the times did the rest, inclined to accept uncritically, as a meritorious work, anything miraculous. The apparition of Our Lady of Guadalupe had been told to a pastor, and the Indian witnesses of the Inquiry of 1666 would know it from their ancestors, the circumstances that were already in circulation with general acceptance would be easily accommodated to it. Dating the event on December 12 undoubtedly came from the fact that on the same day in 1527 Señor Zumárraga was nominated as bishop, something that in those days was the same as a formal appointment. What I do not manage to explain to myself satisfactorily is why the event was situated in the year 1531. A rare coincidence, however, should be noted. Sahagún mentions (book 8, chapter 2) that Don Martín **Ecatl** was the second governor of Tlaltelolco [*sic*], after the conquest: he governed three years "and in his time the devil, disguised as a woman, would walk and appear by day and by name, and she was called **Cioacoatl**." Calculating the time that the said Don Martín was governor, according to the data offered by Sahagún in the same chapter, it turns out that they were 1528 to 1531; and from another passage by the same author (book 1, chapter 6) we know that the goddess **Cioacoatl** was also called **Tonantzin.** Here we have the fact that during those years there was talk among the Indians of apparitions by **Tonantzin,** the name by which they know Our Lady of Guadalupe, according to the same Father Sahagún.

69. I have finished, Your Excellency, the examination of the history of the Apparition from the point of view of history. I did not want to write a dissertation but some points to smooth the way for Your Excellency, if you wish, to examine for yourself this serious business. I am not permitted to enter into the theological argument; Your Excellency will know if the miracles are duly proven, if in case of being so they prove the Apparition; if the Holy See makes statements about **facts**; if the granting of the office and *patronato* is an explicit approval;

if breviaries have not often been corrected; and if sometimes a mass has not been forbidden, after a better examination, that was already granted a long time before.

70. I am a Catholic, although not a good one, Your Excellency, and a devotee, as much as I am able, of the Most Holy Virgin; I would not want to take this devotion away from anyone: the image of Guadalupe will always be the most ancient, devout, and respectable one of Mexico. If, contrary to my intention, out of pure ignorance, some ill sounding word has escaped me, from this point on I consider it not to have been written. Of course I do not deny the possibility and reality of miracles: he who laid down the laws can very well suspend or repeal them; but Divine Omnipotence is not a mathematical quantity susceptible of increase or decrease, and one miracle more or less does not add or detract anything from it. With all my heart I would like one that honors our fatherland to be certain, but I do not find it to be so; and if we are obliged to believe and proclaim true miracles, we are also forbidden to spread and uphold false ones. When it is not admitted that the Apparition of Our Lady of Guadalupe (as it is recounted) is one of these latter, at least, it cannot be denied that it is subject to the most serious objections. If these are not refuted (which up to now has not been done), the defenses will produce the opposite effect. In my youth I believed, like all Mexicans, in the truth of the miracle; I do not remember where my doubts came from, and in order to remove them, I went to the defenses: these converted my doubts into the certainty of the falsity of the fact. And I have not been the only one. For that reason I judge that it is a very delicate thing to continue defending the history. If I have written about it here, it has been in obedience to the command repeated by Your Excellency. I ask you, for the same reason, with all the urging of which I am capable, that this writing, the child of obedience, not be given to other eyes nor pass to other hands: Your Excellency has promised me this.

Again, Your Excellency's most devoted friend and obedient servant, who kisses your pastoral ring.

Joaquín García Icazbalceta

Joint Letter to the Congregation
for the Causes of the Saints, 9 March 1998

Most Eminent Señor Alberto Cardinal Bovone
Titular Archbishop of Caesarea in Numidia
Pro-Prefect of the Congregation for the Causes of the Saints
Vatican City

Your Eminence:

We, a small group of scholars, both priests and lay, have met together in order to examine in more depth the "Guadalupan Event." The names of some of those could be mentioned — for example, Father Stafford Poole, C.M., an American historian whose book has been published by the University of Arizona in 1995 and which has the title *Our Lady of Guadalupe: The Origins and Sources of a Mexican National Symbol, 1531–1797.*

Also with us was Doctor Xavier Noguez, doctor in history from Tulane University in New Orleans. The title of his doctoral dissertation is "Documentos Guadalupanos: A Study on the Early Sources of Information in Regard to the Marian Apparitions at Tepeyac" (El Colegio Mexiquense, A.C., Fondo de Cultura Económica, Mexico, 1993).

These two persons whom we have just cited reach the same conclusions as other historians, both ancient and contemporary — for example, Doctor Richard Nebel, a German theologian and historian, whose work of revisionism has the title (translated into Spanish) of *Santa María Tonantzin Virgen de Guadalupe: Continuidad y transformación en México.* These conclusions are: historically speaking the apparitions of the Most Holy Virgin Mary to a supposed real person,

Juan Diego, cannot be proven since there exists a documentary vacuum of more than a century in regard to it. We do have a precious image of the Most Holy Virgin Mary under the invocation of Guadalupe, which is very probably a picture from the mid–sixteenth century. In addition, the famous account of the apparitions written in the Nahuatl language, called the *Nican mopohua*, from its opening words which mean "Here is recounted, here is named," whose date of composition and whose true authority we do not know, except that some believe it was written toward the end of the sixteenth century and attributed it to an Indian named Antonio Valeriano. None of these things can be proved from the perspective of history; and of that contemporary authors are sure with regard to documents, although affirmations to the contrary continue to be made.

Is it a question of a literary catechesis with respect to the Most Holy Virgin in order to instruct the natives, or is it perhaps a theatrical presentation in four acts, written for this same purpose by some one of the great missionaries of the sixteenth century? We do not know. The testimonies that are put forth to defend the historicity of this beautiful and pious account are not conclusive. It is clear to us that it was published for the first time in the Nahuatl language by the Bachelor Luis Lasso [*sic*] de la Vega in 1649, that is, 117 years after the supposed apparitions of Our Lady of Guadalupe.

Luis Lasso de la Vega says that he is the author of this narrative, in order to recall to the Indians "what they had forgotten." We do not have any other valid testimony up to this date so that we could date with precision both its closeness to the supposed events of 1531 and its author.

Those who try to defend the opposite are not convincing and do no more than repeat the answers that they have always given. In that regard the now old objections of Don Joaquín García Icazbalceta, who in 1883 wrote the "Letter Concerning the Origin of the Image of Our Lady of Guadalupe" continue to be valid. Don Joaquín was a man eminent for his knowledge, a Catholic of deep faith, and an absolutely honest man. A great Spanish writer, Don Marcelino Menéndez y Pelayo, called Don Joaquín a "master of all learning." Nevertheless, the apparitionists (since in Mexico there will always be apparitionists and anti-apparitionists, and of course Catholic devotees of Our Lady of Guadalupe, since Guadalupanism is not the same as apparitionism; nor anti-Guadalupanism as anti-apparitionism) try to minimize the great personality of Don Joaquín García Icazbalceta in order to distort his objections.

Among the priests are the archpriest of the Basilica and doctor in canon law, Canon Carlos Warnholtz Bustillos; Father Esteban Martínez de la Serna, a great devotee of history, librarian of the Basilica, and also one of its canons; the priest Don José de Martín Rivera, a great student of history, bibliophile, and very knowledgeable about Mexico in the sixteenth century.

Don Rafael Tena, M.A., specialist in the Nahuatl language, Doctor Ana Rita Valero de García Lascuráin, also an outstanding Christian and student of our past history, and the Abbot Emeritus of Guadalupe and Prothonotary Apostolic, Monsignor Guillermo Schulenburg Prado, who since he was named secular abbot of the Famous and National Basilica of Guadalupe, has been deeply interested in the Guadalupan Event, because for him it was very important to have a clear vision of that devotion of the people of Mexico toward the Most Holy Virgin under the invocation of Guadalupe.

From the point of view of conscience we are seriously distressed that after the recognition of the cultus, or rather, the "equivalent" beatification of the alleged visionary, without clear evidence of his historical existence, appealing to a miracle worked through the intercession of this native, we repeat that it distresses us because if this canonization is carried out, it would cast doubt before all these scholars, Mexican or non-Mexican, believing Catholics, on the seriousness and credibility of our Church, to which we belong and which we defend in an absolutely resolute way.

We must add — in order to speak with absolute truthfulness — that there are many of our people who, without being students of history, consider the Guadalupan Event as a pious tradition, which is not opposed to a deep devotion to Our Lady, under the invocation of Guadalupe, so linked to our past history, to Mexican nationalism, and to our Marian piety. One could speak of this at great length.

We do not know if that Congregation has at hand the books of at least three of the authors we have mentioned. We know that some time ago the book of Doctor O'Gorman *Destierro de sombras*, arrived there, but nothing more. We are very concerned that it may be said that "for that Congregation the subject of the existence of Juan Diego is completely closed."

We repeat again that the cultus of Our Lady under the invocation of Guadalupe is beyond doubt, but that the cultus to Juan Diego cannot be proven, for whose personal existence they try to adduce iconographic and archeological proofs that did not exist for more than a hundred years, since we can call the famous "four evangelists of Guadalupanism" (Miguel Sánchez, Luis Lasso de la Vega, Luis Becerra Tanco, and Francisco de Florencia) the creators of the Guadalupan Event as a supernatural phenomenon.

The documental and historical vacuum of more than a century is still standing: the total silence of the first missionaries in relation to the historicity has not changed: they knew absolutely nothing of the alleged fact — for example, Fray Juan de Zumárraga, the number one witness of the Event, since according to the narrative of the *Nican mopohua*, when the native opened his *tilma*, the image of Our Lady appeared before him and he venerated it on his knees. Nevertheless, sixteen years later, in the catechism *Regla Cristiana breve* (1547), he affirmed, "The Redeemer of the world no longer wants miracles to be worked because they are not necessary; since this holy faith of ours, based so much on so many thousands of miracles such as we have in the Old and New Testaments . . ."

And thus we could speak, for example, of Fray Bernardino de Sahagún, Jerónimo de Mendieta, Fray Bartolomé de las Casas, of the same Father Juan González, who supposedly was the interpreter between the Indian and the bishop, since the Indian did not know Spanish and the bishop did not know Nahuatl. Nevertheless, Juan González, in spite of gratuitous suppositions and iconographic forgeries, never said anything in that regard, as Doctor O'Gorman proves very well in his book that has been cited. We believe that the Congregation knows all this perfectly well, that it has taken notice of it, and that they will have studied it in depth.

It would be very long for us to refer — as we announced above — to the famous iconographic and archeological proofs which are a true invention as far as the sixteenth century and a good part of the seventeenth century are concerned. Some of our well-known historians have refuted such assertions.

Finally, we have no desire to stretch out these letters, but simply to manifest for the last time our serious disquiet of conscience and our sincere desire to defend the prestige of our Catholic Church, which we love and serve.

It is not our function to give careful advice to that Congregation, but normally canonizations come long after the beatification. Nevertheless, miracles were found at a short distance from the recognition of the cultus, in spite of the fact that many of us continue to have serious doubts about the real existence of the Indian Juan Diego, who previously was a humble native, and now turns out to be a man "white, bearded, noble, and rich," according to the assertions that appeared in the weekly journal *Proceso*, of which we enclose a copy.

Some of those who were present at the meeting of which we spoke at the beginning can send to that Congregation a personal work about this subject.

May our letters be read and given serious consideration.

Your Eminence's servants in Christ,

Father Stafford Poole, C.M.

Señor Don Rafael Tena

Very Illustrious Señor Doctor Carlos Warnholtz,
Archpriest of the Basilica of Guadalupe

Señor Doctor Xavier Noguez

Most Illustrious Monsignor Doctor Guillermo Schulenburg,
Abbot Emeritus of Guadalupe, Prothonotary Apostolic

Very Illustrious Señor Esteban Martínez de la Serna[1]

Joint Letter of 27 September 1999

27 September 1999

His Eminence
Angelo Sodano
Secretary of State
Vatican City

Cc: His Excellency Tarcisio Bertone, S.D.B.
Archbishop Emeritus of Vercelli
Secretary for the Congregation for the Doctrine of the Faith

Cc: His Excellency José Saraiva Martins
Prefect of the Congregation for the Causes of the Saints
Piazza Pío XIII, 10 Rome

Your Eminence:

We are pained and worried, both as priests and scholars, that a pious belief, such as the apparition of the Virgin of Guadalupe to the Indian Juan Diego, so preserved in this way for centuries, recently, that is, some fifteen or sixteen years ago, would be promoted by the Cardinal Archbishop Primate of Mexico, Don Ernesto Corripio Ahumada and endorsed with the signatures of a group of priests of the archdiocese of Mexico, in order to bring about the beatification of the alleged visionary, the Indian Juan Diego.

The majority of the members of the Chapter of Guadalupe at that time (with the exception of two canons) expressed to the Cardinal Archbishop by letter our disagreement with recommending the said possible beatification because of the lack of truly historical documents that would prove the real existence of the Indian Juan Diego. Many lay scholars, who were knowledgeable about this historical problem, were of the same opinion. We believed, and thus we expressed it, that the said cause could not be seriously accepted by the Congregation for the Causes of the Saints because of the lack of documentation — we say it again — that is historical, decisive, and strongly believable in order to arrive at proof of this alleged historical fact.

To our great surprise, and having read and analyzed the entire text of the *Positio*, we nevertheless beheld the fact of the "Recognition of Cult" of the Indian Juan Diego, effected in the Basilica of Guadalupe by His Holiness John Paul II on May 6, 1990. We have to say, in all honesty and in homage to the truth, that the said *Positio* seems to us to be tendentious, since it was filled with inaccuracies and pure suppositions.

Therefore we thought that all would end there and that the cause would sleep the sleep of the centuries. As a matter of fact, there were in Mexico Monsignor Oscar Sánchez Barba, promoter of Mexican causes in Rome, Father Fidel Fernández González, consulter for the Congregation for the Causes of the Saints, and His Eminence Cardinal Don Darío Castrillón Hoyos, prefect of the Congregation for the Clergy, invited by His Eminence the Cardinal Archbishop Primate of Mexico, Don Norberto Rivera Carrera. The presence of these persons who came from Rome was due to the fact that on August 24 of this year, in a room of the curia of the archdiocese of Mexico, the book *El encuentro de la Virgen de Guadalupe y Juan Diego*, written by the priests Fidel González Fernández, Eduardo Chávez Sánchez, and José Luis Guerrero Rosado, was publicized. They kept the book a secret and did not make it known until the meeting.

In fact those invited were the clergy of the archdiocese of Mexico, whose attendance was minimal, a group of religious women, a group of laypersons, and some of the communications media.

In the presidium were the cardinals, the apostolic nuncio, the authors of the book, Monsignor Sánchez Barba, and one of the episcopal vicars who acted as master of ceremonies.

In the said presentation there was no opportunity for questions or objections, and it was simply announced that the new book resolved all the existing difficulties and that the preparations for the canonization of the Indian Juan Diego were ready, once the last customary procedures were finished in Rome.

In reality this event was little noticed in the media, and the critics did not give it any greater importance.

We said in the introduction to this letter that we are disturbed, within the orthodoxy of our faith, by the fact that an alleged "salvific event," as it is called in the *Positio*, whose historicity has been widely disputed since at least the beginning of the eighteenth century and continues to be the subject of serious differences, in the following year — according to reports — during the month of May, comes the canonization of this Indian, who, for many, did not exist. The book that was presented added nothing new to what was said in the *Positio*, outside of the often superficial refutation of the books of Doctor Richard Nebel and of the American priest Stafford Poole, both serious and profound researchers, even if with different methodologies. Rather, the new book suffers from the inaccuracies and errors of the *Positio* itself. Of Doctor Noguez, whose historical thesis is of the highest scholarly interest and absolute honesty, nothing is said, outside of an occasional allusion.

With regard to the image of Our Lady itself, which has been venerated in the Basilica since time immemorial, and which allegedly is the *ayate* of Juan Diego, made from maguey fiber, it was known quite well ever since the eighteenth century that "the material on which the holy image is painted," as says Don Mariano Fernández de Echeverría y Veytia, a fervent Guadalupan apparitionist, in his work *Baluartes de México (1775–1779)*, is not of *ixtle* or maguey fiber, but of palm or cotton fiber, since its weave is denser than the *ayate*, which is wider and thinner.

For the purpose of work of preservation we ordered a new analysis of some of the threads and we found that they were canvas.

In fact, when we transferred the image of Our Lady from the old to the new Basilica, and out of a desire to give it the best protection possible, we examined it quite closely, both some of our best experts in the preservation of works of art and the archpriest Don Carlos Warnholtz, and a servant, at that time the abbot of the Basilica [Schulenburg], and we realized that it combined all the characteristics of a picture made by human hands, with the deterioration proper to the antiquity of the image itself. We sent the said critical examination to the Apostolic See as a sign of honesty and love for the truth. Nevertheless, the authors of the new book, together with a group of persons they took to the Basilica by night, did not want to examine the image and viewed it only through the glass.

On pages 193–214 of the new book there is an attempt to present the image of Our Lady as a "trustworthy document" and as an authentic message for whom it was intended. Nevertheless, there was no such technical and scientific examination; those present could realize that it was a question of a true human picture. Some historians as serious as Father [Ernest] Burrus, S.J.(†), who did not know the image directly and close-up, affirm that "the number one document is precisely the Holy Image." Since, then, it is a human pictorial work, that argument loses all is documental and iconographic value.

Before all else our questions are: What kind of assent in a canonization does the Catholic Church demand of a totally orthodox believer? Is it perhaps a matter of faith to accept the authenticity of this canonization, which as we learned in theology, should be considered a "dogmatic fact"? Is it possible, by way of theology, to arrive at the historic truth of an "event" that could not be proved by way of the documentation that gives us moral certitude?

And as the great historian and scholar, Don Joaquín García Icazbalceta, whom Don Marcelino Menéndez y Pelayo called "master of all learning," said in response to the Most Illustrious Señor Archbishop of Mexico, Don Pelagio Antonio Labastida y Dávalos, who wanted to know his opinion about a defense of the apparitions of Our Lady of Guadalupe of Mexico, "Your Excellency, I am not a theologian or canon lawyer, but I am an historian. As a result I do not wish to pass judgment on this defense." Señor Labastida insisted, since he apparently had his doubts, and answered him, "I do not ask your opinion as theologian or canonist, but as a person well versed in the history of this country. I ask you as a friend and command you as a prelate." All this is quoted from Labastida. In the end Don Joaquín yielded and wrote his famous letter, which has been the material for so many disputes.

Our present question can be the same: If the famous canonization takes place, with perfect knowledge of the serious and grave historical problem, what ought to be our assent of faith? We say again: Can something be resolved by way of faith that has not been able to be resolved by way of history? What is the credibility and seriousness of the Church in such a case? Is the hierarchy of the persons pushing the canonization enough, without the historicity of the personage and of the events that are in legend attributed to such a personage enough?

We have never received any answer, official or unofficial, whether from the Secretariat of State or from the Congregation for the Causes of the Saints. Books and evidence have been sent. This is the last time that we will write about the topic, moved only by our love for the Church and for the truth. We believe that we deserve an answer, since we did not appeal to our hierarchy, but simply to our sharing in the priesthood of Christ, whether ministerial or baptismal, within the Church to which we belong.

We have followed carefully the human process of this problem in Rome, and we are saddened by the way in which it has been carried out.

We dare to make a modest suggestion: if in Rome the Congregation for the Causes of the Saints would in all honesty want to entrust its study and commentaries to an authentic doctor in Church history, one with a profound knowledge of the history of the Church on our Latin

American continent, especially Mexico, to evaluate in an independent and objective way, without showing partiality either to the group that supports the apparitions of Our Lady to an Indian nor to the authorized writers who maintain the opposite, to comment, for example, on the book of Doctor Xavier Noguez, whose text seems to us to be of great value for the subject of Guadalupe, especially in the most ancient testimonies both native and Spanish, we think that the said study would shed notable light on the criteria of that Congregation for something as momentous as is whether to canonize the Indian Juan Diego or not.

We could have many priests and non-priests endorse this document, since they have thus made clear to us, but we do not want to compromise anyone.

Thanking beforehand your fine and care attention to this letter and in hope of your response, we sign

Your Eminence's attentive and certain servants in the Lord,

Monsignor Guillermo Schulenburg Prado,
Prothonotary Apostolic Abbot Emeritus of Guadalupe

Reverend Doctor Carlos Warnholtz B.,
Archpriest of the Basilica of Guadalupe

Canon Esteban Martínez de la Serna,
Librarian of the Basilica[1]

Notes

Abbreviations Used in the Notes

AAS   *Acta Apostolicae Sedis: Commentarium Officiale*
(Vatican City, 1909–   )

ASV   Archivio Segreto Vaticano, Vatican City

THG   *Testimonios históricos guadalupanos*, ed. Ernesto de la Torre Villar
and Ramiro Navarro de Anda

Introduction

1. Poole, *Our Lady of Guadalupe*.
2. Hernández Chávez, "¡Qué pena Señor Abad!" 12.

Chapter 1. From the Beginning

1. Reprinted as "Imagen de la Virgen María Madre de Dios de Guadalupe
(1648)," in *THG*, 152–281. See also López Beltrán, *La primera historia guadalupana de México impresa*.

2. Sánchez erroneously identified Zumárraga as the bishop of Mexico; he was
only bishop-elect.

3. Sánchez, "Imagen de la Virgen María Madre de Dios de Guadalupe
(1648)," in *THG*, 181.

4. Ibid., 187.

5. Ibid., 190 (emphasis in original).

6. Ibid.

7. This was an anachronism on Sánchez's part, for there was no ecclesiastical
cabildo at that time.

8. For a detailed analysis of these miracles, see Sousa, Poole, and Lockhart,
The Story of Guadalupe, 14–17.

9. A good translation of this book into Spanish is Velázquez, *Hvei Tlamahvicoltiça* [*sic*]. A critical edition of the work, together with a precise translation, is
Sousa, Poole, and Lockhart, *The Story of Guadalupe*. There are Spanish transla-

tions by Guillermo Ortiz de Montellano, Jesús Galera Lamadrid, and Miguel León-Portilla (titled *Tonantzin Guadalupe*).

10. Sousa, Poole, and Lockhart, *The Story of Guadalupe*, 63.

11. Ibid., 43–47.

12. Sánchez, "Imagen de la Virgen María Madre de Dios de Guadalupe (1648)," in *THG*, 158.

13. On this, see Poole, *Our Lady of Guadalupe*, 102, 105–6, 108; and Robles, *Diario*, 1:145.

14. Gutiérrez Dávila, *Memorias historicas*, 254.

15. On the scarcity of paper, see Beristáin de Sousa, *Biblioteca hispanoamericana septentrional*, 2:116.

16. Sousa, Poole, and Lockhart, *The Story of Guadalupe*, 116–17.

17. On the inquiry, see Poole, *Our Lady of Guadalupe*, 128–43; and Noguez, *Documentos guadalupanos*, 124–32. The documents of the inquiry have been reproduced in Sada Lambretón, *Las informaciones jurídicas*; and Chávez Sánchez, *La Virgen de Guadalupe y Juan Diego en las informaciones jurídicas de 1666*.

18. On this, see Noguez, *Documentos guadalupanos*, 161; and Poole, *Our Lady of Guadalupe*, 139–42. Poole's judgment on the testimony of Diego Cano Moctezuma needs to be modified: the witness's claim to have been a *nieto* of the Mexica emperor could mean that he was only a descendant, not a grandson (140).

19. On Becerra Tanco's testimony, see Poole, *Our Lady of Guadalupe*, 144–51; and Noguez, *Documentos guadalupanos*, 132–37, 181, 247.

20. In *THG*, 309–33.

21. In this context, the term "Mexico" referred to the city, not the modern nation.

22. For a summary of these, see Poole, *Our Lady of Guadalupe*, 145–51.

23. Sada Lambretón, *Las informaciones jurídicas*, facsimile no. 275; [Vera], *Informaciones sobre la milagrosa aparicion de la Santísima Virgen de Guadalupe*, 138–39.

24. Becerra Tanco, "Origen milagroso del Santuario de Nuestra Señora de Guadalupe (1666)," in *THG*, 325.

25. Sada Lambretón, *Las informaciones jurídicas*, facsimile nos. 306–7; [Vera], *Informaciones sobre la milagrosa aparicion de la Santísima Virgen de Guadalupe*, 149.

26. On Florencia, see Poole, *Our Lady of Guadalupe*, 156–65; and Brading, *Mexican Phoenix*, 101–14.

27. Florencia, *La estrella del norte de Mexico*, 6.

28. Gama had subsidized the publication of Becerra Tanco's *Felicidad de México*.

29. Florencia, *La estrella del norte de Mexico*, 41–42.

30. Ibid., 50–51.

31. Ibid., 314–16.

32. Ibid., 316.

33. The standard reference for his life is Irving Leonard, *Don Carlos de Sigüenza y Góngora*; see also Alicia Mayer, "El guadalupanismo en Carlos de Sigüenza y Góngora."

34. Noguez believes that it was probably written between 1688 and 1693 and published between 1694 and 1700 (*Documentos guadalupanos*, 144). Alicia Mayer says that it was not printed until 1790 (personal communication).

35. Sigüenza y Góngora, *Piedad heroyca de Don Fernando Cortés*, 63.

36. There is some question as to how Sigüenza y Góngora would have obtained these papers, since he would have been no more than six years old at the time of Alva Ixtlilxochitl's death. The papers may have come to Sigüenza y Góngora through Ixtlilxochitl's son, Juan de Alva y Cortés.

37. This was the edition of *Felicidad de México* published in Seville in 1685 (see Becerra Tanco, "Origen milagroso del Santuario de Nuestra Señora de Guadalupe [1666], in *THG*, 326).

38. Sigüenza y Góngora, *Piedad heroyca de Don Fernando Cortés*, 65.

39. This was one of the factors that led Garibay to be skeptical about Sigüenza y Góngora's attribution of the authorship to Valeriano. "Confusions such as this at least make the testimony very suspect, if they do not totally invalidate it" (*Historia de la literatura náhuatl*, 2:264).

40. Noguez, *Documentos guadalupanos*, 137. Noguez deals with the confusion created by Florencia with regard to these documents (ibid., 139).

41. Escamilla González, "Máquinas troyanas."

42. Boturini Benaduci, *Idea de una nueva historia general de la América septentrional* [edición facsímil], 2–3.

43. Escamilla González, "Máquinas troyanas," 15.

44. On this, see Poole, *Our Lady of Guadalupe*, 177.

45. Escamilla González, "Máquinas troyanas," 19.

46. Bartolache, "Manifiesto satisfactorio u opúsculo guadalupano (1790)," in *THG*, 603.

47. Ibid., 603 n. 4.

48. Velázquez, *La aparición*, 337.

49. Muñoz, "Memoria sobre las apariciones y el culto de Nuestra Señora de Guadalupe (1794)," in *THG*, 691–701.

50. Ibid., 691.

51. Ibid., 692.

52. Ibid., 693.

53. On this, see Poole, *Our Lady of Guadalupe*, 69–77.

54. Muñoz, "Memoria sobre las apariciones y el culto de Nuestra Señora de Guadalupe (1794)," in *THG*, 699.

55. Ibid., 701.

56. Quoted in Altamirano, "La Fiesta de Guadalupe (1884)," in *THG*, 1177.

57. Extensive quotations from this interview can be found in ibid., 1177–78.

58. Mier, fifth letter to Muñoz, in *THG*, 831; Altamirano, "La Fiesta de Guadalupe (1884)," in ibid., 1177–78.

59. Mier Noriega y Guerra, "Cartas a Juan Bautista Muñoz (1797)," in *THG*, 757–861

60. Fernández de Uribe, *Sermon*; Escamilla González, *José Patricio Fernández de Uribe*, 61.

61. Fernández de Uribe, *Sermon*, 3.

62. Ibid., 17–18.

63. On this will, see Poole, *Our Lady of Guadalupe*, 195–200.

64. Escamilla González says that Omana y Sotomayor played no role in composing the report, but he does not cite any source (*José Patricio Fernández de Uribe*, 248 n. 32).

65. Ibid., 256–57. Escamilla González believes that this edict actually hurt the Guadalupan cause by shutting off intellectual debate on the subject and leaving it entirely to popular piety (259).

66. Ibid., 245–49. In 1750 the church at Guadalupe was given a chapter of canons. Chapters are usually attached to cathedrals, and the canons have two functions: singing the canonical hours in common and acting as an advisory board to the ordinary. Chapters in non-cathedral churches have only the first function and are called collegiate chapters, hence the shrine at Guadalupe was called La Colegiata. The presiding officer of a collegiate chapter is called a secular abbot.

67. Fernández de Uribe, *Disertacion historico-critica*, 16.

68. Ibid., 21.

69. Ibid., 71.

70. Ibid., 77.

71. Ibid., 79. It should be noted that Uribe must have taken this from Becerra Tanco's *Origen milagroso* rather than the *Felicidad de Mexico*.

72. Sherman, Meyer, and Deeds, *The Course of Mexican History*, 279.

73. Velázquez, *La aparición*, 295.

74. Guridi y Alcocer, "Sermón de Nuestra Señora de Guadalupe (1804)," in *THG*, 863–74.

75. Ibid., 864.

76. Ibid., 872.

77. See Guridi y Alcocer, "Apología de la aparición (1820)," in *THG*, 874–974, especially 896–900.

78. Ibid., 874–974.

79. Ibid., 903.

80. Ibid., 904.

81. According to Altamirano, Bustamante first wrote this as *Disertación guadalupana*, which preceded his edition of book 12 of Sahagún's *Historia general*. He revised this work and published it in 1840 with "the strange title" of *La aparición* ("La fiesta de Guadalupe [1884]," in *THG*, 1201 n. 124).

82. Reprinted in *THG*, 1007–56.

83. Grajales and Burrus, *Bibliografía guadalupana, 1531–1984*, s.v. no. 357.

84. Bustamante, "Elogios y defensa Guadalupana (1831–1843)," in *THG*, 1012 (emphasis in original).

85. Ibid. (emphasis in original).

86. In *THG*, 1056–91. Grajales and Burrus cite Bustamante as the author (*Bibliografía guadalupana, 1531–1984*, s.v. no. 343).

87. Bustamante, "La aparición," in *THG*, 1020–21 (emphasis in original).

88. *Informe critico-legal*, 6 (emphasis in original). The other two commissioners were Father José Ortigosa and Licenciado Luis González Movellán.

89. Lucas Alamán, *Disertaciones* (Mexico City, 1969), 2:157, quoted in Brading, *Mexican Phoenix*, 265.
90. See Brading, *Mexican Phoenix*, 242–43; Fowler, *Tornel and Santa Anna*.
91. Tornel y Mendívil, *La aparición*, 1:5–18.
92. Ibid., 2:1.
93. In a letter to the Jesuit Basilio Arrillaga, quoted in Brading, *Mexican Phoenix*, 266.

Chapter 2. The Controversy Is Ignited

1. See Sherman, Meyer, and Deeds, *The Course of Mexican History*, 376–81.
2. For a good brief survey of these differing attitudes, see Weiner, "Trinidad Sánchez Santos," 328.
3. On this, see Roger Aubert, "Aspects divers du néo-thomisme." Mazzella (1833–1900) had spent ten years (1869–79) at Woodstock, New York, organizing their Jesuit system of studies before being called back to Rome to do the same there. During his stay at Woodstock, he became an American citizen.
4. Hill, *Lord Acton*, 145.
5. O'Dogherty, "El ascenso de una jerarquía intransigente," 180. This article is an excellent brief summary of the ecclesial situation in Mexico and the part played by the Colegio Pío Latinoamericano.
6. On this, see Hurtado, *El cisma mexicano*.
7. On the history of the Colegio and its alumni, see Cavalli, "Cent'anni"; Gómez Rodeles, "El Colegio Pío-Latino-Americano"; Maina, "Il Pontificio Collegio Pio Latino Americano"; Medina Ascensio, *Historia del Colegio Pio Latino Americano*. Of special importance because it deals with the alumni who became bishops in Mexico is O'Dogherty, "El ascenso de una jerarquía intransigente."
8. Quoted in Cavalli, "Cent'anni," 261.
9. Ibid.
10. Plancarte y Navarrete, *Antonio Plancarte y Labastida*, 336.
11. Ibid.
12. Tapia Méndez, *El siervo de Dios*, 128.
13. Mexico, in this context, refers to the city, not the nation.
14. Antícoli, *Historia*, 2:322–23.
15. For biographical data, see Carreño, "Notas biográficas." Some sources give his full last name as Andrade Pau, his mother's name having been Eleonora Pau de Andrade (see Dios, *Historia de la familia vicentina en México*, 1:589–90). His first name is often given as Vicente de Paula, although he himself always wrote it as Vicente de Paúl.
16. Carreño, "Notas biográficas," 14.
17. This is according to Carreño, "Notas biográficas," 14. Valverde Téllez says he entered on November 8 (*Bio-Bibliografía eclesiástica*, 1:35), as does Carreño ("Notas biográficas," 13); Dios says November 12 (*La familia vicentina en México*, 1:589), as do the records in the General Curia (Curia Generalizia della Missione, Rome, *Dictionnaire du Personnel*, troisième série, 1851–1900).
18. Carreño says December 18 ("Notas biográficas," 14).

19. This date is according to the records of the General Curia, Curia Generalizia della Missione, Rome, *Dictionnaire du Personnel*, troisième série, 1851–1900. Valverde Téllez says 1870 (*Bio-Bibliografía eclesiástica*, 1:36); as does Dios (*La familia vicentina en México*, 1:589).

20. Records of the General Curia (Curia Generalizia della Missione, Rome, *Dictionnaire du Personnel*, troisième série, 1851–1900); the date was 1873 according to Valverde Téllez (*Bio-Bibliografía eclesiástica* 1:36), or 1872 according to Dios (*La familia vicentina en México*, 1:589).

21. Records of the General Curia (Curia Generalizia della Missione, Rome, *Dictionnaire du Personnel*, troisième série, 1851–1900). The date was 1878 according to Dios (*La familia vicentina en México*, 1:590).

22. Bravo Ugarte, *Diócesis y obispos*, 84.

23. Unfortunately, information on García Icazbalceta is not as plentiful as one would like. Among the works consulted for this study were Galindo y Villa, *Don Joaquín García Icazbalceta*, which this author found at the Biblioteca Nacional de México in Mexico City, bound in with a copy of Agüeros, *Album de la coronación*. Another version, perhaps the original, is "Don Joaquín García Icazbalceta, His Life and Works." This biographical sketch was first published in 1889, during García Icazbalceta's lifetime. It was somewhat revised in 1903 and appeared as a pamphlet in 1905. See also Martínez, *Don Joaquín García Icazbalceta*; Bernal, *Correspondencia de Nicolás León con Joaquín García Icazbalceta*; Wagner, *Joaquín García Icazbalceta*; "Noticia biográfica," 1:v–xvi; Camelo, "Joaquín García Icazbalceta," 13–21. A listing of biographical events and dates can be found in Valton, *Homenaje*, 70–11.

24. Galindo y Villa, *Don Joaquín García Icazbalceta*, 524.

25. Martínez, *Don Joaquín García Icazbalceta*, 8.

26. Wagner, *Joaquín García Icazbalceta*, 11.

27. Keen, *The Aztec Image in Western Thought*, 433–34.

28. González Fernández, Chávez Sánchez, and Guerrero Rosado, *El encuentro*, 11.

29. *Diccionario Porrúa*, s.v. García Icazbalceta.

30. Montes de Oca y Obregón, "Breve elogio," 349–55.

31. Ibid., 350–51.

32. "Noticia biográfica," 1:xv.

33. Montes de Oca y Obregón, "Breve elogio," 353.

34. Francisco de Paula Verea y González (1813–84) was consecrated bishop of Linares in the church at Guadalupe in 1853, and was bishop of Puebla from 1879 to 1884. See also Brading, *Mexican Phoenix*, 261–62.

35. Antícoli, *Defensa*, 307 n. 1.

36. Ibid., 122 (emphases is Antícoli's).

37. Quoted in Antícoli, *Historia*, 2:236.

38. Altamirano, "La fiesta de Guadalupe (1884)," in *THG*, 1156.

39. Antícoli, *La Virgen del Tepeyac*.

40. Gutiérrez Casillas, *Jesuítas en México*, 254.

41. Iguíniz, *Disquisiciones biblográficas*, 196, quoting José María Vigil. Iguíniz cited Primo Feliciano Velázquez as theorizing that the archbishop's motive

was to give García Icazbalceta an opportunity to break his silence on the Guadalupe question (ibid., 197). This does not seem plausible in view of the fact that the letter was supposed to remain confidential and did remain so for a long time.

42. See Appendix 1. This aspect of the controversy has never been the subject of full scholarly research. A summary of it can be found in Brading, *Mexican Phoenix*, chapter 11. Gutiérrez Casillas devotes a few paragraphs to it (*Historia*, 359–64). He was not sympathetic to García Icazbalceta, "The most serious thing was that a practicing Catholic and famed historian came to be the head of the anti-apparitionist school" (ibid., 359), and "He did not want to take away anyone's devotion but in reality he did so, and thus came to be the object of violent polemics and attacks" (360). And, "With regard to señor García Icazbalceta, wounded in the innermost depth of his sensitivity, before the tacit censures of the hierarchs of the Church and the 'indecency' of Father Antícoli, he enclosed himself in a contemptuous silence and killed time like someone who could entertain himself in making cages and mousetraps" (361).

43. García Icazbalceta, *Carta*, 51; "Carta" in *Investigación histórica y documental*, 70.

44. García Icazbalceta, *Carta*, 11; "Carta," in *Investigación histórica y documental*, 22.

45. Sosa, *El episcopado mexicano*, 5–16.

46. "La Virgen de Guadalupe: Entrevista," *El Universal*, August 30, 1896.

47. The area at Guadalupe is often referred to as La Villa de Guadalupe, or simply La Villa.

48. "La leyenda guadalupana: Opinión del Sr. Agreda," *El Universal*, September 4, 1896. There is no clue as to who the elderly canon was.

49. He was bishop of Sonora from 1852 to 1868, and of Guadalajara from 1868 until his death in 1898 (Bravo Ugarte, *Diócesis y obispos*, 54). Valverde Téllez gives 1868 as the date when he became bishop of Guadalajara (*Bio-Bibliografía eclesiástica*, 2:50).

50. See Escalada, *Enciclopedia guadalupana*, vol. 2, s.v. Santa María de Guadalupe, patrona de los mexicanos. On Sabás Camacho, see Valverde Téllez, *Bio-Bibliografía eclesiástica*, 1:169–78; on Ramón Camacho García, see ibid. 1:178–82. Because of his learning and influence, the latter had the nickname of "mentor del Episcopado Mexicano" (Munguía, *La obra*, 9).

51. Iguíniz, *Disquisiciones bibliográficas*, 200.

52. González, *Santa María de Guadalupe*, introduction.

53. Ibid., 324–34.

54. Ibid., 324.

55. Ibid.

56. Ibid., 328.

57. Interview, *El Universal*, August 30, 1896. As will be mentioned, the purpose of this and similar interviews was to testify to the authenticity of the recently published letter.

58. Interview, *El Universal*, September 1, 1896, quoted in Iguíniz, *Disquisiciones bibliográficas*, 201.

59. According to Carreño, it was García Icazbalceta himself who showed the

letter to José María de Jesús, Agreda y Sánchez, and Paso y Troncoso, at their own request (Carreño, "Notas biográficas," 25).

60. The papers of this controversy are published in *THG*, 36–72; Romero Salinas, *Eclipse guadalupano*, 219–61; and Miranda Godínez, *Dos cultos fundantes*, 421–38. For an analysis of the incident, see Poole, *Our Lady of Guadalupe*, 58–64; Noguez, *Documentos guadalupanos*, 89–91; and Lundberg, *Unification and Conflict*, 204–12.

61. Agreda y Sánchez, "Carta a los editores," in *Investigación histórica y documental*, 83–84. Ramírez (1804–1871) was one of the most distinguished Mexican historians of the nineteenth century. Because he served the imperial government of Maximilian, he was forced into exile and died in Germany (Torre Villar, *Mexicanos ilustres*, 2: 221–53).

62. Agreda y Sánchez, "Carta a los editores," 84. Agreda y Sánchez says that he heard the story from José Guadalupe Arriola, a friend of Ramírez. He also says that a "person of trust" told him that the same thing had happened to Rafael Adorno. A certain degree of skepticism is in order.

63. Agreda y Sánchez, "Carta a los editores," 84.

64. Ibid., 84–85.

65. Ibid., 85–86.

66. *Información*, 1888 ed., v–ix. The *aditamentos* are found on pp. 55–102, together with a listing of authors who did not favor the apparitions. See also O'Gorman, *Destierro de sombras*, 265–71. Surprisingly, the editors of *THG* have included the *aditamentos* after the text in their publication (pp. 72–99), and the notes (pp. 99–141). The *Investigación histórica y documental* does not include the notes. Felipe Teixidor, in his notes to García Icazbalceta's letter to Nicolás León, March 9, 1889, says that most of the *aditamentos* were written by Paso y Troncoso (García Icazbalceta, *Cartas*, 182 n. 4).

67. Antícoli, *Historia*, 333.

68. Especially by Romero Salinas (*Eclipse guadalupano*, 23–39, 157–59).

69. On this, see Poole, *Our Lady of Guadalupe*, 64.

70. García Icazbalceta to Aquilés Gerste, April 4, 1894, in García Icazbalceta, *Cartas*, 271.

71. Miranda Godínez, *Dos cultos fundantes*, 266 n. 14.

72. Ibid.

73. Grajales and Burrus, *Bibliografía guadalupana*, 14.

74. Velázquez, *La aparición*, 301.

75. Agustín de la Rosa y Serrano (1824–1907) was a canon of the Cathedral chapter of Guadalajara and a defender of Guadalupe. In 1887 he published a criticism of García Icazbalceta's letter, titled *Disertatio historico-theologica de apparitione B. M. V. de Guadalupe*, and would publish another in 1896, *Defensa de la aparición de Ntra. Sra. de Guadalupe*. For some basic facts of his life, see Valverde Téllez, *Bio-Bibliografía eclesiástica*, 3:403–9.

76. Matins was one of seven parts of the Roman Breviary and on feasts was divided into three nocturns. The second nocturn had three readings, called historical lessons, which dealt with the history and meaning of the feast.

77. According to González Fernández, Chávez Sánchez, and Guerrero

Rosado, Andrade broke into the archbishop's office (*El encuentro*, 13). According to Nicolás León, the copy was stolen from Agreda y Sánchez (García Icazbalceta, *Cartas*, 235 n. 4). Tapia Méndez gives an entirely different account as to how Andrade got Icazbalceta's letter: Don Joaquín had given the key of his home to Vivanco, Andrade borrowed it, and "removing some boards from the writing desk" took out the text of the letter (*El siervo de Dios*, 208).

78. However, Nicolás León also considered it to be a bad translation (Iguíniz, *Disquisiciones biblográficas*, 206). From what I have seen, the translation seems to be adequate.

79. Though the first volume is dated 1887, the introduction by José de Jesús Cuevas is dated November 25, 1889, and the dedication to Archbishop Labastida y Dávalos, December 1, 1889.

80. García Icazbalceta to Nicolás León, October 9, 1887, in García Icazbalceta, *Cartas*, 141.

81. Gutiérrez Casillas says that it was Loza y Pardavé who took the first steps toward a new mass and office, on November 27, 1889 (*Jesuítas en México*, 252).

82. Antícoli, *Historia*, 2:391; Velázquez, *La aparicion*, 302.

83. Tapia Méndez, *El siervo de Dios*, 208. Antícoli also says that he combined the two (*Historia*, 2:392).

84. Tapia Méndez, *El siervo de Dios*, 208.

85. Antícoli, *Historia*, 2:392; Velázquez, *La aparición*, 302–3. The three archbishops were Alarcón y Sánchez de la Barquera of Mexico, Loza y Pardavé of Guadalajara, and José Ignacio Arciga y Ruiz de Chávez of Michoacán. In that same year, three new metropolitan sees were erected: Oaxaca, Durango, and Linares. The bishops' petition and the supporting arguments were printed in *Sacra Rituum Congregatione*.

86. Cuevas said that he would not give the name of the representative because the man later regretted his role in the campaign (Cuevas, *Album histórico guadalupano del IV centenario*, 258).

87. Interview with Agreda y Sánchez, *El Universal*, September 4, 1896.

88. Velázquez, *La aparición*, 303; Antícoli, *Historia*, 2:392–93. Vannutelli was one of the cardinal members of the Congregation of Rites (see *La gerarchia cattolica*, 645).

89. Velázquez, *La aparición*, 303.

90. Ibid., 303.

91. For a summary of these, based on Antícoli's responses, see Velázquez, *La aparición*, 303–4. The promotor of the faith was sometimes called the devil's advocate. This was not an ad hoc position, but rather a permanent one entrusted to one of the consultors (see *La gerarchia cattolica*, 648).

92. Interview in *El Universal*, September 4, 1896.

93. Valverde Téllez, *Bio-Bibliografía eclesiástica*, 1:171; Antícoli, *Historia*, 2:394. While in Rome, he also worked toward the erection of the diocese of Durango and the appointment of Fortino Hipólito Vera as the first bishop of Cuernavaca (Salinas, *Bosquejo biográfico*, 27).

94. Velázquez, *La aparición*, 305. There is no indication as to who wrote this letter.

95. Quoted in Iguíniz, *Disquisiciones biblográficas*, 208.

96. This material is taken from Plancarte y Navarrete's own account, "Apuntes históricos," 335–45.

97. Plancarte y Navarrete to Alarcón, 16 December 1893, cited in Plancarte y Navarrete, "Apuntes históricos," 336.

98. Same to same, ibid., 337. Quoted in Iguíniz, *Disquisiciones bibliográficas*, 208.

99. Plancarte y Navarrete to Alarcón, December 16, 1893, in Plancarte y Navarrete, "Apuntes históricos," 337.

100. Plancarte y Navarrete to Alarcón, January 13, 1894, in ibid., 338.

101. Plancarte y Navarrete to Alarcón, February 28, 1894, in ibid., 339.

102. Ibid.

103. Ibid.

104. Plancarte y Navarrete to Alarcón, March 7, 1894, in ibid., 342.

105. Plancarte y Navarrete to Alarcón, March 7, 1894, in ibid., 340; see also Antícoli, *Historia*, 2:400–8.

106. The Vannutelli report (*Sacra Rituum Congregatione*) contains the most important papers of the process. These include an introduction by Mariani (4–11), a summary of the request to the pope by the three archbishops of Mexico, February 12, 1892 (13–14), Leo XIII's approval of the coronation, February 7, 1887 (14–16), the office granted by Benedict XIV (16–24), the decree authorizing that office, April 24, 1754 (24–25), the proposed new office (25–32), the observations by the promotor of the faith (1–19 of a separate foleto), refutation of the observations by Mariani (1–74, new foleto), a Latin translation of the *Nican mopohua* (19–30), and an Italian translation of some of the testimonies from the capitular inquiry of 1666. It is of interest that the historical lessons in the proposed new office do not correspond to those of 1754, or those eventually approved by the Holy See.

107. Brief accounts of the coronation can be found in Bravo Ugarte, *Diócesis y obispos,* 47–50; and López Beltrán, *Album del LXXV aniversario de la coronación guadalupana,* 194–226.

108. López Beltrán, *Album del LXXV aniversario de la coronación guadalupana,* 217; Tapia Méndez, *El siervo de Dios,* 26; Salinas, *Bosquejo bibliográfico.* See also Banegas, "Patriota y guadalupano," 39–50. There is no good, objective biography of Plancarte, one of the most controversial figures in recent Mexican Church history. Those that have been written are usually hagiographic in character. The biography by his nephew, Francisco Plancarte y Navarrete, *Antonio Plancarte y Labastida,* is detailed but also favorable to his uncle. It also stops at the year 1889.

109. He was director of the Colegio de San Luis in Jacona, and later of San Joaquín; first bishop of Campeche, 1896 (or 1895?)–1898; second bishop of Cuernavaca, 1899–1911; archbishop of Monterrey (Linares), 1912–1920. Around 1914, he was exiled and lived at DePaul University in Chicago, together with Orozco y Jiménez and Leopoldo Ruiz. There was another nephew, the priest Miguel Plancarte, about whom I have been able to find very little. For biographical details, see Valverde Téllez, *Bio-Bibliografía eclesiástica,* 2:234–40.

110. Tapia Méndez, *El siervo de Dios*, 24.

111. Ibid., 31.

112. Plancarte y Navarrete, *Antonio Plancarte y Labastida*, 10.

113. Montes de Oca y Obregón, "Elogio fúnebre . . . Plancarte," 221. Saint Mary's College was opened in 1794 at a time when Catholics were not admitted to Oxford or Cambridge. By the mid–nineteenth century it had achieved a high degree of prestige. The future Cardinal Nicholas Wiseman was president from 1840 to 1847, and the noted architect Augustus Pugin taught there. The famed English Catholic historian Lord Acton was also an alumnus.

114. Ibid., 222. Montes de Oca had resided in England for so long that he was beginning to forget Spanish. Montes de Oca would later make Plancarte an honorary canon of the Cathedral of San Luis Potosí.

115. Valverde Téllez, *Bio-bibliografía eclesiástica*, 3:99.

116. Tapia Méndez, *El siervo de Dios*, 64–65.

117. Ibid., 75–76.

118. Plancarte y Labastida's obituary, submitted by Vicente de P. Andrade, stated that he also studied at the Colegio Pío Latinoamericano (*El Tiempo*, April 27, 1898).

119. Quoted in Tapia Méndez, *El siervo de Dios*, 69.

120. Ibid., 68–69.

121. The statue of Plancarte y Labastida in the old Basilica at Guadalupe shows him dressed in the Roman style, down to the shoe buckles.

122. The term is derived from Malintzin, also known as Malinche, the native interpreter and mistress of Hernando Cortés; she is viewed by Mexican nationalists as a traitor to her people. The term refers to anyone who shows too great a fondness for things foreign or non-Mexican.

123. Montes de Oca y Obregón, "Elogio Fúnebre . . . Plancarte," 237.

124. For his years in Jacona, see Plancarte y Navarrete, *Antonio Plancarte y Labastida*, 75–86. Jacona is an ancient town, having been founded in 1555 by Fray Sebastián de Trastierra.

125. On his use of theater and the reaction to it, see ibid., 82–83.

126. Tapia Méndez, *El siervo de Dios*, 123.

127. Brading says that it was the bishop who closed the school (*Mexican Phoenix*, 294). This is possible, but unfortunately the actual course of events is not clear.

128. Tapia Méndez, *El siervo de Dios*, 126–27.

129. Plancarte y Navarrete, *Antonio Plancarte y Labastida*, 88–92.

130. Montes de Oca y Obregón, "Elogio Fúnebre . . . Plancarte," 238–39.

131. The story of the railroad is told by Plancarte y Navarrete, *Antonio Plancarte y Labastida*, 159–66. It is not clear if it was a true railway or a trolley system.

132. For data on him, see Valverde Téllez, *Bio-Bibliografía eclesiástica*, 1:227–29.

133. Tapia Méndez, *El siervo de Dios*, 145.

134. Plancarte y Navarrete, *Antonio Plancarte y Labastida*, 165.

135. Treviño, *Antonio Plancarte y Labastida, Abad de Guadalupe*, 55–56.

Though he is listed only as "Señor Munguía," it is clearly the first archbishop of Michoacán, who lived from 1810 to 1868. He was from Zamora, and was a close friend of Archbishop Labastida y Dávalos (see *Diccionario Porrúa*, s.v. Munguía; Munguía, *La obra*; and Montes de Oca y Obregón, "Elogio fúnebre . . . Labastida y Dávalos," 165–66).

136. Plancarte y Navarrete, *Antonio Plancarte y Labastida*, 169.

137. Ibid., 170.

138. Tapia Méndez, *El siervo de Dios*, 115.

139. The monument to Plancarte in the old Basilica of Guadalupe gave the date of establishment as February 2, 1878 (Munguía, *La obra*, 7).

140. The notice in López Beltrán, *Album del LXXV aniversario de la coronación guadalupana*, 218, says the opposite. It was originally called the Daughters of Mary Immaculate, and the name of Daughters of Mary Immaculate of Guadalupe was given to it when Plancarte and his community moved to Mexico City in 1885.

141. Tapia Méndez, *El siervo de Dios*, 155–56.

142. Visita Apostolica nel Messico di Nicola Averardi (1896–1900), in ASV, Busta 1: Istruzioni; Posizione 2ª, fascicolo 1º: Affari speciali, Antonio Plancarte. The story of this affair can be found in Treviño, *Antonio Plancarte y Labastida, Abad de Guadalupe* 52–55. This version of the story indicates that two girls were involved. See also Plancarte y Navarrete, *Antonio Plancarte y Labastida*, 179–91.

143. Letter of support for Plancarte, in Latin, to Averardi, from Orizaba, April 15, 1896, from a priest named Wilde, in ASV, Visita Apostolica nel Messico di Nicola Averardi (1896–1900), Busta 1: Istruzioni; Posizione 2ª, fascicolo 1º: Affari speciali, Antonio Plancarte.

144. According to O'Dogherty, the bishop disapproved of the kind of instruction given in the Colegio and looked askance at Plancarte's attempt to found a congregation of nuns ("El ascenso de una jerarquía intransigente," 182).

145. Munguía, *La obra*, 9.

146. It can be found in Tapia Méndez, *El siervo de Dios*, 145–46, 149–53.

147. According to Plancarte y Navarrete, this occurred in 1882 (*Antonio Plancarte y Labastida*, 181).

148. Ibid.

149. According to Brading, one of the accusations was that "Plancarte had married her in a civil ceremony, taking the view that the proceedings had no canonical validity. It was further alleged that he had been alone for a brief time with the young woman" (*Mexican Phoenix*, 306). Brading's phraseology makes it sound as if Plancarte had contracted civil marriage with Concepción.

150. It is not clear when he made this journey, but it may have been in 1891, when he went to Europe to purchase artwork for the restoration of the church at Guadalupe.

151. José Adrián Plancarte to Averardi, from Atzcapotzalco, September 1, 1899, in ASV, Visita Apostolica nel Messico di Nicola Averardi (1896–1900), Busta 1: Istruzioni; Posizione 2ª, fascicolo 1º: Affari speciali, Antonio Plancarte, folio 64r–v.

152. Ibid., folio 64v. The accusation that Antonio Plancarte had been expelled

from Zamora rather than leaving voluntarily would surface again during the coronation controversy. Montes de Oca glossed over all this in his eulogy of Plancarte, saying simply that he went to a new residence that "God was pointing out to him" (Montes de Oca y Obregón "Elogio fúnebre," 239).

153. These were Antonio's nephew, Francisco Plancarte y Navarrete, bishop of Cuernavaca, first cousin to the heirs; Leopoldo Ruiz y Flores; and a lawyer, Manuel Dávalos, who may also have been a relative (José Adrián Plancarte to Averardi, from Atzcapotzalco, September 1, 1899, in ASV, Visita Apostolica nel Messico di Nicola Averardi [1896–1900], Busta 1: Istruzioni; Posizione 2ª, fascicolo 1º: Affari speciali, Antonio Plancarte, folio 64r). Ruiz y Flores was bishop of León, 1900–1907, and was succeeded by Mora y del Río. Later, he was archbishop of Monterrey/Linares, 1907–11, and then Michoacán, 1911–41.

154. José Adrián Plancarte y Labastida to Averardi, September 3, 1899, in ASV, Visita Apostolica nel Messico di Nicola Averardi (1896–1900), Busta 1: Istruzioni; Posizione 2ª, fascicolo 1º: Affari speciali, Antonio Plancarte, folio 68v; José Adrián Plancarte y Labastida to Averardi, 1 September 1899, in ibid., folio 65r.

155. Agustín Verdugo to Averardi, August 5, 1896, in ibid., folio 37r; Agustín León to Averardi, December 15, 1896, in ibid., folio 46r–47v; Agustín León to Averardi, April 25, 1898, in ibid., folio 61r–v.

156. Tapia Méndez, *El siervo de Dios*, 167.

157. Ibid., 169.

158. For an overview of one aspect of clerical education in Mexico City, see Lee, "Clerical Education in Nineteenth-Century Mexico"; and Sánchez, *Historia del seminario conciliar de México*.

159. On all this, see Dios, *Historia de la familia vicentina en México*, 1:162–67.

160. Plancarte y Navarrete, *Antonio Plancarte y Labastida*, 294.

161. Tapia Méndez, *El siervo de Dios*, 206. Valverde Téllez gives the date of Labastida's death as February 4, 1891 (*Bio-Bibliografía eclesiástica*, 2:15; see also Agüeros, *Album de la Coronación*, 129–48). Alarcón was archbishop from 1891 until 1908 (see Valverde Téllez, *Bio-Bibliografía eclesiástica*, 1:80–93).

162. O'Dogherty gives the date as 1882, but this appears to be a typographical error ("El ascenso de una jerarquía intransigente," 183).

Chapter 3. Coronation and Controversy

1. Tapia Méndez, *El siervo de Dios*, 186. The story of the church is covered by Plancarte y Navarrete, *Antonio Plancarte y Labastida*, 284–93.

2. The site chosen for the church was immediately adjacent to the Church of San Francisco de Asís on what is now Avenida Madero in Mexico City. This required razing part of the old church's enclosure. The Church of San Francisco was roughly on the site of the famed Franciscan Church of San José de los Naturales.

3. Plancarte y Navarrete, *Antonio Plancarte y Labastida*, 290.

4. Tapia Méndez, *El siervo de Dios*, 175–77. Miguel Plancarte Garibay later became a canon of Guadalupe.

5. Plancarte to *El Tiempo*, July 18, 1895; Tapia Méndez, *El siervo de Dios*, 194–95; Plancarte to Victoriano Agüeros, from Tacuba, July 18, 1886, repro-

duced in López Beltrán, *Album del LXXV aniversario de la coronación guadalupana*, 196. Among those present was Montes de Oca. Gutiérrez Casillas says, probably incorrectly, that the idea came from the bishops of Mexico in 1885 (*Jesuítas en México*, 252). The image of Our Lady of Hope is in the present Church of San Agustín in Jacona. It is surprisingly small, probably not more than three or four feet, with the crown perched at a rather precarious angle. It is disconcerting to realize that from this small image came such a major controversy.

6. The other two archbishops were José Ignacio Arciga of Michoacán and Pedro Loza y Pardavé of Guadalajara. Their letter is reproduced in López Beltrán, *Album del LXXV aniversario de la coronación guadalupana*, 199–202.

7. Velázquez, *La aparición*, 300; Tapia Méndez, *El siervo de Dios*, 197.

8. The brief is reproduced in full in Velázquez, *La aparición*, 300. The three archbishops made the plans known to the Catholics in Mexico in a pastoral letter, March 19, 1887, which is reproduced in López Beltrán, *Album del LXXV aniversario de la coronación guadalupana*, 199–202.

9. López Beltrán, *Album del LXXV aniversario de la coronación guadalupana*, 197.

10. Plancarte y Labastida, *Catecismo*.

11. This is the date given by Antícoli (*Historia*, 1:88 n. 1). See also Brading, *Mexican Phoenix*, 304; and Tapia Méndez, *El siervo de Dios*, 201.

12. According to Velázquez, the absence of the crown was noticed when the image was returned to the church on September 30, 1895 (*La aparición*, 306).

13. Antícoli, *Historia*, 1:88 n. 1.

14. Quoted in Antonio Bertrán, "Reclama Guadalupana Su Corona," *Reforma*, May 22, 2000; see also Tapia Méndez, *El siervo de Dios*, 221.

15. Antonio Bertrán, "Reclama Guadalupana Su Corona," *Reforma*, May 22, 2000.

16. Ibid.

17. Chávez, *Celeste o terrestre*, 9, 10, 11.

18. Velázquez, *La aparición*, 306.

19. Montes de Oca y Obregón, "Elogio Fúnebre . . . Plancarte," 244.

20. This description is taken from López Beltrán, *Album del LXXV aniversario de la coronación guadalupana*, 220.

21. Tapia Méndez, *El siervo de Dios*, 205; Plancarte y Navarrete, *Antonio Plancarte y Labastida*, 395.

22. Plancarte y Navarrete, *Antonio Plancarte y Labastida*, 413.

23. Antonio Bertrán, "Reclama Guadalupana Su Corona," *Reforma*, May 22, 2000.

24. Brading, *Mexican Phoenix*, 295; as sources he cites Agüeros, *Album de la coronación*, 120; and Antícoli, *Historia*, 2:449–52.

25. Tapia Méndez, *El siervo de Dios*, 225–26.

26. López Beltrán, *Album del LXXV aniversario de la coronación guadalupana*, 203.

27. "La Carta del Nuestro Ilmo. Prelado," *El Nacional*, February 1, 1887. The letter was written from Yautepec.

28. López Beltrán, *Album del LXXV aniversario de la coronación guadalu-

pana, 219. The same story is told almost verbatim in *Vigésimo quinto aniversario*, 49; and also by Tapia Méndez, *El siervo de Dios*, 213.

29. Quoted in López Beltrán, *Album del LXXV aniversario de la coronación guadalupana*, 220. The whole incident seems too outlandish to be credible.

30. Tapia Méndez specified a canon named Angel Vivanco y Esteve as one of the most fervent anti-apparitionists and an enemy of Plancarte (*El siervo de Dios*, 208). I have not encountered that name elsewhere.

31. "Inimicus homo" was the phrase used in the Vulgate translation of the Bible to refer to the person who sowed weeds among wheat: "Inimicus homo hoc fecit" (An enemy has done this) (Matthew 13:28).

32. *El obispo de Tamaulipas*, 36.

33. Ibid.

34. Biographical data by Guillermo Prieto in *El Universal*, September 6, 1896.

35. Data on his life can be found in Zorrilla and González Salas, *Diccionario biográfico de Tamaulipas*, 431–34.

36. Bravo Ugarte has a confused entry on this (*Diócesis y obispos*, 85). He lists Montes de Oca and Sánchez Camacho as being respectively the first and second bishops of Tampico. He does not list Tamaulipas as a diocese, though later on a map/appendix he does.

37. Tapia Méndez, *El diario*, 86.

38. Sánchez Camacho, *Pastoral del Obispo de Tamaulipas*. The story of this part of the controversy is found in Antícoli, *Historia*, 2:306–11; Antícoli quotes from the pastoral on 307–8.

39. The archbishops' letter was dated September 24, 1886; the pope's response was February 8, 1887. Both had been published in *La Voz de México*, March 27, 1887.

40. Sánchez Camacho, *Pastoral del Obispo de Tamaulipas*, 15.

41. *El obispo de Tamaulipas*, 8.

42. Ibid., 15.

43. Ibid., 17–18.

44. Ibid., 40–43.

45. Ibid., 33.

46. Montes de Oca's position regarding Guadalupe seems to have been cautious. He went along with the other bishops regarding the coronation, but there is evidence that toward the end of his life he was anti-apparitionist, at least in sympathy. He was also a staunch defender of García Icazbalceta, as will be seen below. Antícoli was perplexed by his attitude (*Historia*, 2:309–10 n. 1).

47. This was most probably Cardinal Raffaele Monaco la Vallella (*La gerarchia cattolica*, 641).

48. Antícoli, *Historia*, 2:310.

49. In *La Verdad*, August 17, 1888, quoted in Antícoli, *El magisterio de la iglesia*, no pagination; and Velázquez, *La aparición*, 300–301.

50. Carrillo y Ancona was born at Izamal, April 19, 1837, and died in Mérida, Yucatán, March 19, 1897. He was consecrated bishop of Lero in the parish church of Guadalupe on July 6, 1884 and appointed bishop of Yucatán three years later. He was bishop from 1887 until 1897. See Agüeros, *Album de la*

coronación, 165; Bravo Ugarte, *Diócesis y obispos*, 95; Escalada, *Enciclopedia guadalupana*, s.v. Carrillo y Ancona; and Rivero Figueroa and Cantón Rosado, *Dos vidas ejemplares*. Unfortunately, the last book makes no reference to the bishop's role in the Guadalupan controversy. See also Valverde Téllez, *Bio-Bibliografía eclesiástica*, 1:193–99.

51. It is also quoted in Carrillo y Ancona, *Don Joaquín García Icazbalceta y la historia guadalupana*. The letter was addressed to Archbishop Alarcón, August 12, 1896, and contains several references to the previous letter.

52. Carrillo y Ancona, *Carta de actualidad*, 1–2.

53. Ibid., 3.

54. Ibid.

55. Ibid., 6.

56. Quoted in Carrillo y Ancona, *Don Joaquín García Icazbalceta y la historia guadalupana*, 6–7 (emphasis in original).

57. García Icazbalceta to Carrillo y Ancona, December 29, 1888, in Carrillo y Ancona, *Don Joaquín García Icazbalceta y la historia guadalupana*, 9.

58. García Icazbalceta to Nicolás León, March 9, 1889, in García Icazbalceta, *Cartas*, 182 (emphasis in original).

59. The letter is quoted in Antícoli, *El magisterio*, no pagination; and Antícoli, *Historia*, 2:331; it was reprinted in *El Universal*, September 10, 1896.

60. Emphasis in original.

61. *El Universal*, February 9, 1889.

62. Biographical data can be found in Gutiérrez Casillas, *Jesuítas en México*, 284, 252–58; Escalada, *Enciclopedia guadalupana*, s.v. Antícoli.

63. Gutiérrez Casillas, *Jesuítas en México*, 253; paraphrased in Escalada, *Enciclopedia guadalupana*, 1:46.

64. Gutiérrez Casillas, *Jesuítas en México*, 284; Escalada, *Enciclopedia guadalupana*, 1:46.

65. Antícoli, *La Virgen del Tepeyac, patrona principal de la nacion mexicana*. The introduction was by Archbishop Loza y Pardavé of Guadalajara; it was reprinted in 1956 by Editorial Nacional in Mexico City.

66. Antícoli, *El magisterio*.

67. Ibid., 10 (emphasis in original).

68. Ibid., 11 (emphasis in original).

69. Ibid., 21–22 (emphases in original).

70. Ibid., 73.

71. Ibid., 75 (emphasis in original).

72. This is taken from Felipe Teixidor's notes to García Icazbalceta's letter of March 9, 1889, to Nicolás León (García Icazbalceta, *Cartas*, 183 n. 4). He says that the quotation is taken from the correspondence of Agreda and León, specifically a letter of February 1, 1890, but he does not specify which of the two wrote it. From the context, it appears to have been Agreda. Agreda offered to buy fifty copies of the new edition so that he could send them to friends in Rome.

73. Carrillo y Ancona to Vera, October 15, 1890, in García Icazbalceta, *Cartas*, 185 n. 4. According to Teixidor, the original was in the Archivo García Gutiérrez.

74. Ibid.

75. "Notas á esta segunda edición," *Información* (1891), 103–65.
76. Andrade, "Ciertos aparicionistas," *Información* (1891), 126–47; *THG*, 109–29.
77. "Noticas del indio Marcos y de otros pintores del siglo XVI, *Información* (1891), 167–88; *THG*, 129–41.
78. Note by Felipe Teixidor to García Icazbalceta's letter of 9 March 1889 to Nicolás León, García Icazbalceta, *Cartas*, 183 n. 4. See also Brading, *Mexican Phoenix*, 273.
79. *THG*, 36–141. Grajales and Burrus have confused matters by not including Vera's *La milagrosa aparición* in their bibliography and attributing the 1891 republication of the *Información* to him (#444).
80. García Icazbalceta, *Cartas*, 249 n. 2.
81. Ibid., 249; Gutiérrez Casillas, *Jesuítas en México*, 255.
82. Antícoli, *Defensa de la aparición*, 15.
83. Ibid., 16 (emphasis in original).
84. Ibid., 23.
85. Ibid., 108, 120, 121.
86. *Aquello,* his code word for the Guadalupe question.
87. García Icazbalceta to León, 28 March 1890, García Icazbalceta, *Cartas*, 202; Iguíniz, *Disquisiciones bibliográficas*,197.
88. García Icazbalceta to León, 24 May 1893, García Icazbalceta, *Cartas*, 249; quoted in Iguíniz, *Disquisiciones bibliográficas*, 197 (emphases in original). Though García Icazbalceta did not mention the book's name, *La defensa* was the only one of Antícoli's books to be published in Puebla in 1893. León specifically identified it as the work that García Icazbalceta was referring to (García Icazbalceta, *Cartas*, 249 n. 2).
89. García Icazbalceta to León, 20 June 1893, García Icazbalceta, *Cartas*, 250. According to León, citing a letter from Agreda y Sánchez to Justo Zaragoza, December 1895, the work that García Icazbalceta abandoned was *Documentos para nuestra historia* (ibid., 250–51, n. 1)
90. García Icazbalceta to León, 24 May 1893, in Bernal, *Correspondencia de Nicolás León con Joaquín García Icazbalceta*, 307.
91. García Icazbalceta, *Cartas*, 251 n. 1. Aquilés (Achille) Gerste was a Belgian Jesuit who had been a consulter for the Bollandists. He came to Mexico in 1866 and was a close friend of both García Icazbalceta and Paso y Troncoso. He wrote about medicine and botany among the Mexicans and also about the Tarahumaras. He returned to Europe in March of 1893, never to return to Mexico (ibid., 212, note 3; Gutiérrez Casillas, *Jesuítas en México*, 250–51, 413).
92. García Icazbalceta, *Cartas*, 251; Gutiérrez Casillas, *Jesuítas en México*, 257.
93. The more correct form of the phrase is "donec corrigatur."
94. Quoted in García Icazbalceta, *Cartas*, 252 n. 1.
95. Gutiérrez Casillas, *Jesuítas en México*, 257.
96. That is, darnel, a poisonous weed. The reference is to the parable of the wheat and the weeds, Matthew 13: 24–30.
97. Quoted in García Icazbalceta, *Cartas*, 252 n. 1. According to the note, the letter was in the Archivo F. Pérez Salazar.

98. These can be found in Vera, *Contestación*, 629–77.

99. Antícoli, *Defensa*, 11 n. 1. It is interesting that Antícoli emphasized the anonymity of his opponents, since all his works were published in the same way.

100. "La cuestión guadalupana," *El Universal*, 1 September 1896.

101. "La leyenda guadalupana: opinión del Sr. Agreda," *El Universal*, 4 September 1896.

102. García Icazbalceta to Nicolás León, 13 July 1892, in García Icazbalceta, *Cartas*, 232; Bernal, *Correspondencia de Nicolás León con Joaquín García Icazbalceta*, 282.

103. García Icazbalceta to León, 5 October 1892, García Icazbalceta, *Cartas*, 235; Bernal, *Correspondencia de Nicolás León con Joaquín García Icazbalceta*, 288.

104. Nicolás León wrote "Don Joaquín insists on his singular attitude of feigning an absolute ignorance about the text of the Exquisitio. He was covering himself and at the same time he wanted to explore the attitude of his correspondent" (García Icazbalceta, *Cartas*, 235 n. 4).

105. García Icazbalceta, *Cartas*, 183; Gutiérrez Casillas, *Jesuítas en México*, 254.

106. Andrade, *Ciertos aparicionistas*. The book carried no date or publisher. Nicolás León said that it was published in Mexico City and that Andrade was the author (García Icazbalceta, *Cartas*, 233 n. 4). It has been reprinted, together with the Montúfar–Bustamante *Información*, in THG, 109–22.

107. This edition contains numerous footnotes by Andrade, some of which correct Vera's translation.

108. *Apuntes históricos.*

109. Ibid., 3–24.

110. Ibid., 25–30.

111. Ibid., 36. This section was written by P. Flores Valderrama.

112. Quoted in Iguíniz, *Disquisiciones bibliográficas*, 212.

113. "La Virgen de Guadalupe: Entrevista," interview with Francisco Sosa, *El Universal*, August 30, 1896; "La Cuestión Guadalupana: Otra Entrevista," with Galindo y Villa, *El Universal*, September 1, 1896; "La Leyenda Guadalupana: Opinión del Sr. Agreda," with Agreda y Sánchez, *El Universal*, September 4, 1896.

114. Quoted in Iguíniz, *Disquisiciones bibliográficas*, 212.

115. Ibid., 217.

116. Ibid.

117. Quoted in Carrillo y Ancona, *Don Joaquín García Icazbalceta y la historia guadalupana*, 11.

118. Quoted in Iguíniz, *Disquisiciones bibliográficas*, 217.

119. "Advertencia a los Católicos," *El Tiempo*, August 11, 1896; Iguíniz, *Disquisiciones bibliográficas*, 215. According to Vera, on April 12, 1894 the archbishop ordered that "none of his *diocesanos* should presume to write or read anything that in any way would be contrary to this important truth of the apparition" (Vera, *Contestación a una hoja anónima*, introduction, unpaginated).

120. Montes de Oca y Obregón, *Obras pastorales y oratorias* (Mexico City, 1898), 5:67, quoted in Iguíniz, *Disquisiciones bibliográficas*, 215.

121. Iguíniz, *Disquisiciones bibliográficas*, 215, citing Cuevas, *Album histórico guadalupano del IV centenario*, but without giving a page number. I have been unable to verify the citation.

122. Quoted in Iguíniz, *Disquisiciones bibliográficas*, 219–20. The decree was undated but was published on September 10, 1896.

123. *Acta et decreta*, 134–35, decree 438.

124. Ibid., 144, decree 480; 134, decree 435.

125. Ibid., 135–36, decree 440.

126. "Los Esclarerecidos [*sic*] Príncipes del Tepeyac: El Edicto del 10 de septiembre," *El Universal*, October 27, 1896.

127. Ibid. (emphasis in original).

128. Iguíniz, *Disquisiciones bibliográficas*, 216.

129. V. Salado Alvarez, "Un Obispo Frondista," *El Correo de Jalisco*, September 19, 1901. "Frondista" refers to the Fronde, the seventeenth-century civil war in France in which some clergy played a major role. On Montes de Oca, see Valverde Téllez, *Bio-Bibliografía eclesiástica*, 2:98–116.

130. Salado Alvarez, "Un Obispo Frondista," *El Correo de Jalisco*, September 19, 1901. A joke at the time said that the bishop's signature "I[gnacio], obispo de San Luis Potosí," actually stood for "I[ncrédulo] de San Luis Potosí."

131. Antícoli, *Defensa*, 55.

132. Montes de Oca y Obregón, "Breve elogio," 349–55.

133. Ibid., 353; Galindo y Villa, *Don Joaquín García Icazbalceta*, 529 (emphasis in orginal).

134. Montes de Oca y Obregón, "Breve elogio," 353.

135. The "Nota" that follows the "Breve elogio" indicates that the chapter dealt with the same subject as García Icazbalceta's letter to Archbishop Labastida y Dávalos (Montes de Oca y Obregón, *Oraciones fúnebres*, 355).

136. Montes de Oca y Obregón, "Breve elogio," 354; V. Salado Alvarez, "Un Obispo Frondista," *El Correo de Jalisco*, September 19, 1901.

137. López Beltrán, *Album del LXXV aniversario de la coronación guadalupana*, 221.

138. Vargas y Gutiérrez was bishop of Colima (1883–88), then Puebla (1888–96) (Bravo Ugarte, *Diócesis y obispos*, 39).

139. López Beltrán, *Album del LXXV aniversario de la coronación guadalupana*, 197–98.

140. According to Velázquez, the work was completed in April 1895 (*La aparición*, 306).

141. Quoted in *El Tiempo*, September 27, 1895.

142. His proposal, dated August 1895, can be found in detail in López Beltrán, *Album del LXXV aniversario de la coronación guadalupana*, 205–6. When he presented it to the Mexican hierarchy, he was accompanied by Plancarte (Munguía, *La obra*, 10).

143. One notable absence was that of Montes de Oca, who was "far, very far away" (Montes de Oca y Obregón, "Elogio funebre . . . Plancarte," 250). Bishops from the United States who attended were Michael Corrigan of New York; William Elder of Cincinnati; Francis Janssens of New Orleans; Theo Meerschaert,

vicar apostolic of Indian Territory (Oklahoma); Peter Verdaguer, the vicar apostolic of Brownsville (Texas); Thomas Heslin of Natchez; John Watterson of Columbus; Thomas Byrne of Nashville; Henry Gabriel of Ogdensburg; Peter Bourgade, vicar apostolic of Arizona; Edward Dunne of Dallas; and Nicholas Gallagher of Galveston.

144. This can be found in Carrillo y Ancona, *Panegírico*, v. The plan was dated October 7, 1895, and signed by Antonio J. Paredes.

145. Nones and Vespers were parts of the canonical hours that were recited each day by persons in major orders, and which were sung by canons of chapters. Nones corresponded to early afternoon and Vespers to early evening. On the eve of an especially solemn feast, the Vespers would be those of the following day and were called First Vespers. Those sung on the feast itself were Second Vespers.

146. López Beltrán, *Album del LXXV aniversario de la coronación guadalupana*, 210.

147. Did Andrade sign the oath? Father Esteban Martínez de la Serna, former archivist of the Basilica of Guadalupe, says no (personal communication).

148. Grajales and Burrus reproduce one of these with a very free translation by Archbishop Loza y Pardavé of Guadalajara (*Bibliografía guadalupana*, no. 485). The Latin, however, contains one error. The correct version can be found in Plancarte y Navarrete, "Apuntes históricos," 345; and Antícoli, *Historia*, 2:408:

> *Mexicus heic populus mira sub imagine gaudet*
> *Te colere, Alma Parens, praesidioque frui.*
> *Per te sic vigeat felix, teque auspice Christi*
> *Immotam servet firmior usque fidem.*

> Here, under a wondrous image, the Mexican people
> Rejoice to worship you, Gracious Mother, and to
> Enjoy your protection; through you may it flourish happily
> And with you as guide, may it more firmly
> Keep continuously the faith of Christ.

149. López Beltrán, *Album del LXXV aniversario de la coronación guadalupana*, 211.

150. Ibid., 209. Béguerisse was a prominent Catholic laymen who had connections with many Mexican bishops. He was a particular friend of Labastida y Dávalos.

151. Carrillo y Ancona, *Panegírico*, vi.

152. Ibid., 6, 13.

153. Ibid., 15, 21, 22.

154. López Beltrán, *Album del LXXV aniversario de la coronación guadalupana*, 11, 12.

155. Ibid., 26.

156. Rivera, *El intérprete Juan González*.

Chapter 4. The Visitation of Archbishop Averardi

1. Romero de Solís, "Apostasía episcopal en Tamaulipas," 240.

2. *El Tiempo*, September 15, 1895.

3. Romero de Solís, "Apostasía episcopal en Tamaulipas," 240.

4. Plancarte y Navarrete, *Antonio Plancarte y Labastida*, 539, 544.

5. Romero de Solís, "Apostasía episcopal en Tamaulipas," 242.

6. Ibid., 243.

7. These letters are in printed form and are found in ASV, Visita Apostolica nel Messico di Nicola Averardi (1896–1900), Busta 1: Istruzoni, no. 31; Posizione 2ª, fascicolo 2°, folio 162r.

8. Averardi to Rampolla, June 15, 1896, in ASV, Visita Apostolica di Nicola Averardi (1896–1900), Busta 1: Istruzioni, no. 452, Posizione 2ª, fascicolo 4°, folio 90v (emphasis in original).

9. Ibid.

10. Ibid.

11. Ibid.

12. Ibid., folio 91v–92r.

13. Romero de Solís, "Apostasía episcopal en Tamaulipas," 250.

14. Ibid., 252.

15. Averardi to Sánchez Camacho, June 10, 1896, in ASV, Visita Apostolica nel Messico di Nicola Averardi (1896–1900), Busta 1: no. 17, Posizione 2ª, fascicolo 2°, folio 163r; Averardi to Rampolla, June 15, 1896, in ASV, Visita Apostolica di Messico di Nicola Averardi (1896–1900), Busta 1: Istruzioni, no. 452, Posizione 2ª, fascicolo 4°, folio 92r.

16. The letter was reprinted in *El Universal*, 2 September 1896.

17. Averardi to Rampolla, September 16, 1896, in ASV, Visita Apostolica nel Messico di Nicola Averardi (1896–1900), Busta 1: no. 17, Posizione 2ª, fascicolo 2°; Romero de Solís, "Apostasía episcopal en Tamaulipas," 259. In all probability this was a reprint of the pamphlet *El obispo de Tamaulipas y la coronación y aparición de Nuestra Señora de Guadalupe*, first published at Ciudad Victoria in 1888.

18. In ASV, Visita Apostolica nel Messico di Nicola Averardi (1896–1900), Busta 1: no. 17, Posizione 2ª, fascicolo 2°, folio 93r. The folio has no label as such and immediately follows Averardi's letter to Rampolla of June 15, 1896. In the pamphlet mentioned in note 17, Sánchez Camacho said that it was an article in *La Voz de México*, December 2, 1887.

19. Romero de Solís leans to the opinion that it was the pastoral letter of the bishop of Yucatán ("Apostasía episcopal en Tamaulipas," 259). However, Carrillo y Ancona's letter to Alarcón was not a pastoral. Sánchez Camacho's reference to "the last paragraph of number 12" does not seem to correspond to Carrillo y Ancona's letter.

20. Carrillo y Ancona, *Don Joaquín García Icazbalceta y la historia guadalupana*, 5.

21. Ibid., 10–11. See Iguíniz, *Disquisiciones bibliográficas*, 209.

22. Averardi to Rampolla, September 16, 1896, in ASV, Visita Apostolica nel Messico di Nicola Averardi (1896–1900), Busta 1: no. 17, Posizione 2ª, fascicolo 2°, folios 95v–96r.

23. In *Investigación histórica y documental*, 71–78. Apparently, it was printed on September 2. Strangely, it was also included in the first publication of

García Icazbalceta's letter to Archbishop Labastida y Dávalos (García Icazbalceta, *Carta*, 55–62).

24. On Sánchez Santos, see Weiner, "Trinidad Sánchez Santos."

25. *Investigación histórica y documental*, 73.

26. Ibid.

27. Ibid.

28. Ibid.

29. Sánchez Camacho seems to be referring to Carrillo y Ancona's letter of August 12, 1896 to Archbishop Alarcón.

30. *Investigación histórica y documental*, 74.

31. Ibid., 75.

32. Ibid., 75–76 (emphasis in original).

33. None of the published citations of the Inquisition's rebuke include any suggestion of a resignation.

34. *Investigación histórica y documental*, 77.

35. Ibid., 77–78.

36. Tomás Barón Morales was bishop of Chilapa (1876–82) and León (1883–98).

37. *Investigación histórica y documental*, 78. Eulogio Gillow y Zavalza was appointed bishop of Oaxaca in 1887, and then archbishop in 1892. He died in 1922.

38. The newspaper received financial aid from the Porfirian regime (see Weiner, "Trinidad Sánchez Santos," 330).

39. Averardi to Sánchez Camacho, September 5, 1896, in ASV, Visita Apostolica nel Messico di Nicola Averardi (1896–1900), Busta 1: no. 17, Posizione 2ª, fascicolo 2°, folios 103r–104r; Romero de Solís, "Apostasía episcopal en Tamaulipas," 254.

40. Sánchez Camacho to Averardi, September 10, 1896, in ASV, Visita Apostolica nel Messico di Nicola Averardi (1896–1900), Busta 1: no. 17, Posizione 2ª, fascicolo 2°, folios 163–64; Romero de Solís, "Apostasía episcopal en Tamaulipas," 255–56.

41. Romero de Solís, "Apostasía episcopal en Tamaulipas," 256.

42. Averardi to Rampolla, September 16, 1896, in ASV, Visita Apostolica nel Messico di Nicola Averardi (1896–1900), Busta 1: no. 17, Posizione 2ª, fascicolo 2°, folios 95r–96v; Romero de Solís, "Apostasía episcopal en Tamaulipas," 256–57.

43. Averardi to Rampolla, September 16, 1896, in ASV, Visita Apostolica nel Messico di Nicola Averardi (1896–1900), Busta 1: no. 17, Posizione 2ª, fascicolo 2°, folio 95r. If Averardi is correct, one would be justified in asking how Sánchez Camacho ever became a bishop.

44. Averardi to José Mora del Río, September 23, 1896, quoted in Romero de Solís, "Apostasía episcopal en Tamaulipas," 271 n. 68.

45. Averardi to Montes de Oca, October 30, 1896, quoted in ibid., 278.

46. Felipe de Velázquez to Jacinto López, from Victoria, September 18, 1896, in ASV, Visita Apostolica nel Messico di Nicola Averardi (1896–1900), Busta 1: no. 481, Posizione 2ª, fascicolo 2°, folios 99–100.

47. Romero de Solís, "Apostasía episcopal en Tamaulipas," 271.

48. Averardi to Rampolla, September 16, 1896, in ASV, Visita Apostolica nel Messico di Nicola Averardi (1896–1900), Busta 1; Romero de Solís, "Apostasía episcopal en Tamaulipas," 263 n. 38.

49. *El Imparcial*, October 3, 1896, in ASV, Visita Apostolica nel Messico di Nicola Averardi (1896–1900), Busta 1; Romero de Solís, "Apostasía episcopal en Tamaulipas," 262–63.

50. Romero de Solís, "Apostasía episcopal en Tamaulipas," 263.

51. Ibid., 264.

52. Ibid.

53. Ibid., 262.

54. Plancarte to Averardi, March 3, 1896, in ASV, Visita Apostolica nel Messico di Nicola Averardi (1896–1900), Busta 1: Affari speciali, Antonio Plancarte, folios 15r–16r.

55. Plancarte to Averardi, March 3, 1896, in ASV, Visita Apostolica nel Messico di Nicola Averardi (1896–1900), Busta 1: Affari speciali, Antonio Plancarte, folio 4v.

56. Ibid. It is certainly interesting to speculate on the relationship between Plancarte and Andrade on the chapter.

57. Tapia Méndez, *El siervo de Dios*, 215.

58. ASV, Visita Apostolica nel Messico di Nicola Averardi (1896–1900), Busta 1: Affari speciali, Antonio Plancarte, folio 4r. López Beltrán (*Album del LXXV aniversario de la coronación guadalupana*, 222) gives the date as September 27. Montes de Oca said that the brief of appointment was dated September 17, 1895 (Montes de Oca y Obregón, "Elogio," 251). At an earlier date, Bishop Rafael Sabás Camacho of Querétaro had included Plancarte's name in his *terna*, or list of three candidates to succeed him in his diocese (Munguía, *La obra*, 10). A titular bishop does not have his own active or existing diocese, nor does he have any ecclesiastical jurisdiction by reason of office. However, since a bishop should always be attached to a diocese, he is given one that has been suppressed or is no longer extant. Since these are often in countries conquered from Christians by non-Christians, he is often said to be a bishop *in partibus infidelium* ("in the areas of nonbelievers").

59. Tapia Méndez, *El siervo de Dios*, 217.

60. Ibid., 218.

61. Ibid., 221.

62. The information in this paragraph is taken from an undated, unsigned, and unaddressed report in Italian (see ASV, no. 91, Posizione 2ª, fascicolo 1º, "Affari speciali Antonio Plancarte," folios 4r–6v.

63. Plancarte y Navarrete, *Antonio Plancarte y Labastida*, 530–31. The letter is quoted in its entirety.

64. Bishop of Zamora to Averardi, April 28, 1896, in ASV, no. 91, Posizione 2ª, fascicolo 1º, "Affari speciali Antonio Plancarte," folios 11v–12r. One of Cázares's partisans, the priest Luis Arceo, gave his version of Averardi's trip to Zamora. When the delegate came to Zamora, he stayed with Arceo's cousin, where Arceo also lived. Averardi asked Arceo about Cázares's health and how much he worked, which Arceo interpreted as a question about Cázares's resigna-

tion. Arceo said his health was all right, as he would soon see. He said that Cázares made a good impression on Averardi in their interview. Arceo absolved Cázares of being an accuser or calumniator. He wrote those notes November 3, 1940 (quoted in Tapia Méndez, *El siervo de Dios*, 240–41).

65. Tapia Méndez, *El siervo de Dios*, 248.

66. Ibid., 249.

67. Ibid., 249 n. 50.

68. Ibid., 251.

69. This is a theory advanced by Treviño, *Antonio Plancarte y Labastida, Abad de Guadalupe*, 140.

70. Ibid., 140.

71. ASV, no. 91, Posizione 2ª, fascicolo 1°, "Affari speciali Antonio Plancarte," folio 16r; unnamed newspaper, September 6, 1896, in Biblioteca Nacional de Antropología e Historia, Mexico City, Papeles varios 44. Montes de Oca gave the date as May 10, 1896 (Montes de Oca y Obregón, "Elogio," 252).

72. Undated document, in ASV, no. 91, Posizione 2ª, fascicolo 1°, "Affari speciali Antonio Plancarte," folio 25v.

73. Orozco y Jiménez later became bishop of Guadalajara, and was exiled to the United States around 1914. He was intellectual and controversial. Like Plancarte y Navarrete, he spent his exile at DePaul University in Chicago.

74. Ruiz to Averardi, from Guadalupe, July 28, 1896, in ASV, no. 91, Posizione 2ª, fascicolo 1°, "Affari speciali Antonio Plancarte," folio 42r.

75. Rampolla to Averardi, July 7, 1896, in ASV, no. 91, Posizione 2ª, fascicolo 1°, "Affari speciali Antonio Plancarte," folios 33r–v; Averardi to Plancarte, July 27, 1896, in ibid., folio 35r.

76. Averardi to Plancarte, from Tacuba, July 27, 1896, in ASV, no. 91, Posizione 2ª, fascicolo 1°, "Affari speciali Antonio Plancarte," folio 35r.

77. Shortly after this, Averardi received a letter from a lawyer in Mexico City named Agustín Verdugo, who wanted his help in collecting a bill for 5,000 pesos from Plancarte. Averardi referred him to the archbishop of Mexico (Verdugo to Averardi, August 5, 1896; and Averardi to Verdugo, August 10, 1896, both in ASV, no. 424, Posizione 2ª, fascicolo 1°, 37r–38r, folio 37r.

78. Tapia Méndez, *El siervo de Dios*, 262.

79. Averardi to Rampolla, September 15, 1896, in ASV, no. 91, Posizione 2ª, fascicolo 1°, "Affari speciali Antonio Plancarte," folios 44r–45r.

80. Ibid., folio 44r. It is not clear whether the reference is to uncle or nephew, probably the latter.

81. Ibid., folio 45r–v.

82. Ibid.

83. Rampolla to Averardi, December 12, 1896, in ASV, no. 91, Posizione 2ª, fascicolo 1°, "Affari speciali Antonio Plancarte," folios 49r–50v.

84. Plancarte y Navarrete, *Antonio Plancarte y Labastida*, 553, 554–56.

85. Munguía, *La obra*, 8.

86. Ibid., 11.

87. Averardi to Leopoldo Ruiz, July 11, 1896; Ruiz to Averardi, July 12,

1896, both in ASV, Affari Speciali: Antonio Plancarte, tittulo 341, Posizione 2ª, fascicolo 1°.

88. Averardi to Ramón Ybarra, bishop of Chilapa, July 18, 1896, in ibid.

89. Martínez, *Don Joaquín García Icazbalceta*, 16.

90. Wagner, *Joaquín García Icazbalceta*, 16.

91. Quoted in García Icazbalceta, *Cartas*, 261.

92. According to Rivera, *El intérprete Juan González*, 7 n. 1.

93. Tapia Méndez, *El siervo de Dios*, 270; *El Tiempo*, April 27, 1898.

94. *El Tiempo*, April 29, 1898.

95. V. Chiriet to Averardi (in French), April 26, 1898, in ASV, no. 91, Posizione 2ª, fascicolo 1°, "Affari speciali Antonio Plancarte," folio 54r; Andrade to Averardi, undated, in ibid., folio 56r; V. Chiriet to Averardi, from Guadalupe, April 26, 1898, in ibid., folio 57r; Averardi to Andrade, April 28, 1898, in ibid., folios 59r–v. The newspaper accounts of the funeral do not mention Alarcón's presence.

96. *Reforma*, May 22, 2000.

97. Antícoli, *Historia*; Gutiérrez Casillas, *Jesuítas en México*, 258.

98. Plancarte y Navarrete, *Antonio Plancarte y Labastida*, 552–53.

99. On this, see Hurtado, *El cisma mexicano*, 84–86.

100. Romero de Solís, "Apostasía episcopal en Tamaulipas," 263.

101. In Archivo Histórico, Archdiocese of Mexico, Secretería Episcopal, 1883, caja 18, expediente 20.

102. Ibid., Secretería Episcopal, licencias, caja 18, expediente 16.

103. Reprinted in *THG*, 1287–1337.

104. This is the conclusion of Carreño ("Notas biográficas," 24).

105. For this information, see Valverde Téllez, *Bio-Bibliografía*, 3:35–41.

106. Carreño, "Notas biográficas," 32.

107. Dios, *La familia vicentina en México*, 1:590.

108. Bravo Ugarte, *Diócesis y obispos*, 66, 85, 83.

109. Vera, *Apuntamientos históricos*; Vera, *Compendio histórico del tercer concilio provincial mexicano*.

Chapter 5. An Uneasy Calm

1. For a useful survey of this period, see Sherman, Meyer, and Deeds, *The Course of Mexican History*, chapters 7, 8, 9; and Knight, *The Mexican Revolution*, vol. 1, *Porfirians, Liberals, and Peasants*.

2. On this, see Brading, *Mexican Phoenix*, 314–17.

3. In a sermon delivered in the metropolitan cathedral on March 30, 2003, Cardinal Norberto Carrera Rivera quoted the pope as crediting the Virgin of Guadalupe with guiding him in the leadership of the church for twenty-four years. "Ever since I went on pilgrimage for the first time to the splendid Shrine of Guadalupe on January 29, 1979, she has guided my steps in these almost twenty-five years of service as Bishop of Rome and universal pastor of the church," the pope was quoted as saying. "I wish to invoke her, the sure way to encounter

Christ, and who was the first evangelizer of America, as the 'Star of Evangelization,' entrusting to her the ecclesial work of all her sons and daughters of America" ("Cardinal Notes Pope's Debt to the Virgin of Guadalupe," http://www.zenit .org, April 1, 2003). It is hardly accurate to call Guadalupe the first evangelizer of America.

4. Cervantes de Conde, Torre Villar, and Navarro de Anda, *Album conmemorativo*, 291.

5. Iguíniz, *Disquisiciones bibliográficas*, 222.

6. Valton, *Homenaje*, 11.

7. For biographical data on Cuevas, see Gutiérrez Casillas, *Jesuítas en México*, 314–16; Torre Villar, *Mexicanos ilustres*, 2:102.

8. For a listing of these works, see the Bibliography.

9. For more details on this, see Poole, *Our Lady of Guadalupe*, 11–12, 39, 46, 57, 168–69, 198–99, 238 n. 32, and 243 n. 4

10. Cuevas, *Album histórico guadalupano del IV centenario*, 10. It is not clear whom he was referring to.

11. This was particularly true of his analyses of the Monumentos Guadalupanos in the New York Public Library (see Poole, *Our Lady of Guadalupe*, 115–16).

12. For a listing of these, see the Bibliography.

13. *New Catholic Encyclopedia*, s.v. Guadalupe. For a listing of his works, see the Bibliography.

14. O'Gorman lists them: Mario Rojas Sánchez, Luis Medina Ascensio, J. Jesús Jiménez, Manuel Robledo Gutiérrez, Ramón Sánchez Flores, Ernesto de la Torre-Villar, and Ramiro Navarro de Anda (*Destierro de sombras*, 206, n. 72).

15. O'Gorman, *Destierro de sombras*, 165–94; Noguez, *Documentos guadalupanos*, 34; Poole, *Our Lady of Guadalupe*, 41–42. See also Rivera, *El intérprete Juan González*.

16. León-Portilla, *Tonantzin Guadalupe*, 31.

17. Ibid., 52.

18. Ibid.

19. Ibid., 61.

20. Brading, *Mexican Phoenix*, 344.

21. Escalada, *Enciclopedia guadalupana*, 1:50; Brading, *Mexican Phoenix*, 344.

22. Siller A., "La evangelización guadalupana," 5. He also says that it is written in different styles but does not specify them.

23. Ibid.

24. Elizondo, *Guadalupe*, 134.

25. Ibid., xviii.

26. Ibid., 35.

27. Ibid., xviii.

28. Brading, *Mexican Phoenix*, 350. The letter, with the title "A todos los sacerdotes y fieles de la Arquidiócesis de México, y a todos los mexicanos de buena voluntad" (To all the priests and faithful of the archdiocese of Mexico and to all Mexicans of good will) is included in Rivera Carrera, *Juan Diego*, 103–14. For

some time, Louise M. Burkhart, Barry D. Sell, and I have been preparing an edition and translation of the only two existing Nahuatl dramas that deal with the Guadalupe apparitions (forthcoming from the University of Oklahoma Press). One of these, the "Coloquios de la aparición," makes extensive use of texts from the *Nican mopohua*. The anonymous author felt no such exaggerated reverence for these texts, and edited, changed, and revised them at will. In fact, both plays take great dramatic license with the story of Guadalupe.

29. Brading, *Mexican Phoenix*, 356, citing Guerrero Rosado, *El nican mopohua*, 152–65, 173–77, 188, and 330–33.

30. Brading, *Mexican Phoenix*, 357.

31. Chávez Sánchez, *La Virgen de Guadalupe y Juan Diego en las informaciones jurídicas de 1666*, 42–44, 47–49, 66–67.

32. Taylor, "The Virgin of Guadalupe," 11.

33. Ibid., 14.

34. Ibid., 23.

35. Ibid., 15.

36. Poole, *Our Lady of Guadalupe*, 4–14.

37. Allan Figueroa Deck, "Review of *Our Lady of Guadalupe*, by Stafford Poole," *America*, September 30, 1995 (emphasis in original).

38. John Gledhill, "Review of *Our Lady of Guadalupe*, by Stafford Poole," *American Anthropologist* 98, no. 3 (September 1996): unpaginated.

39. Thomas Ascheman, "Review of *Our Lady of Guadalupe*, by Stafford Poole," *Anthropos Institut*, 92 (1997): unpaginated.

40. Richard Nebel, "Review of *Our Lady of Guadalupe*, by Stafford Poole," *Notas/Frankfurt* 6, no. 1 (1999): unpaginated.

41. Richard Salvucci, " 'He hath not dealt so with any nation': Three recent books on Religion, Economy, and Society in Colonial Mexico," *Colonial Latin American Review* 5, no. 2 (1996).

42. Guerrero Rosado, *El "Nican mopohua."*

43. Ibid., 465–626. "The degree to which Poole's critique disconcerted Guadalupan scholars in Mexico can be best observed in *The Nican Mopohua*, where José Luis Guerrero added a substantial appendix to answer the American priest" (Brading, *Mexican Phoenix*, 353).

44. Zires, "Los mitos de la Virgen de Guadalupe," 281–313.

45. Ibid., 285.

46. Miranda Godínez, *Dos cultos fundantes*, 240, 257, 258.

47. Brading, *Mexican Phoenix*, 11.

48. Ibid., 59.

49. Ibid., 75.

50. Ibid., 146.

51. Ibid., 148.

52. On this, see the review by Stafford Poole in the *Catholic Historical Review* 87, no. 4 (October 2001): 773–77.

53. Brading, *Mexican Phoenix*, 73–74.

54. Ibid., 361.

55. Ibid., 362.

56. Ibid., 363.

57. Ibid., 366.

58. Ibid., 345.

59. For a largely negative review, see Stafford Poole, "Our Lady of Guadalupe: The Enduring Enigma," *Catholic Historical Review* 81, no. 4 (October 1995): 588–99.

60. Rodriguez, *Our Lady of Guadalupe*, 47.

61. Ibid., 127.

62. Nebel, *Santa María Tonantzin*, 145–46.

63. Ibid., 126–27, 182–83.

64. Ibid., 240–41. I am grateful to Father Thomas Anslow, C.M., who compared and corrected my translation of the Spanish with the German original.

65. Personal communication, quoted with permission.

66. Elizondo, *Guadalupe*, 26.

67. Ibid., 31.

68. Ibid., xvii.

69. Ibid., 8 n. 8.

70. Ibid., 10 n. 10.

71. On this, see Poole, *Our Lady of Guadalupe*, 22–23.

72. Elizondo, *Guadalupe*, 10 n. 11. Although he claims to be reflecting the ideas of Siller Acuña, Elizondo goes far beyond him in his assertions (see Siller A., "La evangelización guadalupana," 99–100).

73. Elizondo, *Guadalupe*, 10 n. 12.

74. Ibid., 12 n. 14.

75. Ibid., 12 n. 16.

76. Similar conventions are abundant in the Bible. The reader is referred to Genesis 18:22–32.

77. Elizondo, *Guadalupe*, xi.

78. Ibid., 93.

79. For a discussion of the works of Mauro Rodríguez, Donald Kurtz, Patricia Harrington, and Ena Campbell, see Poole, *Our Lady of Guadalupe*, 6, 8–10.

80. Liss, "A Cosmic Approach Falls Short."

81. In Catholic liturgy, a thurifer is a person who carries the thurible, or incense holder.

82. On these previous examinations, see Poole, *Our Lady of Guadalupe*, 142, 202–5.

83. This statement is based on Abbot Schulenburg's report to Archbishop Corripio y Ahumada of Mexico City, *Informe de actividades de los años 1963 a 1988*, 290–97; and Schulenburg Prado, *Memorias*, 161–71. For an excellent summary of the scientific and artistic questions surrounding the image, see Peterson, "Creating the Virgin of Guadalupe."

84. *Informe de actividades de los años 1963 a 1988*, 292.

85. One of these pieces, enclosed in a reliquary, was sent on a pilgrimage to various American cities in the Fall of 2003.

86. Personal communication.

87. On the Códice, see Escalada, *Enciclopedia guadalupana*, appendix; and González Fernández, Chávez Sánchez, and Guerrero Rosado, *El encuentro*, 340–52.

88. Antonio Bertrán, "Encuentran el Códice Más Antiguo sobre Aparición," *Reforma*, August 3, 1995.

89. Ibid.

90. Valeriano's name is given as Vareliano. The confusion of liquids was not unusual at that time.

91. Sigüenza y Góngora, *Piedad heroyca*, 63.

92. González Fernández, Chávez Sánchez, and Guerrero Rosado, *El encuentro*, 341. The correct form of the verb is *omomiquili*. *Omomoquili* is the form given in *El encuentro* (ibid.), but it is not certain if this is a mistake in transcription.

93. Escalada, *Enciclopedia guadalupana*, Appendix, 5.

94. Ibid., 44 (where Dibble's fax is reproduced). Earlier in the text, however, Escalada omits the qualification about the date (Appenidix, 6).

95. Ibid., Appendix, 6.

96. Alfonso M. Santillana Rentería to Salvador Sotomayor Jiménez, September 18, 1996; Escalada, *Enciclopedia guadalupana*, Appendix, 48–49.

97. Escalada, *Enciclopedia guadalupana*, Appendix, 7.

98. Ibid., 8–9.

99. Ibid., 75.

100. Ibid., 75.

101. Reproduced in Boturini Benaduci, *Idea de una nueva historia general de la América septentrional* [edición facsímil].

102. On Sahagún's opposition to the devotion at Guadalupe, see Poole, *Our Lady of Guadalupe*, 77–81.

103. Antonio Bertrán, "El Misterio de Su Procedencia," *Reforma*, May 5, 2002.

104. Antonio Bertrán, "Arrojan Nuevos Datos Sobre 'Códice 1548,'" *Reforma*, May 5, 2002. As of that date, Castaño was the director of the Department of Applied Physics and Advanced Technology of the Instituto de Física of the Universidad Nacional y Autónoma de México.

105. Ibid.

106. Ibid.

107. Ibid.

108. Ibid. This quotation was taken from an earlier interview (Antonio Bertrán, "Cuestionan Autenticidad del 'Códice 1548,'" *Reforma*, December 8, 1997).

109. Antonio Bertrán, "Arrojan Nuevos Datos Sobre 'Códice 1548,'" *Reforma*, May 5, 2002. This quotation was taken from an earlier article by Antonio Bertrán ("Cuestionan Autenticidad del 'Códice 1548'", *Reforma*, December 8, 1997).

110. Xavier Escalada, S.J., "Innecesaria Contienda Sobre la Guadalupana," *Excelsior*, January 15, 2000, 1B.

111. Xavier Escalada, S.J., "Guadalupe Es Mensaje de Amor," *Excelsior*,

August 3, 2001, 1B. Other articles included "Juan Diego, Voluntad Indomable" (July 6, 2001, 1); and "Lourdes y Guadalupe, Cadena Admirable de Valiosos Favores" (May 28, 2001), 1-B.

112. Xavier Escalada, S.J., "Nuevas Pruebas de Las Apariciones Guadalupanas," *Excelsior*, July 12, 2000, 1-B.

113. Xavier Escalada, S.J., "Medallas de Guadalupe y Juan Diego en Excavaciones en EU," *Excelsior*, July 19, 2000, 1-B.

114. Xavier Escalada, S.J., "La 'Placa de Coosawattee,'" *Excelsior*, July 27, 2000, 1-B.

115. Ibid.

116. Leticia Sánchez, "Sobrevive a Los Ataques," *Reforma*, December 8, 2001.

117. The article also spoke of attackers, both physical and ideological, of the Guadalupe tradition, and specifically mentioned Schulenburg.

118. Escalada, *Juan Diego*, 35–40; Carmen Álvarez, "Ofrece Nueva Hipótesis Sobre Las Apariciones," *Reforma*, December 12, 2001.

Chapter 6. The Beatification of Juan Diego

1. Fitzpatrick, "Glossary of Terms," in Woestman, *Canonization*, 138–39.

2. Ibid., 139.

3. These works are Romero Salinas, *Juan Diego*, 5–64; Salazar Salazar, "Inicio y desarrollo"; González Fernández, Chávez Sánchez, and Guerrero Rosado, *El encuentro*, xiii–xvii; and Chávez Sánchez, "Proceso."

4. See the Apostolic Constitution *Divinus Perfectionis Magister*, January 25, 1983; and the norms issued by the Congregation on February 7, 1983 (*AAS* 75, paragraph 1, no. 4, pp. 349–50, 396–404).

5. Fitzpatrick, "Glossary of Terms," in Woestman, *Canonization*, 146; and Fitzpatrick, "Outline and Summary of the Procedures of Canonization," in ibid., 76.

6. According to Chávez Sánchez, this was done at the Marian Congress that was celebrated in Morelia in October 1904 ("Proceso").

7. Ibid.

8. Manríquez y Zárate, *Carta pastoral*; López Beltrán, *Orto, cenit y ocaso*, 54–55.

9. Manríquez y Zárate, *Carta pastoral*, 5.

10. Salazar Salazar, "Inicio y desarollo," 4. He says that there was no follow-up to López Beltrán's urgings.

11. Salazar Salazar says simply that there was no follow-up ("Inicio y desarrollo," 4). García Gutiérrez was a priest who was the author of two Guadalupan books. Bravo Ugarte was a well known Jesuit historian and author of *Cuestiones históricas guadalupanas*. In 1940 Iguíniz was director of the Biblioteca Nacional in Mexico City.

12. López Beltrán, *Orto, cenit y ocaso*, 54–55. Manríquez y Zárate was said to have delivered more than two thousand Guadalupan sermons (ibid., 32).

13. Salazar Salazar says that again it was López Beltrán who interested the

archbishop in the cause, and that again there was no follow-up ("Inicio y desarrollo," 4).

14. Congregatio pro Causis Sanctorum Officium Historicum, *Positio*, 723–24. Medina Ascensio was the author of "Las fuentes esenciales de la historia guadalupana," in López Beltrán, *Album del LXXV aniversario de la coronación guadalupana*, 83–113; and "Las informaciones guadaluapanas de 1666 y de 1725," in *THG*, 1339–77.

15. Congregatio pro Causis Sanctorum Officium Historicum, *Positio*, 724; Salazar Salazar, "Inicio y desarrollo," 5.

16. Salazar Salazar, "Inicio y desarrollo," 5–6.

17. Ibid., 6. Chávez Sánchez has a somewhat differing chronology, saying that Corripio Ahumada took these steps in 1981 and that the Congregation for the Causes of the Saints informed him of the necessary procedures in June 1982 ("Proceso").

18. Congregatio pro Causis Sanctorum Officium Historicum, *Positio*, 724.

19. Romero Salinas, *Juan Diego*, 28; Congregatio pro Causis Sanctorum Officium Historicum, *Positio*, 724; Salazar Salazar, "Inicio y desarrollo," 6.

20. The documents in the *acta* are listed in Romero Salinas, *Juan Diego*, 29–32.

21. Congregatio pro Causis Sanctorum Officium Historicum, *Positio*, 724; Chávez Sánchez, "Proceso."

22. Romero Salinas, *Juan Diego*, 32.

23. Salazar Salazar, "Inicio y desarrollo," 8.

24. Ibid.

25. Ibid., 9.

26. Ibid., 33; Congregatio pro Causis Sanctorum Officium Historicum, *Positio*, 724. It is difficult to tell if this was the same historical commission described by Chávez Sánchez and presided over by Romero Salinas. He indicates that the commission was formed in 1984, or thereabouts ("Proceso").

27. Although all early sources, including the *Nican mopohua*, are unanimous in saying that Juan Diego lived in Cuauhtitlán, some of the witnesses in the capitular inquiry of 1666 said that he lived in Tlayac or Tlayacac, a barrio of Cuauhtitlán. This place cannot today be identified with certainty, nor is it listed in Gerhard, *A Guide to the Historical Geography of New Spain* (see Poole, *Our Lady of Guadalupe*, 139 n. 61). In contrast, Luis Becerra Tanco said that he lived in a town called Tolpetlac ("Origen milagroso," in *THG*, 312, 314). Supposedly he arrived at this conclusion after studying the possible routes that Juan Diego could have taken, and concluding that he could not have lived in Cuauhtitlán. In this he was followed by Florencia ("La estrella del norte de México [1688]," in *THG*, 365). Fernández de Echeverría y Veytia gave the form Tolpetlatl ("Baluartes de México," in *THG*, 533), as did Juan Bautista Muñoz ("Memoria," in *THG*, 692). Another explanation was that if Juan Diego lived in Cuauhtitlán, where there was a Franciscan convent, it would have been pointless for him to go to Tlatelolco. Some commentators later claimed that he was born in Cuauhtitlán but lived in Tolpetlac.

28. "A relator is an expert in theology, history and procedures of the Congregation for the Causes of the Saints who is assigned to study and to guide the

progress of a cause through its Roman phase. He prepares, with the help of collaborators, or arranges to have prepared by others, the *study on the virtues/martyrdom/miracle.* . . . . He makes sure that all requisite conditions are fulfilled, he directs the work of collaborators, sorts out difficulties, and prepares all that is necessary for the smooth passage of the cause" (Fitzpatrick, "Glossary of Terms," in Woestman, *Canonization,* 147; emphasis in original).

29. Salazar Salazar, "Inicio y desarrollo," 10. Salazar Salazar consistently spells the name "Papap."

30. Congregatio pro Causis Sanctorum Officium Historicum, *Positio,* 724–25; Salazar Salazar, "Inicio y desarrollo," 10. Chávez Sánchez gives the date of the appointments as January 19, 1984 ("Proceso").

31. Romero Salinas was the author of *Precisiones históricas de las tradiciones guadalupana y juandieguina; Eclipse guadalupano: La verdad sobre el antiaparicionismo;* and *Juan Diego: Su peregrinar a los altares.*

32. Congregatio pro Causis Sanctorum Officium Historicum, *Positio,* 725.

33. This promotor of the faith should not be confused with the promotor of the faith found in the canonization process of the 1917 Code of Canon Law. Also known as the "devil's advocate," his function was "to weaken the cause at every stage as far as possible by challenging the admissibility of this or that document, by exposing flaws in the evidence submitted by the postulator, by producing witnesses and documents of his own, etc. In a word, his duty was to oppose the cause" (Woestman, "Codification of the Norms for Beatification and Canonization and Changes Prior to 1983," in *Canonization,* 35).

34. Romero Salinas gives his name as Palassini (*Juan Diego,* 42).

35. González Fernández, Chávez Sánchez, and Guerrero Rosado specifically mention Schulenburg and Warnholtz (*El encuentro,* xv n. 9). Salazar Salazar speaks only of secret opposition ("Inicio y desarrollo," 11).

36. Romero Salinas, *Juan Diego,* 43.

37. Ibid., 43–45. According to Romero Salinas, the members of the Congregation were asking why, five years after signing a *carta postulatoria,* Schulenburg would now present objections? Was it possible that he doubted the tradition? Why did he not address the Congregation rather than the archbishop? Why did the archbishop seek to advance the cause when he knew of the serious difficulties? Why did the archivist of the Cathedral chapter send his arguments to Schulenburg rather than the archbishop? Why were the arguments not presented in the diocesan inquiry? Why was he so sure of the arguments that he could function independently as a Devil's Advocate? (Ibid., 44).

38. See Chapter 1; also, Poole, *Our Lady of Guadalupe,* 128–43.

39. Romero Salinas maintained that the documents of this dispute (which has been treated previously), were not authentic (*Juan Diego,* 48), but the authors of *El encuentro* do not question their authenticity and explain them in detail (252–66).

40. On Freire and the shrine, see Poole, *Our Lady of Guadalupe,* 67. Also, at this stage, Romero Salinas found a small image of Guadalupe that may have been one of the first copies of the original and which, according to tradition, had belonged to Juan Diego, who bequeathed it to his son or someone considered as such. It was in the possession of the Meade family, which gave it to Pope John II

on the occason of his first visit to Mexico in 1979. Some authors have found it necessary to formulate tortuous explanations as to how a celibate Juan Diego could have bequeathed an image to his heirs.

41. "His wife died a virgin. He too lived as a virgin; he never knew a woman" (Laso de la Vega, *The Story of Guadalupe*, 113).

42. At a later stage in the Nahuatl language, it was also synonymous with Indian.

43. According to a published report, the president of Mexico, Carlos Salinas de Gortari, intervened in 1990 to ask Schulenburg and the nuncio Prigione to withdraw their objections to the beatification, and they complied (Bill Coleman and Patty Coleman, "Guadalupe Caught in Clerical Struggle," *National Catholic Reporter*, June 14, 1996). The source for this was the Jesuit Father Antonio Roqueni Ornelas, then legal counsel for the archdiocese of Mexico.

44. Romero Salinas, *Juan Diego*, 52.

45. Ibid.

46. Ibid., 54; Chávez Sánchez, "Proceso."

47. Schulenburg, *Memorias*, 292.

48. Chávez Sánchez, "Proceso."

49. According to Woestman (*Canonization*), there is no requirement of an examination of the *Positio* by historians, only by theologians. In the case of Juan Diego, this may have been a response to the doubts about his historicity.

50. *Divinus perfectionis magister*, section II, paragraph 11.

51. Actually, the *Annuario Pontificio* lists no relator general for 1990 and lists Eszer only in the following year. It is difficult to say when the change was made.

52. Romero Salinas, *Juan Diego*, 58. It is possible that this is an error (since Papa had retired), or that Papa put the finishing touches to something begun while he was relator.

53. According to the *Annuario Pontificio*, Petti was the promotor of faith or theological prelate in 1988 and 1989.

54. Romero Salinas, *Juan Diego*, 60.

55. Ibid., 62. See also *AAS* 82, no. 9 (September 4, 1990): 855.

56. *AAS* 82, no. 9 (September 4, 1990): 853–55. Chávez Sánchez ("Proceso") called it a decree of beatification, but it was not quite that. It was titled "Cultus liturgicus in honorem Beati Ioannis Didaci conceditur" (Liturgical Cultus Granted in Honor of Blessed Juan Diego).

57. González Fernández, Chávez Sánchez, and Guerrero Rosado, *El encuentro*, xv. The Latin text of the decree is in *AAS* 82, no. 9 (September 4, 1990): 853–55. A Spanish translation is in Romero Salinas, *Juan Diego*, 5–9.

58. Schulenburg had also made a point of this in his interview with *Ixtus*. However, the decree of beatification reproduced by Romero Salinas does mention Juan Diego and calls him a *beato*.

59. *AAS* 82, no. 9 (September 4, 1990): 853, 854; Romero Salinas, *Juan Diego*, 6–7.

60. Romero Salinas, *Juan Diego*, 63.

61. *AAS* 82, no. 9 (September 4, 1990): 853, 855.

62. Romero Salinas, *Juan Diego*, 9.

63. Biographical data can be found in Schulenburg, *Memorias*, 9, 25–32.

64. Nebel, *Santa María Tonantzin*, 9.

65. "El milagro de Guadalupe: Entrevista con Guillermo Schulenburg," *Ixtus: Espíritu y Cultura* 3, no. 15 (Winter 1995): 28–35; reprinted in Schulenburg, *Memorias*, 331–41.

66. "El milagro de Guadalupe: Entrevista con Guillermo Schulenburg," *Ixtus: Espíritu y Cultura* 3, no. 15 (Winter 1995): 28.

67. Callahan, *The Tilma under Infra-Red Radiation;* Smith, *The Image of Guadalupe: Myth or Miracle?*; and Smith, *The Image of Guadalupe.*

68. "El milagro de Guadalupe: Entrevista con Guillermo Schulenburg," *Ixtus: Espíritu y Cultura* 3, no. 15 (Winter 1995): 31.

69. Ibid.

70. Ibid., 32.

71. Ibid.

72. Ibid., 32–33.

73. Ibid., 33.

74. Ibid. (emphasis added).

75. Schulenburg, *Memorias*, 287.

76. I have used the reprint of Tornelli's article in Guerrero Rosado, *¿Existió Juan Diego?*, 26–30. See also Schulenburg, *Memorias*, 288.

77. Guerrero Rosado, *¿Existió Juan Diego?*, 26.

78. Ibid., 28.

79. Ibid., 29–30.

80. "Piden el Retiro del Abad de la Basílica de Guadalupe," *La opinión* (Los Angeles), May 28, 1996.

81. Quoted in Esther Schrader, "Niegan la existencia de la Virgen de Guadalupe," *Vida Nueva* (section of the *San José Mercury-News*), June 7, 1996.

82. *New York Times*, June 21, 1996; *La Opinión* (Los Angeles), May 28 and 29, June 3, 7, and 26, 1996; *National Catholic Reporter*, June 14, 1996; *Chicago Tribune*, June 6 and 24, 1996; *Washington Post*, date unknown; *Boston Globe*, June 1, 1996; *San Diego Union-Tribune*, September 7, 1996; *San José Mercury News*, June 7, 1996. The story was also carried by Reuters.

83. "Mexicans Outraged in Defense of Icon," *San José Mercury News*, June 7, 1996.

84. Bill Coleman and Patty Coleman, "Guadalupe Caught in Clerical Struggle," *National Catholic Reporter*, June 14, 1996.

85. Published in May 1996, the pamphlet had sold out four editions of 5,000 copies each by August.

86. Guerrero Rosado, *¿Existió Juan Diego?*, 4 (boldface type in original).

87. "Cardenal Recomienda Dejar a un Lado Polémica por Declaraciones del Abad," *La Opinión* (Los Angeles), June 7, 1996.

88. "Vaticano Estudia el Caso del Abad," *La Opinión* (Los Angeles), May 29, 1996.

89. Ibid.

90. *Proceso*, June 3, 1996, quoted in Bill Coleman and Patty Coleman, "Guadalupe Caught in Clerical Struggle," *National Catholic Reporter*, June 14, 1996.

91. *Proceso*, June 3, 1996, quoted in ibid.

92. "Mexico's Faithful Rally around Virgin," Washington Post News Service, published in the *Boston Globe*, June 1, 1996.

93. Bill Coleman and Patty Coleman, "Guadalupe Caught in Clerical Struggle," *National Catholic Reporter*, June 14, 1996.

94. Cited in "A Costa de la Basílica, el Abad se Ha Enriquecido," *Vida Nueva* (section of the *San José Mercury News*), June 7, 1996. The article in *Proceso* also claimed that Schulenburg had owned a Ferrari which he turned in for a Mercedes similar to those owned by the richest bankers in the country, and that he was preparing to purchase a BMW. The newspaper *El Día de México* claimed to have located a third residence in the exclusive Bosque de Chapultepec.

95. Quoted in Francisco Robles, "Abad Urge a No Dejarse Arrebatar la Virgen de Guadalupe, Núcleo de la Unidad Nacional," *La Opinión* (Los Angeles), June 26, 1996. Later in the article Robles wrote that Schulenburg's "harang" was given at a "mass loaded with self-praise."

96. "Carta pastoral," in Rivera Carrera, *Juan Diego*, 104, 105, 107.

97. The article was reprinted as a pamphlet, "¡Qué pena señor Abad!" (July 12, 1996).

98. Hernández Chávez, "¡Qué pena señor Abad!" 11.

99. Ibid., 12 (emphasis in original).

100. "López Dóriga, Norberto Rivera y el Caso Schulenburg," *Reforma*, February 16, 2002.

101. Ibid.

102. Ibid.

103. Ibid.

104. The text of his resignation to the Collegiate chapter can be found in Schulenburg, *Memorias*, 133–35.

105. Ibid., 135.

Chapter 7. History versus Juan Diego

1. "El milagro de Guadalupe: Entrevista con Guillermo Schulenburg," *Ixtus: Espíritu y Cultura* 3, no. 15 (Winter 1995): 33. See also Margaret O'Gara, "Counter-Evidence of Infallibility's Exercise."

2. Fitzpatrick, "Outline and Summary of the Procedures in the Process of Canonization," in Woestman, *Canonization*, 88.

3. González Fernández, Chávez Sánchez, and Guerrero Rosado, *El encuentro*, xvi.

4. Quoted in ibid.

5. The *Annuario Pontificio* for 1998 lists González Fernández as a consultor to the Congregation for the Causes of the Saints.

6. "Juan Diego existió: Las pruebas," Zenit News Service, December 19, 1999. This dispatch contains the full report plus an introduction whose author is not identified. The introduction states that González Fernández was studying the social origins of Juan Diego. "It is not known if he was a noble Indian or a 'poor' Indian. It is a question of confusion caused by the translations of the *Nican mopohua* into

Castilian." On the contrary, the *Nican mopohua* says nothing of possible noble origins and consistently refers to Juan Diego as a commoner (*macehualli*).

7. On the basis of the *Annuario Pontificio* of 1998, I surmise that the previous prefect was Alberto Bovone, S.D.B., and that Saraiva Martins received the appointment late in the year or at some time after the *Annuario* was prepared.

8. *The Tidings*, September 3, 1999.

9. Héctor Moreno and Eduardo Lliteras, "Claman ante el Papa Canonizar a Juan Diego," *Reforma*, May 22, 2000.

10. González Fernández, Chávez Sánchez, and Guerrero Rosado, *El encuentro*, 16.

11. Ibid.

12. Ibid.

13. Ibid., 17, 363 n. 16, 365 n. 20, 375.

14. Ibid., 372 n. 34.

15. Ibid., 19–20.

16. Ibid., 31.

17. See Appendix 3.

18. Francisco Robles, "Salen en Defensa de Juan Diego," *La Opinión*, December 3, 1999.

19. Ibid. Incoming canons took two oaths. The first, in Latin, included a pledge to obey the capitular statutes, to keep secret the deliberations of the *cabildo*, to render obedience to the archbishop of Mexico, and to avoid all factions and conspiracies against the archbishop or any fellow canons. The second, in Spanish, was a declaration of belief in the historical and supernatural nature of the apparitions and the image, "a truth proven by a most ancient, constant, and uniform tradition, and approved by the Roman Pontiffs in a multitude of documents. . . . I solemnly promise and swear to defend this pious belief with all the strength of my soul" (*Estatutos capitulares*, 104–5).

20. James F. Smith and Margaret Ramirez, "Challenge to Sainthood Evokes Charges of Racism," *Los Angeles Times*, December 11, 1999. At a later date he was quoted as saying that the opponents of the canonization were merely anti-Indian racists. "They can't understand how an Indian, who was nothing, could ever have been chosen by God" (Kevin Sullivan, "Myth versus Miracle: Debate Rages Over Likely Canonization," *Washington Post*, February 5, 2002).

21. Catholic News Service, December 7, 1999.

22. Susan Ferriss, "Faithful Stunned At Priests' Doubts About Juan Diego," *The News: Mexico*, December 11, 1999; María Elena Medina, "Las Dudas del ex Abad," *Reforma*, December 12, 1999. See also Homero Aridjis, "Schulenburg, ¿El último hereje?", *Reforma*, December 12, 1999.

23. María Elena Medina, "Exigen Que Pida Perdón el ex Abad Schulenburg," *Reforma*, December 8, 1999.

24. Tania Gómez and María Elena Medina, "Se Reúnen en Nunciatura Mullor y Schulenburg" *Reforma*, December 13, 1999. The article contained no details of the meeting.

25. Alejandro León, "El Enigma de Juan Diego," *Contenido*, February 2000, 32–33. This article contains several errors of fact, such as saying that the *Huei*

tlamahuiçoltica contained texts in Spanish, giving the wrong date for García Icazbalceta's letter, attributing Sánchez Camacho's resignation to his anti-Guadalupan stand, and saying that he died soon after, perhaps of sorrow. His account of the beatification process is garbled.

26. "Mexican Church Officials Surprised at Nuncio's Transfer," *The Tidings*, February 18, 2000, citing Bernardo Barranco, head of Mexico's Center for the Study of Religion, writing in *La Jornada*, February 12, 2000.

27. Ernesto Núñez, "Defiende Fox Canonización," *Reforma*, December 9, 1999.

28. María Elena Medina and Marcela Turati, "El Papa Está Convencido de la Aparición — Rivera," *Reforma*, December 13, 1999.

29. "Disparate, Cuestionar Apariciones," *Reforma*, December 12, 1999.

30. *Reforma*, December 23, 1999.

31. http://www.princeofeden.com.

32. E-mail message, May 1, 2000, forwarded to the author by Professor John Frederick Schwaller of the University of Montana, Morris.

33. Laso de la Vega, *The Story of Guadalupe*, 69, 71.

34. "Juan Diego's Historicity Verified," http://www.zenit.org, August 25, 2000.

35. The letter was addressed to Archbishop Tarcisio Bertone, S.D.B., secretary of the Congregation, and was signed by Tena, Martínez de la Serna, Miranda Godínez, Noguez, González de Alba, Olimón Nolasco, Warnholtz, Schulenburg, and Poole. Bertone was the former archbishop of Vercelli and also secretary for the Congregation for the Doctrine of the Faith. The letter is reproduced in Olimón Nolasco, *La Búsqueda de Juan Diego*, 178–83.

36. Ibid., 177.

37. The Collegiate chapter had three *dignidades*, or higher offices: the abbot, the archpriest (*arcipreste*), and the *sacristán mayor*.

38. Olimón Nolasco, *La búsqueda de Juan Diego*, 179–80.

39. Ibid., 178, 181.

40. Sastre Santos, "La cuestión de Guadalupe vista desde España," 3. All quotations are from the copy that was sent to Poole.

41. Ibid. In 1570 Freire, who was the vicar of Guadalupe, drew up a report for the Council of the Indies in which he said that the *ermita* had been founded by Archbishop Montúfar about the years 1555–56. His report was incorporated with others into a document called *Descripción del arzobispado de Mexico*. In his letter to Archbishop Labastida y Dávalos, García Icazbalceta said that the *Descripción* contained no mention of Guadalupe. Freire's report was not included in the version of the *Descripción* published by García Icazbalceta's son, Luis García Pimentel, in 1897, but was included in that published by Francisco del Paso y Troncoso in 1905. On this rather mysterious question, see Poole, *Our Lady of Guadalupe*, 66–67.

42. Sastre Santos, "La cuestión de Guadalupe vista desde España," 4.

43. Ibid., 5.

44. Ibid., 8–9.

45. Ibid., 9–10.

46. Ibid., 14.

47. Ibid.

48. Ibid., 16–17. On Verdugo Quetzalmamalitzin, see Poole, *Our Lady of Guadalupe*, 87; Noguez, *Documentos guadalupanos*, 60–61. On Bartolomé López, see Noguez, *Documentos guadalupanos*, 86; and González Fernández, Chávez Sánchez, and Guerrero Rosado, *El encuentro*, 360–61.

49. Sastre Santos, "La cuestión de Guadalupe vista desde España," 17; Poole, *Our Lady of Guadalupe*, 95–96.

50. Sastre Santos, "La cuestión de Guadalupe vista desde España," 17–18.

51. Miles Philips was an English corsair captured by the Spanish in 1568; he visited the shrine at Guadalupe in 1573 on his way to Mexico City for trial. On this, see Poole, *Our Lady of Guadalupe*, 69–71.

52. Sastre Santos, "La cuestión de Guadalupe vista desde España," 19–20.

53. Ibid., 20.

54. Alcalá Alvarado, "Breves observaciones," 1. All quotations are from the copy sent to Poole. For Poole's comments on the argument from silence, see *Our Lady of Guadalupe*, 219–20.

55. Alcalá Alvarado, "Breves observaciones," 1.

56. Ibid., 2.

57. For more details on this point, see Poole, *Our Lady of Guadalupe*, 102, 105–6, 108–9.

58. Alcalá Alvarado, "Breves observaciones," 4.

59. Ibid., 8.

60. Eduardo Lliteras and Héctor Moreno, "Avanza Caso de Juan Diego," *Reforma*, May 23, 2000. The same issue carried a story about the pope's surprise visit to the Mexican bishops at the Collegio Pontificio in Rome. During the course of a meal at the Collegio, "the pope received petitions to speed up the beatification [*sic*] of Juan Diego. . . . Sources indicated that everything would be ready to raise the Mexican saint to the altars before the end of the present year. Nevertheless, it was made clear that there was still no official date" (Eduardo Lliteras, "Sorprende Visita de Juan Pablo II," *Reforma*, May 23, 2000).

61. "Sin Fecha, Aún, la Canonización del Beato Juan Diego, Afirma Navarro Valls," *Excelsior*, September 23, 2000.

62. Sergio Javier Jiménez, "Tardará Canonización de Juan Diego," *El Universal*, September 20, 2000.

63. "Sin Fecha, Aún, la Canonización . . . ," *Excelsior*, September 23, 2000.

64. Olimón Nolasco, "Carta/Sólo es Honestidad Intelectual y Moral," *Reforma*, June 24, 2001.

65. "Avanza la Canonización del Indio Juan Diego," *Reforma*, June 26, 2001. Chávez Sánchez succeeded Oscar Sánchez Barba.

66. Ibid.

67. Quoted in Chávez Sánchez, "Proceso." In the text he gives the date as August 21, 2000, but in the footnote he gives it as 2001.

68. "El Acontecimiento Guadalupano Hoy," quoted in Chávez Sánchez, "Proceso."

69. Zenit International News Agency, October 30, 2001.

70. See Burkhart, *The Slippery Earth*; Burkhart, *Holy Wednesday*; and Burkhart, *Before Guadalupe*.

71. Burkhart to Poole, personal communication, November 1, 2001.

72. Burkhart to Poole, personal communication, December 10, 2001.

73. *Reforma*, date unknown.

74. *Reforma*, date unknown; forwarded to this author via e-mail, January 22, 2002.

75. Vicente Guerrero, "Ven la Canonización como Algo Consumado," *Reforma*, December 12, 2001.

76. On these wills, see Poole, *Our Lady of Guadalupe*, 195–200.

77. "Juan Diego, Josemaría Escrivá, and Padre Pio Headed for Canonization," http://www.zenit.org, December 20, 2001; Chris Kraul, "Pope Endorses Mexico's First Indian Saint," *Los Angeles Times*, December 21, 2001; "Reconoce el Vaticano Milagro de Juan Diego," *Reforma*, December 21, 2001; Ignacio Herrera Alcántara, "Aprueba Juan Pablo II la Canonización de Juan Diego," *Excelsior*, December 21, 2001.

78. "Reconoce el Vaticano Milagro de Juan Diego," *Reforma*, December 21, 2001.

79. "Drug Addict Proves Mexican Indian Juan Diego's Sanctity," http://www.zenit.org, December 20, 2001. According to Chávez Sánchez, the fall took place on May 3 and the cure on May 6 ("Proceso").

80. Chávez Sánchez, "Proceso."

81. Ibid.

82. Gerardo Jiménez, "Nadie Frena el Proceso — Diego Monroy," *Reforma*, December 21, 2001.

83. "Reconoce el Vaticano Milagro de Juan Diego," *Reforma*, December 21, 2001.

84. Personal communication, December 28, 2001. For reasons of confidentiality, the name is not given.

85. "La Vergine di Guadalupe del Messico e l'Indio Juan Diego: Mito, Simbolo o Storia," *L'Osservatore Romano*, December 20, 2001 (published in English as "Our Lady of Guadalupe: Blessed Juan Diego, the Indian, and Our Lady's Love for Native Peoples," January 23, 2002).

86. Olimón Nolasco, "Juan Diego: ¿Personaje histórico?" *Nexos* 291 (March 2002): 37, citing the printed version of the interview, which appeared in *Milenio*, January 22, 2002.

87. Olimón Nolasco, "Juan Diego: ¿Personaje histórico?" *Nexos* 291 (March 2002): 37.

88. Ibid., 38.

89. Olimón Nolasco, "Juan Diego: ¿Personaje histórico?" *Nexos* 291 (March 2002): 38, citing "¿Verdaderamente existió?" *Reforma*, January 30, 2002.

90. "Mexico Beginning to Prepare for Possible Papal Visit," http://www.zenit.org, January 21, 2002.

91. Francisco Robles, "Juan Pablo II Vuelve a México: La Quinta Visita al

País Será para Canonizar a Juan Diego en Julio," *La Opinión* (Los Angeles), January 18, 2002.

92. Possibly this was a reference to the apparition to an aged Indian, Miguel de San Gerónimo, October 12, 1576, during the epidemic of that year (Mendieta, *Historia eclesiástica indiana*, book 4, chapter 24, 453).

93. John Allen, "Maybe He Isn't Real But He's Almost a Saint," *National Catholic Reporter*, January 25, 2002.

94. Marcela Turati, "Ignoran a Promotor de Beato en Proceso," *Reforma*, date unknown.

95. Luis Reyes de la Maza, "Guillermo Schulenburg: El Derecho de No Callar," *Excelsior*, January 30, 2002.

96. *Reforma*, undated.

97. Kevin Sullivan, "Myth versus Miracle: Debate Rages over Likely Canonization," *Washington Post*, February 5, 2002.

98. Marcela Turati/Grupo Reforma, "Retrasó ex Abad la Canonización," interview with José Luis Guerrero, February 14, 2002.

99. Jay Root, "Mexican Visionary on Way to Sainthood May Be Just a Legend," Knight Ridder/Tribune Information Services, 2002.

100. Ibid.

101. "Ven Historiadores Racismo en Imagen de Juan Diego," *Reforma*, March 8, 2002.

102. "Mexico Bracing for What Could Be the Largest Mass in History," http://www.zenit.org, March 1, 2002.

103. Jo Tuckman, "Mexican Church Plans Scaled-Down Canonization Mass for Juan Diego," Catholic News Service, March 22, 2002.

104. Ibid.

105. "Mexico Already Considers Juan Diego a Saint," http://www.zenit.org, March 6, 2002.

106. Fernando Cervantes, "Did the Mexican Moses Exist?" *The Tablet*, January 1, 2002, 32–33.

107. Ibid., 32.

108. Ibid., 33.

109. Ibid.

110. Ibid.

111. Brading, "Can We Canonize a Myth?" *The Tablet*, February 2, 2002.

112. Dummet, "Keep Infallibility Clear," *The Tablet*, March 22, 2002.

113. McBrien, ibid.

114. *Nexos* 291 (March 2002): 21–55.

115. González de Alba, "El *affaire* Juan Diego," *Nexos* 291 (March 2002): 39–40.

116. Ibid., 40.

117. Ibid.

118. Ibid.

119. Olimón Nolasco, "Juan Diego: ¿Personaje histórico?" *Nexos* 291 (March 2002): 35–38.

120. "El Falso Debate Sobre la Existencia de Juan Diego," *La Jornada*, January 30, 2002, cited in ibid., 36.

121. "Juan Diego y la Intolerancia," *El Universal*, January 29, 2002, cited in ibid., 36

122. Olimón Nolasco, "Juan Diego: ¿Personaje histórico?" *Nexos* 291 (March 2002): 36. In a note, Olimón Nolasco points out that two versions of this interview were published. A brief, more or less unedited one, in *Novedades*, January 23, 2002, with the title "Cardenal"; and another, longer and better edited, interview, with the title "Arzobispo" which appeared in *El Universal* on the same date.

123. Olimón Nolasco, "Juan Diego: ¿Personaje histórico?" *Nexos* 291 (March 2002): 36 n. 5.

124. Thomas J. Reese, S.J., to Poole, March 5, 2002, personal communication.

125. According to an article in *Reforma*, Barragán Silva had migrated to the United States and was working in a restaurant in Anaheim, California. In an interview, his mother stated that the only persons who had profited by the miracle were reporters and churchmen (Alhelí Lara/Grupo Reforma, "Huyen del Milagro de Juan Diego," *Reforma*, January 16, 2002).

Chapter 8. A Sign of Contradiction

1. Laso de la Vega, *The Story of Guadalupe*, 117.

2. See Poole, *Our Lady of Guadalupe*, 138–39.

3. Ibid., 143.

4. González Fernández, Chávez Sánchez, and Guerrero Rosado, *El encuentro*, 19–20.

5. Ibid., 31.

6. Chávez Sánchez, "Proceso."

7. Poole, *Our Lady of Guadalupe*, 195–200.

8. López Beltrán calls Boturini Benaduci the "protomartyr of Guadalupe," and Plancarte the "the second protomartyr [*sic*] of the Guadalupan cause" (*Album del LXXV aniversario de la coronación guadalupana*, 195).

9. Gutiérrez Casillas has a somewhat more benign opinion. "In the field of history competent ecclesiastics were opposed to him [García Icazbalceta], among whom the most impassioned and fearsome was Father Esteban Antícoli of the Society of Jesus" (*Historia de la Iglesia en México*, 360). He seems to have found it difficult to be critical of a fellow Jesuit.

10. Romero, *Breve historia de las apariciones*, 88, quoted in Senott, *Acheiropoeta*, 31.

11. Antícoli, *El magisterio*, 75.

12. Quoted in S. Lynne Walker, "Pope's Mission Clouded by Doubts about Beloved Figure," Copley News Service, July 27, 2002.

13. Cited in Rodríguez, *Our Lady of Guadalupe*, 47.

14. In no source is Juan Diego ever identified as a *tameme*, or native cargo carrier. This idea may have originated from his statement in the *Nican mopohua*,

"I carry burdens with the tumpline and carrying frame" (Laso de la Vega, *The Story of Guadalupe*, 69). This, however, was a conventional Nahuatl statement of self-deprecation.

15. Fuentes, *The Buried Mirror*, 145–46.

16. Rodríguez, *Our Lady of Guadalupe*, 73.

17. Lockhart, *The Nahuas after the Conquest*, 5. For more on Native–Spanish contact and early interaction, see Lockhart, *We People Here*, 4–8. For a detailed overview of this, issue see Restall, *Seven Myths*, chapter 6.

18. Ricard, *The Spiritual Conquest of Mexico*.

19. Lockhart, *The Nahuas after the Conquest*, 205.

20. Laso de la Vega, *The Story of Guadalupe*, 79.

21. Cardinal Roger Mahony, homily for the Feast of Our Lady of Guadalupe, quoted in *Vida Nueva* (Los Angeles), December 12, 2002.

22. "Virgin of Guadalupe, the Apostle to Latin America," http://www.zenit .org, March 25, 2003.

23. Sánchez, "Imagen de la Virgen," in *THG*, 179.

24. Laso de la Vega, *The Story of Guadalupe*, 112, 113.

25. Ibid., 115.

26. Becerra Tanco, "Origen milagroso," in *THG*, 331.

27. Poole, *Our Lady of Guadalupe*, 159, 163–64.

28. Boturini Benaduci, "Catalogo," in *Idea* 26, no. 4: 90.

29. Clavigero, "Breve noticia," in *THG*, 589.

30. Sigüenza y Góngora, *Piedad heroyca*, 63. This work was written in 1689 but not published until 1790.

31. Poole, *Our Lady of Guadalupe*, 195–200.

32. Chávez Sánchez, "Proceso."

33. Carrera Rivera, *Juan Diego*, 112, 113.

34. Both Warnholtz Bustillos and Martínez de la Serna were compelled by the archbishop to leave the priests' residence at Guadalupe (see Olimón Nolasco, *La búsqueda de Juan Diego*, 171–75; L. A. G. Bilbao, "Los disidentes mexicanos blanco de represalias," *El Correo* (Bilbao, Spain), July 27, 2002.

Appendix 1

1. [Notes enclosed in brackets are those of the translator.]

2. [Antícoli, *La Virgen del Tepeyac*.]

3. [On this, see Poole, *Our Lady of Guadalupe*, 36.]

4. [The printed version consistently gives this form of the name.]

5. [Zumárraga, *Regla cristiana breve*, 36.]

6. [Apparently the reference is to Antícoli.]

7. [There is some confusion about this; see Poole, *Our Lady of Guadalupe*, 66–67.]

8. [Julián Garcés, bishop of Tlaxcala.]

9. [Mendieta, *Historia ecclesiástica indiana*, book 4, chapter 24, 453–54.]

10. "On the hill of Guadalupe where the celebrated sanctuary of the Most Holy Virgin of Guadalupe is they had an idol of a goddess called Ylamateuchtli

or Casamihauh or by another name and the more ordinary one Tonantzin, to whom they celebrated a feast in the month called Tititl. 17th on one calendar, and 16th on the other. And when they go to the feast of the Most Holy Virgin they say that they are going to the feast of Totlaznantzin and the intention is directed in the evil one to the goddess and not to the Most Holy Virgin or to both intentions, thinking that one or the other can be done" (Serna Manual de Ministros de Indios, fol. 90), [manuscript].

11. [Andrés Cavo, S.J., *Tres siglos de México durante el gobierno español hasta la entrada del ejército trigarante*. Publícala con notas y suplemento, el Lic. Carlos María Bustamante (Mexico City: L. Abadiano y Valdés, 1836)].

12. ["Without knowing it" is not in Laso de la Vega's original letter.]

13. [The parchments of the Turpiana tower were discovered in 1588 and the lead plates in 1595. They were forgeries intended to show the antiquity of the diocese and its line of bishops and to add to their glory. Pope Innocent XI condemned them as false in 1682.]

14. [Jerónimo Ramón de la Higuera (1538–1611) was a Spanish Jesuit, forger of some chronicles published in 1611, which he claimed to have found in the monastery of Fulda in Germany, written by ancient authors and with flattering pictures of the Spanish Church. Antonio Lupián Zapata (?–1667), Spanish priest and historian, was also noted for falsifying documents. José Pellicer de Ossau Salas y Tovar (1602–79) was a prolific Spanish author and the official chronicler of both Castile and Aragón.]

15. [The text in *THG*, 1112, has "extractos más seguros."]

16. [That is, Plácido.]

Appendix 2

1. Taken from Olimón Nolasco, *La búsqueda de Juan Diego*, 165–70.

Appendix 3

1. Taken from Olimón Nolasco, *La búsqueda de Juan Diego*, 158–64.

Bibliography

Acta et decreta Concilii Provincialis Mexicani Quinti celebrati An. Dom. MDC-CCXCVI metropolita Illustrissimo ac Reverendissimo D. D. Prospero Maria Alarcon y Sanchez de la Barquera. Editio secunda. Mexico City: Herrera Hermanos, 1899.

Agreda y Sánchez, José María. "Carta a los editores." In *Investigación histórica y documental sobre la aparición de la Virgen de Guadalupe de Mexico,* 83–84. Mexico City: Ediciones Fuente Cultural, n.d.

Agüeros, Victoriano, ed. *Album de la coronación de la Sma. Virgen de Guadalupe. Reseña del suceso mas notable acaecido en el Nuevo Mundo. Noticia histórica de la milagrosa aparición y del santuario de Guadalupe, desde la primera ermita hasta la dedicación de la suntuosa basílica.* Mexico City: Imprenta de "El Tiempo," 1895.

Album conmemorativo del centenario del natalicio del Ilmo. Sr. D. Antonio Plancarte y Labastida: 23 de diciembre 1840–1940. Mexico City: n.p., 1941.

[Alcalá Alvarado, Alfonso]. "Breves observaciones sobre la ciencia de la historia y su método con algunas referencias al libro de Stafford Poole C.M., *Our Lady of Guadalupe.* . . ." Unpublished manuscript, in author's possession.

Altamirano, Ignacio Manuel. "La fiesta de Guadalupe (1884)." In *Testimonios históricos guadalupanos,* edited by Ernesto de la Torre Villar and Ramiro Navarro de Anda, 1127–1210. Mexico City: Fondo de Cultura Económica, 1982.

———. *Paisajes y leyendas, tradiciones y costumbres de México.* Mexico City: Imprenta y Litografía Española, 1884.

[Andrade, Vicente de P.]. *Ciertos aparicionistas, obrando de mala fe: 1°(inventan algunos episodios, 2°(desfiguran otros, y 3°(mancillan las reputaciones mejor sentadas.* N.p., n.d.

———. *De B. M. V. Apparitione in Mexico sub titulo de Guadalupe exquisitio historica.* Mexico City: Epifanio Orozco, 1888.

———. *Ensayo bibliográfico mexicano del siglo XVII.* Mexico City: Imprenta del Museo Nacional, 1900.

———. *Exquisitio histórica anónimo escrito en Latín sobre la Aparición de la B. V. M. de Guadalupe.* Traducido al español por Fortino Hipólito Vera. Segunda edición. Jalpa [*sic*]: Tipografía de Talonia, 1893.

[Antícoli, Esteban]. *Algunos apuntamientos en defensa de la Virgen del Tepeyac contra una obra recién impresa en México.* Mexico City: Círculo Católico, 1892.

———. *Defensa de la aparicion de la Virgen Maria en el Tepeyac, escrita por un sacerdote de la Compañia de Jesus contra un libro impreso en Mexico el año de 1891.* Puebla: Imprenta del Colegio Pío de Artes y Oficios, 1893.

———. *Historia de la aparición de la Sma. Virgen María de Guadalupe en México desde el Año de MDXXXI al del MDCCCXCV, por un sacerdote de la Compañía de Jesús.* 2 vols. Mexico City: Tip. y Lit. "La Europea" de Fernando Camacho, 1897.

———. *El magisterio de la iglesia y la Virgen de Tepeyac, por un sacerdote de la Compañía de Jesús.* Querétaro, 1892.

———. *La Virgen del Tepeyac: Disertación sobre la aparición de Nuestra Señora de Guadalupe en México.* Puebla: Imp. del Colegio Pío de Artes, 1882.

———. *La Virgen del Tepeyac, patrona principal de la nacion mexicana: Compendio historico-critico por un sacerdote residente en esta arquidiocesis.* Guadalajara: Tip. de Ancira y Hno., 1884.

Apuntes históricos y críticos sobre la aparición de la Virgen de Guadalupe. Mexico City: Imprenta Evangélica, 1895.

Aubert, Roger. "Aspects divers du néo-thomisme sous le pontificat de Léon XIII." In *Aspetti della cultura cattolica nell'età di Leone XIII,* 133–227. Rome: Edizione 5 Lune, 1961.

Banegas, Francisco. "Patriota y guadalupano." In *Vigésimo quinto aniversario de la muerte del M. I. Sr. Abad Don Antonio Plancarte y Labastida, 1898–1923.* Tacuba, D.F., 1923.

Bartolache y Díaz de Posadas, José Ignacio. "Manifiesto satisfactorio u opúsculo guadalupano (1790)." In *Testimonios históricos guadalupanos,* edited by Ernesto de la Torre Villar and Ramiro Navarro de Anda, 597–651. Mexico City: Fondo de Cultura Económica, 1982.

Becerra Tanco, Luis. *Felicidad de Mexico.* Mexico City: Viuda de Bernardo Calderón, 1675, 1685, 1745. [Revised edition of *Origen milagroso del Santuario de Nuestra Señora de Guadalupe,* originally published in 1666.]

———. "Origen milagroso del santuario de Nuestra Señora de Guadalupe" (1666). In *Testimonios históricos guadalupanos,* edited by Ernesto de la Torre Villar and Ramiro Navarro de Anda, 309–33. Mexico City: Fondo de Cultura Económica, 1982.

[Bera Cercada, Antonio, pseud. Cayetano Cabrera y Quintero]. *El patronato disputado, dissertacion apologetica, Por el Voto, Eleccion, y Juramento de Patrona, a Maria Santissima, venerada en su imagen de Guadalupe de Mexico, e invalidado para negarle el rezo del Comun (que à Titulo de Patrona electa, y jurada, segun el Decreto de la Sagrada Congregacion de Ritos) se le ha dado en esta Metropoli, por el Br. D. Jvan Pablo Zetina Infante, Mro. de ceremonias en la Cathedral de la Puebla.* Mexico City: Imprenta Real del Superior Gobierno, y del Nuevo Rezado de Doña Maria de Rivera, 1741.

Beristáin de Sousa, José Mariano. *Biblioteca hispanoamericana septentrional.* 5 vols. Mexico City: Ediciones Fuente Cultural, 1883.

Bernal, Ignacio, ed. *Correspondencia de Nicolás León con Joaquín García Icazbalceta.* Mexico City: Universidad Nacional Autónoma de México, Instituto de Investigaciones Antropológicas, 1982.

Boturini Benaduci, Lorenzo. "Catálogo de obras guadalupanas." In *Testimonios históricos guadalupanos,* edited by Ernesto de la Torre Villar and Ramiro Navarro de Anda, 407–12. Mexico City: Fondo de Cultura Económica, 1982.

———. *Historia de la América Septentrional por el caballero Lorenzo Boturini Benaducci, señor de la Torre y de Hono, cronista real en las Indias, edición, prólogo y notas por Manuel Ballesteros Gabrois.* Madrid, 1948.

———. *Idea de una nueva historia general de la América septentrional.* 1746; edición facsímil, Mexico City: Instituto Nacional de Antropología e Historia, Consejo Nacional para la Cultural y las Artes, 1999.

———. *Idea de una nueva historia general de la América Septentrional fundada sobre material copioso de figuras, symbolos, caractères, y geroglificos, cantares, y manuscritos de autores indios ultimamente descubiertos. Dedicala al Rey n.tro Senor en su real y supremo consejo de las Indias el cavallero Lorenzo Boturini Benaduci, Señor de la Torre y de Hono.* Madrid: En la Imprenta de Juan de Zunniga, 1746.

Brading, David. *Mexican Phoenix: Our Lady of Guadalupe: Image and Tradition across Five Centuries.* Cambridge: Cambridge University Press, 2001.

Bravo Ugarte, José. *Cuestiones históricas guadalupanas.* Mexico City: Editorial Jus, 1966.

———. *Diócesis y obispos de la Iglesia Mexicana (1519–1965).* Mexico City: Editorial Jus, 1965.

Burkhart, Louise M. *Before Guadalupe: The Virgin Mary in Early Colonial Nahuatl Literature.* Institute for Mesoamerican Studies, monograph 13. Albany, NY: University at Albany, 2001.

———. *Holy Wednesday: A Nahua Drama from Early Colonial Mexico.* Philadelphia: University of Pennsylvania Press, 1996.

———. *The Slippery Earth: Nahua–Christian Moral Dialogue in Sixteenth-Century Mexico.* Tucson: University of Arizona Press, 1989.

Burrus, Ernest J., S.J. *A Major Guadalupan Question Resolved: Did General Scott Seize the Valeriano Account of the Guadalupan Apparitions?* CARA Studies on Popular Devotion, no. 2; Guadalupan Studies, no. 2. Washington, DC, 1979.

———. *La continuidad y congruencia de los documentos de la historia guadalupana.* Congreso Mariológico. Mexico City, 1982.

———. "La copia más antigua del Nican Mopohua." *Histórica: Organo del Centro de Estudios Guadalupanos* (1986): 5–27.

———. "Historia del culto guadalupano." In *Album conmemorativo del 450 aniversario de las apariciones de Nuestra Señora de Guadalupe.* Mexico City: Ediciones Buena Nueva, 1981.

———. *The Oldest Copy of the Nican Mopohua.* CARA Studies on Popular Devotion, no. 4; Guadalupan Studies, no. 4. Washington, DC, 1981.

Bustamante, Carlos María de. *La aparicion de N.tra Señora de Guadalupe de México, comprobada con la refutacion del argumento negativo que presenta*

D. Juan Bautista Muñoz, fundandose en el testimonio del P. Fr. Bernardino de Sahagun; ó sea: Historial original de este escritor que altera la publicada en 1829 en el equivocado concepto de ser la unica y original de dicho autor. Publícala, precediendo una disertación sobre la aparicion Guadalupana, y con notas sobre la conquista de México, Carlos Ma. de Bustamante, individuo del supremo poder conservador. Mexico City: Impreso por I. Cumplido, 1840.

————. "La aparición guadalupana de México." In *Testimonios históricos guadalupanos*, edited by Ernesto de la Torre Villar and Ramiro de Anda, 1007–56. Mexico City: Fondo de Cultura Económica, 1982. [Originally published as *La aparición guadalupana de México: Vindicada de los defectos que le atribuye el Dr. D. Juan Bautista Muñoz en la disertación que leyó en la Academia de la Historia de Madrid, en 18 de abril de 1794, comprobada con nuevos descubrimientos* (México: J. M. F. de Lara, 1843).]

————. "Elogios y defensa guadalupanos (1831–1843)." In *Testimonios históricos guadalupanos*, edited by Ernesto de la Torre Villar and Ramiro Navarro de Anda, 1007–91. Mexico City: Fondo de Cultura Económica, 1982.

————. "Manifiesto de la Junta Guadalupana a los mexicanos, y disertación histórico-crítica sobre la aparición de Nuestra Señora en Tepeyac." In *Testimonios históricos guadalupanos*, edited by Ernesto de la Torre Villar and Ramiro de Anda, 1057–91. Mexico City: Fondo de Cultura Económica, 1982. [Originally published as *Manifiesto de la Junta Guadalupana a los mexicanos, y disertacion historico-critica sobre la aparicion de Nuestra Señora en Tepeyac* (Mexico City: A. Valdés, 1831).]

Bustamante, Fray Francisco de, and Fray Alonso de Montúfar. "Información por el sermón de 1556." In *Testimonios históricos guadalupanos*, edited by Ernesto de la Torre Villar and Ramiro Navarro de Anda, 36–141. Mexico City: Fondo de Cultura Económica, 1982.

Cabrera, Miguel. *Maravilla americana y conjunto de raras maravillas observadas con la direccion de las reglas del Arte de la Pintura en la prodigiosa imagen de N.ra Señora de Guadalupe de Mexico por D. Miguel Cabrera, pintor del Ilustrisimo Señor D. D. Manuel Josef Rubio y Salinas, dignisimo Arzobispo de Mexico, y del Consejo de su Magestad, etc., a quien se la consagra.* Mexico City: Imprenta del Real y Más Antiguo Colegio de San Ildefonso, 1756.

Cabrera y Quintero, Cayetano. *Escudo de armas de México: Celestial proteccion de esta nobilissima ciudad, de la Nueva-España, y de casi todo el Nuevo Mundo, Maria Santissima en su portentosa imagen del Mexicano Guadalupe, milagrosamente apparecida en el palacio arzobispal el Año de 1531. y jurada su principal patrona el passado de 1737. En la angustia que ocasionò la Pestilencia, que cebada con mayor rigor en los Indios, mitigò sus ardores al abrigo de tanta sombra: describiala de orden, y especial nombramiento . . . D. Cayetano de Cabrera, y Quintero, Presbytero de este arzobispado.* Mexico City: Por Viuda de D. Joseph Bernardo de Hogal, 1746.

Callahan, Philip Serna. *The Tilma under Infra-Red Radiation.* CARA Studies on Popular Devotion, no. 2; Guadalupan Studies, no. 3. Washington, D.C., 1981.

Camelo, Rosa. "Joaquín García Icazbalceta." In *Historiadores de México en el siglo XX*, edited by Enrique Florescano and Ricardo Pérez Montfort, 13–21.

Mexico City: Consejo Nacional para la Cultura y las Artes, Fondo de Cultura Económica, 1995.

Carreño, Alberto María. "Don Fray Alonso de Montúfar, the Second Archbishop of Mexico, and the Devotion to Our Lady of Guadalupe." *The Americas* 2, no. 3 (January 1946): 280–95.

———. "Notas biográficas." In *Sesión celebrada la noche del día 9 de septiembre de 1915 por la Sociedad Mexicana de Geografía y Estadística en memoria del socio honorario sr. lic. Canónigo don Vicente de P. Andrade (1844–1915)*, 10–35. Mexico City: Imprenta Stephan y Torres, n.d.

Carrillo y Ancona, Crescencio. *Carta de actualidad sobre el milagro de la Aparición Guadalupana en 1531*. Mérida, Yucatán: "Imprenta Mercantil" a Cargo de José Gamboa Guzmán, 1888.

———. *Don Joaquín García Icazbalceta y la historia guadalupana. Carta escrita por el Ilustrísimo Señor Doctor Don Crescencio Carrillo y Ancona, obispo de Yucatán*. Mérida, Yucatán: Imprenta "Gamboa Guzmán," 1896.

———. *Panegírico de Nuestra Señora de Guadalupe en la singular y solemne fiesta de su coronación celebrada el 12 de octubre de 1895 en la nacional é insigne colegiata de México por el Illmo. Señor Doctor Don Crescencio Carrillo y Ancona Obispo de Yucatán*. Mérida, Yucatán: Imp. y Lit. de R. Caballero, 1895.

Cavalli, Fiorello, S.J. "Cent'anni di vita del Pontificio Collegio Pio Latino-Americano." *La Civiltà Cattolica*, anno 110, vol. 1 (1959): 260–73.

[Cawley, Martinus]. *Guadalupe: From the Aztec Language*. CARA Studies on Popular Devotion, no. 2; Guadalupan Studies, no. 6. Lafayette, OR, 1983.

Cervantes de Conde, María Teresa, Ernesto de la Torre Villar, and Ramiro Navarro de Anda, eds. *Album conmemorativo del 450 aniversario de las apariciones de Nuestra Señora de Guadalupe*. Mexico City: Ediciones Buena Nueva, 1981.

Chávez, Gabino. *Catecismo de controversia guadalupana*. Guadalajara: Ant. Imp. de N. Parga — D. Juan Manuel, E., 1893.

———. *Celeste y terrestre o las dos coronas guadalupanas: Reflexiones acerca de la desaparición de la corona en la imagen de Nuestra Señora de Guadalupe*. Mexico City: Guillermo Herrero y Comp., 1895.

Chávez Sánchez, Eduardo. "Proceso de beatificación y canonización de Juan Diego," 2004, http://www.virgendeguadalupe.org.mx/juandiego/proceso_c.htm.

———, ed., with the collaboration of Alfonso Alcalá Alvarado, Raúl Soto Vázquez, José Luis Guerrero Rosado, and Peter Gumpel. *La Virgen de Guadalupe y Juan Diego en las informaciones jurídicas de 1666, con facsímil del original*. 2nd ed. Mexico City, 2002.

Clavigero, Francisco Javier. *Breve ragguaglio della prodigiosa e rinomata immagine della Madonna di Guadalupe di Messico*. Cesena, Italy: Gregorio Biasini, 1782.

———. "Breve noticia sobre la prodigiosa y renombrada imagen de Nuestra Señora de Guadalupe (1782)." In *Testimonios históricos guadalupanos*, edited by Ernesto de la Torre Villar and Ramiro Navarro de Anda, 578–96. Mexico City: Fondo de Cultura Económica, 1982.

Colección de obras y opúsculos pertenecientes a la milagrosa aparición de la bellísima imagen de Nuestra Señora de Guadalupe, que se venera en su santuario extramuros de México. Madrid: Lorenzo de San Martín, 1785.

Conde y Oquendo, Francisco Javier. *Disertación histórica sobre la Aparición de la portentosa Imagen de María Sma. de Guadalupe de México.* Mexico City: Imprenta de la Voz de la Religión, 1852.

Congregatio pro Causis Sanctorum Officium Historicum, 184: Mexicana: Canonizationis Servi Dei Ioannis Didaci Cuauhtlatoatzin viri laici (1474–1548). *Positio super fama sanctitatis, virtutibus et cultu ab immemorabili praestito ex officio concinnata.* Rome, 1989.

"Critique d'un sermon sur N.D. de Guadalupe et divers autres sujets (1794–1795)." Mexicains 270, Bibliothéque Nationale de France, Paris.

[Cruz, Mateo de la]. *Relación de la milagrosa aparición de la Santa Virgen de Guadalupe de México, sacada de la historia que compuso el Br. Miguel Sánchez.* Puebla de los Angeles: Viuda de Borja, 1660.

Cuevas, Mariano, S.J. *Album histórico guadalupano del IV centenario.* Mexico City, 1930.

———. "Documentos escritos en pro de la historicidad de las apariciones guadalupanas: Su autenticidad. Su valor." In *Memoria del Congreso Nacional Guadalupano: Discursos, conclusiones, poesías.* Mexico City: Escuela Tipográfica Salesiana, 1931.

———. *Documentos inéditos del siglo XVI para la historia de México.* Mexico City: Museo Nacional de Arqueología y Etnología, 1914.

———. *Historia de la Iglesia en México.* 4 vols. Tlalpam, D.F.: Impr. del Asilo Patricio Sanz, 1921–24.

Diccionario Porrúa de historia, biografía y geografía de México. 5th ed., corrected and augmented. 3 vols. Mexico City: Editorial Porrúa, 1986.

Dios, Vicente de. *Historia de la familia vicentina en México, 1844–1894.* 2 vols. Salamanca: Editorial CEME, 1993.

Dos relaciones históricas de la admirable aparición de la Virgen Santíssima y Soberana Madre de Dios baxo el título de Santa María de Guadalupe, acaecida en esta Corte de México el año de mil quinientos treinta y uno. Mexico City: Imprenta de Felipe de Zúñiga y Ontiveros, 1781.

Elizondo, Virgil. *Guadalupe: Mother of the New Creation.* Maryknoll, NY: Orbis Books, 2001.

Escalada, Xavier, S.J. *Enciclopedia guadalupana.* 4 vols. in 2. Mexico City, 1995.

———. *Juan Diego: Escalerilla de Tablas.* Mexico City: Enciclopedia Guadalupana, n.d.

Escamilla González, Francisco Iván. *José Patricio Fernández de Uribe (1742–1796): El cabildo eclesiástico de México ante el Estado Borbónico.* Mexico City: Conaculta, 1999.

———. "'Máquinas troyanas': El guadalupanismo y la ilustración novohispana." *Relaciones* (publication of the Colegio de Michoacán), forthcoming.

Estatutos capitulares de la Insigne Secular Colegiata Iglesia Basílica de Santa María de Guadalupe. Aprobados por el Excmo. Y Revmo. Señor Arzobispo

Doctor Don Luis María Martínez, según su Decreto expedido el día 24 de septiembre del Año 1942. N.d.

Fernández de Echeverría y Veytia, Mariano. "Baluartes de México (1775–1779)." In *Testimonios históricos guadalupanos*, edited by Ernesto de la Torre Villar and Ramiro Navarro de Anda, 529–77. Mexico City: Fondo de Cultura Económica, 1982.

Fernández de Uribe, José Patricio. *Disertacion historico-critica en que el autor del sermon que precede sostiene la celestial imagen de Maria Santísima de Guadalupe de México, milagrosamente aparecida al humilde neófito Juan Diego. Escribiase por el año de 1778.* [Mexico City: M. de Zúñiga y Ontiveros, 1801.]

———. *Sermon de Nuestra Señora de Guadalupe de Mexico, predicado en su santuario el año de 1777 dia 14 de diciembre en la solemne fiesta con que su ilustre congregacion celebra su aparicion milagrosa, por el señor Doctor y maestro D. Joseph Patricio Fernandez de Uribe, Colegial Real de Oposicion en el mas antiguo de San Ildefonso, Cura propio de la Catedral, y despues Canónigo Penitenciario de la misma Metropolitana Iglesia de Mexico. El que dió motivo para escribir la adjunta Disertacion, como en ella misma se expresa. Sale á luz á expensas de dicha I. y V. Congregacion año de 1801.* Mexico City: En la Oficina de D. Mariano de Zúñiga y Ontiveros, 1801.

Florencia, Francisco de. *La estrella del norte de Mexico aparecida al rayar el dia de la luz Evangelica en este Nuevo Mundo, en la cumbre del cerro de Tepeyacac, orilla del mar Tezcucano, à un Natural recien convertido; pintada tres dias despues milagrosamente en su tilma ò capa de lienzo delante del Obispo y de su familia, en su casa Obispal, para luz en la fé à los Indios; para rumbo cierto à los Españoles en la virtud, para serenidad de las tempestuosas inundancias de la Laguna. En la historia de la milagrosa imagen de nuestra Señora de Guadalupe de Mexico Que se apareció en la manta de Juan Diego Compusola el Padre Francisco de Florencia de la extinguida Compañia de Jesus.* 1688; reprinted, Madrid: En la Imprenta de Lorenzo de San Martin, Impresor de la Secretaría de Estado y del Despacho Universal de Indias y de Otras Varias Oficinas de S. M., 1785.

Fowler, Will. *Tornel and Santa Anna: The Writer and the Caudillo, Mexico, 1795–1853.* Westport, CT: Greenwood Press, 2000.

Fuentes, Carlos. *The Buried Mirror: Reflections on Spain in the New World.* Boston: Houghton Mifflin, 1992.

Galera Lamadrid, Jesús. *Nican mopohua: Breve análisis literario e histórico.* Mexico City: Editorial Jus, 1991.

Galindo y Villa, Jesús. *Don Joaquín García Icazbalceta: Biografía y bibliografía.* N.p., n.d. [Found at the Biblioteca Nacional de México, Mexico City, bound with a copy of the *Album de la coronación.*]

———. "Don Joaquín García Icazbalceta, His Life and Works." *Inter-America* (New York) 9, no. 4 (April 1926).

García Gutiérrez, Jesús. *Apuntamientos para una bibliografía crítica de historiadores guadalupanos.* Mexico City, 1940.

————. *Primer siglo guadalupano: Documentación indígena y española (1531–1648).* 2nd ed. Mexico City: Librería Editorial San Ignacio de Loyola, 1945. [First edition published 1931 by Imprenta "Patricio Sanz" Tlalpan, D.F.]

García Icazbalceta, Joaquín. *Carta acerca del origen de la imagen de Nuestra Señora de Guadalupe de México escrita por D. Joaquín García Icazbalceta al Ilmo. Sr. Arzobispo D. Pelagio Antonio de Labastida y Dávalos seguida de la Carta Pastoral que el señor arzobispo [sic] de Tamaulipas don Eduardo Sanchez Camachio dirigio al mismo eminente prelado.* Mexico City, 1896.

[————]. *Cartas de Joaquín García Icazbalceta a José Fernández Ramírez, José María de Agreda, Manuel Orozco y Berra, Nicolás León, Agustín Fischer, Aquilés Gertes, Francisco del Paso y Troncoso.* Compiladas y anotadas por Felipe Teixidor; prólogo por Genaro Estrada. Mexico City: Ediciones Porrúa, 1937.

————. *Don Fray Juan de Zumárraga, primer obispo y arzobispo de México.* Edición de Rafael Aguayo Spencer y Antonio Castro Leal. 4 vols. Mexico City: Editorial Jus, 1947.

García Pimentel, Luis, ed. *Descripción del arzobispado de México hecha en 1570 y otros documentos.* Mexico City: José Joaquín Terrazas e Hijos Imprs., 1897.

García Pimentel y Elguero, Luis. *Don Joaquín Icazbalceta como católico: Algunos testimonios publicados por su nieto.* Mexico City: Editorial "Clásica," 1944.

Garibay K., Angel María. *Historia de la literatura náhuatl.* 2 vols. Mexico City: Editorial Porrúa, 1961.

————. Los manuscritos en lengua náhuatl de la Biblioteca Nacional de México. *Boletín de la Biblioteca Nacional* 17 (January–June 1966): 5–19.

————. "La maternidad de María en el mensaje guadalupano." In *La maternidad espiritual de María*, 187–202. Mexico City, 1961.

————. "Temas guadalupanos I: Los anales indígenas." *Abside* 9, no. 1 (1945): 37–46.

————. "Temas guadalupanos II: El diario de Juan Bautista." *Abside* 9, no. 2 (1945): 155–69.

————. "Temas guadalupanos III: El problema de los cantares." *Abside* 9, no. 3 (1945): 243–59.

————. "Temas guadalupanos III: El problema de los cantares (prosigue)." *Abside*, 9, no. 4 (1945): 381–420.

La gerarchia cattolica: La famiglia e la cappella pontificia per l'anno 1895. Rome: Tipografia Vaticana, 1895.

Gerhard, Peter. *A Guide to the Historical Geography of New Spain.* Cambridge: Cambridge University Press, 1972.

Gómez Marín, Manuel. *Defensa guadalupana, escrita por el P. dr. y Mtro. D. Manuel Gomez Marin, Presbítero del Oratorio de S. Felipe Neri de Méjico, contra la disertacion de D. Juan Bautista Muñoz.* Mexico City: A. Valdes, 1819.

Gómez Rodeles, Cecilio. "El Colegio Pío-Latino-Americano." *Razón y Fe* 1, no. 4 (December 1901): 485–95.

[González, José María Antonino]. *Santa María de Guadalupe, patrona de los mexicanos: La verdad sobre la aparición de la Virgen de Tepeyac. Opúsculo escrito por X.* Guadalajara: Ancira y Hno., Antigua de Rodríguez, 1884.

González Fernández, Fidel, Eduardo Chávez Sánchez, and José Luis Guerrero Rosado. *El encuentro de la Virgen de Guadalupe y Juan Diego.* Mexico City: Editorial Porrúa, 1999.

Grajales, Gloria, and Ernest J. Burrus, S.J., comps. and eds. *Bibliografía guadalupana, 1531–1984 (Guadalupan Bibliography, 1531–1984).* Washington, DC: Georgetown University Press, 1986.

Gruzinski, Serge. *Images at War: Mexico from Columbus to Blade Runner (1492–2019).* Translated by Heather MacLean. Durham, NC: Duke University Press, 2001.

Guerrero Rosado, Luis. *¿Existió Juan Diego?* Mexico City: Obra Nacional de Buena Prensa, 1996.

———. *El "Nican mopohua": Un intento de exégesis.* Mexico City: Universidad Pontificia de México, 1996.

Guridi y Alcocer, José Miguel. *Apología de la aparición de Nuestra Señora de Guadalupe de Méjico: En respuesta a la disertación que la impugna.* Mexico City: Alejandro Valdés, 1820.

———. "Apología de la aparición (1820)." In *Testimonios históricos guadalupanos,* edited by Ernesto de la Torre Villar and Ramiro Navarro de Anda, 874–974. Mexico City: Fondo de Cultura Económica, 1982.

———. "Sermón de Nuestra Señora de Guadalupe (1804)." In *Testimonios históricos guadalupanos,* edited by Ernesto de la Torre Villar and Ramiro Navarro de Anda, 863–74. Mexico City: Fondo de Cultura Económica, 1982.

Gutiérrez Casillas, José, S.J. *Jesuítas en México durante el siglo XX.* Mexico City: Editorial Porrúa, 1972.

———. *Historia de la Iglesia en México.* 2nd ed., revised and enlarged. Mexico City: Editorial Porrúa, 1984.

Gutiérrez Dávila, Julián. *Memorias historicas de la Congregacion de el Oratorio de la Ciudad de Mexico . . . recojidas, y pvblicadas por el P. Julian Gutierrez Davila, Presbytero Preposito, que fue, de dicha Congregacion del Oratorio de Mexico.* Mexico City: En la Imprenta Real del Superor Govierno, y del Nuevo Rezado, de Doña Maria de Rivera, 1736.

Hernández Chávez, Prisciliano. "¡Qué pena Señor Abad!" Offprint from *Observador* 47 (June 2, 1996).

Las Hijas de María Inmaculada de Guadalupe a la venerada memoria del M. I. Sr. Abad Don Antonio Plancarte y Labastida su insigne fundador. Tacuba, D.F., 1923.

Hill, Roland. *Lord Acton.* New Haven, CT: Yale University Press, 2000.

Hurtado, Arnulfo. *El cisma mexicano.* Mexico City: "Buena Prensa," 1956.

Iguíniz, Juan B. *Disquisiciones bibliográficas: Autores, libros, bibliotecas, artes gráficas.* Mexico City: El Colegio de Mexico, n.d.

Ilmo. Y Revmo. Abad Mitrado don Antonio Plancarte y Labastida: Sintesis de su vida. N.p.: Formación del Comité Pro-Monumento, n.d.

Información que el arzobispo de México D. Fray Alonso de Montúfar mandó practicar con motivo de un sermón que en la fiesta de la Natividad de Nuestra Señora (8 de septiembre de 1556) predicó en la capilla de San José de Naturales del Convento de San Francisco de México su Provincial Fray Francisco de

Bustamante, acerca de la devoción y culto de Nuestra Señora de Guadalupe.
Madrid: Imprenta de la Guirnalda, 1888.

*Información que el arzobispo de México don fray Alonso de Montúfar mandó
practicar con motivo de un sermon que en la fiesta de la Natividad de Nuestra
Señora (8 de Septiembre de 1556) predico en la capilla de San José de los Naturales del Convento de San Francisco de Méjico, el Provincial Fray Francisco
de Bustamante acerca de la devoción y culto de Nuestra Señora de Guadalupe.*
2nd ed. Mexico City: Imprenta, Litografia y Encuadernacion de Irineo Paz,
1891.

*Informe critico-legal dado al muy Ilustre y Venerable Cabildo de la Santa Iglesia
Metropolitana de Mexico por los comisionados que nombró para el
reconocimiento de la Imagen de nuestra Señora de Guadalupe de la Iglesia de
San Francisco, pintada sobre las tablas de la mesa del Illmo. Sr. Obispo D. Fr.
Juan de Zumárraga, y sobre la que puso su tilma el venturoso Neófito Juan
Diego, en que se pintó la Imagen de nuestra Señora de Guadalupe, que se
venera en la Colegiata de la Ciudad de Hidalgo.* Mexico City: Imprenta de la
Testamentaria de Valdés á Cargo de José Maria Gallegos, 1835.

*Informe de actividades de los años 1963 a 1988 publicado por el Venerable
Cabildo con motivo del XXV° aniversario de la toma de posesión como Abad
de Guadalupe de Monseñor Guillermo Schulenburg Prado.* Privately printed,
n.d.

*Interesantísimas cartas sobre la aparición de la Imagen de Guadalupe escritas por
el Illmo. Obispo de Tamaulipas D. Eduardo Sánchez Camacho por el renom-
brado historiador católico D. Joaquín García Icazbalceta y por el presbítero
Xavier Baldragas.* Colección de La Patria. N.p.: Imprenta, Litografía y
Encuadernación de Ireneo Paz, 1896.

*Investigación histórica y documental sobre la aparición de la Virgen de
Guadalupe de Mexico.* Mexico City: Ediciones Fuente Cultural, n.d.

Keen, Benjamin. *The Aztec Image in Western Thought.* New Brunswick, NJ: Rut-
gers University Press, 1971.

Knight, Alan. *The Mexican Revolution.* Vol. 1, *Porfirians, Liberals, and Peasants.*
New York: Cambridge University Press, 1986.

Lafaye, Jacques. *Quetzalcóatl et Guadalupe: La formation de la conscience
nationale au Mexique (1531–1813).* Paris: Éditions Gallimard, 1974. [Trans-
lated by Benjamin Keen as *Quetzalcoatl and Guadalupe: The Formation of
Mexican National Consciousness, 1531–1813* (Chicago: University of
Chicago Press, 1976).]

Laso de la Vega, Luis. *Huey tlamahuiçoltica omonexiti in ilhuicac tlatocaci-
huapilli Santa Maria totlaçonantzin Guadalupe in nican huey altepenahuac
Mexico itocayocan Tepeyacac.* Mexico City: Imprenta de Iuan Ruiz, 1649.

———. *Hvei Tlamahvicoltiça [sic] . . . Libro en Lengua Mexicana, que el Br. Luis
Lasso de la Vega hizo imprimir en Mexico, el año de 1649 ahora traducido y
anotado por el Lic. Don Primo Feliciano Velazquez. Lleva un prólogo del
Pbro. Don Jesus Garcia Gutierrez Secretario de la Academia, Academia Mexicana de Santa María.* Mexico City: Carreño e Hijos, Editores, 1926.

———. *Nican mopohua.* Edited and translated by P. Mario Rojas Sánchez. Mexico City: Imprenta Ideal, 1978.

————. *The Story of Guadalupe: Luis Laso de la Vega's "Huei tlamahuiçoltica" of 1649.* Edited and translated by Lisa Sousa, Stafford Poole, C.M., and James Lockhart. Stanford, CA: Stanford University Press; Los Angeles: UCLA Latin American Center Publications, University of California, Los Angeles, 1998.

Lee, James H. "Clerical Education in Nineteenth-Century Mexico: The Conciliar Seminaries of Mexico City and Guadalajara, 1821–1910." *The Americas: A Quarterly Review of Inter-American Cultural History* 36, no. 4 (April 1980): 465–77.

León, Alejandro. "El enigma de Juan Diego." *Contenido* (February 2000): 30–39.

León-Portilla, Miguel. *Tonantzin Guadalupe: Pensamiento náhuatl y mensaje cristiano en el "Nican mopohua."* Mexico City: El Colegio Nacional; Fondo de Cultura Económica, 2000.

Leonard, Irving A. *Don Carlos de Sigüenza y Góngora: A Mexican Savant of the Seventeenth Century.* University of California Publications in History, no. 18. Berkeley: University of California Press, 1929.

Liss, Peggy. "A Cosmic Approach Falls Short: A Review of Jacques Lafaye's *Quetzalcóatl and Guadalupe: The Formation of Mexican National Consciousness, 1531–1813.*" *Hispanic American Historical Review* 57, no. 4 (November 1977): 707–11.

Lockhart, James. *The Nahuas after the Conquest: A Social and Cultural History of the Indians of Central Mexico, Sixteenth through Eighteenth Centuries.* Stanford, CA: Stanford University Press, 1992.

————. *We People Here: Nahuatl Accounts of the Conquest of Mexico.* Berkeley: University of California Press, 1993.

López Beltrán, Lauro. *La historicidad de Juan Diego.* Obras guadalupanas de Lauro López Beltrán, no. 5. Mexico City: Editorial Tradición. 1981.

————. *Orto, cenit y ocaso de Monseñor Manríquez y Zárate.* Mexico City: Editorial Tradición, 1989.

————. *La primera historia guadalupana de México impresa.* Obras guadalupanas de Lauro López Beltrán, no. 4. Mexico City: Editorial Tradición, 1981.

————. *La protohistoria guadalupana.* 2nd rev. ed. Mexico City: Editorial Tradición, 1981.

López Beltrán, Lauro, ed. *Album del LXXV aniversario de la coronación guadalupana.* Mexico City: Editorial Jus, 1973.

Lundberg, Magnus. *Unification and Conflict: The Church Politics of Alonso de Montúfar OP, Archbishop of Mexico, 1554–1572.* Studia Missionalia Svecana, no. 86. Lund, Sweden: Lund University, 2002.

Maina, Pietro, S.I. "Il Pontificio Collegio Pio Latino Americano nel LXXV anniversario della sua fondazione in Roma (1858–1933)." *La Civiltà Cattolica,* anno 84, vol. 4 (1933): 272–82.

Manríquez y Zárate, José de Jesús. *Carta pastoral que el Excmo. Y Rvmo. Obispo de Huejutla dirige a sus diocesanos sobre las necesidades de trabajar ahincadamente por la Glorificación de Juan Diego en este mundo.* N.p., April 12, 1939.

Martínez, Manuel Guillermo. *Don Joaquín García Icazbalceta: His Place in Mexican Historiography.* Studies in Hispanic-American History, no. 4. Washington, DC: Catholic University of America, 1947.

Mayer, Alicia. "El guadalupanismo en Carlos de Sigüenza y Góngora." In *Carlos de Sigüenza y Góngora: Homenaje, 1700–2000*, edited by Alicia Mayer. Mexico City: Universidad Nacional Autónoma de México, 2000.

Maza, Francisco de la. *El guadalupanismo mexicano.* Mexico City: Fondo de Cultura Económica, 1981.

Medina Ascensio, Luis, S.J. *Historia del Colegio Pío Latino Americano: (Roma: 1858–1978).* Mexico City: Editorial Jus, 1978.

Mendieta, Gerónimo de. *Historia eclesiástica indiana: Obra escrita a fines del siglo XVI.* Tercera edición facsimilar, y primera con la reproducción de los dibujos originales del códice. Mexico City: Editorial Porrua, 1980.

Mier Noriega y Guerra, Servando Teresa de. "Cartas a Juan Bautista Muñoz (1797)." In *Testimonios históricos guadalupanos*, edited by Ernesto de la Torre Villar and Ramiro Navarro de Anda, 757–861. Mexico City: Fondo de Cultura Económica, 1982.

———. *Cartas del Doctor Fray Servando Teresa de Mier al cronista de Indias Doctor D. Juan Bautista Muñoz, sobre la tradición de Ntra. Sra. de Guadalupe de Mexico, escrita desde Burgos, año de 1797.* Mexico City: Imp. de "El Porvenir," 1875.

———. *El heterodoxo guadalupano: Estudio preliminar y selección de textos de Edmundo O'Gorman.* Nueva Biblioteca Mexicana, no. 83. Mexico City: Universidad Nacional y Autónoma de México, 1981.

Miranda Godínez, Francisco. *Dos cultos fundantes: Los Remedios y Guadalupe (1521–1649).* El Colegio de Michoacán, 2001.

Montes de Oca y Obregón, Ignacio. "Breve elogio del Excmo. Sr. D. Joaquín García Icazbalceta, pronunciado en la asamblea general de las conferencias de San Vicente de Paúl, de San Luis de Potosí, el 23 de diciembre de 1894." In *Oraciones fúnebres por D. Ignacio Montes de Oca y Obregón, obispo de San Luis de Potosí.* Colección de escritores castellanos, vol. 119, Oradores, 349–57. Madrid: Est. Tipográfico "Sucesores de Rivadeneyra," 1901.

———. "Elogio fúnebre del Ilmo. Y Excmo. Sr. Dr. D. Pelagio Antonio de Labastida y Dávalos, arzobispo de México, pronunciado en Méjico el 18 de abril de 1891." In *Oraciones fúnebres por D. Ignacio Montes de Oca y Obregón, obispo de San Luis de Potosí. Colección de escritores castellanos,* vol. 119, *Oradores,* 157–215. Madrid: Est. Tipográfico "Sucesores de Rivadeneyra," 1901.

———. "Elogio fúnebre del Ilustrísimo señor don Antonio Plancarte y Labastida, abad de Guadalupe, predicado en San Luis de Potosí el 27 de mayo de 1898." In *Oraciones fúnebres por D. Ignacio Montes de Oca y Obregón, obispo de San Luis de Potosí. Colección de escritores castellanos,* vol. 119, *Oradores,* 217–57. Madrid: Est. Tipográfico "Sucesores de Rivadeneyra," 1901.

Munguía, Cesáreo. *La obra del Ilustrísimo Sr. don Antonio Plancarte y Labastida, Abad de Guadalupe, en Querétaro.* Monografias Históricas de la Diócesis de Querétaro; Colección Primer Centenario. Querétaro: Editorial Jus, 1963.

Muñoz, Juan Bautista. "Memoria sobre las apariciones y el culto de Nuestra Señora de Guadalupe (1794)." In *Testimonios históricos guadalupanos*, edited by Ernesto de la Torre Villar and Ramiro Navarro de Anda, 689–701. Mexico City: Fondo de Cultura Económica, 1982.

Muriel, Josefina. *Las indias caciques de Corpus Christi.* Instituto de Historia, Serie Histórica, no. 6; UNAM Publicaciones del Instituto de Historia 1, serie no. 83. Mexico City: Universidad Nacional Autónoma de México, 1963.

Nebel, Richard. *Santa María Tonantzin, Virgen de Guadalupe: Continuidad y transformación religiosa en México.* Traducción del alemán por el Pbro. Dr. Carlos Warnholtz Bustillos, arcipreste de la Insigne y Nacional Basílica de Guadalupe, con la colaboración de la señora Irma Ochoa de Nebel. Mexico City: Fondo de Cultura Económica, 1995.

New Catholic Encyclopedia. 15 vols. Washington, DC: Catholic University of America–McGraw Hill, 1967.

Noguez, Xavier. *Documentos guadalupanos: Un estudio sobre las fuentes de información tempranas en torno a las mariofanías en el Tepeyac.* Mexico City: El Colegio Mexiquense; Fondo de Cultura Económica, 1993.

"Noticia biográfica." In *Obras de D. J. García Icazbalceta.* Vol. 1, *Opúsculos varios,* v–xvi. 2nd ed. Mexico City: Tipografía de Victoriano Agüeros, Editor, 1905.

El obispo de Tamaulipas y la coronación y aparición de Nuestra Señora de Guadalupe. Ciudad Victoria: Imprenta Católica de Telésforo Velázquez, 1888.

O'Dogherty, Laura. "El ascenso de una jerarquía intransigente, 1890–1914." In *Memoria del I Coloquio Historia de la Iglesia en el Siglo XIX,* edited by Manuel Ramos Medina, 179–98. Mexico City: Servicios Condumex, 1998.

O'Gara, Margaret. "Counter-Evidence of Infallibility's Exercise." *The Jurist* 59 (1999): 448–68.

O'Gorman, Edmundo. *Destierro de sombras: Luz en el origen y culto de Nuestra Señora de Guadalupe de Tepeyac.* Mexico City: Universidad Nacional Autónoma de México, 1986.

Olimón Nolasco, Manuel. *La búsqueda de Juan Diego.* Mexico City: Plaza Janés, 2002.

———. "Juan Diego: ¿Personaje histórico?" *Nexos* 291 (March 2002): 35–38.

Ortiz de Montellano, Guillermo. *Nican mopohua.* Mexico City: Universidad Iberoamericana, Departamento de Ciencias Religiosas, Departamento de Historia, 1990.

Panegírico de Nuestra Señora de Guadalupe en la singular y solemne fiesta de su coronación celebrada el 12 de octubre de 1895 en la nacional é insigne colegiata de México por el Illmo. Señor Doctor Don Crescencio Carrillo y Ancona Obispo de Yucatán. Mérida, Yucatán: Imp. y Lit. de R. Caballero, 1895.

Peterson, Jeanette Favrot. "Creating the Virgin of Guadalupe: The Cloth, the Artist, and Sources in Sixteenth-Century New Spain." *The Americas* 61, no. 4 (April 2005): 571–610.

Plancarte y Labastida, Antonio. *Cartas selectas a sus congregantes.* Monterrey: Tip. de Arzobispado, 1912.

———. *Catecismo de la coronación de Ntra. Sra. de Guadalupe.* N.p.: Díaz de León, Imp., 1886.

Plancarte y Navarrete, Francisco. *Antonio Plancarte y Labastida, Abad de Santa María de Guadalupe: Su vida sacada principalmente de sus escritos.* Mexico City: Imprenta Franco Mexicana, 1914.

———. "Apuntes históricos sobre la concesión del nuevo oficio guadalupano,

1884–1894." In *Cartas de Joaquín García Icazbalceta a José Fernández Ramírez, José María de Agreda, Manuel Orozco y Berra, Nicolás León, Agustín Fischer, Aquilés Gertes, Francisco del Paso y Troncoso,* compiladas y anotadas por Felipe Teixidor; prólogo por Genaro Estrada, 335–45. Mexico City: Ediciones Porrúa, 1937.

Pompa y Pompa, Antonio. *El gran acontecimiento guadalupano.* Mexico City: Editorial Jus, 1967.

Poole, Stafford, C.M. *Our Lady of Guadalupe: The Origins and Sources of a Mexican National Symbol.* Tucson: University of Arizona Press, 1995.

Restall, Matthew. *Seven Myths of the Spanish Conquest.* New York: Oxford University Press, 2003.

Ricard, Robert. *The Spiritual Conquest of Mexico.* Translated by Lesley Byrd Simpson. Berkeley: University of California Press, 1966.

Rivera, Agustín. *El intérprete Juan González es una conseja. Folleto escrito por Agustín Rivera, quien lo deddica a su sabio medico y amigo el Sr. Dr. D. Eugenio Moreno.* Lagos de Moreno: Ausencio López Arce e Hijo, Typógrafos, 1896.

Rivera Carrera, Norberto, Cardenal. *Juan Diego: El águila que habla.* Mexico City: Plaza Janés, 2002.

Rivero Figueroa, José D., and Francisco Cantón Rosado. *Dos vidas ejemplares: Ensayos biográficos del Ilmo. Sr. Obispo de Yucatán Don Crescencio Carrillo y Ancona y de Monseñor Norberto Domínguez.* Havana: Imprenta "Avisador Comercial," 1918.

Robles, Antonio de. *Diario de sucesos notables (1665–1703).* Edición y prólogo de Antonio Castro Leal. 2 vols. Mexico: Editorial Porrúa, 1964.

Rodriguez, Jeanette, *Our Lady of Guadalupe: Faith and Empowerment among Mexican-American Women.* Austin: University of Texas Press, 1994.

Romero Salinas, Joel. *Eclipse guadalapano: La verdad sobre el antiaparicionismo.* Mexico City: Editorial El Nacional, 1992.

———. *Juan Diego: Su peregrinar a los altares.* Mexico City: Ediciones Paulinas, 1992.

———. *Precisiones históricas de las tradiciones guadalupana y juandieguina.* Mexico City: Editorial Centro de Estudios Guadalupanos, 1986.

Romero de Solís, José Miguel. "Apostasía episcopal en Tamalaupias, 1896." *Historia Mexicana* 37, no. 2 (October–December 1987): 239–82.

Ronan, Charles, S.J. *Francisco Javier Clavigero, S.J. (1731–1787): Figure of the Mexican Enlightenment: His Life and Works.* Bibliotheca Instituti Historici S.I., no. 40. Rome: Institutum Historicum S.I.; Chicago: Loyola University Press, 1977.

Rosa y Serrano, Agustín de la. *Defensa de la aparición de Ntra. Sra. de Guadalupe y refutación de la carta en que la impugna un historiógrafo de México.* Guadalajara: Luis G. González, 1896.

———. *Disertatio historico-theologica de apparitione B. M. V. de Guadalupe.* Guadalajara: Typographia Narcisi Parga, 1887.

Sacra Rituum Congregatione Emo. ac Rmo. Domino Cardinali Vincentio Vannutelli Relatore. Mexicana concessionis et approbationis officii proprii in honorem Beatae Mariae Virginis de Guadalupe Patronae primariae mexicanae regionis. Instantibus archiepiscopis et episcopis omnibus Mexicanae ditionis. Rome: Typis Perseverantiae, 1892.

Sada Lambretón, Ana María, ed. *Las informaciones jurídicas de 1666 y el beato indio Juan Diego.* Mexico City, 1991.

Salazar Salazar, Roberto. "Inicio y desarrollo del proceso canónico de beatificación y canonización del Siervo de Dios Juan Diego." *Historica,* colección II (n.d.): 1–12.

Salinas, Miguel. *Bosquejo biográfico del Illmo. Sr. Dr. D. Francisco Plancarte y Navarrete: Geógrafo, historiador y arqueólogo.* Tlalpam, D.F.: Imprenta del Asilo "Patricio Sanz," 1923.

Sánchez, Miguel. "Imagen de la Virgen María Madre de Dios de Guadalupe (1648)." In *Testimonios históricos guadalupanos,* edited by Ernesto de la Torre Villar y Ramiro Navarro de Anda, 152–281. Mexico City: Fondo de Cultura Económica, 1982.

———. *Imagen de la Virgen Maria, Madre de Dios de Gvadalvpe, milagrosamente aparecida en la civdad de Mexico. Celebrada en su historia, con la Profecia del capitulo doce del Apocalipsis. A devocion del Bachiller Miguel Sanchez Presbitero. Dedicada al Señor Don Pedro de Barrientos Lomelin.* Mexico City: Imprenta de la Viuda de Bernardo Calderón, 1648.

Sánchez, Pedro. *Historia del seminario conciliar de México.* Mexico City: Escuela Tip. Salesiana "Cristóbal Colón," 1931.

[Sánchez Camacho, Eduardo]. *Pastoral del Obispo de Tamaulipas relativa a la coronación de Nuestra Señora de Guadalupe, Edición de "La Verdad,"* Ciudad Victoria: Imp. Católica de Telésforo Valázquez, 1887.

Sastre Santos, Eutemio. "La cuestión de Guadalupe vista desde España." Unpublished ms. (in author's possession).

Schulenburg Prado, Guillermo. *Memorias del "último abad de Guadalupe."* Mexico City: Miguel Ángel Porrúa, Librero-Editor, 2003.

Senott, Thomas Mary. *Acheiropoeta: Not Made by Hands.* New Bedford, MA: Franciscan Friars of the Immaculate, 1998.

Sesión celebrada la noche del día 9 de septiembre de 1915 por la Sociedad Mexicana de Geografía y Estadística en memoria del socio honorario sr. lic. Canónigo don Vicente de P. Andrade (1844–1915). Mexico City: Imprenta Stephan y Torres, n.d.

Sherman, William L., Michael C. Meyer, and Susan Deeds. *The Course of Mexican History.* 7th ed. New York: Oxford University Press, 2003.

Sigüenza y Góngora, Carlos de. *Piedad heroyca de Don Fernando Cortés.* Edición y estudio por Jaime Delgado. Colección Chimalistac de libros y documentos acerca de la Nueva España, no. 7. Madrid: José Porrúa Turanzas, Editor, 1960.

Siller A., Clodomiro L. "La evangelización guadalupana." Offprint from *Cuadernos Estudios Indígenas* 1 (December 1984).

Smith, Jody Brant. *The Image of Guadalupe.* [Macon, GA]: Mercer University Press, in association with Fowler Wright Books, 1994.

———. *The Image of Guadalupe: Myth or Miracle?* Garden City, NY: Image Books, 1984.

Sosa, Francisco. *El episcopado mexicano.* Litografeias del Taller de Hesiquio Iriarte y Santiago Hernandez. [Mexico City]: Editorial Innovación, 1978.

Sousa, Lisa, Stafford Poole, C.M., and James Lockhart, eds. and trans. *The Story of Guadalupe: Luis Laso de la Vega's "Huei tlamahuiçoltica" of 1649.* Stanford, CA: Stanford University Press; Los Angeles: UCLA Latin American Center Publications, University of California, Los Angeles, 1998.

Tapia Méndez, Aureliano. *El diario de Don José Ignacio Montes de Oca y Obregón — Ipandro Acaico.* Monterrey: Producciones Al Voleo-El Troquel, 1988.

———. *El siervo de Dios, José Antonio Plancarte y Labastida, profeta y mártir.* 2nd ed. Mexico City: Editorial Tradición, 1987.

Taylor, William. "The Virgin of Guadalupe: An Inquiry into the Social History of Marian Devotion." *American Ethnologist* 20 (1986): 9–33.

Testimonia authentica fidei mexicanorum antistitum circa apparitiones B. V. Mariae de Guadalupe et miraculosam imaginis ipsius picturam a Raphaele S. Camacho episcopo de Queretaro collecta. Querétaro, 1887.

Tornel y Mendívil, José Julián. *La aparición de Nuestra Señora de Guadalupe de México, comprobada con documentos históricos y defendida de las impugnaciones que se la han hecho.* 2 vols in one. Orizava: J. M. Naredo, 1849.

Torre Villar, Ernesto de la. *Mexicanos ilustres.* 2 vols. Mexico City: Editorial Jus, 1979.

Torre Villar, Ernesto de la, and Ramiro Navarro de Anda, eds. *Testimonios históricos guadalupanos.* Mexico City: Fondo de Cultura Económica, 1982.

Treviño, José Guadalupe. *Antonio Plancarte y Labastida, Abad de Guadalupe.* 2nd ed. Mexico City: Administración de "La Cruz," 1948.

Valton, Emilio. *Homenaje al insigne bibliógrafo mexicano Joaquín García Icazbalceta.* Contribución de la Hemeroteca Nacional a la VI Feria Mexicana del Libro. Mexico City: Imprenta Universitaria, 1954.

Valverde Téllez, Emeterio. *Bio-Bibliografía eclesiástica mexicana (1821–1943).* Dirección y prólogo de José Bravo Ugarte, S.J. 3 vols. Mexico City: Editorial Jus, 1949.

Velázquez, Primo Feliciano. *La aparición de Santa María de Guadalupe.* Reproducción facsimilar de la primera edición de 1931. Introducción y bibliografía de J. Jesús Jiménez López. Mexico City: Editorial Jus, 1981.

———. "Comentario a la historia original guadalupana." In *La protohistoria guadalupana*, by Lauro López Beltrán, 140–73. 2nd rev. ed. Obras guadalupanas de Lauro López Beltrán, no. 3. Mexico City: Editorial Tradición, 1981.

Vera, Fortino Hipólito. *Apuntamientos históricos de los concilios provinciales mexicanos y privilegios de América: Estudios previos al primer concilio provincial de Antequera.* Mexico City, 1893.

———. *Colección de documentos ecclesiásticos de México o sea antigua y moderna legislación de la Iglesia mexicana. Comprende: Encíclicas, bulas, breves, rescriptos y decisiones de la Sagrada Congregación de Roma; pastorales, edictos, exhortaciones, circulares, avisos, decretos de la sagrada mitra; algunas disposiciones de otras diócesis, y doctrinas tomadas del Fasti Novi Orbis, notas del Concilio III Mexicano, colección del P. Hernáez &c., compilados por El Pbro. Br. Fortino H. Vera.* 2 vols. Amecameca: Imprenta del Colegio Católico, a Cargo de Jorge Sigüenza, 1887.

————. *Compendio histórico del tercer concilio provincial mexicano.* Amecameca: Colegio el Católico, 1879.

————. *Contestación a una hoja anónima y clandéstina contra la maravillosa aparición de la Santíssima Virgen del Tepeyac, escrito por Fortino Hipólito Vera canónigo de la insigne colegiata de Guadalupe.* Querétaro: Imprenta de la Escuela de Artes, 1894.

————. *Contestación histórico-crítica en defensa de la maravillosa Aparición de la Santísima Virgen de Guadalupe al anónimo intitulado: Exquisitio historica y a otro anónimo también que se dice Libro de sensación.* 2 vols. Querétaro: Escuela de Artes, 1892.

[————]. *Informaciones sobre la milagrosa aparicion de la Santísima Virgen de Guadalupe, recibidas en 1666 y 1723, publicalas el presbítero Br. Fortino Hipólito Vera.* Amecameca: "Imprenta Católica," a Cargo de Jorge Sigüenza, 1889.

————. *La milagrosa aparición de Nuestra Señora de Guadalupe comprobada por una información levantada en el siglo XVI contra los enemigos de tan asombroso acontecimiento.* Amecameca, 1890.

————. *Tesoro guadalupano. Noticia de los libros, documentos, inscripciones &c. que tratan, mencionan ó aluden á la Aparición y devoción de Nuestra Señora de Guadalupe.* 2 vols. Amecameca: Imprenta del "Colegio Católico," 1887–89.

Vigésimo quinto aniversario de la muerte del M. I. Sr. Abad Don Antonio Plancarte y Labastida, 1898–1923. Tacuba, D.F., 1923.

Wagner, Henry R. *Joaquín García Icazbalceta.* Reprinted from the Proceedings of the American Antiquarian Society for April 1934. Worcester, MA, 1935.

Weiner, Richard. "Trinidad Sánchez Santos: Voice of the Catholic Opposition in Profirian Mexico." *Mexican Studies/Estudios Mexicanos* 17, no. 2 (Summer 2001): 321–49.

Woestman, William H., O.M.I., ed. *Canonization: Theology, History, Process.* Ottawa: Faculty of Canon Law, Saint Paul University, 2002.

Wolf, Eric. "The Virgin of Guadalupe: A Mexican National Symbol." *Journal of American Folklore* 71 (1958): 34–39.

Zetina Infante, Pablo de. *Parecer sobre si se puede rezar de N. Señora de Guadalupe el dia 12. De Diziembre con rito de 1. Classe y Octava, por averse jurado Patrona de este Reyno Que en cumplimiento de su oficio, diò el Br. Juan Pablo de Zetina, Mrò. De ceremonias de la Cathedral de la Puebla.* 1738.

Zires, Margarita. "Los mitos de la Virgen de Guadalupe: Su proceso de construcción y reinterpretación en el México pasado y contemporáneo." *Mexican Studies/Estudios Mexicanos* 10, no. 2 (Summer 1994): 281–313.

Zorrilla, Juan Fidel, and Carlos González Salas, eds. *Diccionario biográfico de Tamaulipas.* Ciudad Victoria, Tamaulipas, 1984.

[Zumárraga, Juan de]. *Regla cristiana breve.* Edición crítica y estudio preliminario por Ildefonso Adeva. Pamplona: Ediciones EUNATE, 1994.

Index